THE NEW YORK MONEY MARKET

PREPARED UNDER THE AUSPICES OF THE

COLUMBIA UNIVERSITY COUNCIL FOR RESEARCH
IN THE SOCIAL SCIENCES

EDITED BY

BENJAMIN HAGGOTT BECKHART

ASSOCIATE PROFESSOR OF BANKING IN COLUMBIA UNIVERSITY

VOLUME II

BY

BENJAMIN HAGGOTT BECKHART

AND

JAMES G. SMITH

Courtesy Irving Trust Company

THE HEAD OF WALL STREET IN 1930

FROM AN ETCHING BY ANTON SCHUTZ

The New York Money Market

VOLUME II

SOURCES AND MOVEMENTS OF FUNDS

BY

BENJAMIN HAGGOTT BECKHART

AND

JAMES G. SMITH

NEW YORK

COLUMBIA UNIVERSITY PRESS

1932

Published September, 1932

PRINTED IN THE UNITED STATES OF AMERICA
BY THE VAIL-BALLOU PRESS, INC., BINGHAMTON, N. Y.

PREFACE

This volume is one of a series of studies on the New York money market conducted under the auspices of the Council for Research in the Social Sciences of Columbia University and under the immediate supervision of a subcommittee on economics composed of Professors R. C. McCrea, W. C. Mitchell, and E. R. A. Seligman. The generous support of the Council and the coöperative attitude of the members of the subcommittee on economics have greatly facilitated the work. The members of the subcommittee on economics, however, are not to be held responsible for opinions expressed or judgments rendered.

Volume I of this series covered the development of the New York money market from 1791 to 1913.

The period from 1913 to 1931 inclusive constitutes the basis for the discussion in Volumes II, III and IV. In the case of certain topics, which involved a radical change in the situation, the discussion is carried into 1932.

In the preparation of this volume, the authors have had associated with them in various stages of the work Messrs. Alfred J. Casazza, H. E. Cooper, Frank T. de Vyver, Richard H. Garlock, Abram L. Harris, Heyman Jarrett, Vladimir Kazakévich, Richard A. Lester, Duncan Merriwether, D. W. Michener, Gilbert Sussman, C. H. Tsai, Eric C. Vance and Misses Mabel Lewis, Elizabeth Rumpf, Mary N. Swinney and Caroline Whitney.

In particular, the authors are indebted to Cornelia Bruère Rose, Jr., for a very painstaking and critically constructive reading of the manuscript. The suggestions made assisted greatly in the manuscript revisions.

The authors have had the benefit of counsel of Professor H. Parker Willis of Columbia University, and of Dr. Margaret G. Myers, the author of the first volume in the series; and in addition are indebted to various banks and bankers and officials of the United States government and of the Federal Reserve system who aided the study. In footnote references, acknowledgment is rendered for the assistance given.

Special mention is due Miss Georgia W. Read of the Columbia University Press for a meticulous and interested editing of the manuscript.

CONTENTS

CHARTS

PART ONE

INTRODUCTION

CHAPTER I

INTRODUCTION

Definition and meaning of the term "money market"

To define the money market in terms at once inclusive and delineating leads one into the expression of a truism or into confusing complexities. The intricacies of the money market, its multitude of functions and services, elude any attempt at a simple definition. A certain precision can be given to the conception of the money market, without arbitrary simplication, if it is described simply as the field of operation of a group of institutions and occupations specializing in the function of bringing together the supply of short- and long-term funds for distribution to those types of activity which bid successfully for their use. Such a definition suggests the variety a. 1 complexity of the constituent elements of the money market and suggests further the essential function of the institutions of the money market, namely, the bringing together of bids and offers for the *use* of funds for a certain period of time. The term "credit market" might be more exact, but the term money market in this connection is too strongly sanctioned by usage for us to attempt a change.

The institutions of the money market

The field of operation, in which the specialized institutions and occupations of the money market are concentrated, covers but a small area in New York City, running from the Battery north to Fulton Street, hemmed in on one side by the East River and on the other by the Hudson. Assuming no handicap of the rush-hour crowds, one may comfortably traverse the entire distance, from north to south or from east to west, in fifteen minutes. No other area in the world represents such a concentration of financial and credit activities and functions, or houses such a concentration of the executive offices of leading industries, railroads and public utilities. About halfway down to the Battery, running from Broadway to the East River, is Wall Street, which, from the time of the establishment of the first credit institution in New York, has been the heart of the financial district. Though the residences, the hotels, the shops, have migrated, by successive steps, farther and farther north on the Island, the financial district has not moved, nor is it likely to do so. Historically it was the child of the port, and was located within easy reach of the wharfs, the commission merchants, and the auctioneers. The increasing volume of the activities of the market has been housed, not by spreading over a much larger area, but by the rebuilding of "the Street" and the district. Perpendicular elasticity has provided the space needed.[1]

The incorporated banks

Among the institutions of the money market there are, in the first place, the incorporated banks—national banks, state banks and trust companies—which, with their affiliated investment companies, their trust, foreign, savings, commercial banking, bond, and a multitude of other departments, stand ready to serve every credit need. The resources of the incorporated banks of New York City constitute about 15 per cent of the banking resources of all banks in the United States.[2] They form a huge pool of credit, deriving funds from all parts of the world, and meeting the credit needs of domestic [3] and foreign customers, of individuals, firms, corporations, banks and governments.

The unincorporated banks

In addition to the incorporated banks, those owing their existence to State or Federal law, there are the unincorporated banks, existing as partnerships with unlimited liability, performing much the same function as do the incorporated banks, but with greater

[1] See Davenport, Donald H., Lawrence M. Orton, and Ralph W. Roby, "The Retail Shopping and Financial Districts in New York and Its Environs," *Regional Plan of New York and Its Environs*, New York (1927).
[2] Excluding private banks not under state supervision.
[3] Only about one-half of their domestic depositors have New York addresses.

emphasis on the investment phases of banking. They are among the oldest and the most powerful of the credit institutions, and have figured prominently in the history of the Street in times of crisis, or in various battles waged for the control of different corporations. The private banks, through interlocking directorates, are linked with domestic and foreign industrial concerns and railroads and utilities. So close is the relationship in some cases that a corporation may be known as the protégé of one of the private banks. Even some of the incorporated banks are thought of as being particularly close to certain of the private banks. Several of the unincorporated banks have served as fiscal agents of foreign governments, and have played important rôles in the post-war financial rehabilitation of Europe. Their financial statements are never published, though their power is not to be measured in terms of their assets alone, but in the prestige of the firms and the personal connections and fortunes of the partners.

Agencies of foreign banks

With the growth in the international connections and importance of the New York money market, numerous foreign banks have established agencies or maintain representatives in the financial district. Many years ago the Canadian banks, which have been heavy lenders in the call loan market and important participants in the foreign exchange market, took the lead in establishing such agencies. The close ties between the United States and Canada, of a commercial, economic and financial nature, made this inevitable. In more recent years, agencies of Japanese, British, French, German, Italian, and Greek banks, to cite but a few, have been established, though not all of the important foreign banks are so represented, since many conduct their American business entirely through a correspondent New York institution.

Acceptance corporations

Another phase of the growing international importance of the Street has been the development of the discount market. The rôle that it has played in the financing of international trade has given rise to the establishment of at least three specialized acceptance corporations. These have come to occupy positions of importance in the market and through their efforts have contributed to the use of the dollar acceptance.

The Federal Reserve bank

The keystone of the arch is the Federal Reserve bank, exercising a predominant influence over the credit volume and on market rates of interest. Though only incorporated domestic banks are members, the credit operations of the Reserve bank, changes in the bank rate and changes in its open-market portfolio, affect to some degree the policies of member and non-member banks, of domestic and foreign banks, of incorporated and unincorporated banks.

The Clearing House

The Clearing House, established in 1853 on the basis of recommendations made many years earlier by Albert Gallatin, still exists to handle the clearance of checks among member institutions. The functions it formerly exercised during crises, in the issuance of Clearing House loan certificates, Clearing House certificates, and in the pooling of reserves, have been assumed in a different form and with a different technique by the Federal Reserve bank. Even though stripped of its central banking functions, the Clearing House still is used by its members for the promulgation of uniform rules relative to the rates of interest to be paid on deposits, collection charges and charges imposed for the placing of loans for out-of-town banks on the brokers' loan market. In the establishment of uniform rules and regulations, some of which have been adopted to supplement the credit control policies of the Reserve bank, it thus still exercises considerable influence.

The intermediaries

To facilitate the relations between the various parts and parties to the market, there have been called into being a host of intermediaries. Among these are stock and bond brokers, produce brokers, money brokers, note brokers, bill brokers, foreign exchange brokers, insurance brokers, ship brokers, custom house brokers, freight brokers, merchandise brokers, and commission merchants of various and sundry types. In the history of the money market, one class of brokers has disappeared, and that is the bullion brokers, who flourished during the gold suspension period from 1861 to 1879.

The specialists

Added to the intermediaries are other specialized vocations, such as those of lawyers, accountants, statisticians, economists and investment counselors, vocations called forth by the demand for specialized services. In the financial district, within a short distance of one another, may be found those with expert knowledge of domestic and foreign money market conditions, of the conditions of different industries at home and abroad, of economic conditions in various countries, which makes the money market the repository of a greater volume of information, of domestic and foreign economic and financial conditions, than any other single center with the possible exception of London.

The exchanges

In concluding the category of the financial institutions of the money market, the organized exchanges must be mentioned. These have been established to furnish rooms for the convenient consummation of transactions among the member brokers. The conduct of members and of their transactions is regulated and supervised in the interests of the maintenance of high standards of economy, efficiency and honesty. The organized exchanges include the New York Stock Exchange, the New York Curb Association, the New York Cotton Exchange, the New York Produce Exchange, the New York Coffee and Sugar Exchange, the New York Cocoa Exchange, the Rubber Exchange of New York, etc.

Divisions of the money market

The great variety of different instruments subject to money market supply and demand obviously cannot be adequately dealt with in any one general market and, as a result, the student of the New York money market finds himself confronted with, not one, but many money markets, each with its own machinery for bringing together bids and offers for a particular kind of instrument. These different submarkets of the New York money market include, for example, the market for Federal funds, the call loan money market, the commercial paper market, the discount market, the government bond market and the general securities market.

On the basis of the length of the loan, the money market is conventionally divided into the following groups. the call loan market, including brokers' loans and to a minor extent call loans against acceptances, the short-term market, including time security loans, commercial paper, bankers' acceptances and short-term government securities, and the long-term market or capital market including the bond market. As a matter of logic, and viewing the situation as a whole, there is but one money market, of which the above three elements are parts. The supply of loanable funds is available for the use of any one of the three and that one which is the highest bidder (in relation to all circumstances) will obtain the use of the funds offered. This does not mean that one rate would logically obtain synchronously in all three elements of the money market, inasmuch as the length of the loan is, in itself, a partially determining factor With a rising time price, there is likely to be a greater tendency to apply "free capital" to short-term contracts in preference to long-term contracts. The result may be a relative increase in the supply of loanable funds for short-term credits and a relative decrease in the supply of funds for long-term credits. Thus a rising general time price may result in an actual decline in the call loan rate if the above tendency is sufficiently marked. With a very rapid decline in the general time price, the reverse would be likely to occur

With the general time price changing only slowly, the equilibrium between short-term loans and long-term loans will tend to be maintained, and the three series of rates will tend to correlate positively Sudden and violent changes in general time prices, however, may tend to cause a negative correlation between short-term and long-term interest rates.[4]

[4] Smith, James G., "The Measurement of Time Valuation," *American Economic Review*, Vol. XVIII, p. 247, June, 1928.

Doctrine of "non-competing groups" in the money market

Viewed as a general proposition of logic, then, the call loan market, the short-term market, and the long-term market, are all one money market; and among these the available funds of the money market would be distributed in accordance with the fundamental principles of time price, assuming perfect competition and an organization of money market institutions in such a way as to allow a free flow of funds from one to another. As a matter of practical significance, money market institutions and financial customs have developed in such a manner that freedom in the flow of funds from one to another of the three elements of the money market—e. g., from the call loan market to the short-term market or from the call loan market to the long-term or investment market—is hampered to a degree. To the extent that this is true, the three elements of the money market constitute "non-competing groups."

Primarily this volume will deal with the short-term money markets, which are the more immediately affected by increments and decrements of money market funds. In general the shorter the term of the instrument dealt in, the more responsive the market to strictly monetary phenomena.

This completes the brief catalogue of the divisions and institutions of the money market, a picture that has been painted purposely in broad strokes to convey an idea of the magnitude of its operations, the specialization of its functions, the world-wide ramifications of its activities.

Before proceeding to an analysis of the forces operative in the several short-term money markets, the factors which affect the basis of the credit employed in the money markets will first receive attention. This will be followed in turn by an analysis, first of the concentration, and then of the ebb and flow, of domestic and foreign funds. Proceeding from this, in Volume III, the uses of the funds of the money market in the form of brokers' loans, commercial paper and bankers' acceptances will be analysed. The importance of the Federal Reserve banks and the Federal government as factors in the money market and in money market changes warrants the inclusion in Volume IV of sections dealing with their activities. The study will conclude with an analysis of money market interrelationships and periodicities.

PART TWO

THE BASIS OF MONEY MARKET FUNDS

Chapter II

MEMBER BANK RESERVE BALANCES—STATUTORY REQUIREMENTS

Underlying the credit employed in money market and other transactions, is a stock of reserve funds, to which the total funds of the money market bear a definable relationship. The term "reserve funds" has been used to refer to the gold and lawful money reserves of the Federal Reserve banks, as well as to reserves which commercial banks hold against their own deposit liabilities and which in the case of member banks consist of realized deposit balances with the Reserve banks. From a statistical point of view, the analysis of the credit structure of the money market may be broadly divided, therefore, somewhat as follows: (1) statistics dealing with the volume and movement of primary reserve funds; (2) statistics dealing with the volume and movement of member bank deposits with the Federal Reserve banks; and (3) statistics dealing with the volume and movement of bank credit, as related to one of the various divisions of the money market.

The analysis of statistics of the volume and movement of bank credit as related to the money market constitutes a study of the actual credit in use; whereas the study of the first two alone is a study of underlying "protective" or regulatory funds, not actually in use in the money market; but serving as a base for the funds employed.

The total reported volume of bank loans and investments in the United States on June 30, 1931, came to 55 billions of dollars, and total deposits to 52 billions of dollars. Inasmuch as nonmember banks maintain their reserves in the main in the form of deposit accounts with member institutions,[1] directly or indirectly the entire amount of bank credit of the country rests on the reserves of the member institutions, deposit balances which they maintain

[1] See p. 33.

with the Federal Reserve banks and which amounted on the date of these figures to 2,381 millions of dollars.

By reason of the fact that member banks seldom maintain reserve balances larger than that prescribed by law, an increase in their own deposit liabilities requires an increase in their reserves. On the other hand, an increase in member bank reserves will permit a multiple expansion in bank credit in the form of loans and (or) investments accompanied by a multiple increase in bank deposits. The exact form which expansions in bank credit take will depend on the intensity of demand of the various credit markets, within the limitation set by bank portfolio policies, by the desire of banks to satisfy the needs of commercial customers and by any loan or investment restrictions incorporated in the banking statutes.

It is not the amount of bank loans and investments, of bank deposits, or of member bank reserve balances which are of prime importance to the money market. Rather it is the increases and decreases in the reserve balances, fluctuations at the margin, which are of greatest significance.[2] The money market is the focal point of those factors which induce fluctuations in bank reserves. Increments in bank reserves will permit the extension of a greater volume of credit and tend to ease rates. Decreases in bank reserves may lead to a sharp upward movement in money market rates, and to a restriction of credit or to a slackening in its rate of growth. The fact that member bank reserves constitute the basis of credit, whether employed in money market or other use, the fact that increases and decreases are likely to affect the money market first and are likely to be synchronous with changes in money rates and the volume of credit employed in the money market, necessitate the inclusion of a discussion of these in a volume treating of the money market.[3]

[2] See Chap. VII for an elaboration of this point.

[3] "A bank can increase its loans or investments only when it is in a position either to pay out cash or to create a new deposit liability, and its ability to do either of these things depends upon its cash reserves. The circumstances which tend to generate bank expansion, the creation of additional loans, discounts and investments, and additional bank deposits, are thus bound up in the circumstances governing the volume of bank reserves." B. M. Anderson, "An Analysis of the Money Market," *The Chase Economic Bulletin*, June 4, 1928, pp. 4–5.

Reserve provisions of National Bank Act

To trace the historical background in the character and amount of reserves required to be maintained, it will be recalled that the provisions of the National Bank Act of 1863 simply embodied customary usage. That this was the case is shown by the analysis, appearing in Volume I of these studies, of the actual situation existing prior to the passage of the Act and of the provisions of the measure itself. In the revision enacted in 1864, the reserves of the country national banks were lowered somewhat below the amounts habitually maintained. This was done to entice state banks into the system and was the first in a never-ending series of measures of the Federal and the state governments to lower standards in order to compete for bank membership.

In both the law of 1863 and that of 1864, the threefold classification of cities in the United States for purposes of determining reserve requirements was introduced, a classification that has continued to the present time. New York was designated as a Central Reserve city and continued as the only one in this group until 1887, when Chicago and St. Louis were added. Including Richmond and Charleston, added after the close of the Civil War, eighteen other cities were specifically named in the National Bank Act of 1864 as Reserve centers. Immediately prior to the establishment of the Federal Reserve system, on September 12, 1914, the number of Reserve cities, exclusive of Central Reserve cities, had increased to forty-nine. With subsequent additions, including St. Louis, which gave up its status as a Central Reserve city on July 1, 1922, there are at the present time 61 such centers. National banks located elsewhere are known as country banks.

Against all deposits, exclusive of deposits of public funds by the United States in designated depositaries, the country national banks prior to the introduction of the Reserve system, were to maintain at all times a reserve of 15 per cent, and national banks in the Reserve and Central Reserve cities a reserve of 25 per cent. Two-fifths of the reserves of the country national banks were to be maintained on hand in the form of lawful money, and one-half of the reserves of the national banks in the Reserve cities were to be maintained in such form. The reserves of national banks in Central Reserve cities were to consist wholly of lawful money. Lawful money for purposes of reserve requirements, as defined by the amended provisions of the Act, included United States notes, the treasury notes of 1890, gold and silver coin, gold and silver certificates, and Clearing House specie certificates. National banks in the country towns were allowed to maintain the balance of their reserves in the form of deposits with national banks in Reserve or Central Reserve cities; and national banks in the reserve cities, in the form of deposits with national banks in Central Reserve cities.

Under the National Bank Act, the reserve basis of the banking system consisted in part of cash on hand and in part of deposits with other banks. Reserves were customarily pared down to the legal minimum, and to the extent that excess reserves were maintained, these were held in the form of deposit balances rather than in the form of cash. It is true that in the early history of the national banking system, excess cash reserves were held, a situation which arose from the fact that under the provisions of the 1864 enactment these were fixed under the amount customarily held. This excess was reduced through the years until the Act of June 20, 1874, released the cash reserves held against national bank notes. This increased the excess somewhat but thereafter, as before, the trend was steadily downwards. Even the banks in the Central Reserve cities, which were performing the functions of central banks, maintained cash reserves only slightly above the legal minimum. Any excess in deposited reserves was maintained for the most part by the country national banks. However, even that did not necessarily represent realized balances, since the float was customarily included and a check in the process of collection might serve double and triple duty as reserve funds.

The deposited reserves were themselves a function of the amount of cash held by the banks, so that the credit superstructure including the deposited reserves rested on cash in vault. Disregarding the effect of the silver legislation, the cash base could increase only through augmentations in the gold stock. Rediscount agencies empowered to enlarge bank reserves through credit extensions were lacking. This in part accounted for the reliance which existed upon the elasticity of foreign money markets, particularly the London market, from which gold was imported in event of emergencies. The rigidity of the system made for certain advantages, in that inflationary or speculative forces were soon checked and the readjustments following a crisis were made the more quickly. This hardly was sufficient to offset the advantage of elasticity to be obtained under a well managed central banking system, which through its open-market and discount policies would be in a position to check expansions, to mitigate the effects of gold imports and exports on the credit superstructure, and to perform that miscellany of functions generally lumped under the term of credit control.

Provisions of the Federal Reserve Act

Without stopping to recount the many changes which took place in the member bank reserve provisions of the Federal Reserve Act during its consideration by Congress, it is sufficient to state that the final measure constituted a distinct break with the past. In the completeness of this severance, it was hoped that the evils which had developed from the old redeposited reserve situation would be corrected, including the pyramiding of funds, and their concentration in the security loan markets of New York City. After a preliminary period of thirty-six months, the reserves of national banks and other member institutions were to consist entirely of vault cash or of balances with the Reserve banks. The framers of the Reserve Act looked upon the reserves required to be held in vault as primary reserves, and balances with the reserve banks as secondary reserves. Concentration of a part of the reserves with the regional banks was required in order that these might serve as clearing balances for member institutions [4] and provide a sufficiency of funds for effective open-market and discount operations on the part of the Reserve banks. To render

[4] In this connection it might be noted that the practice of the joint-stock banks in London of keeping reserves with the Bank of England had its origins in the practice of these banks of settling clearing balances on the books of the Bank of England.

the change less distasteful to the banking community and to avoid the contraction of credit which would have resulted, if the existing reserve ratios had been continued, the reserve requirements were reduced, and a differentiation introduced in the percentage of reserves to be held against demand and time deposits. The strength given to the banking system through the concentration of a part of the reserves with the central institutions was believed to justify the lower reserve percentages. The change was not to be effective immediately, but was to take place gradually over a three-year period.[5] The member bank reserve provisions of the original enactment are given on page 19. There was considerable dispute at the time over the inflationary or deflationary effects of the new legislation, with general agreement that the immediate result would be in the direction of credit expansion.

Deposit classifications and reserve balances

By section 19 of the Federal Reserve Act, deposits of national banks were for the first time classified under those of a demand and those of a time category, with a differentiation in the amount of reserves to be maintained against each type. This change arose from a desire to place national banks on a competitive footing with state institutions and from a recognition of the increasing importance of their savings and investment functions. Linked to this deposit classification was the provision in the original Reserve Act giving to national banks outside of the three Central Reserve cities the power to lend against farm mortgages up to one-fourth of capital and surplus or one-third of time deposits. The purpose of this was to permit the financing of local farm mortgage needs from local savings. By enlarging opportunities for the local employment of savings, it was expected that funds would be diverted from the money market, an advantage which was emphasized among others by Professor Sprague.

The proportion of time to total deposits has grown steadily since the enactment of these provisions. In 1914 time deposits

[5] See Warburg, Paul M., *The Federal Reserve System*, Vol. I, pp. 95–96. Willis, H. P., *The Federal Reserve System*, p. 349.

MEMBER BANK RESERVE REQUIREMENTS

Cities	Total required reserve		Distribution of reserve		
	Demand (payable within 30 days)	*Time (payable after 30 days)*	*In own vault*	*With Reserve banks*	*Balance*
Central Reserve cities	18 per cent	5 per cent	6/18	7/18	Balance in own vaults or with Federal Reserve bank at the option of the member bank
Reserve cities	15 per cent	5 per cent	6/15 for 36 months, thereafter 5/15	3/15 for first 12 months, to be increased by 1/15 each succeeding 6 months, until 9/15 shall have been deposited	For first 36 months balance in own vaults, or with Federal Reserve bank, or with national banks in Reserve, or Central Reserve cities. Thereafter balance was to be kept in own vaults or with Federal Reserve bank, or in both, at option of member bank
Country towns	12 per cent	5 per cent	5/12 for first 36 months, thereafter 4/12	2/12 for first 12 months, to be increased by 1/12 each succeeding 6 months, until 5/12 shall have been deposited	For first 36 months balance in own vaults, or with Federal Reserve bank, or with national banks in Reserve, or Central Reserve cities. Thereafter balance was to be kept in own vaults, or with Federal Reserve bank, or in both, at option of member bank

amounted to but 16.5 per cent of total deposits. The decline in demand deposits through the post-war inflation period, with the continued increase in time deposits, raised the proportion to 30.9 per cent by December 31, 1921, while at the close of 1930 time deposits accounted for nearly 40 per cent of total deposit liabilities.

Between the end of 1921, when the post-war forces of deflation had run their course, and 1930, net demand deposits increased by 36 per cent, while time deposits reflected a growth of 108 per cent. If demand deposits had increased as rapidly as time deposits, reserve balances would have had to have been approximately 900 millions of dollars larger in 1930 than was actually the case. If, on the other hand, time deposits had increased as slowly as demand deposits, reserve balances would have been smaller by only 135 millions of dollars.

It was the very rapid increase in time deposits that permitted a huge credit expansion to take place, with only a moderate increase in reserve balances. At the end of 1917, member bank reserves with the reserve banks came to 1,497 millions of dollars or to an amount equal to 9.6 per cent of total deposit liabilities. Despite an increase in total deposits of 18 billions of dollars through the succeeding eleven years, reserve balances increased by only 912 millions of dollars. The percentage of reserves fell from 9.6 to 7.2. If till money, *i. e.,* cash in vault, is added to reserve balances at each date, the percentage decline is even greater, which is accounted for by an absolute decline that had taken place in till money.

Nature of time deposits

The genesis and nature of time accounts has been the subject of considerable discussion during the past few years.[6] Analyses of available evidence indicate that they are more closely linked to bank lending operations, stimulated in part by the "easy-money"

[6] The most thorough study of the nature of time deposits is that which was prepared by Professor William Howard Steiner of the College of the City of New York and filed with the United States Senate Committee on Banking and Currency in Feb. 1926. See also "Member Bank Reserves," *Report of the Committee on Bank Reserves of the Federal Reserve System.* Washington: Government Printing Office, 1931.

policies of the Federal Reserve banks than to the accumulations of savings by workingmen and other wage earners. Reference to the table below brings out the fact that while time deposits increased continuously through the period, except through 1929 and

ALL MEMBER BANKS
(In millions of dollars)

Call date	Net demand deposits	Time deposits	Net demand plus time deposits	Reserve with Federal Reserve banks	Cash in vault	Per cent of reserve with Federal Reserve banks to net demand plus time deposits	Per cent of reserve with Federal Reserve banks plus cash in vault to net demand plus time deposits
1914 Dec. 31	6,235	1,233	7,468				
1915 Dec. 31	7,971	1,506	9,477				
1916 Dec. 27	9,502	1,983	11,485				
1917 Dec. 31	12,487	3,156	15,643	1,497		9.6	
1918 Dec. 31	14,563	3,834	18,397	1,655	675	9.0	12.7
1919 Dec. 31	16,576	5,305	21,881	1,904	691	8.7	11.9
1920 Dec. 29	15,345	6,188	21,533	1,763	678	8.2	11.3
1921 Dec. 31	14,449	6,451	20,900	1,758	478	8.4	10.7
1922 Dec. 29	16,203	7,645	23,848	1,939	562	8.1	10.5
1923 Dec. 31	16,376	8,651	25,027	1,900	561	7.6	9.8
1924 Dec. 31	18,468	9,805	28,273	2,228	597	7.9	10.0
1925 Dec. 31	19,260	10,653	29,913	2,238	575	7.5	9.4
1926 Dec. 31	18,922	11,440	30,362	2,210	523	7.3	9.0
1927 Dec. 31	20,105	12,765	32,870	2,514	523	7.6	9.2
1928 Dec. 31	19,944	13,453	33,397	2,409	564	7.2	8.9
1929 Dec. 31	19,797	13,233	33,030	2,374	558	7.2	8.9
1930 Dec. 31	18,969	13,546	32,516	2,475	593	7.6	9.4
1931 Dec. 31	15,716*	11,316	27,032	1,975	523	7.3	9.2

* Estimated.

1931, the greatest absolute annual increases (those totaling a billion dollars or over) took place in 1917, 1919, 1922, 1923, 1924 and 1927. With the exception of 1923, those were the years that were also characterized by maximum expansions taking place in demand deposits.

The statement that the growth in time deposits is related in part at least to the easy-money policies of the Reserve banks, *i. e.*, to their open-market purchases, receives substantiation by developments taking place through 1924 and 1927. In each of these years the Reserve banks greatly expanded their open-market portfolios, placing banks in possession of excess reserves, upon the basis of which they expanded their loans and investments to a multiple extent. Reflecting or accompanying the increases in these bank asset items, both demand and time deposits rose rapidly. The growth in time deposits was specially marked in the case of those banks located in towns of 100,000 or more persons, which were the very institutions experiencing the greatest growth in demand deposits. If time deposits represented true savings, the great increase in 1924 would be difficult to explain in view of the decline in production and employment as compared with 1923. Nor may the large increase in 1927 be explained on the basis of increased production, employment or pay rolls, indices for which were all lower than during the preceding year.

If increases in time accounts, as some allege, are simply reflective of monetary savings, one would expect the rate of increase to be somewhat similar to that of mutual savings banks' deposits, taking into consideration the fact that in those sections in which they are found, mutual savings banks generally pay a higher rate of interest than do national banks on time deposits and therefore possess a competitive advantage. Yet despite this, we find through the post-war period that the annual rate of increase in time deposits has greatly exceeded that of mutual savings banks' deposit totals. In the years of greatest expansion, the average rate of increase has been twice as great.[7]

[7] A study pointing to the same conclusion, that time deposits are not wholly the result of savings, was that involving a statistical comparison of the activity of the accounts in the mutual savings banks of Massachusetts with the activity of the savings accounts in the commercial banks. The results revealed that the velocity of the latter greatly exceeded that of the former.

The lack of similarity between time deposits and those of mutual savings-banks, is illustrated by the fact that while a substantial decline took place in the time deposits of member banks in the Boston Federal Reserve district between May and November, 1928, the deposits of mutual savings banks increased at the usual rate. (*Monthly Review*, Federal Reserve Bank of Boston, Dec. 1, 1928, p. 3.) See also *Monthly Review of Business and Credit Conditions*, Federal Reserve Bank of New York, April, 1929, p. 1.

The inescapable conclusion is that time deposits have not resulted solely from savings. They have reflected in no small degree larger extensions of bank credit based on the easy-money policies of the Federal Reserve banks. As Dr. Anderson puts it: "the great growth of time deposits has been in periods of monetary ease and rapid bank expansion, and not in periods of relatively firmer money and retarded bank expansion." [8]

To recapitulate, an important factor in the growth of time deposits has been increases taking place in the open-market portfolio of the Federal Reserve banks. The growth in member bank reserve balances led to an expansion of bank credit in the form of loans and investments. The bonds purchased by banks placed corporations, foreign governments and central banks in possession of an increased volume of bank deposits. Some part of these funds were either invested in money market use or transferred to time deposits. To the extent that they were shifted into time deposits, additional excess reserve balances were created on the basis of which the banking system could expand still further. Mr. Curtiss, of the Federal Reserve Bank of Boston, dealt on this point in an address delivered before the fifth annual meeting of stockholders: [9]

There is nothing better for a community than the accumulation of real savings in the savings departments of member banks, for many of the people whom these departments are supposed to serve have no other equally safe facilities for investing their money, and therefore have been too frequently an easy prey to sellers of speculative, unsound, and even fraudulent, securities. I see evidence, however, of a large amount of this increase in savings deposits coming from conversion of accounts which would ordinarily go into demand or commercial departments of banks. I refer especially to the large sums of money that are put either into savings deposits or into certif-

[8] Anderson, B. M., "Bank Expansion versus Savings," *The Chase Economic Bulletin*, June 25, 1928, pp. 14–15.

[9] *Proceedings of the Fifth Annual Meeting of Stockholders of the Federal Reserve Bank of Boston*, Held at the Banking House, Friday, Nov. 11, 1927, pp. 8–11. See testimony of Governor Harrison of the Federal Reserve Bank of New York, *Hearings before a Subcommittee of the Committee on Banking and Currency*, United States Senate, Seventy-first Congress, Third Session Pursuant to S. Res. 71, Part I, p. 35.

icates of deposit without definite maturity,—deposits that are really subject to immediate demand and represent unemployed working capital.

Of course all of these deposits and certificates are supposedly subject to thirty days' notice, but you and I know that no bank would take advantage of this provision except under very unusual circumstances. This conversion has come about in order that the banks may have the benefit of the three percent reserve provision for time deposits instead of the higher reserve called for against demand deposits. These large deposits are competed for even more keenly than the smaller ones, and the fact that such deposits may constitute a demand liability should be given most careful consideration by the management of every bank. I am led to believe that the competition in this district for this class of account is fully as keen as, if not keener than, in other sections of the country. The only exception perhaps is the San Francisco districts where, through rather unusual circumstances, there have been large increases in such accounts.

The difference in reserve requirements has been great enough to induce banks to encourage the shifting of deposits from the demand to the time category.[10] No impediment has been placed in the way of this process, through a limitation on the maximum volume of time deposits that might be received from any one interest or through segregation of time deposits and of the offsetting assets. Through such shifting, excess bank reserves are created, money market rates of interest lowered, and a further expansion in bank credit made possible. The reverse movement, the shifting of deposits from the time to the demand category, in forcing member banks to build up their reserve balances through rediscounts, if the reserve banks are not putting funds into the market and in the absence of gold imports or currency retirement, serves to tighten market rates of interest. In periods of high money rates, the shifting from demand to time accounts would prevent interest rates from reaching the heights that would otherwise be the case, whereas, in periods of low money rates, shifts in this direction would make money rates still easier.

The experience through the years with the shifting of deposits

[10] An advantage offset to a minor extent by the difference in rates of interest paid on time and demand accounts.

bears out the wisdom of the framers of the Glass Bill (the Federal Reserve Act as enacted by the House of Representatives) in requiring a complete segregation of the liabilities and the offsetting assets of the savings departments.[11] An assignment of a specified amount of capital was provided. The Federal Reserve Board was given the power to prepare rules and regulations for the conduct of the savings departments. The employment of time deposits in investments of a type approved by the Board was to have been required. Furthermore, in event of insolvency the assets held in the savings departments were to be used for the repayment of time deposit liabilities. The wisdom of this last provision has been demonstrated by the fact that in the thousands of bank failures taking place in the United States since 1920 the time depositor, to the extent that his funds represented actual savings, has received less proportionately in the final liquidation of assets than the demand depositor.[12] The reasons are that the demand depositor is frequently a person of sufficient contacts or knowledge to withdraw his account prior to failure; or he is, at the same time, a borrower and his deposits are offset against his own liability to the bank. In its failure to provide for such departmentalization, the final Federal Reserve Act must be held accountable for the lack of sufficient protection for the savings depositor and for that portion of credit inflation or expansion, in the money market or elsewhere, made possible through a shifting of slow demand accounts into the time category.

The transfer of reserves

On the day, November 16, 1914, designated by the Secretary of the Treasury, Mr. McAdoo, for the opening of the Reserve

[11] In this provision the Glass Bill was following the recommendations of various students of banking reform. As far back as 1910, Professor E. W. Kemmerer wrote: "Finally, let me say that I heartily sympathize with Professor Sprague's proposal that national banks be authorized to establish true savings departments 'with segregated deposits payable at notice, which might be invested in mortgages.' In the carrying out of such a plan, it is perhaps needless to say, great care should be taken to prevent the juggling of accounts." ("The Reform of the Currency," *Proceedings of the Academy of Political Science in the City of New York*, Jan. 1911, p. 253.)

[12] For a recommendation of Mr. Joseph Broderick, Superintendent of Banks,

banks, member banks were to make their first transfer of reserves to the new institutions. The Federal Reserve Board had requested that it be made in gold and gold certificates. The Act required that payments on account of capital stock take this form and the first of these had been made on the second of November. By suggesting that member banks build up their reserve balances in the same fashion, the Reserve Board hoped to accumulate a large stock of gold to form the basis of note issues, rediscounts and open-market operations.

To induce each member bank to ship specie from its own holdings, the Reserve banks agreed to assume express charges. Otherwise it was feared that some member banks might dispatch drafts on their correspondents, the collection of which by the Reserve banks would involve a heavy additional strain on the specie holdings of banks in Reserve and Central Reserve cities.[13] In other words, it was desired that the withdrawal of funds from the vaults of member banks be as nearly uniform as possible and geographically so evenly distributed that no section would bear an unusual burden.

The aggregate amount of cash required to be transferred to the Reserve banks and to be held in the vaults of member banks was substantially below the amount of cash reserves formerly maintained, 713 millions of dollars as compared with 903 millions of dollars. This meant a release of 190 millions of dollars of reserve cash, to which must be added an additional 275 millions of dollars representing a release of deposited reserves. The total reduction in member bank reserves in the form of cash and deposited reserves amounted thus to about 465 millions of dollars.[14] The expectation of those that the new system would initially, at least, tend towards monetary ease rather than tension was fulfilled. In itself the release of reserves would have brought about a sharp decline in rates of interest, which in normal times would have

---

New York State, relative to segregation of thrift accounts, see *The New York Times*, March 25, 1931, p. 2.

[13] Willis, *The Federal Reserve System*, Chap. XXIX, *First Annual Report of the Federal Reserve Board*, p. 167.

[14] *Annual Report of the Comptroller of the Currency*, Dec. 7, 1914, Vol. I, pp. 31–33.

been accompanied by an expansion in credit and a rise in prices and gold exports. However, with the outbreak of the World War, the times were anything but normal. The immediate effect of the War was to plunge this country into a severe economic crisis and industrial depression. International economic relationships were disrupted, the foreign exchanges were demoralized, a temporary suspension of international trade occurred, and the stock exchanges were closed in the financial centers of the world. Following the acute immediate requirements of the crisis for currency and credit, the demand fell and this was an additional easing factor in the situation towards the close of 1914. Owing to these complicating factors the effects of the payment of the first installment of reserves are not clearly discernible.

When the time came, November 16, 1915, for the payment of the second installment on the part of the country and Reserve city banks, the economic situation had completely changed. The composite index of business activity compiled by the American Telephone and Telegraph Company stood 9 per cent above "normal" as compared with 17 per cent below during the same month of the previous year. The increase in business activity reflected the intense war demand for the impedimenta of conflict. To pay for the goods purchased, the Allies resorted to a variety of expedients. During the early days of the War, they canceled America's floating indebtedness on open account. Later gold was exported, American securities returned and loans floated. It was the influx of gold that permitted member banks to meet the second and subsequent transfers of reserves without tightening the money market or reducing the volume of credit. Had it not been for this, the carrying out of the reserve provisions of the original Federal Reserve Act, though the immediate effect was inflationary, would at the end of the three year period have resulted in considerable tension.

In view of the increase in the monetary gold stock the problem became one, not of relieving the market, but of endeavoring to check price inflation. In order not to further expansionist tendencies, the Federal Reserve banks exercised great moderation in their open-market operations, utilizing them simply to cover their expenses of operation.[15]

Pre-war credit expansion

On the basis of an increase of 1,330 millions of dollars in the monetary gold stock from June, 1914, to June, 1917, concomitant with a release of member bank reserves and a reduction in the reserve requirements in the provisions of the banking laws of many states, the total superstructure of credit expanded rapidly. An increase of 7.5 billions of dollars took place in the loans and investments of all banks. Despite a deposit increase of 7.8 billions of dollars and an increase of 700 millions of dollars in the amount of money in circulation, the gold influx was of such large proportions that the ratio of gold to total bank deposits plus money in circulation advanced from 8.2 to 10 per cent.

Lowering and changing the character of the reserve requirements

By an amendment enacted on June 21, 1917, the reserves required of member banks were lowered to the following percentages, the entire amount of which was to be maintained as deposit accounts with the Reserve banks:

Type of deposit	*Central Reserve cities*	*Reserve cities*	*Country towns*
Demand	13	10	7
Time	3	3	3

It had been ruled previously by the Federal Reserve Board that deposited reserves must consist of realized balances, which meant that the checks sent to the Reserve banks for collection by member banks were not to be credited until actually collected. To facilitate this, tables were prepared by each Reserve bank of the time required to collect checks drawn on banks in various parts of the United States. Settlement between the Reserve banks was to take place through the gold settlement fund.

The 1917 enactment had been foreshadowed to some extent by the amendment of September 7, 1916, which empowered the Re-

[15] See Beckhart, B. H., *Discount Policy of the Federal Reserve System*, for discussion of methods used as suggested to neutralize the effect of the gold inflow.

serve Board, upon the affirmative vote of not less than five members, to permit member banks to carry with their respective Reserve banks any portion of their reserves then required to be held in their own vaults.[16] On the following day, the Board ruled that any member bank that desired might take such action. There was no response to these permissive provisions. In consequence the mandatory provisions were enacted, with which member banks located in the Federal Reserve bank cities were to comply immediately. Elsewhere they were given until July 15, 1917,[17] to satisfy the requirements of the amendment.

The amendment followed in every particular but one the recommendations made by the Federal Reserve Board in 1916.[18] The one exception was the omission of the requirement that member banks should hold in their own vaults an amount of specie or currency equal to at least 5 per cent of demand deposits, less the amount of excess balances held with the Reserve banks. The inclusion of this provision for a minimum till money requirement would, in the opinion of the Board, result in only a slight reduction in required reserves.[19] The reduction would arise from the difference in the reserve requirement of 3 as against 5 per cent to be held against time accounts, and from the absence of a provision in the case of time deposits for the maintenance of a minimum amount of till money.

Not confronted by a minimum till money requirement, member banks have pared their vault cash down to a very small percentage of total deposits. In the reduction that has been taking place in vault cash, the ease of obtaining currency from the Reserve banks and their many branches has been a factor of prime importance. In this, those member banks located in the Federal Reserve and branch cities have profited most, and the country banks the least. For example, as of December 31, 1929, the vault cash of the country member banks amounted to 321 millions of dollars, of member banks in Reserve cities to 156 millions of dollars, and of mem-

[16] *Federal Reserve Bulletin*, 1916, p. 508.
[17] *Federal Reserve Bulletin*, 1917, p. 503.
[18] *Third Annual Report of the Federal Reserve Board*, 1916, pp. 143–44.
[19] Willis, *The Federal Reserve System*, pp. 1183–84. For recommendation of the Federal Advisory Council, see *Fifth Annual Report of the Federal Reserve Board*, 1918, pp. 819–20.

ber banks in Central Reserve cities to 81 millions of dollars, a total of 558 millions of dollars. In per cent of demand deposits, these amounts were respectively 5.5, 2.6 and 1.14; while relative to total deposits, time and demand, they came to 2.8, 1.43 and 0.919 per cent. The holdings of vault cash as of this date on the part of the country member banks slightly exceeded the recommendation of the Reserve Board of a 5 per cent minimum against demand deposits. The cash holdings of member banks in Reserve and Central Reserve cities were considerably below the recommendation. If those institutions had held cash equal to the amount recommended by the Board, the volume of till money would have amounted to 943 millions of dollars instead of 558 millions of dollars, assuming, of course, that member banks were not maintaining excess balances with the Reserve banks. The omission of this recommendation of the Board, which should have applied equally to time and demand deposits, made for a very real reduction in reserve requirements, though the framers of the measure did not foresee the extent to which vault cash would be reduced.

The mandatory concentration or mobilization of member bank reserves with the Reserve banks must be looked upon as a part of the war finance program of the United States government and was for the purpose of bringing about an impounding of the gold stock of the country with the Federal Reserve banks. On the basis of concentrated reserves and impounded gold, the total volume of bank credit could be enlarged still further. War inflation was rendered the easier. Consequently the concentration of member bank reserves had far-reaching consequences. It increased the potential expansibility of the credit superstructure, even more than did the reduction in reserve percentages, and placed the responsibility for control over fluctuations in the volume of credit more completely in the hands of the Reserve officials. In no other country, and certainly not before the War, had such a marked degree of concentration of authority taken place.

Changes needed in present reserve requirements

From the fact that the 1917 amendments were purely a war measure, one must not conclude that, with the Armistice behind us by fifteen years, they should be repealed forthwith. To do so and to revert to the provisions of the original Federal Reserve Act, now that the superstructure of credit has adjusted itself to the lower reserve base, would involve deflationary consequences of a magnitude that would be extremely harmful and unnecessary. Even if the law should be changed, as many have suggested, to require the same percentage of reserves against time as are required against demand deposits, considerable time must be allowed for the banking system to adjust itself to the new requirements.

There is no question but that the present member bank reserve requirements are extremely deficient. This conclusion is reached in an elaborate study of the whole situation by the Committee on Bank Reserves of the Federal Reserve system.[20] The committee indicated that the tripartite classification of cities into Central Reserve cities, Reserve cities, and country towns, for purposes of reserve requirements, is obsolete and actually makes for an unfair and inequitable situation as between various types of member banks. Furthermore, the conclusion was reached that there is no practicable way of defining demand and time deposits in order to prevent the abuses arising from the shifting of slow demand accounts into the time category. That all time deposits do not represent genuine savings was shown by the fact that out of 13 billions of dollars of time deposits in May, 1931, 3 billions of dollars consisted of deposit balances of $25,000 or more in amount. The conclusion was reached that present reserve requirements do not take into account genuine differences in the character of banking entered into by individual member banks and are not such as to relate expansions in credit to the needs of trade and industry. Furthermore, the volume of reserves required may be affected by such extraneous considerations as the geographic location of the deposit accounts. In periods of low money rates, member banks located in smaller centers are apt to build up their bankers' balances with banks in metropolitan centers, which forces an increase in the volume of reserves maintained. The opposite is apt to be the case in periods of high money rates. The high money rates

[20] "Member Bank Reserves." *Report of the Committee on Bank Reserves of the Federal Reserve System.* Washington, Government Printing Office, 1931.

then prevailing might reflect Federal Reserve credit policies, and the fact that bankers' balances are drawn out of banks located in Reserve and Central Reserve cities lowers reserve requirements and to an extent nullifies Federal Reserve credit policies of the moment.

In an effort to solve the problems presented, the Federal Reserve Board suggests changes in reserve requirements which are made uniformly applicable to all member banks and to all types of deposits. Even the deposits of the United States government are brought under the proposed provisions. The tripartite classification of cities is done away with, as is the artificial distinction between demand and time deposits. It is suggested that all member banks maintain against all deposits a reserve of 5 per cent, plus an additional reserve equal to 50 per cent of average daily debits to deposit accounts. Changes in the definition of net demand deposits are proposed and suggestions made that a part of the reserves required be maintained in the form of cash in member banks' vaults.

While doubtless there would be differences of opinion as regards the technical details of the Board's proposals, the principle that member bank reserves should be related mainly to velocity of turnover rather than to volume is sound. The principle involved is somewhat akin to that to be found in the proposals of Professor John Maynard Keynes included in his *Treatise on Money*, but the technique is much more automatic in operation.[21] If the Board's proposal had been in force through 1929, member bank reserves would have been larger by several hundred millions of dollars, by reason of the increase in the activity of deposit accounts. This would have assisted in making Federal Reserve credit policies the more effective. As was actually the case, the deposit volume did not increase through 1929 so that the reserves maintained by member banks sagged until the time of the panic. The proposed requirements possess the merit of forcing an increase in member bank reserves during inflationary periods, when deposit activity is increasing, even though deposit volume may be falling, and of permitting a decrease during deflationary periods when the activity of deposit accounts is declining. Not that these

[21] Vol. II, Chap. XXXII.

proposed changes in reserve requirements may be considered as a substitute for central bank credit policies but rather should be viewed in the light of significant hand-maidens.

Summary

Bank credit, whether employed in money market or other use, rests on member bank reserve balances.[22] From the point of view of the money market increments and decrements in these are of the greatest significance. The money market is the focal point of those forces inducing increases or decreases in member bank reserves and is likely to experience the initial effects of such changes.

Inasmuch as the amount and character of reserves held by member banks is determined entirely by law, it was necessary for us to review changes in the legislation affecting these. The effect of such during the past seventeen years has been entirely in the direction of increasing the potential expansibility of a given increase in reserves. For fifty years the reserve requirements of the National Banking Act stood without material modification. This period of quiescence was followed by the enactments of 1913 and 1917, which altered completely the composition and reduced drastically the amount of the reserves required. With the concentration of member bank reserves brought about by the war amendments, with the absolute and relative declines in vault cash and currency in circulation, and with the increase in time deposits, the potential effects of a gold influx and of Federal Reserve open-market operations has been made the greater.

[22] The validity of this statement is not affected by the number of nonmember banks, inasmuch as these institutions maintain their reserves in the form of deposit balances with member institutions. See testimony of Mr. B. W. Trafford, *Hearings before a Subcommittee of the Committee on Banking and Currency*, United States Senate, Seventy-first Congress, Third Session, Pursuant to S. Res. 71, Part I, p. 242.

Chapter III

MEMBER BANK RESERVE POLICIES

Under the provisions of the National Bank Act, reserves at all times were required to equal the stipulated percentages. In order to provide for temporary deficiencies, reserve balances today are computed on an average basis. Deficiencies of member banks in those cities in which Federal Reserve banks and branches are located and in such other Reserve cities as the Federal Reserve Board may from time to time designate are computed on the basis of average daily net deposit balances covering semiweekly periods. Deficiencies in the reserve balances of member banks in all other Reserve cities are computed on the basis of average daily net deposit balances covering weekly periods, and deficiencies in the reserve balances of member banks located in country towns are computed on the basis of average daily net deposit balances covering semimonthly periods. In computing such deficiencies the required reserve balance of the member bank taken at the close of each business day is based upon the amount of its net deposit balances at the opening of business the same day.[1]

In the Federal Reserve district of New York, the semiweekly periods are fixed to end on Tuesday and Friday nights,[2] and the semimonthly periods are fixed to cover the first fifteen days and

[1] The change in reserve computation from the basis of the volume of deposits at the close of the day to that at the opening of the day's business was initiated on October 31, 1930. The change took place by reason of the fact that deposit fluctuations particularly towards the close of a day made it difficult for many banks to forecast their reserve requirements. *Federal Reserve Bulletin,* October, 1930, p. 645.

[2] Prior to January 3, 1928, reserve balances of member banks in the largest centers were computed on the basis of weekly averages. The change to semiweekly periods was made to eliminate the "jig-saw" practice of member banks in allowing their reserves to fall for a few days far below the legal minimum to be built up substantially above the minimum at the close of the period. A discussion of the staggering of reserve periods over the country in order to make for less disturbance in the money market is contained in Governor Strong's testimony in *Hearings before the Committee on Banking and Currency,* House of Representatives, Sixty-ninth Congress, First Session, on H. R. 7895, p. 453.

the balance of each month. This means that the New York City banks must maintain over Saturday, Monday and Tuesday, and over Wednesday, Thursday and Friday, an average balance with the Federal Reserve bank, taken as of the close of each day, equal to that required against average deposit liabilities taken as of the opening of business each day. Penalties on reserve deficiencies are assessed monthly on the basis of the average daily deficiencies. The penalty imposed is assessed at a basic rate of 2 per cent per annum above the Federal Reserve bank discount rate on 90-day commercial paper in effect on the first day of the calendar month in which the deficiencies occurred.[3]

Maintaining reserves at a minimum

The practice of American banks has not changed from that followed prior to the passage of the Federal Reserve Act in paring reserves down to the legal minimum. Statistical verification of this is to be found in the data compiled by the Comptroller of the Currency and the Federal Reserve Board, which reveal that the country banks maintain proportionately larger excess reserves than the Reserve city or Central Reserve city institutions.[4] The country bank excess ranges from 3 to 5 per cent, while that for the Reserve city banks does not ordinarily exceed 2 per cent.

For many years it had been possible to follow changes in the reserve position of the New York City Clearing House banks from the Saturday condition statement. Data were given of the weekly average surplus or deficit in reserves, as well as of the actual condition on Saturday. The last of the Clearing House statements to contain this information was published for the week ending March 24, 1928. The reason given by the Clearing House authorities for eliminating the data was that these had lost their significance and were consequently subject to misinterpretation.[5] There was much truth in their contention. Inas-

[3] For long continued deficiencies progressive penalties may be imposed and drastic action taken. See Regulation "D" of the Federal Reserve Board.

[4] *Sixteenth Annual Report of the Federal Reserve Board,* 1929, p. 108. In 1931 member banks in New York City and Chicago did maintain excess reserves in relatively large amounts.

[5] See *New York Times,* financial section, April 1, 1928, p. 16. *Commercial and Financial Chronicle,* March 31, 1928.

much as the required reserves of the New York City banks are now computed on a semiweekly average basis, a Saturday deficit or surplus has little meaning. Furthermore the reserve is no longer a cash reserve, as it had been up to 1914, but a deposit credit on the books of the Reserve bank. Since this may be augmented at will by increased borrowings on the part of member institutions or by purchases of Federal funds,[6] there is really little excuse for a bank to experience a reserve deficiency. Reserve deficiencies reflect themselves in the item "bills discounted" on the Federal Reserve statement or in increases in the Federal funds' rate. Despite the cogency of these arguments, the dropping of the data at this particular time was interpreted as the result of a succession of Saturday deficits in reserves and as a concession to the speculative group.

How closely the New York City banks pare their reserves down to the legal minimum is illustrated in the accompanying chart in which monthly averages of the weekly averaged reserve position of the Clearing House banks are depicted. The data for the years prior to 1920 illustrate the policy of the banks in working reserves down to a minimum whether the excess be due to gold imports or to a change in legal reserve requirements.[7] In recent years the average monthly excess has risen only occasionally above 10 millions of dollars. The increase in the summer months of 1924 reflected the expanding open-market portfolio of the Reserve system and the increase in the monetary gold stock.

The fact that banks pare reserves down to a minimum is very important in an understanding of money market fluctuations. Obviously the reason is that the Reserve banks do not pay interest on deposits and that they should not do so is a cardinal principle in central banking practice.[8] Despite this member banks might maintain excess reserves if, in their opinion, dictates of prudence required them to do so. Though this was the practice followed in the early days of the Reserve system, member banks have come

[6] See pp. 40–48.

[7] Source of data: weekly Clearing House statements appearing in *The Commercial and Financial Chronicle*.

[8] Incidentally it has been suggested that as one instrument of credit control the Reserve banks pay interest at varying amounts on the excess balances.

so to depend upon the resources of the Federal Reserve banks to meet any need, that surplus reserves for the system as a whole seldom amount to more than 3 per cent of the reserves required.

Factors affecting reserve balances

To some official in each of the New York banks is delegated the task of adjusting the bank's reserve position. The reserve

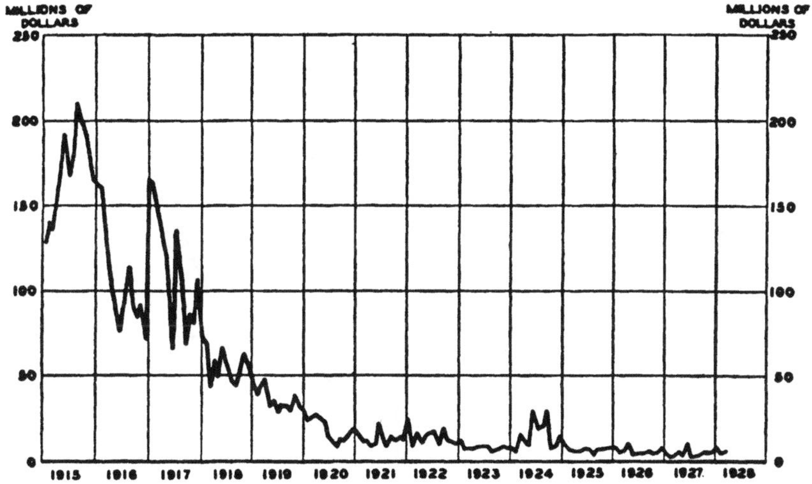

CHART I. EXCESS RESERVES OF THE NEW YORK CITY CLEARING HOUSE BANKS, 1915–1928.
MONTHLY AVERAGES OF WEEKLY DATA.

balance of the individual bank fluctuates with the local ebb and flow of funds, since Clearing House balances are settled on the books of the Federal Reserve bank, and with the sectional ebb and flows which would not only result in changes in the reserve balances of the individual banks but also in changes of ownership in the gold settlement fund of the Federal Reserve banks affected.[9] In addition to the local and sectional inflow and drain of funds, the reserves of the individual bank are influenced by all those factors that affect the banking system, fluctuations in the monetary stock of gold, fluctuations in the volume of currency in circulation, and changes that take place in various items on the

[9] See Chaps. XVI and XVII for further discussion.

statement of condition of the Reserve banks. A decline in the gold stock, an increase in the amount of money in circulation (since vault cash is maintained at a minimum), a decline in holdings of securities or bankers' bills by the Federal Reserve banks, a decline in the Federal Reserve float account, an increase in gov-

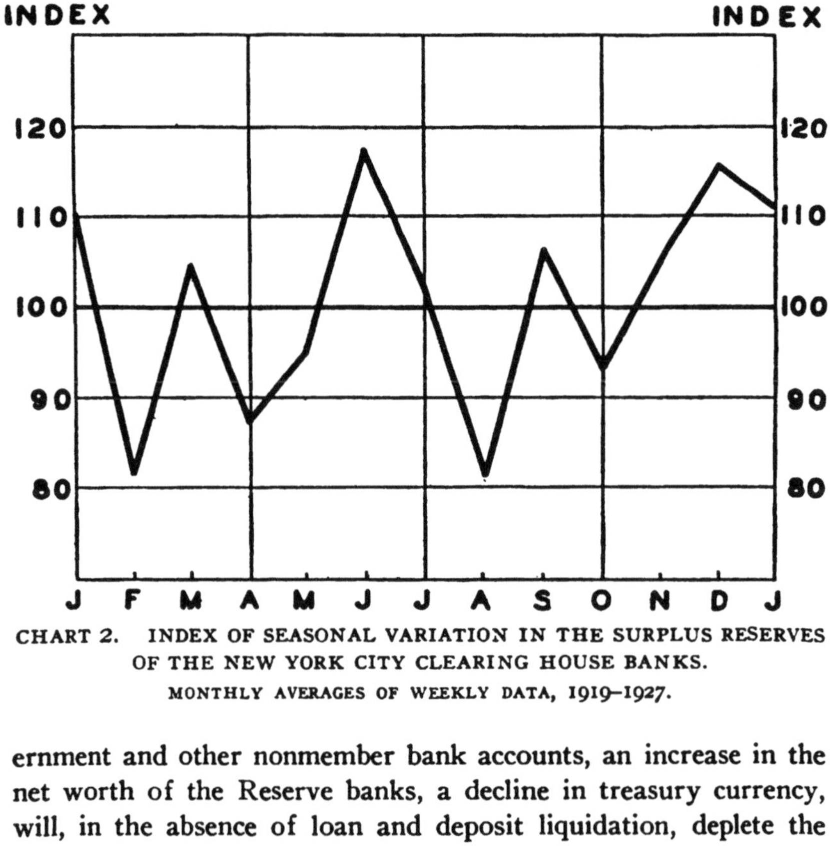

CHART 2. INDEX OF SEASONAL VARIATION IN THE SURPLUS RESERVES OF THE NEW YORK CITY CLEARING HOUSE BANKS.
MONTHLY AVERAGES OF WEEKLY DATA, 1919–1927.

ernment and other nonmember bank accounts, an increase in the net worth of the Reserve banks, a decline in treasury currency, will, in the absence of loan and deposit liquidation, deplete the member bank reserve account, and the reverse movement in each of these factors will swell member bank reserves. In the next few chapters detailed consideration will be given to these factors and the effect of their fluctuations on member bank reserve balances.

The effect of certain of these forces may be foreseen. The official in charge of the adjustment of the reserve balance may estimate the inflow of funds resulting from the repayment of loans, from the maturity of bond holdings, from government fiscal operations, and from periodic movements of the currency. The drain of funds away from the bank may be estimated on the basis of new loans made, of increases in investment holdings, of government operations and of periodicities in the sectional ebb and flow. Since it is the function of this official to maintain the reserve balance at the legal minimum, the anticipated receipt of a large volume of funds is the occasion for allowing the reserve balance to fall below the legal minimum on a particular day provided that the expected inflow is of sufficient proportions so that the average for the period will be equal to the amount required.

Employing excess reserves

Excess reserves are employed immediately. Considerations of profit require that this be done. On the first day they might be sold as Federal funds, and thereafter used as the basis for increased extensions of credit to the brokers' loan market, increased investments in commercial paper, in bankers' acceptances, of increases in loans to customers, or of increased investments in government bonds and notes and other types of funded obligations. Whether the excess is diverted to one use or to another would depend largely on the judgment of the "surplus funds committee" of the bank regarding the relative profit possibilities of the different loan markets and of the length of time for which the excess reserves will be available.

Excess reserves might be used also to reduce the indebtedness of the member bank if it is in debt to its Reserve bank. In this connection borrowings of member banks are likely to be a most responsive item on the Federal Reserve statement. These rise in response to factors depleting reserves and fall in response to fluctuations in factors making for an increase in reserve balances.

Replenishing of reserves

Reserves depleted through the shifting of funds, fluctuations in the currency, changes in the monetary stock of gold, in the open-market portfolio of the Reserve banks, etc., are ordinarily restored, as indicated previously, by member banks increasing their borrowings or rediscounts with their Reserve bank. Occasionally member banks sell securities or bills outright or under resale agreement to the Reserve banks. Only a few, however, carry a bill portfolio and fewer still make use of their portfolio in the adjustment of their reserve balances. In addition to these direct methods, an individual bank might replenish its reserves in a manner that would shift the burden to other units of the banking system. The sale of securities, the calling of Stock Exchange loans, and the transfer of deposit balances maintained with larger member banks to the Reserve bank are examples in point. In all of these cases the increase in the reserve balance of one bank results in a decrease in the reserve balance of some other unit in the banking system.

The market for Federal funds

There is still another method by which a member bank may increase its reserve balance, a method which has given rise to the development of a new "market" within that congeries of institutions known as the money market.[10] This is the practise of buying and selling Federal funds, so that an excess balance standing to the credit of one bank on the books of the Federal Reserve bank is shifted to another which is experiencing a deficit.[11] While it is true that the excess balances of the banking system as a whole are negligible in amount, it is also true that in the shifting of funds within a given locality and from section to section, individual banks from time to time find themselves in possession of excess balances with their Reserve bank of which they may make most profitable disposal at the moment by selling to other banks.

The market for Federal funds arises from the fact that while Reserve banks give immediate credit to checks drawn on them-

[10] The authors have been assisted in this section by the work of one of the graduate students in Columbia University, Mr. F. H. N. Hawkins. Reference should also be made to Miss Bernice C. Turner's detailed treatment of the subject in her work *The Federal Fund Market,* New York, Prentice-Hall, Inc., 1931.

[11] By a ruling of the Federal Reserve Board, a purchase of Federal funds must be shown on the member bank statement as bills payable and a sale of Federal funds as a grant of a loan.

selves and on the United States government, those drawn upon commercial banks are credited only as collected, in accordance with a definite time schedule. In New York, for example, Clearing House checks are one-day items unless received before 9 A. M., while checks drawn upon banks outside of the city are not credited until from one to eight days later. Consequently a New York bank which on a Tuesday or Friday finds its reserve balance deficient for the semiweekly period, but does not wish to borrow from, or sell bills and securities to, the Reserve bank, must buy Federal funds from some other bank in order to avoid the heavy penalties imposed for reserve deficiencies.

Mechanics of trading in Federal funds

If the bank in need of Federal funds deals directly with the institution possessing excess reserves, it would simply give its own check, a cashier's check with interest added for one day, in exchange for a check on the Federal Reserve bank.[12] The rate of interest agreed upon by the two institutions is commonly termed the Federal funds' rate. The check drawn on the Reserve bank is deposited there by the buying bank and becomes effective immediately, while the cashier's check received by the selling bank passes through the Clearing House the next day and cancels the indebtedness.

The increasing activity of the Federal funds' market has given rise to the handling of the transactions by intermediaries, so that the operation is customarily not direct, but rather triangular in nature. The function of intermediary has been assumed, among other institutions, by the discount corporations, *i.e.*, by the bill brokers;[13] since they have accounts with the Reserve banks and are in a position to sell their own checks on the Reserve bank. The deposit accounts of the discount corporations are built up through the purchase of excess balances from member institutions or through the sale of bills or securities, direct or under resale agreement, to the Reserve banks.

[12] This could be effected as well by entries on the books of the Federal Reserve bank.

[13] See Vol. III, Chap. XII.

In purchasing Federal funds, discount corporations give a cashier's check or else a check drawn on a commercial bank, with interest added for one day. Small amounts of Federal funds are purchased outright, whereas large blocks are customarily acquired on an option basis. Against their balance with the Reserve bank, increased through the purchase of Federal funds, they sell their own check and receive the cashier's check of the buying bank in return. The differential established between the rates at which the discount corporations buy and sell usually ranges from 1/4 to 3/8 of one per cent, but is not sufficient to eliminate the dealer.

The volume of Federal funds handled in the money market in any one day ranges up to 250 millions of dollars, with 100 millions of dollars representing a normal day's trading. The volume handled naturally mounts on the settlement days, Tuesdays and Fridays, inasmuch as the greatest demand for Federal funds arises from banks desirous of adjusting their reserve balances. Some banks, however, adjust their position constantly, so that there is a continuous demand from this source.

Other sources of the supply and demand for Federal funds in the money market arise from the clearing accounts of the nonmember institutions, from the open-market operations of the Reserve banks, from transactions between dealers in United States securities and in bankers' acceptances with the Reserve banks, and from certain of the transactions of foreign banks with the Reserve banks.

A large amount of intercity trading in Federal funds is carried on, especially between banks in Boston, New York, Philadelphia, Chicago and San Francisco, either directly, through correspondents or through one of the dealers possessing a network of branches. Since trading in Federal funds is on a day-to-day basis, transactions between distant points involve complexities in the multilateral nature of the transactions.

Differences in rates of rediscount at the different Federal Reserve banks tend to stimulate an interdistrict flow of Federal funds. Such transactions, however, occur only between the better known banks in the larger centers.

In an effort to ascertain the extent of trading in Federal funds and the reasons for the practice, the United States Senate Committee on Banking and Currency incorporated a query along these lines in a questionnaire which it sent in 1931 to the various Federal Reserve banks. Five Reserve banks, those of Atlanta, Dallas, Minneapolis, Richmond and St. Louis, reported that the transactions were negligible among the member banks of those districts. The replies received from the other Federal Reserve banks follow: [14]

Boston–Dealing in Federal funds has undoubtedly relieved member banks, particularly large city banks, from the necessity of rediscounting, although it would be difficult to determine just how extensive the effects have been. Practically all of the dealings in Federal funds in this district have been carried on either between Boston banks or between Boston banks and banks in other large financial centers, although there are indications that these dealings are beginning to extend to banks in this district outside of Boston. As Boston is an industrial center, the city banks have in portfolio varying amounts of eligible paper, and the motive for dealing in Federal funds has not been the lack of eligible paper, but rather a matter of rates—the member banks purchasing Federal funds when they may be secured at a rate lower than the established rediscount rate.

Chicago–Dealings in Federal reserve funds are confined principally to the larger banks in the important financial centers. This practice which we believe to be legitimate has relieved the large member banks from the necessity of borrowing at the Federal reserve banks for their temporary requirements. In our opinion this has been beneficial inasmuch as it conserves the use of Federal reserve credit by decreasing the amount of Federal reserve credit which would otherwise go into the market. In our experience, we know of no cases where member banks have resorted to the use of Federal reserve funds because of their lack of eligible paper.

Cleveland–Dealings in Federal funds to a limited extent have been resorted to by some of our larger member banks. Such deal-

[14] "Federal Reserve Questionnaires," Appendix, Part 6, *Hearings before a Subcommittee of the Committee on Banking and Currency*, Seventy-first Congress, Third Session, Pursuant to S. Res. 71, pp. 725–27.

ings have no doubt relieved them from the necessity of borrowing from us temporarily, but we are without information as to the volume. These purchases have been made because of a saving in cost as against borrowing and not necessarily because of a lack of eligible paper.

Kansas City–Dealings in Federal funds in this district have been confined almost entirely to transactions between banks located in Kansas City or our branch cities and we doubt whether any such transactions have in recent years been resorted to because of lack of eligible paper by such member banks. Ordinarily purchases of Federal exchange have been made by one member bank from another merely to cover a very temporary shortage in reserve and in no instance have we learned of any member bank being a regular purchaser of Federal exchange for any considerable period of time. These transactions have, perhaps, resulted in some slight reduction in member bank rediscounting, but if member banks could not sell their excess reserve balances locally, they would merely transfer them by wire to some other point and the net result would be the same.

New York–In order to make clear the discussion of this question it seems desirable first to explain how Federal funds originate. Federal funds are in effect the excess reserves of one bank or group of banks, which are made available to other banks. In the conduct of their business, member banks frequently find upon adjustment of their reserve position that they have an excess of reserves for the day. Ordinarily if the bank with an excess reserve is borrowing at the reserve bank, such excess will be used to reduce or eliminate its indebtedness, but if the bank is not in debt to the reserve bank, or if the excess reserve exceeds its indebtedness, the bank will naturally seek to employ the funds. The ordinary employment of funds by a member bank does not require actual payment until the business day following the commitment, since normally it either issues a check payable through the clearing house or establishes a credit on its books. In either case it does not actually lose the funds until the following day, so that the usual methods of employing its excess reserves would still leave the bank with the excess for one day. In order to employ these funds for that one day, there has developed a market in Federal funds. The natural market for such funds is with banks which are deficient in reserves, as such banks are of course generally glad to purchase

Federal funds if they can do so upon advantageous terms, rather than to borrow at the reserve bank.

Dealings in such funds have relieved member banks from the necessity of rediscounting only to a relatively slight extent. When such funds are scarce the demand is at the maximum, and when they are in supply there generally exists little demand for them. There has not come to our notice any cases where member banks have resorted to the purchase of Federal funds because they lack eligible paper, and such transactions are unlikely because of the risk of placing dependence on a source of credit which may fail when most needed. As a matter of fact, trading in Federal funds in this district is limited to banks of the highest credit standing, because the bank selling Federal funds is in effect making an unsecured loan for one day, and the class of banks entitled to this type of accommodation generally have an ample supply of eligible paper. There appears also to be a growing tendency to deal in Federal funds between Federal reserve districts; and it is not unlikely, when there is a difference in reserve bank rates, that such inter-district transactions may be the means of member banks in the district having the higher rate obtaining Federal reserve funds more cheaply than they could otherwise be obtained. A market in Federal funds, if limited to banks of unquestioned credit standing, should on the whole be a desirable thing, since it should be of assistance in making funds available where needed, and should make for a greater fluidity of credit.

Philadelphia–It is impossible for us to state to any degree of accuracy the extent to which Federal reserve funds were used as a substitute for rediscount, but we do know that this method of borrowing has been used quite extensively by the large city banks, and on one or two occasions, as near as we can estimate, they were indebted to the New York banks and dealers to the extent of $50,000,000. This method of borrowing is confined mostly to the large city banks and the question of rate, not the lack of eligible paper, is the dominating factor in such transactions.

San Francisco–To a considerable extent. A number of banks in eastern cities follow the practice of transferring their surplus funds to correspondent banks on the Pacific coast, with the request that the identical amount be re-transferred East early the following day. Frequently, banks transfer practically the same amount back and forth day after day for a considerable time.

Funds transferred by wire at 3:00 P. M. eastern standard time reach the Pacific coast at say 12:30 P. M. Pacific standard time. Immediately trading commences for the purpose of adjusting reserves and borrowing.

In some instances, the funds are transferred as the result of a specific purchase by the Pacific coast bank, or in the normal course to augment interest-bearing balances, or, in some cases, are transferred to be sold "at the best price available."

Obviously, these "low-rate" funds in the San Francisco market have an important effect on the volume of Federal reserve bank credit outstanding.

No instance is known of a member bank using Federal reserve funds in an amount greater than that for which it could have furnished eligible paper or security.

Federal funds' rate

In the accompanying chart is depicted the weekly average of the daily closing bid and asked rate on Federal funds since April, 1928, when data for the series first began to be published in *The New York Herald-Tribune*. While the rate quoted exhibits wide fluctuations through the course of a day's trading, the chart is no doubt accurate in its depiction of the major sweeps, even if it fails to convey an idea of the extreme daily sensitiveness of the rate.

Normally the Federal funds' rate would be expected to parallel the bank rate in its major fluctuations. At times an increase above the bank rate might be expected since it is more convenient for a bank to purchase Federal funds than to rediscount, particularly if it possessed no United States obligations and were forced to send in customers' paper. The unusually wide differential which prevailed between the two rates in 1928 and 1929 was due to the fact that certain banks lacked paper eligible for rediscount and others, which were lending heavily on call, preferred to replenish their reserves in this way. Otherwise they would risk the displeasure of the Federal Reserve authorities through increasing their borrowings at the time that they were lending heavily for speculative purposes. After the panic of October, 1929, the rate on Federal funds dropped sharply. According to official explanations this reflected a heavy inflow of funds from the interior in answer to margin calls. The low rates prevalent through 1930 were the result of a cyclical currency retirement, increases in the monetary stock of gold, and the easy-money policy of the Federal Reserve system. On several occasions the asked rate fell as low as ¼ of one per cent.

Viewed in comparison with other money rates, the Federal

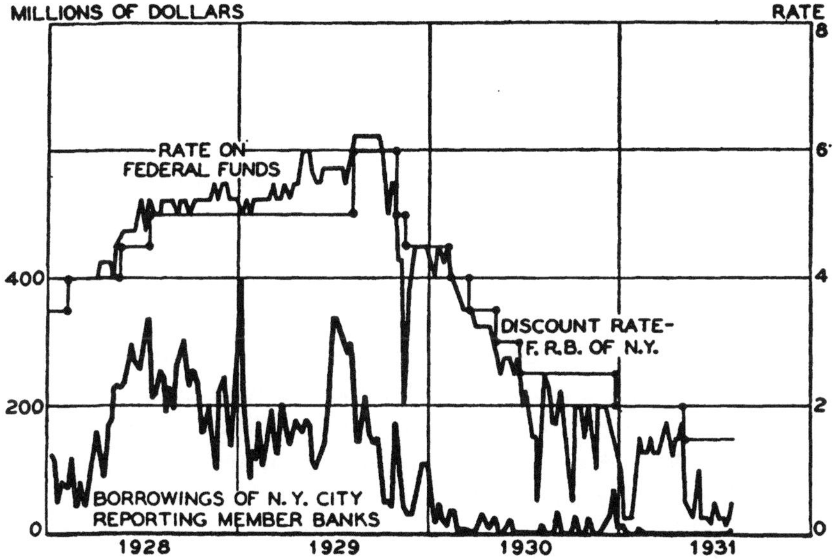

CHART 3. THE RATE ON FEDERAL FUNDS, NEW YORK CITY.

funds' rate is more sensitive, and tends to anticipate changes in money market conditions. It is the rate which is most immediately responsive to changes in the reserve position of the banks, and to the factors which affect that position. Trading in Federal funds has permitted banks to figure more closely on their reserves and doubtless has been a factor in the paring of these down to a minimum. Inasmuch as the amount of excess reserves maintained is negligible, the purchase and sale of Federal funds does not relieve the banking system, however much it may relieve the individual bank, of the necessity of reliance on or borrowing from the Federal Reserve banks. Excess reserves of the banking system are so small that gold exports, increases in the amount of money in circulation, decreases in treasury currency, and appropriate changes in various items on the Federal Reserve statement of condition, will force increases in member bank borrowings. The purchase and sale of Federal funds, therefore, may simply be looked upon as a further refinement in the clearance mechanism, without having any more than a temporary effect on member bank borrowings.

Summary

Under the provisions of the National Bank Act, bank reserves had at all times to be maintained at the stipulated percentages. To provide a certain flexibility, member bank reserves at the present time are computed on an average basis over longer or shorter periods of time. Banks pare their reserves down to a minimum now just as they did prior to the establishment of the Federal Reserve system. The excess maintained by the banking system is negligible. From the point of view of the individual bank, reserve balances fluctuate with the ebb and flow of funds, and with changes in the monetary gold stock, volume of currency in circulation, and items on the statement of condition of the Federal Reserve banks. A depleted reserve balance of an individual member bank may be replenished by drawing in funds from the rest of the banking system, by borrowing from or selling bills or securities to the Federal Reserve system, and through the purchase of Federal funds. These latter represent the excess bank balances possessed by some other unit of the banking system.

In the next few chapters, detailed consideration will be given those factors which affect the bank reserves of the entire banking system. These include changes in the gold stock, in the currency, and in items on the statement of condition of the Federal Reserve banks. It is the changes in these various factors which increase or decrease the marginal funds of the credit organization and in particular of the money market.

Chapter IV

THE MONETARY GOLD STOCK AS RELATED TO MEMBER BANK RESERVES

As long as the United States retains the gold standard, domestic and world gold production, gold earmarking operations,[1] gold imports and exports, industrial gold consumption, in short any factor that affects the monetary stock of gold in the United States, will affect the specie reserves of the Federal Reserve banks and, in the absence of offsetting factors, the reserve balances of member banks. Indeed it is by virtue of their influence on the member bank reserve account that changes in the monetary stock of gold influence the superstructure of credit.

Gold imports

The effects of changes in the gold stock on the statements of the United States treasury, the Federal Reserve banks, member banks and so on the credit system, may be visualized through a depiction of the accounting sequences. In the case of an increase in the gold stock through imports, consisting of American gold coins and bars and bars of the Bank of England, the procedure is very simple. Gold coming into the country in this form is sent by a member institution, acting on its own behalf or on behalf of a nonmember institution or other client, directly to its Federal Reserve bank, where it receives an immediate credit.

To illustrate the balance sheet changes involved, let us assume that the "A" National Bank of New York City has imported $10,000,000 of gold for client "X." The effect on its own statement and that of the Federal Reserve bank is as follows:

[1] See p. 65.

"A" National Bank		*Federal Reserve Bank of New York*	
Assets	*Liabilities*	*Assets*	*Liabilities*
Due from Federal Reserve bank + $10,000,000	Due to client "X" + $10,000,000	Gold + $10,000,000	Due to "A" National Bank + $10,000,000

After setting aside a reserve of 13 per cent, the excess reserves of the "A" National Bank, in consequence of this operation, amount to $8,700,000 which it could use in any manner it chose, to reduce bills discounted, to meet currency demands or to expand its loans and investments. If the "A" National Bank had imported the gold on its own initiative, drawing on its foreign-deposit balances to do so, its excess reserves would in such case amount to the full sum imported.

Gold imports which take the form of foreign gold coin and foreign bars, other than those of the Bank of England, are sent upon arrival to the assay office. An immediate advance in the form of a check on the United States Treasury Department, varying from 90 to 98 per cent of the estimated value of the gold, pending final adjustment, is customarily granted the importer.

Assuming that the gold imported by the "A" National Bank is sent to the assay office and that, contrary to usual practice, the bank receives a check for the full amount, the effect on the daily treasury statement would be as follows:

Gold Account—United States Treasury Department

(In millions of dollars)

Assets	*Liabilities*
Gold bullion + 10	Gold in general fund + 10

When the "A" National Bank deposits the check drawn on the United States Treasury Department with the Reserve bank (which it would do immediately since this constitutes Federal funds), the following changes take place on the Federal Reserve statement:

Federal Reserve Bank of New York

(In millions of dollars)

Assets	*Liabilities*	
	Due to the United States government	— 10
	Due to the "A" National Bank	+ 10

The treasury department must necessarily replenish its account with the Reserve bank, and probably would do so by shifting the gold purchased from the general fund to the gold settlement fund of the Federal Reserve bank of New York:

Gold Account—United States Treasury Department

(In millions of dollars)

Assets	*Liabilities*	
	Gold fund—Federal Reserve Board	+ 10
	Gold in general fund	— 10

Gold exports

Quite generally member banks secure gold for export from the Federal Reserve banks, where it is packed for shipment at their expense. Assuming that the reserves of the member bank were at the legal minimum, this operation would leave the member bank with a deficiency in its reserve account. The deficiency would equal the full amount exported provided that the member bank were exporting for its own account. If the exportation were conducted on behalf of a client, the deficiency would not amount to the entire sum exported since the deposit account of the client with the member bank would be debited and reserves set free to a proportionate amount. But in either event the member bank would have to borrow or rediscount with the Reserve bank to repair whatever deficiency existed, unless there were offsetting factors such as a currency inflow or purchases of bills or securities by the Federal Reserve banks. For the member bank to call loans or to sell securities to replenish the deficiency would simply force some other unit of the banking system to borrow from the Reserve banks.

Offsetting changes in the monetary gold stock

Whether an efflux of gold or an increase in the amount held under earmarked account [2] are provocative of deflationary tendencies, credit strains, higher rates of interest, etc., depends on whether or not member banks are forced to increase their borrowings to repair the deficiency in reserves induced by the decline in the monetary stock of gold. If they are relieved from so doing through the purchase of securities or acceptances by the Reserve banks, member bank borrowings will not rise and interest rates will be unaffected. In this sense the Reserve banks may offset the effect of gold exports or of gold imports, though their power to do so is not unlimited. Limits to the ability of the Reserve banks to offset gold exports are set by the amount of gold collateral and reserves which they must maintain against their note and deposit liabilities. On the other hand the volume of their earning assets sets a very definite limit to their ability to offset gold imports. Furthermore the Federal Reserve banks are quite unable to offset the effect of gold exports or imports on the credit systems of foreign nations. If the opposite offsetting process is not carried on by the foreign central bank, the change taking place in interest rates in the country concerned will eventually react on the balance of payments of the United States and exert a reflex action on the American money market. Within the limitations stated, which at times are quite narrow, the Reserve banks may offset the effect of changes in the monetary stock of gold on

[2] See p. 65. The earmarking of gold is usually preliminary to exporting though it may result from the desire of a central bank to build up its specie holdings to the legal minimum.

Occasionally gold is earmarked over the end of a month for a member bank requesting this on behalf of one of the chartered banks of Canada indulging in a bit of "window dressing" preparatory to the issuance of its end-of-the-month statement.

member bank reserves and consequently on the money market. One may not relish the policies adopted or the economic consequences thereof, one may conclude that they have but postponed an inevitable readjustment in the credit structure, but this is beside the point in a recognition of the results achieved.

Cases in point

Since America's return to the gold standard in June, 1919, following war-time deviation from the paths of monetary rectitude, there have been some eight major waves of gold imports and exports. Certain of these were stimulated by Federal Reserve policy, while others were due to factors beyond the control of the Federal Reserve banks. On occasion, the effect of the changes taking place in the monetary stock of gold on member bank borrowings has been offset by Federal Reserve open-market policy. At other times the Reserve banks' open-market holdings of securities and bills have been so manipulated as to intensify the effect of gold movements. Gold imports at times have been utilized to finance increases in the volume of money in circulation and consequently have exerted no effect on the credit structure. On occasion gold imports have taken place during a cyclical decline in the volume of currency in circulation.

For illustrative purposes, taking the period from June, 1919, to June, 1931, the gold stock of the United States increased by 1,696 millions of dollars. Any effect that this increase might have upon the volume of credit would be exerted through increasing member bank reserve balances, which rose between these dates by 708 millions of dollars. On the basis of this increase and the more intensive utilization of member bank balances through the rapid proportionate growth taking place in time deposits, the total loans and investments of all member banks were greater by 11,681 millions of dollars, and of all banks by 18,451 millions of dollars. This represented an increase of about 50 per cent in the total volume of bank credit, based directly or indirectly on an increase of 40 per cent in member bank reserves.

Inasmuch as member bank reserves increased by only 708 millions of dollars between June, 1919, and June, 1931, while the monetary gold stock of the country increased by 1,696 millions of dollars, offsetting factors must have been present. That such was the case is apparent from the following table, where the factors leading to increases and decreases in member bank reserve balances are listed. The classification of items follows the compilation of the Federal Reserve Board.[3]

INCREASE IN MONETARY GOLD STOCK, JUNE, 1919–JUNE, 1931

Items	*Leading to increase in member bank reserves*	*Leading to decrease in member bank reserves*
	Change (In millions of dollars)	
Monetary gold stock	+ 1,696	
Total reserve bank credit		− 1,522
Treasury currency (adjusted)	+ 528	
Money in circulation	− 141	
Nonmember bank balances Federal Reserve banks	− 98	
Unexpended capital funds Federal Reserve banks		+ 233
TOTAL	2,463	1,755
Increase in member bank reserve balances = 708		

It will be noted that the decline in the total volume of Federal Reserve credit was smaller by 174 millions of dollars than the increase taking place in the monetary stock of gold. While the sums are quite similar, there is no logical reason for linking these two particular items. One could as correctly relate the decline in Federal Reserve credit to the increase in treasury currency, to the decline of money in circulation and to the decline in nonmember bank balances.

Of an importance equal to the decline in the total volume of Federal Reserve credit was the change taking place in its composition. Bills discounted declined by 1,652 millions of dollars while other Federal Reserve credit, including the open-market holdings of the Reserve banks, increased by 130 millions of dol-

[3] For meaning of the various items, see *Federal Reserve Bulletin,* July, 1929. In this and in the following tables in this chapter, the data given are monthly averages of daily figures.

lars. The lightening of the burden on the "discount shoulder" accounted for the ease in the money market on the latter as compared with the former date.

The fact that the increase in member bank reserves was only 42 per cent as large as the gold inflow does not mean that gold was consciously sterilized, nor does it necessarily mean that there was an inadequacy of credit for business use through the period. Rather, on occasion, the superstructure of credit expanded too rapidly relative to business requirements and gave rise to speculative waves in real estate, securities and commodities.

The better to follow the use made of the gold imports and changes in the gold policy of the Reserve banks, it is necessary to divide the period from June, 1919 into its several component parts. The points of division were selected on the basis of the high and low points attained in the monetary gold stock in consequence of each of the gold movements.

Period of loss, June, 1919–April, 1920

In this period the monetary gold stock of the United States declined by 348 millions of dollars. The bulk of the loss was accounted for by exports to Japan, Argentina, Spain, China, India, Mexico, Venezuela and Uruguay, with which America had had adverse balances of payments during the war period.

Period of Loss in Gold Stock, June, 1919–April, 1920

Item	*Change (In millions of dollars)*
Monetary gold stock	−348
Member bank borrowings—Federal Reserve banks	+591
Open-market holdings of acceptances and securities and other Reserve bank credit—Federal Reserve banks	+306
Treasury currency (adjusted)	+178
Money in circulation	+481
Member bank reserve balances—Federal Reserve banks	+174
Nonmember bank deposits—Federal Reserve banks	−27
Unexpended capital funds—Federal Reserve banks	+99

The loss of gold was not reflected in a decline of member bank reserve balances. On the contrary these increased by 174 millions of dollars. Nor was it reflected in a contraction of the superstructure of credit. This continued to expand at a rapid rate, forcing at that time the increase which occurred in member bank reserves. Even the increase in member bank borrowings can be ascribed only in part to the decline in the gold stock. Since increases in the open-market holdings of bills and securities by the Federal Reserve banks and in other Federal Reserve credit so nearly equaled the decline in the gold stock (though the similarity of relationship may be wholly fortuitous), it could be concluded that the increase in member bank borrowings was due to the increase in the amount of money in circulation, to the increase in member bank reserve balances, to the increase in unexpended capital funds, offset in part by the increase in treasury currency and the decline in nonmember bank deposits. Setting up the relationship in this particular fashion gives emphasis to the fact that the decline in the gold stock was only one of several factors, and not the most important, making for the increase in member bank borrowings.

Period of gain, April, 1920–August, 1924

Throughout most of this period America represented the most advantageous market for gold, which had lost its world value and, with the exception of a few of the neutral nations, continued demonetized in Europe. In consequence gold came to the United States and was used in the main to pay for commodities and to reduce the indebtedness of the outside world.

This period may be divided into two phases. The first continued until about the end of 1921. During this time the total loans and investments of member banks were shrinking rapidly, accompanying the decline in commodity and other prices and in business activity. The Reserve banks were allowing their open-market portfolio of bills and securities to fall. Reflecting the liquidation in credit, member bank reserves declined 197 millions of dollars. The increase in unemployment and the decline in payroll totals and retail trade were themselves reflected in a decline of 654 millions of dollars of money in circulation.

Period of Gain in Gold Stock

April, 1920–December, 1921

Item	*Change (In millions of dollars)*
Monetary gold stock	+ 822
Member bank borrowings—Federal Reserve banks	− 1,251
Open-market holdings of acceptances and securities and other Reserve bank credit—Federal Reserve banks	− 565
Treasury currency (adjusted)	+ 168
Money in circulation	− 654
Member bank reserve balances—Federal Reserve banks	− 197
Nonmember bank deposits—Federal Reserve banks	− 79
Unexpended capital funds—Federal Reserve banks	+ 104

To the increase of 822 millions of dollars in the monetary stock of gold must be added the other funds released through the increase in treasury currency, the decline of money in circulation, the decline in member bank reserve balances and in nonmember bank deposits, which totaled 1,098 millions of dollars.[4] All were utilized in reducing member bank borrowings and the open-market holdings of securities and bills of the Reserve banks. The only offsetting factor was the important increase in the unexpended capital funds of the Reserve banks.

The huge volume of member bank borrowings at the beginning of the period permitted the absorption and neutralization of the gold inflow. Had it not been for this, the influx of gold would have brought about an expansion of credit, accompanied doubtless by price increases. Indeed this was expectantly awaited by those British observers who desired to have pound sterling buoyed to parity on the basis of a general price increase in the United States. But, as it was, the total volume of credit declined, member bank balances fell, and the gold inflow was neutralized.

The second phase, embracing the period from December, 1921, to August, 1924, was marked by an increase in the gold stock slightly larger than that received during the first period. The increase amounted to 873 as compared with 822 millions of dol-

[4] It is rather interesting that the funds resulting from this miscellaneous group of factors were larger in amount than the gold imports.

lars. This period is differentiated from the first by the rapid expansion taking place in bank credit, and by the huge fluctuations that occurred in the holdings of securities of the Federal Reserve banks. Between December, 1921, and August, 1924, the total loans and investments of the reporting member banks increased by 2,604 millions of dollars. In the first quarter of 1922, the Reserve banks rapidly expanded their holdings of securities. This expansion was followed by a decline reaching its lowest point in August, 1923, and this in turn by another rapid increase which carried total holdings of securities, by the beginning of the fourth quarter of 1924, to a point only slightly under the peak reached in the spring of 1922.

As between the beginning and the end of the period, the open-market holdings of the Reserve banks increased by 245 millions of dollars. It was this, plus the influx of gold, plus the increase in treasury currency, plus the decline in unexpended capital funds, that financed the decline in member bank borrowings, the increase in the volume of money in circulation and the increase in member bank reserve balances.

Period of Gain in Gold Stock

December, 1921–August, 1924

Item	*Change (In millions of dollars)*
Monetary gold stock	+ 873
Member bank borrowings—Federal Reserve banks	− 912
Open-market holdings of acceptances and securities and other Reserve bank credit—Federal Reserve banks	+ 245
Treasury currency (adjusted)	+ 186
Money in circulation	+ 82
Member bank reserve balances—Federal Reserve banks	+ 399
Nonmember bank deposits—Federal Reserve banks	+ 6
Unexpended capital funds—Federal Reserve banks	− 95

If, in an arbitrary fashion, the increase in the gold stock were related to the decline in member bank borrowings, one would conclude that the increase in the gold stock was not used to enlarge member bank reserves and so played no part in the expansion of the superstructure of credit. This would mean that the growth in member bank reserves resulted from the increase in the open-market portfolio of the Reserve banks, the increase in treasury currency and the decrease in unexpended capital funds. Naturally there is no basis for relating the decline in member bank borrowings directly to the increase in the gold stock. The decline taking place could quite as logically be linked to the increase in the open-market holdings of the Reserve banks, the increase in treasury currency and the decline in unexpended capital funds. So far as the gold policy of the Reserve banks through this period may be ascertained, it was not one of sterilizing gold. The increase taking place in their open-market portfolio would belie that.

Period of loss, August, 1924–April, 1925

Convincing evidence that the Reserve banks were not by their own policies attempting in 1924 to sterilize gold is afforded by the fact that in the first half of the year they increased their open-market holdings very rapidly. The primary purpose of this was to make interest rates low enough in New York to discourage further gold imports and encourage capital exports and a transfer of funds to Europe, thus expediting through financial measures Europe's return to the gold standard. This indeed was the result achieved. Money rates prevailing in the money markets made easier the flotation of the Dawes loan, which placed Germany on the gold exchange standard, and sterling exchange rose to parity.

The gold exports that took place in 1925 were in large measure the direct consequence of the easy money policy of the Reserve banks and its effect on exports of capital. Out of the total gold exports of 263 millions of dollars, Germany took 68 millions of dollars which represented a portion of the proceeds of the Dawes loan and was used in building up the gold reserves of the Reichsbank. Exports to Australia, totaling 27 millions of dollars, also followed the flotation of a loan in the American investment market. British India drew 59 millions of dollars of gold, which was not the result of capital imports from the United States, but rather the consequence of competitive forces raising the price of gold in India, which was drawn from the cheapest market. Of the remaining exports, Canada took 46 millions of dollars, which was but one side of the gold shuttle between that country and the United States.

As the following table indicates, the Federal Reserve banks did not entirely offset the effect of the decline in the monetary gold stock upon member bank borrowings. Between August, 1924, and April, 1925, their open-market portfolio of acceptances and securities and other types of Reserve bank credit increased by only 94 millions of dollars, as compared with a decline of 176 millions of dollars in the gold stock. The whole amount of this increase consisted of acceptances inasmuch as the Reserve banks had begun to dispose of their security holdings in November, 1924. The motive for the sale of securities was the fact that the increase in the superstructure of credit, stimulated by the previous purchases, had been utilized in an expansion of bank security loans and investments. Member bank borrowings rose by 135 millions of dollars, reflecting that amount of gold loss not offset by Reserve open-market operations, and reflecting the increase in member bank reserve balances and a slight increase taking place in the currency.

Period of Loss in Gold Stock

August, 1924–April, 1925

Item	*Change (In millions of dollars)*
Monetary gold stock	— 176
Member bank borrowings—Federal Reserve banks	+ 135
Open-market holdings of acceptances and securities and other Reserve bank credit—Federal Reserve banks	+ 94
Treasury currency (adjusted)	+ 6
Money in circulation	+ 3
Member bank reserve balances—Federal Reserve banks	+ 51
Nonmember bank deposits—Federal Reserve banks	— 6
Unexpended capital funds—Federal Reserve banks	+ 11

The experience of the Reserve banks through this period raises the question whether the policy they followed in endeavoring to bring about a redistribution of the gold stock of the world through financial measures was a desirable one, even from the point of view of the European powers. For a time the low money rates in the New York money market buoyed the foreign exchanges. But inasmuch as the absorption of credit in investment operations and security loans made a reversal of the policy imperative, the foreign exchanges were later subjected to considerable pressure. On one occasion Dr. Hjalmar Schacht, then President of the Reichsbank, stated that he would prefer that the reserve banks fix their bank rates with sole reference to the domestic situation. This, he said, would give the European central banks a firm anchorage to which they could relate their own policies and the gold stock of the world would then be redistributed in accordance with relative needs and productive capacities (excepting in so far as interfered with by tariff and other artificial barriers) and in accordance with capital exports, resulting from true savings and not from the creation of fiat bank credit.

If this policy had been followed the intense swings taking place in money market rates of interest might have been avoided. The artificially low rates raised the value of the foreign exchanges. The succeeding artificially high rates, which accompanied restrictive measures adopted by the Federal Reserve banks to curb the speculative tendencies induced by the easy money policies, exposed the foreign exchanges to considerable pressure and forced the Federal Reserve banks to lend support by buying bills in foreign currencies. The one policy unduly stimulated capital exports, the other restricted these. The one gave an unhealthy stimulus to business, the other made for sharp recessions. Stability of policy would have been preferable from the European, no less than from the domestic, standpoint.

Period of gain, April, 1925–May, 1927

The increase in the gold stock through this period represented in large measure imports from Great Britain, Mexico, Chile, Australia and Japan, due to a depreciation of their exchanges or to the inauguration of currency reform measures. The net imports of gold from Canada, which were substantial, represented in effect the annual gold production of the Dominion.

Period of Gain in Gold Stock

April, 1925–May, 1927

Item	*Change (In millions of dollars)*
Monetary gold stock	+311
Member bank borrowings—Federal Reserve banks	+ 70
Open-market holdings of acceptances and securities and other Reserve bank credit—Federal Reserve banks	−139
Treasury currency (adjusted)	− 1
Money in circulation	+ 57
Member bank reserve balances—Federal Reserve banks	+139
Nonmember bank deposits—Federal Reserve banks	+ 12
Unexpended capital funds—Federal Reserve banks	+ 33

Through the greater part of this period no particularly striking changes took place in the open-market holdings of the Reserve banks. The rather substantial decline recorded in the table reflected the decrease which occurred during the first part of 1927. The increase in the gold stock was not used to reduce member bank borrowings, as had been true on some previous occasions. In fact member bank borrowings increased despite the substantial gain of gold. The influx of gold was used to finance the expansion in the currency and the increase in the member bank reserve balances, and to offset the difference between the increase in member bank borrowings and the decline in the open-market portfolio of the Reserve banks.

Period of loss, May, 1927–July, 1928

It was to protect sterling exchange and to induce France to take the gold she desired from New York rather than from London, that the Reserve system, under the leadership of the late Governor Strong, adopted the much discussed cheap-money policy of 1927. This consisted of lowering the rates of rediscount by the Federal Reserve banks and of a purchase of securities in sufficient volume not only to offset the effects of the gold exports taking place but also to increase member bank reserves and to reduce member bank borrowings. This was the policy followed up to the tenth of November, 1927.[5] Beginning then by reason of the rapid absorption of credit in speculative employment, the Reserve banks allowed gold exports to have their full deflationary effect.

From the following table it will be noted that from the beginning to the end of the period the monetary gold stock of the United States declined by 538 millions of dollars, which was the heaviest loss suffered up to that time since the Armistice. Of the amount exported, France drew about 60 per cent, which was for the purpose of building up the gold reserves of the Bank of France and represented a conversion of the foreign credits acquired by the Bank of France through the repatriation of French capital, following the stabilization of the political situation with the advent of the Poincaré coalition government.[6] Of the remainder, the bulk was taken by Argentina, Brazil, Germany and Great Britain. The first two countries had floated stabilization loans in the United States, and Germany's borrowings on short- and long-term account were huge.

Period of Loss in Gold Stock

May, 1927–July, 1928

Item	*Change (In millions of dollars)*
Monetary gold stock	− 538
Member bank borrowings—Federal Reserve banks	+ 617
Open-market holdings of acceptances and securities and other Reserve bank credit—Federal Reserve banks	− 127
Treasury currency (adjusted)	+ 14
Money in circulation	− 114
Member bank reserve balances—Federal Reserve banks	+ 62
Nonmember bank deposits—Federal Reserve banks	− 9
Unexpended capital funds—Federal Reserve banks	+ 27

[5] See testimony of Governor Young of the Federal Reserve Board in *Hearings before the Committee on Banking and Currency*, House of Representatives, Seventieth Congress, First Session, on H. R. 11,806, p. 419. Relative to some of the points treated in this section, see the testimony of Professor O. M. W. Sprague before the *Royal Commission on Indian Currency and Finance*, May 10, 1926, p. 295.

[6] On this point see Dulles, *The French Franc, 1914–1928; Fourteenth Annual Report of the Federal Reserve Bank of New York, 1928*, p. 7; Willis and Beckhart, *Foreign Banking Systems*, Chap. VII.

From the beginning to the end of the period member bank borrowings increased by an amount greater than the decline in the gold stock. This resulted from the efforts of the Reserve banks beginning in November, 1927, to put on the screws in order to divert credit from the security loan markets. The decline in the open-market holdings of the Reserve banks and the increase in member bank reserve balances forced the expansion in borrowings despite the heavy decline in the volume of money in circulation.

Surplus gold thesis

On the basis of the ability of the Reserve banks to offset what would otherwise be the deflationary effect of gold exports or the expansionist effect of gold imports, it was frequently stated, through 1927 and 1928, by persons of importance in official life, that the United States could lose a considerable volume of gold from its excess stock without any serious effect on the credit situation. Without questioning the power of the Reserve banks to offset a certain volume of gold exports and imports, in the enthusiasm of the moment, the limitations imposed by reserve ratios and by the volume of "free gold" was quite generally disregarded by those who stressed this point of view, as was the effect of such export movements on the credit structures of the recipient nations. The amount of possible loss, without important consequences, was generally estimated by the majority of those speaking on the subject to be about one billion dollars. This was the figure given by Governor Young of the Federal Reserve Board in testifying in May, 1928, before the House Committee on Banking and Currency.[7] Since the United States had by that time lost a considerable volume of gold, he indicated that the future losses could possibly amount to 600 millions of dollars. Statements to the same effect were made from time to time by Representative McFadden, Chairman of the House Committee

[7] *Hearings before the Committee on Banking and Currency*, House of Representatives, Seventieth Congress, First Session, on H. R. 11,806, p. 419. In the same hearings, pp. 48–50, Mr. E. A. Goldenweiser, Director, Division of Research and Statistics, Federal Reserve Board, admitted that the growth of credit needs in the United States during the next ten years would require the retention of the surplus stock of gold.

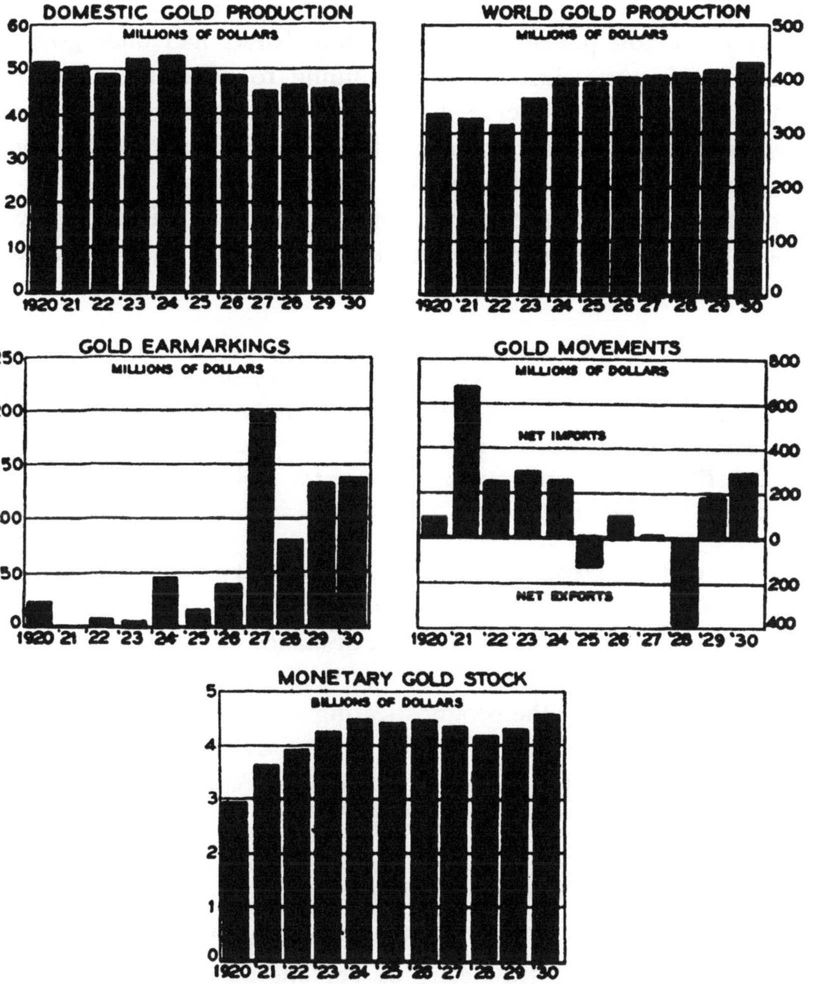

CHART 4. THE MONETARY GOLD STOCK OF THE UNITED STATES AT THE END OF EACH YEAR, TOGETHER WITH RELATED FACTORS.

"GOLD EARMARKINGS" REPRESENT THE GOLD HELD UNDER EARMARKED ACCOUNT AS OF THE CLOSE OF EACH YEAR.

on Banking and Currency, and also by Secretary Mellon. As late as March 29, 1928, the Secretary stated that the loss of additional quantities of gold could take place without any appreciable hardening of interest rates.[8] A few months later the character

[8] *New York Sun*, March 29, 1928, p. 47. See also *Annual Report of the Secretary of the Treasury on the State of the Finances*, 1927, pp. 71–73.

of the statements changed. The reason was that in the meanwhile the credit policies of the Reserve banks had undergone a complete change. Instead of continuing to offset the effect of gold exports, the Reserve banks through 1928 reduced their own portfolio of securities in an attempt to check the use of funds for speculative account. In the *Federal Reserve Bulletin* for September, 1928,[9] an editorial appeared apropos of the suggestion of replacing gold certificates in circulation with Federal Reserve notes:

> It is, therefore, evident that, while the Federal Reserve banks have a considerable volume of excess reserves, or unused lending power, this amount is much smaller than is popularly believed and in the present circumstances can not be materially increased by the device of substituting Federal Reserve notes for gold certificates in the country's circulation.

By the end of December, 1928, the monetary stock of gold of the United States had declined, since the end of July, 1927, when the Reserve banks set out in "the pursuance of a larger plan" of monetary stabilization, by about 433 millions of dollars, less than half of the loss that the prognosticating officials had estimated we could lose without cost. Yet the decline of this amount in our gold stock constituted in the opinion of the Federal Reserve Bank of New York "a considerable drain." [10]

Period of gain, July, 1928–October, 1929

The rising rates of interest brought about by the increase in bills discounted and the desire of persons all over the world to speculate in American securities ultimately proved to be a sufficient deterrent to check the gold outflow and exerted enough magnetic pull to bring about an increase of 268 millions of dollars in the monetary gold stock, with the bulk of the inflow coming from Canada, England, Germany and Argentina.

[9] Page 614.

[10] *Fourteenth Annual Report,* Federal Reserve Bank of New York, 1928, p. 6. For an account of the offsetting of gold imports by the Bank of England, see *Acceptance Bulletin,* May 31, 1929, p. 11.

Period of Gain in Gold Stock

July, 1928–October, 1929

Item	*Change (In millions of dollars)*
Monetary gold stock	+268
Member bank borrowings—Federal Reserve banks	−205
Open-market holdings of acceptances and securities and other Reserve bank credit—Federal Reserve banks	+124
Treasury currency (adjusted)	+ 3
Money in circulation	+ 64
Member bank reserve balances—Federal Reserve banks	+ 62
Nonmember bank deposits—Federal Reserve banks	− 2
Unexpended capital funds—Federal Reserve banks	+ 66

Through a part of this period and particularly through the first half of 1929, the reserve banks offset any effect the gold imports might have had in reducing member bank indebtedness, and so of lowering market rates of interest. This they did by allowing their acceptance holdings to mature. In addition they induced foreign central banks, in particular the Bank of France, to use its dollar credits to earmark gold in New York, and for a time the amount of gold placed under earmarked account was equal to that imported. Beginning the middle of March, imports of gold rapidly exceeded earmarkings and even some of the gold previously earmarked was released by the Bank of France for German account and replaced by gold sent to Paris from Berlin.[11] Even so, through the first half of 1929, the increase in the gold stock was more than offset by declines taking place in the open-market holdings of the Reserve banks.

In the fall of 1929 the Reserve banks increased their acceptance holdings rapidly and by an amount which for some weeks prior to the panic quite definitely eased the money market. As between July, 1928, and October, 1929, the increase in the open-market holdings of the reserve banks and in other Reserve bank credit was sufficient to finance the increase in the currency and in member bank

[11] *Monthly Review*, Federal Reserve Bank of New York, May 1, 1929, p. 36. See also *Commerce Monthly* (National Bank of Commerce, New York City) March, 1929, p. 22; financial notes in *The New York Times*, May 1, 1929.

reserve balances. The increase taking place in the monetary gold stock permitted the decline in member bank borrowings and offset the deflationary effects of the increase in unexpended capital funds.

The rapid decline of interest rates in New York during the last two months of 1929 coupled with a return flow of American securities prompted an outward movement of gold, particularly to France and England, bringing about a reduction amounting to about 100 millions of dollars in the monetary stock of gold.

During the period of high money rates in New York through 1928–1929, foreign governments and foreign central banks made use of moral pressure and gentlemen's agreements to prevent in so far as possible outflows of gold to New York, on the theory that the forces depressing the foreign exchanges were of temporary duration and had developed from a technical situation in the American money market. Foreign observers counted on the ability of the Reserve banks to gain control of the speculative forces, after which they looked for a drop in interest rates, and saw no reason for allowing gold to flow to the United States in response to what were thought to be temporary and artificially induced causes. Canada imposed such an unofficial embargo [12] and other countries as well. The April, 1929, issue of *Commerce Monthly* [13] states that there was reason to believe that considerable amounts of gold, which would normally have come to the United States in response to high interest rates, had been held back by special measures adopted in countries whose exchanges were at or below the gold export point. "Moreover," the bulletin continues, "in some instances where the exchanges were at or near the gold export point the gold has not moved to us because bankers for reasons of policy have refrained from engaging in gold transactions." The bulletin concluded that the

[12] See bulletin of National City Bank, April, 1929, p. 56, where the statement is made: "Canada has been forced to put into effect an unofficial embargo on gold exports in order to check the continued drain of her reserves to this market." The Minister of Finance, Mr. J. A. Robb, was rather equivocal on the subject. See *The Commercial and Financial Chronicle*, May 25, 1929, p. 3433. In *Commerce Monthly* (Feb., 1929, pp. 22–23) it is declared that, though the exchanges of a number of countries had fallen to or were below the gold import point, impediments had been placed in the way of gold movements, the foreign exchanges were manipulated and in the United States alone was there an absolutely free gold market.

[13] Page 24.

accumulating balance of payments due the United States would force the European nations to permit gold exports unless bank rates were raised. Bank rates had finally to be raised in 1929, gold allowed to flow to the United States, and European industry penalized by reason of the New York stock market's demand for funds. The unofficial embargoes through 1929 represented temporary expedients for dealing with a sudden and real peril to the gold standard arising from the credit demands of the New York Stock Exchange.

Period of gain, January, 1930–September, 1931

Between the week ending January 11, 1930, when the monetary gold stock of the United States reached its lowest point following the post-panic exports, and the week ending September 19, 1931, the monetary gold stock of the United States increased by 736 millions of dollars. Total monetary gold holdings were brought to an all-time peak of 5,013 millions of dollars.

Through 1930, the gold received represented a flow from the debtor to the creditor nations and came for the most part from Canada, Mexico, Argentina, Brazil, Colombia, Peru, Uruguay, China and Hong Kong, and Japan. Imports from Japan were particularly heavy and followed upon the reintroduction of the gold standard there and a hammering of Japanese exchange by reason of the decline in cotton and silk exports.

Through the first eight months of 1931 the gold inflow amounted to about 400 millions of dollars. Again gold was received from debtor nations and, in addition, from those countries beset with credit crises and political strife. Argentina, Canada, Japan, Germany, China, Hong Kong, and Colombia contributed the bulk of the gold received. Only a negligible amount was received from England despite the credit crisis there, American banks refraining from withdrawing gold, though frequently it would have been profitable for them to have done so.

The gold outflow from various nations through this period was such as to force the greater part of the world off the gold standard. At the end of 1931 there were but five countries on the gold standard, if this be conservatively defined: the United States,

France, Holland, Belgium and Switzerland. The rest of the world had severed all connection with gold or had so modified the gold standard that free dealings in the foreign exchanges were not permitted.

In an analysis of the developments taking place, the New York money market bears a heavy responsibility for the general suspension of the gold standard and for the loss in the gains made over the preceding six or seven years in the gradual return to gold. The mechanism of the gold standard predicates an even and free flow of capital from the creditor to the debtor nations. Capital exports from the United States have exhibited a highly erratic character. Huge amounts were exported from 1924 to 1929, frequently with little attention to the capacity of the debtor nations to repay or to the use of the funds borrowed. Boom and inflationary conditions were stimulated in the debtor nations, and the rhythm of their economic life given an artificial stimulus. By reason of the widespread adoption of the gold exchange or semigold exchange standard, the capital exports taking place did not force a credit contraction in the United States. In fact the funds utilized in the United States in the purchase of foreign securities were not reflective in their entirety of an increase in savings, but were derived in part from the creation of fiat bank credit based upon an enlargement of the open-market portfolios of the Federal Reserve banks.

The period of inflationary capital outflow was followed by a marked diminution in foreign securities floated in the American market from 1929 through 1931. In 1929 an inflow of short-term foreign funds occurred by reason of the high interest rates prevailing in the money market and the desire of foreigners to speculate in the equity securities of the United States. Debtor nations, unable to borrow on long-term account, were forced to borrow on short-term account and Germany in particular made use of the American acceptance market for this purpose. The cessation of capital exports forced the debtor countries to dump commodities on the world's markets, to export gold, to an eventual abandonment of the gold standard, and to bond defaults. An unduly large capital outflow from creditor nations at one time, followed by a cessation of capital exports at another, will inevitably lead to a breakdown in the gold or gold exchange standards, and a concentration of the world's gold stock in the creditor nations. In other words the maldistribution of gold was not in itself a cause but rather an effect of the disturbed financial and economic relationships over the world.

As will be seen from the accompanying table, the gain in the gold stock was slightly larger than the decline taking place in member bank borrowings and the increase occurring in the volume of money in circulation. This excess, plus the increase in treasury currency, the slight decline in member bank reserve balances, and the decline in unexpended capital funds of the Federal Reserve banks, offset the effects of the increase in nonmember bank deposits at the Federal Reserve banks which was accounted for almost entirely by the growth in the deposits of the Bank of France.

Period of Gain in Gold Stock

From Week Ending January 11, 1930, to Week Ending September 19, 1931

(Weekly averages of daily data, in millions of dollars)

Item	*Change*
Monetary gold stock	+736
Member bank borrowings—Federal Reserve banks	−302
Open-market holdings of acceptances and securities and other Reserve bank credit—Federal Reserve banks	+110
Treasury currency (adjusted)	+ 4
Money in circulation	+386
Member bank reserve balances—Federal Reserve banks	− 3
Nonmember bank deposits—Federal Reserve banks	+191
Unexpended capital funds—Federal Reserve banks	− 26

Period of loss, September 19, 1931–October 31, 1931

Through the latter half of September and through October the United States was subjected to a gold drain of unprecedented dimensions. The suspension of specie payments in England was regarded on the continent of Europe as a harbinger of a similar policy which must needs be followed by the United States. The conviction that such must be the inevitable consequence was translated into action through frantic sales of American dollars in the various European capitals and by the withdrawal of 724 millions of dollars of gold within the space of six weeks. Never had the American banking system relinquished an equal amount of gold in a comparable space of time. Accompanying the foreign drain, a sharp increase occurred in the volume of currency hoarded by American citizens. Estimates placed the amount at well over a billion dollars. An external and internal drain of these proportions before the passage of the Federal Reserve Act would have been disastrous in that it would have forced the banking system to a suspension of specie payments. But as it was, the internal drain was met through the issuance of Federal Reserve notes, which were acceptable to the public inasmuch as confidence had not been lost in the ability of the United States to maintain the gold standard, though confidence in the banking system was impaired, and the external drain was met through the relinquishment of gold on the part of the Federal Reserve banks.

The gold loss was represented by exports to, or gold placed under earmark for the account of France, the Netherlands, Switzerland and Belgium. France withdrew gold not only by reason of the generally expressed fear that the United States would abandon the gold standard, but also by reason of the fact that the French banks were selling their foreign balances in order to acquire funds to meet a domestic currency hoarding demand. To a foreign drain of this type the New York money market was particularly vulnerable. The foreign short-term funds in the money market had reached sizeable proportions and the position of New York was rendered all the more precarious by reason of the fact that the funds for the most part represented French balances, France being a nation to which the United States had not extended credits of comparable proportions on long-term account. Following the visit of Premier Laval, the gold loss subsided, and through November, 1931, the monetary gold stock of the United States increased by 122 millions of dollars, which was accounted for principally by imports from Japan and to releases of gold held under earmarked account.

The loss of gold and the increase in the volume of currency held in hoards through this six weeks' period brought about radical changes in the statements of condition of the Federal Reserve banks.

Changes in Federal Reserve Credit and Related Items
From Week Ending September 19, 1931, to Week Ending October 31, 1931

(Weekly averages of daily data, in millions of dollars)

Demand factors		*Supply factors*	
Monetary gold stock	− 724	Nonmember bank deposits	− 32
Treasury currency (adjusted)	− 28	Unexpended capital funds	− 9
Money in circulation	+ 405	Member bank reserve balances	− 169
United States securities	− 14	Bills discounted	+ 444
		Bills bought	+ 514
		Other Federal Reserve bank credit	+ 3
TOTAL	1,171		1,171

From this table it will be noted that the decline in the gold stock and the increase of money in circulation was financed through increases in borrowings on the part of member banks, purchases of bills on the part of the Federal Reserve banks, and through the decline taking place in the volume of member bank reserve balances. These latter fell in consequence of the reduction in the deposit liabilities of member banks resulting from the decline in the gold stock, the increase in the currency, and the liquidation taking place in bank credit. The expansion in the open-market portfolio of the Federal Reserve banks took the form of an increase in bills purchased. Holdings of United States securities actually declined. The reason was that the Federal Reserve banks desired to maintain the volume of "free gold," which could be accomplished through bill purchases but not through security purchases. The increase in member bank borrowings, as the gold stock declined and the volume of money in circulation increased, led to higher rates of interest in the money market. Bill rates, call loan rates, and commercial paper rates, advanced materially and the rediscount rate at the Federal Reserve Bank of New York was raised on two successive occasions, October 9 and 16, by steps of one per cent at a time.

Summary

Changes in the monetary stock of gold affect the volume of bank credit through their effect on member bank reserve balances. If these increase in consequence of gold imports, releases of gold from earmarked account, or domestic gold production, the superstructure of credit may expand. Not always do member banks make use of an increase in the gold stock to enlarge their reserve balances. They may utilize this to reduce borrowings at the Federal Reserve banks or to purchase acceptances previously held by the reserve banks even if the reserve banks are themselves not following a conscious policy of attempting to "offset" the effects of the larger gold stock. Whether an expansion in bank credit takes place will itself depend upon the use member banks make of an increase in the gold stock, and the particular utilization of such increase in credit as may occur will depend in turn on the demand or lack of demand for credit to be employed in commercial, investment, consumptive or speculative employment.

The developments since 1924 bear out quite forcibly the point that the power of the Federal Reserve banks to bring about a redistribution of the monetary gold stock of the world has not met with the success anticipated. The outflow of gold through 1927 and 1928 was more than made up by imports received from 1929 to the fall of 1931. It is true that the gold obtained in this latter period was not received from the identical countries to which the previous loss had taken place, but the fact remains that the gold stock of the United States was larger than had ever been the case. The rapid drain through the second half of September and through October, 1931, represented in the main a loss to France, which did not stand in need of an increased stock of gold.

The so-called maldistribution of gold, which led to the policy followed by the Federal Reserve banks in 1927 in an effort to correct this, is in itself not an evil, provided that capital flows evenly from those nations, the creditor nations, possessing the gold stock, to those presumably in need of a larger amount. In this respect the New York money market has been extremely culpable and the French money market, as has always been the case, has exported capital mainly to those nations with which it had close political and military alliances.

The widespread suspension of the gold standard through 1930 and 1931 has given rise to much speculation as to the future rôle of gold in the credit structure. At least two alternatives suggest themselves. One is that a reversion be made to the pre-war automatic type of gold standard. The widespread breakdown of the gold exchange standard has brought this suggestion to the fore. It must be remembered though that the pre-war gold standard was never completely automatic in its operation. It was subject to considerable control and manipulation, though to a less degree than has been true with the post-war gold standard. The second alternative is that nations should sever relationship more or less completely with a metallic base and adopt a "managed currency" system. Sweden has already announced her intention of doing so. This involves much more than the management of the volume of credit and currency, which is the type of management usually envisaged by the advocates of this plan. It will involve management of capital issues, of visible and invisible exports and imports, and of the use of credit as well as of its volume. If such plans are adopted, capitalistic nations may find themselves drifting inevitably towards managed, or planned, economies through the route of a managed currency and credit system.

Chapter V

CURRENCY AND DEPOSIT FLUCTUATIONS AS RELATED TO MEMBER BANK RESERVES

Fluctuations in the volume of currency in circulation are a factor of real importance in promoting money market tension or ease. Banks ordinarily keep on hand only enough currency for minimum requirements. For any additional amount member banks are forced to resort to the Reserve banks. These may meet the demand for currency by issuing Federal Reserve notes or by paying out the various types of currency (gold, gold certificates, silver dollars, greenbacks, etc.) that constitute their cash inventory. In either case member banks secure the currency needed by drawing against their reserve accounts. To restore these to the legal minimum, they would be forced to increase their discounts with the Reserve banks, unless the regional banks were purchasing securities or bills or the gold stock were increasing, and an increase in rediscounts is likely to be accompanied by increasing money market tension.

Currency increases, unlike deposit increases, may force an equivalent amount of borrowings; and currency decreases, unlike deposit decreases, may permit an equivalent reduction in member bank indebtedness to the Reserve banks.[1] If a reduced demand for currency were not utilized to reduce borrowings but were allowed to swell the reserve account of member banks, a multiple expansion of bank credit would be made possible. An increasing total of bank credit in the form of brokers' loans or in any other form might very possibly be based on a decline of currency in circulation arising from any one of a number of factors, such as increasing unemployment, declining pay-roll totals, a general decline in the use of currency as purchasing power media, or falling prices. It is the repercussions of currency fluctuations on the

[1] Not exactly equivalent in either case inasmuch as an increase in currency reduces deposit totals and releases a fractional amount of reserves. A reduction in currency volume increases deposits which would require the building up of reserve balances by a fractional amount.

reserve position of member banks, and on member bank borrowings, that necessitates a detailed study of this one factor.

Periodic movements—Intraweek periodicities

Periodicities in currency arise from weekly, monthly, holiday and seasonal monetary requirements. In a chapter entitled "Changes in the Currency," Dr. Burgess, in his volume on the money market, points out that week-end currency demands for pay-roll requirements, retail sales and holiday use, lead to an increasing volume of circulation on Thursdays, Fridays and Saturdays.[2] The currency withdrawn from the Reserve banks to meet this need begins to flow back on Mondays, and continues to do so on Tuesdays and Wednesdays. In a table which he presented, covering the period from April 5 to October 3, 1926, there was a remarkably clear division between the two halves of the week, with net deposits the first three days and net withdrawals the last three days. The same facts were brought out in a study published in the October, 1928, issue of the *Federal Reserve Bulletin,*[3] namely that, barring disturbing influences, due to holiday or other requirements, the weekly low point in currency volume occurs on Wednesday and the weekly high point on Saturday. A table based on the average daily amount of currency in circulation through 1927 showed the following results:

Day of week	*Money in circulation*	*Change from preceding day*
	(In millions	*of dollars)*
Sunday	4,908	
Monday	4,904	— 4
Tuesday	4,879	—25
Wednesday	4,864	—15
Thursday	4,879	+15
Friday	4,902	+23
Saturday	4,908	+ 6

[2] Burgess, W. R., *The Reserve Banks and the Money Market,* pp. 57–60. In the Minneapolis Reserve district there is a net outflow on Fridays, Saturdays and Mondays and a net inflow on Tuesdays, Wednesdays and Thursdays. *Monthly Review of Agricultural and Business Conditions in the Ninth Federal Reserve District,* Dec. 29, 1927.

[3] Pages 684–87.

The decline in currency during the first three working days of the week, amounting to 44 millions of dollars, would tend to increase member bank reserves at the Reserve banks, and the increase in the second half would tend to decrease member bank reserves, in the absence of other factors, to their former level.

Intramonth fluctuations

There is also a noticeable tendency towards increases in the volume of currency in circulation reflected in currency withdrawals from the Reserve banks at the end of each month to meet pay-roll requirements and those monthly bills paid in cash.[4] About the fifteenth of the month a lesser tendency toward withdrawals is in evidence. In January, February, July, and December, the intramonth periodicities are dwarfed by other fluctuations of such magnitude that they are not discernible. In the remaining months, however, this type of fluctuation stands out with more or less definiteness, although not of course with that jig-saw puzzle definiteness that characterizes fluctuations in the note issues of the German Reichsbank. But this is to be expected, since payments in Germany are on a cash basis to a much greater extent than in the United States.

Holiday demand

Superimposed on the intraweek and intramonth currency fluctuations are demands, occurring on such holidays as Easter, the Fourth of July, Labor Day, Christmas and New Year's Day, when large sums are withdrawn from commercial banks and in turn from the Reserve banks, that these festive occasions may be fittingly celebrated. A study by the Division of Research and Statistics of the Federal Reserve Board,[5] showed that in 1927, for example, the Christmas week-end currency needs amounted to 100 millions of dollars. This might not be typical since, in that year, Christmas fell on a Sunday so that Monday was also a holiday. The Fourth of July currency requirements amounted

[4] The intramonth periodicities are particularly noticeable in the Philadelphia Reserve district by reason of the pay-roll requirements in the anthracite coal regions.

[5] See *Federal Reserve Bulletin*, Oct., 1928.

to about 100 millions of dollars, those of Labor Day and Thanksgiving to about 50 millions of dollars, and those of Memorial Day from 30 to 50 millions of dollars.

Holiday currency requirements were visualized by one of the authors, when he happened to be in the money department of the Federal Reserve Bank of New York on a sixth of July. Seeing a huge trunk rolled along the corridor, he was informed that this was filled with one and five dollar bills sent in for deposit by the Bank of Coney Island, this representing funds spent at Coney Island on the Fourth of July. Currency had been withdrawn from banks on the second and third, spent on the fourth, deposited by merchants and concessionaires on the fifth, and on the sixth sent to the Reserve bank by the Bank of Coney Island.

Seasonal fluctuations in currency

In addition to the short-term fluctuations, there are the huge seasonal changes in monetary circulation that are responsible for average variations of close to 400 millions of dollars between the low and high points throughout a year. It was to take care particularly of seasonal demands that currency reformers from the days of the Baltimore plan in 1894 to the Federal Reserve Act made plans for an elastic currency, one which would be related to the commercial assets of banks and which would arise from and fluctuate with the needs of industry, trade and agriculture. If issued on an elastic base, fluctuations in bank notes would respond automatically to business demands. The national bank note, a government bond-secured issue, had become relatively inelastic and a currency reformation was deemed necessary.

Month-to-month analysis of currency seasonals

Starting the analysis of seasonal periodicities with the beginning of the year, the first of the seasonal changes and one of the most important is the January decline. This results from the subsiding of retail trade and employment subsequent to Christmas trade activity and in fact sets in immediately following Christmas Day. Making use of weekly data of the volume of money in circulation published by the Federal Reserve Board, the following table records the decline from the date nearest Christmas Day to the date nearest the end of January:[6]

The January Decline of Money in Circulation
(In millions of dollars)

Year	*Amount*
1924	$353
1925	403
1926	420
1927	398
1928	430
1929	410
1930	472
Mean	412
Median	410

Utilization of January currency decline

The January decline in currency (other factors remaining equal) would increase the member bank reserve account and so permit, if a demand existed, a multiple expansion of member bank loans and investments for money market or other use, giving rise to an enlarged deposit superstructure supported by the increased size of the base. Naturally other things do not remain equal, and hence the actual increases that have taken place in member bank reserve account actually declined, in 1930 by a substantial amount. rency decline. In three of the years listed the member bank reserve accounts have been very small relative to the extent of the cur-

Year	*Decline of money in circulation from date nearest Christmas Day to date nearest end of January*	*Change in member bank reserve account (All Federal Reserve banks)*
	(In millions of dollars)	
1924	−353	+12
1925	−403	−9
1926	−420	+3
1927	−398	+8
1928	−430	+14
1929	−410	−2
1930	−472	−83

[6] Data prior to 1924 are not included in these tables since the seasonal fluctua-

One explanation for the comparatively slight increase in the member bank reserve account is that member banks have utilized in varying degrees the return flow of currency to repay to the Reserve banks those borrowings incurred to finance the currency expansion which begins about July and continues with few abatements to the end of the year. In the past few years the January decline in discounts has varied all the way from a minimum of 87 to a maximum of 376 millions of dollars:

Year	*Decline in total bills discounted by all Reserve banks—from date nearest Christmas Day to date nearest end of January* (*In millions of dollars*)
1924	—309
1925	— 87
1926	—284
1927	—339
1928	—153
1929	—268
1930	—376

A reduction of open-market holdings is peculiarly fitting if the autumnal monetary expansion is financed in part through the purchase of United States securities or bills.[7] In none of the years covered by the table has the January decline in bill holdings even approximated the decline in the currency. The median decline in bills has amounted to 66 millions of dollars as contrasted with a median decline of 410 millions of dollars of currency in circulation.

---

tions were dwarfed by those of a cyclical nature, vitiating the use of the actual data. The data for 1931 were influenced mainly by the hoarding demand.

[7]According to the Reserve authorities a disturbing element in the credit situation in 1928 was the fact that the bills offered to and bought by the Reserve banks in November (1928), were generally of such long maturities that they did not fall due until after the greater part of the January (1929) currency decline had taken place. In other words the excess in funds was not "mopped up." Since the Reserve banks do not customarily sell bills from their portfolio, but allow their bill holdings to mature when they desire to affect the market, the ideal policy is to have bill maturities so arranged that the January decline in currency is matched by the reduction in the bill portfolio.

In 1928 the decline in the bill portfolio was particularly small. On two occasions the Reserve banks increased their holdings of securities during January, adding to the ease in the money market induced by the currency decline. In 1925 and 1928, security holdings were reduced substantially, and in 1927, 1929 and 1930 by a slight amount.

The January Decline in Holdings of Bills and Securities
From Date Nearest Christmas Day to Date Nearest End of January
(In millions of dollars)

Year	*Bills bought in open-market (All Reserve banks)*	*Security holdings (All Reserve banks)*
1924	−63	+ 22
1925	−66	−141
1926	−68	+ 2
1927	−74	− 14
1928	−23	−142
1929	−53	− 28
1930	−91	− 14

The decline in total Federal Reserve credit, including bills discounted, bills purchased, securities and certain miscellaneous items in relation to the January decline in the currency, is given in the table on page 83.[8]

The difference between the January decline in Federal Reserve credit and the volume of money in circulation in 1930 may be accounted for by the change taking place in the member bank reserve account. Ordinarily however the range of fluctuation in this item has been very narrow. The discrepancy in 1925 was due to a decline in the monetary stock of gold; in 1927, to imports of gold; in 1928, to a loss of gold, a decline in treasury currency, and to a lesser extent to the increase in member bank reserve balances; in 1929, to the increase in member bank reserve balances, a loss of gold, and a decline in treasury currency; and in 1930, almost entirely to the decline taking place in member bank reserve balances.

Bearing of January currency decline on Federal Reserve policy

Seasonal variations in the currency may have a significant bearing on Federal Reserve policy, by way of assisting or hampering

[8] As a matter of interest the January decline, in 1929, in the earning assets of the

the means adopted. In 1928 for example the January decline in the currency, 430 millions of dollars, was particularly large, owing to the fact that a cyclical reduction in monetary demand was superimposed on the seasonal decline. The Federal Reserve Board unadjusted index of factory employment was the lowest of any January since 1922. It so happened that this huge decline took place when the Reserve banks were endeavoring to combat an inordinate absorption of credit by stock market speculative activity. As part of their policy the Reserve banks disposed of 142 millions

JANUARY DECLINE IN TOTAL FEDERAL RESERVE CREDIT IN RELATION TO MONEY IN CIRCULATION

FROM DATE NEAREST CHRISTMAS DAY TO DATE NEAREST END OF JANUARY

(In millions of dollars)

Year	*Total Federal Reserve credit*	*Money in circulation*	*Change in total Federal Reserve credit minus change in money in circulation*
1924	− 378	− 353	− 25
1925	− 344	− 403	+ 59
1926	− 419	− 420	+ 1
1927	− 491	− 398	− 93
1928	− 376	− 430	+ 54
1929	− 381	− 410	+ 29
1930	− 535	− 472	− 63
Mean	− 418	− 412	− 6
Median	− 381	− 410	+ 29

of dollars worth of securities. Had this been the only force operative, the member bank reserve account would have increased by 288 millions of dollars, the difference between the decline in currency in circulation and the decline in holdings of United States securities on the part of the Reserve banks. Actually the reserve account increased by only 14 millions of dollars, since total bills discounted fell by 153 millions of dollars, bills purchased by

---

Boston Reserve Bank was less than normally the case by reason of the flow of funds from banks in that district to the New York brokers' loan market. (*Monthly Review of the Federal Reserve Bank of Boston,* Feb. 1, 1929, p. 2.)

23 millions of dollars, other Reserve bank credit by 58 millions of dollars, the gold stock by 23 millions of dollars, and treasury currency by 14 millions of dollars. The net result of these forces was to ease the money market through the reduction in bills discounted, nullifying Reserve policy for the time being. Again in 1929 the January decline in currency was allowed to react on member bank borrowings, easing the money market. This was true to an even greater extent in 1930, although at that time the Reserve banks were following an easy money policy.

To tighten the market in January,[9] the Reserve banks should reduce bills purchased and securities sufficiently (assuming the holdings are large enough) to offset the effect of the retirement in the currency and to bring about an actual increase in member bank borrowings. If the decline in currency were allowed to reduce member bank borrowings, the credit situation would be eased rather than tightened.

The January decline in the currency is one of the factors accounting for the low level of interest rates prevailing in that month. The seasonal index of interest rates is lower then than for any month of the year with the exception of August, which makes January a peculiarly suitable month for the flotation of securities and for the renewal of time loans.

Currency fluctuations in February

The post-Christmas currency decline spends itself by the last week in January. In February manufacturing becomes more active, expressing itself in a rise in pay-roll and employment indices, which in turn translate themselves into a moderate demand for additional currency. The currency increase during the past seven years at the end of February over that at the end of January is given in the following table:

[9] If the Reserve banks are convinced toward the end of the year of the necessity of tightening credit, they frequently defer action until January, doubtless on the ground that restrictive policies will then have the least possible adverse effect on business.

Year	*Increase of currency in circulation at end of February over end of January* (*In millions of dollars*)
1924	110
1925	51
1926	63
1927	39
1928	13
1929	41
1930	17
Mean	48
Median	41

This increase would lead to a decline of a like amount in the member bank reserve account were it not for the other factors in the situation. A principal offsetting factor has been increases taking place in the earning assets of the Reserve banks. Disparities between these and currency increases have been accounted for over the past several years by changes taking place in the government deposits at the Reserve banks, in the float account, in the monetary stock of gold, etc.

Currency changes from March to June

With the exception of the Easter and Memorial Day increases, the volume of money in circulation undergoes no important change from the end of February to the middle of June. The seasonal factors affecting currency volume are either dormant or are mutually offsetting. The net result is that the volume of money generally remains the same, or registers a small net decline at the end as compared with the beginning of the period. This is illustrated in the following tables.

Month to Month Changes in the Volume of Money in Circulation

(In millions of dollars)

Month		*Daily average data*
1924	March	+38
	April	+16
	May	−20
	June	−36
	Net Change	− 2
1925	March	+ 9
	April	−11
	May	−12
	June	− 1
	Net Change	−15
1926	March	+10
	April	+18
	May	−11
	June	+10
	Net Change	+27
1927	March	+13
	April	+23
	May	−19
	June	−29
	Net Change	−12
1928	March	+ 1
	April	+20
	May	− 8
	June	+14
	Net Change	+27
1929	March	+23
	April	−30
	May	+ 5
	June	+ 3
	Net Change	+ 1
1930	March	−22
	April	−14
	May	−21
	June	− 8
	Net Change	−65

On the basis of daily average figures, the mean decline for the four-month period from 1924 through 1930 comes to 5.6 millions of dollars. While the average net change is slight, it should be noted that since 1924 there has been a tendency for the volume of currency to increase slightly in March, less often in April, and to decline in May and June. The seasonal increase in retail trade is probably responsible for the rise, while the decline in employment and the subsiding of retail trade are doubtless responsible for the decline. As based on the monthly averages of daily data, currency tendencies through these months are indicated in the following table.

Number of Increases and Decreases in Monetary Circulation

1924–1930

Month	*Increases*	*Decreases*
March	6	1
April	4	3
May	1	6
June	3	4

The mid-year low point in monetary circulation

Midsummer is the season for the smallest demand for hand-to-hand currency. The seasonal index of retail sales reaches its lowest point in July and employment is at a low ebb. In response to diminishing needs the volume of money in circulation ordinarily declines from the end of June to the end of July. The following table based on the end of the month data depicts the July decline.

THE JULY DECLINE IN THE VOLUME OF CURRENCY
(*In millions of dollars*)

Year	*As compared with the end of June*	*As compared with the end of the preceding December*
1924	−93	−288
1925	−20	−252
1926	+24	−195
1927	−5	−249
1928	−96	−302
1929	−29	−256
1930	−96	−439
Mean . . .	−45	−283
Median . .	−29	−256

August-to-December increase

Beginning early in August the volume of money in circulation begins to increase and with few temporary recessions continues to do so until Christmas week, when it reaches its maximum. The increase in August is very rapid, reflecting a seasonal upward movement in pay-rolls, employment, retail trade, a heavy volume of holiday travel and an increasing total of wage payments in connection with the harvesting of the early cereal and fruit crops. The actual increase in circulation is shown in the following table:

Volume of Currency in Circulation in August as Compared with July

(In millions of dollars)

Year	*End of month data*
1924	+ 103
1925	+ 72
1926	+ 21
1927	+ 8
1928	+ 102
1929	+ 123
1930	+ 107
Mean	+ 77
Median	+ 102

The August increase culminates in a minor peak at the time of the Labor Day currency needs. Of the currency withdrawn from the Reserve banks to meet the monetary demand of that holiday, only a fraction returns from circulation. The large growth in retail sales through September, wage outlays on farms, and a slight seasonal increase in pay rolls are not only sufficient to sustain the volume of currency but in most years actually to force it, by the end of September, above the August total.

Volume of Currency in Circulation in September as Compared with August
(In millions of dollars)

Year	*End of month data*
1924	+ 4
1925	+ 49
1926	+ 48
1927	+ 94
1928	+ 43
1929	— 21
1930	— 32
Mean	+ 26
Median	+ 43

The September increase continues unabated to another minor peak in the second week of October when the harvesting of many crops is completed. This has been followed in recent years by a return flow of currency lasting for about two weeks and then by a rise to another high point in the second week of November. The controlling factor seems to be the increase in retail sales, the seasonal index of which stands at 111 for October and 117 for November as contrasted with 95 for September and 74 for July.

Volume of Currency in Circulation in November as Compared with September
(In millions of dollars)

Year	*End of month data*
1924	+ 189
1925	+ 128
1926	+ 59
1927	+ 4
1928	+ 144
1929	+ 110
1930	+ 159
Mean	+ 113
Median	+ 128

The seasonal index of retail sales reaches a maximum in December, standing 65 per cent above the average for the year. To pay for this huge volume of retail purchases and other expenditures of the holidays, large sums are withdrawn from Christmas savings, from regular savings accounts, and from demand accounts. A larger proportion of retail trade than usual is settled in cash. The following table indicates the extent of the December currency demand which reaches a peak on Christmas Day.

Volume of Currency in Circulation on Date Nearest Christmas Day as Compared with End of November

(In millions of dollars)

Year	*Excess*
1924	+ 129
1925	+ 191
1926	+ 184
1927	+ 168
1928	+ 84
1929	+ 92
1930	+ 317
Mean	+ 165
Median	+ 168

The very large increase in 1930 resulted from the epidemics of bank failures. Banks maintained a larger amount of till money on hand than usual to protect themselves against "runs" and individual depositors, fearful of further bank failures, were hoarding currency.

To review the factors giving rise to the increase in currency circulation from midsummer to the end of the year, it will be remembered that the seasonal index of pay rolls,[10] employment and department store sales each reach a minimum in July. From then until the end of the year the trend is upward in each of these

[10] Illustrating the closeness of the relationship between fluctuations in the currency and pay rolls, it was found for the Chicago Federal Reserve district that the demand for money closely paralleled, with the exception of the Christmas holiday season, fluctuations in the earnings of some 300,000 industrial workers.

indices, and is especially rapid in the case of department store sales. Through the latter part of the summer, vacation demands exert an influence; vast quantities of money are needed to finance automobile or rail travel, and purchases of railway tickets, oil, gasoline, tires, etc., are almost always made with cash. Unfortunately there is no index of the aggregate cash purchases of the nation. In the Richmond, Dallas, Atlanta, Kansas City, Minneapolis, St. Louis, and San Francisco Federal Reserve districts, in which agriculture plays a rôle of greater or lesser importance, wage outlays on the farms are partly responsible for the fall increase. The amount of the currency increase from midsummer (July) to the end of the year is given in the following table.

Increase in Currency from End of July to Date Nearest Christmas Day

(In millions of dollars)

Year	*Amount*
1924	+ 425
1925	+ 440
1926	+ 312
1927	+ 274
1928	+ 373
1929	+ 304
1930	+ 551
Mean	+ 383
Median	+ 373

Seasonal increases in the volume of currency in circulation would, if not offset by other factors, bring about a decline in the member bank reserve position. That this is not the case is well known, since there is no seasonality in the member bank reserve account.[11] In fact the reserve position could withstand no such encroachments, since it is customarily maintained at or only slightly above the legal minimum. Consequently as member banks withdraw currency from the Reserve banks they are forced

[11] See p. 105.

to increase their borrowings unless the Reserve banks are placing funds in the market through the purchase of bills and securities, or unless the expansion in the currency is being financed on the basis of gold imports. There is therefore a close relationship between seasonal changes in the currency and in total bills dis-

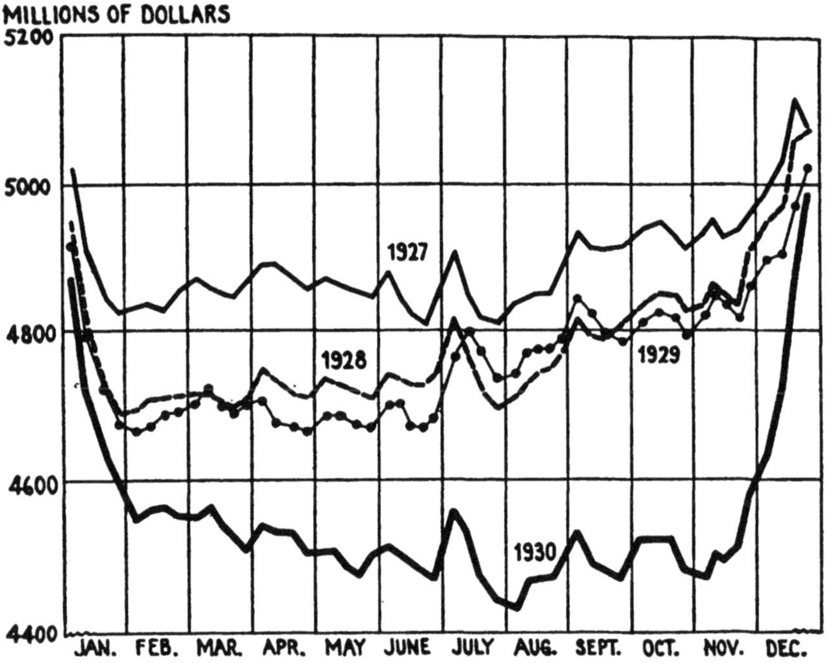

CHART 5. FLUCTUATIONS IN THE VOLUME OF MONEY IN CIRCULATION. WEEKLY AVERAGES OF DAILY DATA.

counted and purchased and total securities held by the Reserve banks as shown by the table on page 93. On the same page are given the actual increases in the currency and in total Federal Reserve credit from July to December over the past eight years. The discrepancy in 1923 is accounted for by the fact that the monetary stock of gold rose by 165 millions of dollars, which financed the currency expansion. In 1924 the Reserve banks were, as a matter of policy, placing funds in the market through purchases of bills and securities sufficient not only to finance the

Index of Seasonal Variation

Month	*Money in circulation* *	*Total bills and securities* (*All Federal Reserve banks*) *
Jan.	99.4	102.0
Feb.	98.4	94.2
March	98.6	98.1
April	99.2	95.8
May	98.6	94.5
June	98.8	93.0
July	99.3	93.1
Aug.	99.4	95.6
Sept.	100.6	100.2
Oct.	101.4	106.0
Nov.	101.9	108.1
Dec.	104.4	119.4

*** Based on monthly averages of daily figures, 1923 through 1928.**

A Comparison of Actual Increases in the Currency and Total Federal Reserve Credit from July to December

(*Monthly averages of daily data, in millions of dollars*)

Year	*Currency*	*Total Federal Reserve credit*
1923	+ 259	+ 81
1924	+ 278	+ 409
1925	+ 325	+ 389
1926	+ 215	+ 224
1927	+ 197	+ 453
1928	+ 262	+ 293
1929	+ 179	+ 263
1930	+ 340	+ 270

expansion in the currency, but also to bring about an actual increase in the member bank reserve account. The disparity in 1927 is accounted for by gold exports as well as by an easy-money policy on the part of the Reserve banks which again had for its effect an increase in the member bank reserve account.

Types of currency used to meet autumnal demand

On occasion the Reserve banks have met autumnal currency requirements by issuing Federal Reserve notes and at other times by payments from their cash holdings. The amount of each issued in recent years is shown in the adjoining table.

END OF JULY TO END OF DECEMBER INCREASE IN CURRENCY

(In millions of dollars)

Year	*Federal Reserve notes*	*Other types of currency*	*Total increase*
1923	+ 64	+ 193	+ 257
1924	+ 96	+ 195	+ 291
1925	+ 214	+ 98	+ 312
1926	+ 145	+ 41	+ 186
1927	+ 95	+ 62	+ 157
1928	+ 216	+ 56	+ 272
1929	+ 114	+ 34	+ 148
1930	+ 321	+ 143	+ 464

There is no apparent correlation between Federal Reserve policy and the particular type of currency issued to meet seasonal needs. In 1924, when the Reserve banks were following an easy-money policy, the monetary demand was met largely through the issuance of other types of currency; in 1927 and 1930, when the same policy was in force, through the issuance of Federal Reserve notes. Federal Reserve notes were issued in 1928 and 1929 when the Reserve banks were following restrictive policies, and other types of currency were used in 1923 when deflationary measures were also in force. No differentiation in currency policy may be made therefore on the basis of credit policies, since in the first two years covered by the table other types of currency were employed to meet the monetary demand, while in the past six years Federal Reserve notes have been more largely used for this purpose.

Decline in the volume of money in circulation

Of great importance to the credit economy up to 1930 was the gradual decline in the absolute amount of money in circulation, which amounted to a very rapid decline relative to the total volume of bank credit. Several factors combined to produce this result. In the first place, since the establishment of the Reserve system,[12] member banks, as indicated previously, have been able to reduce the amount of till money by reason of the promptness with which currency may be procured from the Reserve banks and their branches. In Boston, for example, member banks were said to be in the habit of depositing practically all their till money with the Reserve bank at the end of each business day and of drawing it out the following morning.[13] The Reserve bank was simply used as an overnight depositary. The advantage to the member institution was that the currency so deposited was counted as part of the member bank's reserve account. The same funds were made to serve both as reserves and as till money. Another reason for the declining importance of currency is the growing use of checks, which has been fostered and stimulated by the Federal Reserve collection system.[14] Still another was the inflow of currency from Cuba, as a consequence of trade depression,[15] and the

[12] For discussion see *Federal Reserve Bulletin*, July, 1929, p. 429.

[13] *Hearings before the Committee on Banking and Currency*, House of Representatives, Sixty-ninth Congress, First Session, H. R. 7895, Part 1, pp. 453–54.

[14] This is the point stressed in a letter to the authors by Mr. W. W. Hoxton, Federal Reserve agent and Chairman of the Board at the Richmond Reserve Bank.

[15] Early in 1928 Mr. Guzman estimated that of the total volume of money in circulation in Cuba amounting to 280 millions of dollars, 247 millions of dollars were in the form of United States money and of this total 229 millions of dollars were in the form of Federal Reserve notes which have the legal tender power. (See R. Garcia Guzman, *Cuban Monetary Circulation and the Balance of Trade.*) At the end of 1928 a lower figure for the volume of United States currency in circulation in Cuba was reached by Commercial Attaché Frederick Todd of the United States Department of Commerce in Havana, who estimated the amount to be not far from 122 millions of dollars. Mr. Todd indicated that the amount held in Cuba was the most direct gauge of business turnover there. When business slackened, American currency accumulated in bank vaults which was transferred to New York to be invested. In other words credit expansion in New York City might be based on American currency released by a business depression in Cuba. Cuba has made plans recently to insure her own currency (*New York Times*, February 19, 1931, p. 1.)

In recent years Russia has become a "sink" for American currency. In 1927 and 1928 she received $11,035,000 dollars in currency shipments from fifteen New

inflow from those European countries which made use of American currency when their own monetary systems were in a state of chaos. The amount of the repatriated American currency has been estimated on rather incomplete data by the Federal Reserve Board in recent years to amount to: [16]

Year	*Excess of currency imports over exports* (*In millions of dollars*)
1923	— 18
1924	+ 47
1925	+ 37
1926	+ 24
1927	+ 39
1928	+ 36
1929	+ 27
1930	+ 26
Total	+ 218

A final and an important reason for the decline in currency in circulation until 1930 was the use made of the new credit created during this period. A growing proportion of the nation's credit supply was being used for the carrying of investment securities and this type of business is carried on by means of checks. It is demonstrated in Volume III of these studies that all of the resulting investment credit was not used for the extension of plant by corporations which would have resulted in increased pay-rolls, but that much of it was reinvested in the brokers' loan market, where it was used in the form of bank deposits.

In consequence of all these factors the ratio of bank credit, in the form of deposits, to money in circulation has increased rapidly in recent years.

York banks and returned less than $130,000 by this channel. In addition a large volume of American currency circulates in Canada, taken there by American tourists; and some is in circulation in Panama and the Dominican Republic where it has legal tender power. In Lithuania there is a special tendency for it to remain in circulation, since the national coin is equal to 1/10 of the dollar. (The information embodied in this footnote was supplied by the United States Department of Commerce. See also *Federal Reserve Bulletin*, Oct., 1928, p. 687.)

[16] *Federal Reserve Bulletin*, Jan., 1932, p. 9.

INCREASING RATIO OF BANK CREDIT TO THE VOLUME OF CURRENCY IN CIRCULATION

(In millions of dollars)

Year (End of June)	*Money in circulation*	*Bank credit Individual deposits of all banks excluding interbank deposits*	*Ratio of individual deposits to money in circulation*
1917	4,066	26,352	6.5
1918	4,482	28,765	6.4
1919	4,877	33,603	6.9
1920	5,468	37,721	6.9
1921	4,911	35,742	7.3
1922	4,463	37,615	8.4
1923	4,823	40,688	8.4
1924	4,849	43,405	9.0
1925	4,815	47,612	9.9
1926	4,885	49,733	10.2
1927	4,851	51,662	10.6
1928	4,797	53,398	11.1
1929	4,746	53,852	11.4
1930	4,522	54,954	12.2

If monetary requirements in proportion to the volume of bank deposits had been as large in 1930 as in 1917, an additional volume of currency estimated at 3,932 millions of dollars would have been required.[17] The consequences of this additional demand for currency would have been six times as important in increasing member bank borrowings or inducing a loan liquidation as would the proposed retirement of the national bank note.[18] The increasing credit-currency ratio permits the superstructure of credit to expand to a maximum extent on the basis of gold im-

[17] Even on the basis of minimum gold reserves, the gold stock of the country would not have been adequate to support this volume of currency increase.

[18] In 1924 Secretary of the Treasury Mellon suggested the retirement of the national bank notes when the 2 per cent consols became callable in 1930. This proposal was abandoned by the Secretary in 1928. Had the 700 millions of dollars of national bank notes in circulation then been retired, member banks would have been forced to borrow an equal amount from the Reserve banks in order to obtain currency to fill the monetary void, unless the Reserve banks had been willing to increase their holdings of securities and acceptances by that amount. If securities had been purchased the volume of "free gold" would have been reduced. Any such increase in borrowings would have raised interest rates and tended toward a loan liquidation. At that time (1928) interest rates were high and the treasury probably desired to avoid increasing tension. See *New York Times*, Jan. 22, 1929, p. 37. See article by Jeremiah W. Jenks, entitled "An Analysis of the question of the Retirement of the National Bank Notes," published in the *Bulletin of the Stable Money Association*, Jan.–Feb., 1929, Vol. II, No. 1.

ports or the open-market operations of the Reserve banks.[19] None, or but little, of the additional reserves need to be set aside to finance currency expansion.

Random fluctuations in the currency

As a final type of currency change, there are certain random or non-recurrent fluctuations that arise from special circumstances and which provoke money market fluctuations. A case in point is described in the annual report of the Federal Reserve Bank of San Francisco for 1928. In June of that year there occurred sharp declines in the stocks of certain financial institutions in that reserve district, making for what proved to be an unwarranted loss of confidence and leading to currency withdrawals from some of the banks. To meet this sharp monetary demand, member banks withdrew currency from the San Francisco Reserve Bank, and at the same time drew in funds from the New York money market so that they would not be forced to rediscount to replenish their reserve balances. The borrowing load was thrown on the New York City banks and interest rates rose in the money market.

Another illustration of random currency fluctuations was the increase called for by a run in April, 1926, on the branches of foreign banks located in Cuba. As indicated previously, the currency system of the island consists of American money, and in particular of Federal reserve notes issued by the Atlanta Reserve Bank. When the run began, the New York correspondents of the banks involved requested the New York Reserve Bank to transfer funds to the Atlanta Reserve Bank with instructions that these were to be sent to Cuba in the form of reserve notes. Some

[19] This is a topic which has greatly interested Mr. George J. Seay, Governor of the Federal Reserve Bank of Richmond. In the *Federal Reserve Bulletin* for April, 1929 (p. 242), the point is made that the gold received by the United States from 1922–1927 "gave rise to an expansion at the unusually high rate of $15 of member bank credit to $1 of member bank reserves." The possibility of this ratio of expansion was due, not alone to the declining importance of money as a circulating medium, but also to the increasing importance of time deposits in the bank credit structure. Over the next three years the volume of currency declined by 342 millions of dollars, which would have been a potent source of "surplus funds" if all other factors including member bank borrowings had remained the same. For a discussion of changes taking place in vault cash through this period, see Vol. IV, Chap. XXI.

39 millions of dollars were transferred on April 10 and 12.[20] Rates of interest rose in New York and funds were attracted from other Reserve districts. Another case in point was the curiosity demand for the new-sized money in the summer of 1929, which was an important factor in bringing about a further rise in interest rates.[21]

A final, and the most dramatic example of all, was the hoarding demand[22] in New York City and elsewhere following the largest bank failure ever experienced in this country, in December, 1930. The nonseasonal increase in currency demand continued through the early part of January, 1931. In the latter part of the month, a considerable volume of currency was redeposited with banks and in turn by member banks with the Reserve banks. During February and March, 1931, the volume of money in circulation, adjusted for seasonal requirements, sagged slightly, indicating that some part of the hoarded currency was returning to the banks. In April, May and June further bank failures occurred in the Chicago Reserve district leading to an increased volume of hoarding and to a very sharp increase in the volume of currency, corrected for seasonal changes, particularly in June. Through July the volume of currency as adjusted for seasonal fluctuations changed but little. This period of quiescence was followed by a sharp increase through August, September and October. Through the last two months of the year the currency volume was influenced primarily by seasonal factors. At the end of October, 1931, the volume of currency outstanding exceeded that of the year previous by 1.1 billions of dollars. In view of the decline in employment, pay-roll totals and retail sales in the interim, the volume of money in circulation should have been substantially less, though this natural cyclical decline would have been offset to some extent by the fact that bank failures had left

[20] For an account of this see *Monthly Review of Credit and Business Conditions*, Second Federal Reserve District, May 1, 1926, p. 3.

[21] The demand amounted to about 100 millions of dollars. *Fifteenth Annual Report of the Federal Reserve Bank of New York*, 1929, p. 14.

[22] Estimated to come to 300 millions of dollars. See testimony of Mr. J. H. Case, Chairman, Board of Directors, Federal Reserve Bank of New York, *Hearings before a Subcommittee of Committee on Banking and Currency*, United States Senate, Seventy-first Congress, Third Session, pursuant to S. Res. 71, p. 108.

many communities bereft of a credit mechanism so that a larger amount of hand-to-hand currency was required to effect the exchange of goods. The currency hoarding demand was met through the issuance of Federal Reserve notes. The public, excepting in isolated instances, did not demand gold coins or gold certificates. In fact effort was made by the Federal Reserve banks to reduce the volume of gold certificates in circulation. Confidence was lacking in the financial organization, but not in the monetary standard.

Up to the end of July the increase in the volume of currency in circulation had exerted no effect on the money market, at least no positive effect. The reason was that the increase taking place was financed mainly through imports of gold so that member banks were forced to increase their borrowings but slightly. From February to August, 1931, the reporting member banks of New York City showed no indebtedness to the Federal Reserve Bank. The fact that the gold imports were utilized in the financing of the currency increase is brought out in the following table, which depicts the factors making possible the currency increase, together with certain offsetting factors:

Financing of Currency Hoarding

Week Ending March 28, to Week Ending July 25, 1931

(Weekly averages of daily data; in millions of dollars)

Increase in currency = 240 million dollars

Factors making increase in currency possible		*Offsetting factors*	
Bills discounted *	+ 20	Bills bought *	− 41
United States securities *	+ 74	Treasury currency	− 1
Other Reserve bank credit *	+ 7	Nonmember bank deposits *	+ 65
Monetary gold stock	+ 267	Member bank reserve balances *	+ 35
Unexpended capital funds *	− 14		142
TOTAL	382		

* From Federal Reserve statement.

The hoarding demand from July through October was directly reflected in member bank borrowings and money market tension. Member bank borrowings would have risen to a much higher figure, were it not for purchases of bills on the part of the Federal

Reserve banks. Through the latter part of this period gold was being exported, too, so that the country was subjected to a double drain of considerable magnitude. The increase in the volume of currency held in hoards, and the loss of gold, brought about radical changes in the statements of condition of the Federal Reserve banks through the three months of August, September and October, 1931 and also, as mentioned before, in the general money market situation. The reporting member banks of New York City which were out of debt through the summer were forced to increase their borrowings to a maximum of 121 millions of dollars on October 14. From the accompanying table it will be noted that the increase in the currency and the loss of gold was financed through member bank borrowings, by acceptances purchased by the Federal Reserve banks and by a substantial decline in member bank reserve balances, which fell as member bank deposit liabilities were reduced through currency increases, gold exports and credit liquidation. Total Federal Reserve credit reached the highest point since 1921.

Changes in Federal Reserve Credit and Related Items

From Week Ending July 25, to Week Ending October 31, 1931

(Weekly averages of daily data; in millions of dollars)

Supply factors		*Demand factors*	
Bills discounted *	+536	Monetary gold stock	−667
Bills bought *	+659	Treasury currency	− 19
United States securities *	+ 48	Money in circulation	+696
Other Federal Reserve bank credit *	+ 25		
Member bank reserve balances *	−203	Nonmember bank deposits *	+101
Unexpended capital funds *	− 12		

* From Federal Reserve statement.

Random fluctuations in the currency, like any other type of currency change, will affect the reserve position of member banks and in the absence of offsetting factors will lead to increases or decreases in member bank borrowings and in money market tension or ease.

Deposit periodicities

Much has been written of seasonal changes in credit growing out of seasonal swings in business, and of their effect on rates of interest and the money market. To the extent that seasonal increases in credit give rise to member bank borrowings (as do seasonals in currency in the absence of open-market purchases by the Reserve banks) rates of interest are affected and tension is induced in the money market. Assuming that the "all other loans" of the reporting member banks are representative of the volume of credit

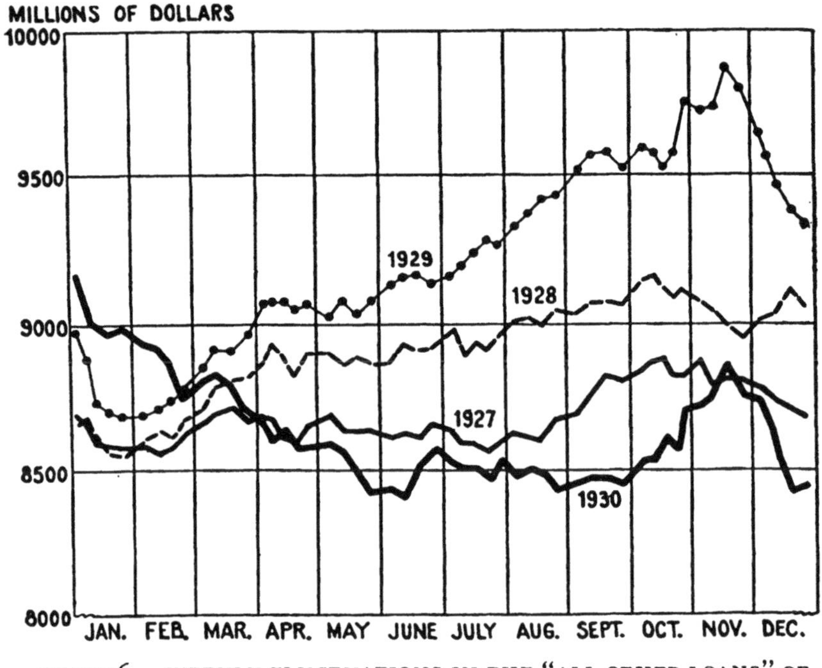

CHART 6. WEEKLY FLUCTUATIONS IN THE "ALL OTHER LOANS" OF ALL REPORTING MEMBER BANKS.

required by seasonal swings in business, the sequence would be from an increase in "all other loans" to an accompanying increase in deposits, to a compulsory increase in member bank reserve balances and consequently to an increase in member bank borrowings as these are required to build reserves to the legal minimum. To the extent that increases in member bank borrowings are induced, there is justification for the frequent assertion that the rise in commercial lending rates in the spring is to be associated with credit requirements.

Relying upon fluctuations in the volume of "all other loans" as indicative of swings in commercial credit needs, we find, upon computing the index of seasonal variation, that in several of the Reserve districts a high point is reached in either March or April, and that so far as those districts are concerned statements of the presence of spring credit seasonals find corroboration.[23] There is a distinct

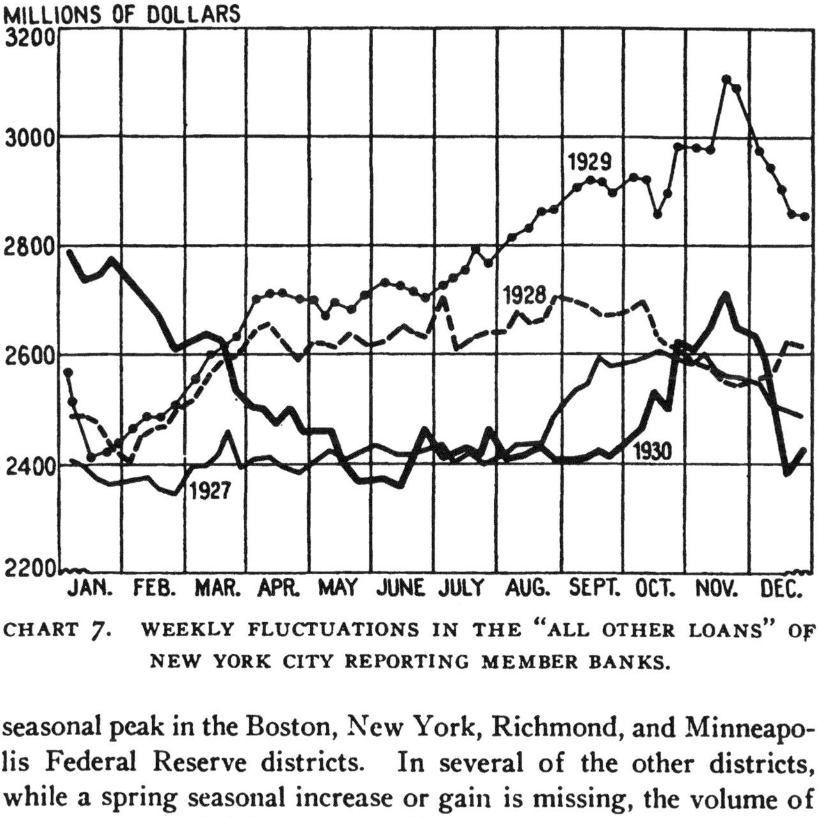

CHART 7. WEEKLY FLUCTUATIONS IN THE "ALL OTHER LOANS" OF NEW YORK CITY REPORTING MEMBER BANKS.

seasonal peak in the Boston, New York, Richmond, and Minneapolis Federal Reserve districts. In several of the other districts, while a spring seasonal increase or gain is missing, the volume of "all other loans" falls away rapidly after March. This appears to be the typical movement in the Atlanta, St. Louis and Dallas districts. For the country as a whole the range of seasonal fluctuation is very limited. The fluctuations in one district neutralize those in another to such an extent that the nationwide index is not particularly significant.

[23] See charts in Vol. IV, Chaps. XIX and XX.

Reserves of course are maintained, not against loans, but against deposits; though not discovering a seasonal fluctuation in "all other loans," it would not be expected that such would be present in deposit totals unless seasonal changes were present in bank security loans or investments. A study of deposit totals for the entire country reveals that there is no significant seasonal variation in either net demand deposits or in net demand plus time deposits. It is less even than the slight amount of seasonal variation in the "all other loans."

Index of Seasonal Variation *

Reporting Member Banks in Leading Cities

(All Federal Reserve districts)

Month	*Net demand deposits*	*Net demand plus time deposits*
Jan.	101	100
Feb.	100	99
March	100	100
April	99	99
May	100	100
June	100	101
July	100	100
Aug.	99	100
Sept.	100	100
Oct.	100	100
Nov.	100	100
Dec.	101	101

* Based on monthly averages of weekly data, 1921 through 1928.

Interestingly enough, in comparing deposit seasonals in the various Federal Reserve districts with those of the "all other loans," the two series reveal an inverse movement in certain districts and at certain seasons. For example, in the spring the loans of the reporting member banks in the Boston, New York and Cleveland Federal Reserve districts reach a fairly high point while deposits are at a low point. Evidently banks in these districts have extended loans to borrowers in other districts, who have withdrawn the resultant deposits for utilization at home.[24] This inference is substantiated in part upon examination of the seasonal movement of funds between New York and the rest of the country through the gold settlement fund. While the index of seasonal variation is not particularly well defined, the maximum loss of funds to New York occurs in February, March, July, October and December and the maximum gain in April, June, September and November. During March the New York banks seemingly are subjected to a double strain, to the increase in loans and to the loss of funds through the

Index of Seasonal Variation *

Reporting Member Banks in Leading Cities

(All Federal Reserve Districts)

Member bank reserve balances

Month	*Index*	*Month*	*Index*
Jan.	101	July	100
Feb.	100	Aug.	98
March	100	Sept.	100
April	98	Oct.	101
May	100	Nov.	100
June	101	Dec.	101

* Based on monthly averages of weekly data, 1921 through 1928.

gold settlement fund. Apparently it is the interdistrict shifting of funds, combined with the seasonal expansion in the currency, which is relatively slight then, that accounts for the March tension in the money market.

Inasmuch as it was found that bank deposits manifest little seasonal variation, it would naturally be expected that the same would be true of member bank reserve balances. Upon computing the index of seasonal variation, it is found that this is actually

[24] In some Reserve districts there is a marked intradistrict shifting of deposits at certain seasons. This is true in the Minneapolis district around May 31, when by reason of tax payments deposits are shifted from country banks to city correspondents, resulting in some repayment of loans at the Reserve bank by the latter.

the case, that the index is not particularly significant and that the spread covers but a three point range, from 98 to 101. The index for March, when the spring credit seasonal would presumably have greatest effect, stands at an average amount. On the basis of the actual amount of reserve balances maintained at the present time the three point spread would mean an absolute maximum variation in member bank reserves of about 60 millions of dollars. Even if member banks were forced to borrow this whole sum from the Reserve banks, the effect on rediscounts would be minor compared with the effect of currency seasonals.

Absolute changes in all other loans

The unimportant effect of seasonal increases in business activity on bank deposits, on member bank reserve balances, and consequently on member bank borrowings, and hence on money market conditions and on interest rates, may be illustrated by use of actual data. From 1922 through 1928,[25] the maximum seasonal spring expansion in "all other loans" has amounted to 460 millions of dollars; and the minimum to 67 millions of dollars. The maximum fall expansion in "all other loans" came to 489 millions of dollars. With the exception of 1923, the spring increase in "all other loans" of the New York City reporting member banks accounted for the bulk of the total.

Assuming that fluctuations in "all other loans" give rise to equivalent deposit fluctuations and assuming that maximum required reserves equal to 13 per cent [26] are maintained against the newly created deposit liabilities, the additional amount required on the basis of the above data, would fluctuate between a low of 9 millions of dollars and a high of 64 millions of dollars. Even granting that the increase in reserves needed to support seasonal credit increases required on all occasions an expansion in member bank borrowings, the maximum amount would come to but 64 millions of dollars. Any tightening of the money market due to

[25] The year 1929 was omitted, since the increase then in all other loans was in the nature of a disguised form of security loan.

[26] This figure was taken since the "all other loans" of the New York City reporting member banks account for the major portion of the increase in loans of this character for all reporting member banks. It represents the maximum required enlargement of member bank reserves.

SEASONAL HIGH AND LOW POINTS IN "ALL OTHER LOANS"

(In millions of dollars)

All reporting member banks			*New York City reporting member banks*		
Date	*Amount*	*Change from preceding date*	*Date*	*Amount*	*Change from preceding date*
1922			1922		
Jan. 4 . .	7,523		Jan. 4 . .	2,198	
Feb. 8 . .	7,301	− 222	Feb. 21 . .	2,140	− 58
April 12 . .	7,368	+ 67	March 15 . .	2,189	+ 49
July 5 . .	7,002	− 366	July 26 . .	1,928	− 261
Nov. 8 . .	7,272	+ 270	Oct. 18 . .	1,976	+ 48
Dec. 6 . .	7,233	− 40	Nov. 29 . .	1,920	− 56
1923			1923		
Jan. 3 . .	7,383		Jan. 3 . .	2,011	
May 16 . .	7,843	+ 460	April 11 . .	2,200	+ 189
July 25 . .	7,743	− 100	July 25 . .	2,130	− 70
Oct. 17 . .	8,038	+ 295	Oct. 17 . .	2,276	+ 146
Dec. 26 . .	7,848	− 190	Dec. 26 . .	2,158	− 118
1924			1924		
Jan. 2 . .	7,798		Jan. 2 . .	2,138	
Jan. 23 . .	7,757	− 41			
April 9 . .	7,999	+ 242	March 26 . .	2,306	+ 168
July 2 . .	7,821	− 178	Sept. 3 . .	2,177	− 129
Nov. 12 . .	8,241	+ 420	Nov. 12 . .	2,336	+ 159
Dec. 24 . .	8,186	− 55	Dec. 17 . .	2,293	− 43
1925			1925		
Jan. 14 . .	8,261		Jan. 7 . .	2,359	
Jan. 28 . .	8,163	− 98	March 25 . .	2,189	− 170
March 11 . .	8,265	+ 102	April 29 . .	2,269	+ 80
June 24 . .	7,999	− 266	July 29 . .	2,123	− 146
Oct. 14 . .	8,488	+ 489	Nov. 11 . .	2,332	+ 209
Dec. 30 . .	8,306	− 182	Dec. 30 . .	2,243	− 89
1926			1926		
Jan. 13 . .	8,321		Jan. 6 . .	2,269	
Jan. 27 . .	8,278	− 43	Feb. 10 . .	2,234	− 35
May 5 . .	8,513	+ 235	May 5 . .	2,402	+ 168
July 21 . .	8,378	− 135	July 21 . .	2,260	− 142
Nov. 17 . .	8,822	+ 444	Dec. 1 . .	2,584	+ 324
Dec. 29 . .	8,717	− 105	Dec. 22 . .	2,526	− 58
1927			1927		
Jan. 5 . .	8,664		Jan. 5 . .	2,407	
Feb. 16 . .	8,558	− 106	Feb. 23 . .	2,344	− 63
March 23 . .	8,707	+ 149	March 23 . .	2,454	+ 110

SEASONAL HIGH AND LOW POINTS IN "ALL OTHER LOANS"
(*Continued*)

(*In millions of dollars*)

All reporting member banks			*New York City reporting member banks*		
Date	*Amount*	*Change from preceding date*	*Date*	*Amount*	*Change from preceding date*
1927			1927		
July 27 . .	8,551	− 156	July 27 . .	2,400	− 54
Oct. 19 . .	8,881	+ 330	Oct. 19 . .	2,607	+ 207
Dec. 28 . .	8,677	− 204	Dec. 28 . .	2,485	− 122
1928			1928		
Jan. 11 . .	8,682		Jan. 4 . .	2,489	
Feb. 1 . .	8,547	− 135	Feb. 1 . .	2,401	− 88
April 11 . .	8,933	+ 386	April 11 . .	2,655	+ 254
May 29 . .	8,857	− 76	July 11 . .	2,605	− 50
Oct. 10 . .	9,160	+ 303	Oct. 10 . .	2,697	+ 92
Nov. 28 . .	8,954	− 206	Nov. 28 . .	2,541	− 156

this factor, then, is negligible when compared to currency demands. Seasonal credit demands, so far as they appear in deposit fluctuations, have so slight an effect on member bank reserves that they possess in themselves little significance from the point of view of the money market. While "all other loans" do customarily reach a high point in the New York district in the spring (though only fractionally higher than in October), it is not the relative or absolute increase in credit that is important, but rather the shifting of funds to the other districts. So far as seasonal money market fluctuations are concerned, emphasis should be placed on the interdistrict shifting of funds and on currency increases.

Summary

An increased demand for currency to meet holiday, seasonal or random needs, as exemplified recently by the volume of hoarded money, forces member banks to resort to the reserve banks. Member bank reserves are reduced and a rising total of rediscounts induced, in the absence of offsetting factors. Unless the reserve banks finance the currency increase through open-market purchases, a money market tension will result. Just as a rising currency demand is met by cashing deposits, so excess currency, deposited by customers with member or nonmember institutions, finds its way to the Federal Reserve banks, where it is employed to reduce member bank borrowings, or is absorbed in a reduction of the bill and security portfolios of the reserve banks, or goes to swell the member bank reserve account and so permits an increase in the superstructure of credit.

Credit seasonals, as distinct from currency seasonals, have a negligible effect on member bank borrowings and interest rates. The spring tension in the money market is due, not to the increase taking place in bank credit, but to a shifting of funds from the money market to the interior.

CHAPTER VI

THE FEDERAL RESERVE STATEMENT AS RELATED TO MEMBER BANK RESERVES—EXPLANATION OF ITEMS

On Thursday evening of each week the statement of condition of each of the Federal Reserve banks and the consolidated statement of all twelve, as of the close of business the preceding day, are released to the press, for publication on Friday. For students of the money market the statements are indispensable in recording developments of the week that has passed and in conveying an idea of future trends. Here are reflected increases and decreases in the monetary stock of gold and fluctuations in the volume of currency in circulation. An imprint is left of the ebb and flow of funds between Federal Reserve districts, of treasury operations, of rising or falling brokers' loan totals, of changes in the commercial demand for funds, and of the investment operations of commercial banks. In short, the Federal Reserve statement is a mirror of banking and financial developments, of which those of the money market constitute an important part.

It must not be imagined that the Reserve banks are entirely passive and that passing business and financial events simply cast their fleeting shadow. Definitely reflected in the statements of condition are the expansionist or restrictionist policies being followed by the reserve banks, their policy in increasing or decreasing their portfolio of acceptances and of United States securities in relation to fluctuations in the volume of money in circulation, in the monetary gold stock and in member bank reserve balances.

The consolidated statement of condition of the twelve Federal Reserve banks, as of December 31, 1930, will be used as the basis for the description of the separate items:

ASSET ITEMS

(1)	Gold with Federal Reserve agents	$1,730,439,000
(2)	Gold redemption fund with United States treasury	35,211,000
(3)	*Gold held exclusively against Federal Reserve notes*	1,765,650,000
(4)	Gold settlement fund with Federal Reserve Board	417,440,000
(5)	Gold and gold certificates held by banks	758,129,000
(6)	*Total gold reserves*	2,941,219,000
(7)	Reserves other than gold	140,298,000
(8)	*Total reserves*	3,081,517,000
(9)	Non-reserve cash	79,932,000
(10)	Bills discounted:	
	Sec. by United States Government obligations	89,421,000
	Other bills discounted	161,977,000
	Total bills discounted	251,398,000
(11)	Bills bought in open market	363,844,000
(12)	United States Government securities	
	Bonds	163,785,000
	Treasury notes	226,473,000
	Certificates and bills	339,209,000
	Total United States Government securities	729,467,000
(13)	Other securities	7,143,000
(14)	*Total bills and securities*	1,351,852,000
(15)	Due from foreign banks	704,000
(16)	Uncollected items	584,783,000
(17)	Federal Reserve notes of other banks	21,993,000
(18)	Bank premises	57,843,000
(19)	All other resources	22,024,000
(20)	Total assets	$5,200,648,000

LIABILITY ITEMS

(21)	Federal Reserve notes in actual circulation	$1,663,538,000
	Deposits:	
(22)	Member bank—reserve account	2,470,583,000
(23)	Government	18,819,000
(24)	Foreign bank	5,761,000
(25)	Other deposits	21,970,000
	Total deposits	2,517,133,000
(26)	Deferred availability items	564,007,000
(27)	Capital paid in	169,640,000
(28)	Surplus	274,636,000
(29)	All other liabilities	11,694,000
(30)	Total liabilities	$5,200,648,000

MEMORANDA ITEMS

(31)	Contingent liability on bills purchased for foreign correspondents	$439,288,000
(32)	Ratio of total reserves to deposit and Federal Reserve note liabilities combined	73.7 per cent

DESCRIPTION OF BALANCE SHEET ITEMS

ASSETS

(1) *Gold with Federal Reserve agents* $1,730,439,000

This represents the gold collateral held by the Federal Reserve agents against all Federal Reserve notes issued to the Reserve banks, whether in actual circulation or not.[1]

Inasmuch as Federal Reserve notes are United States government obligations, the responsibility for holding all the collateral including the gold reserves is delegated to the Federal Reserve agent, an appointee of the Federal Reserve Board.

(2) *Gold redemption fund with the United States Treasury* $35,211,000

The Federal Reserve Act requires each Reserve bank to maintain on deposit in the treasury of the United States a sum in gold sufficient, in the judgment of the secretary of the treasury, for the redemption of the Federal Reserve notes issued to such bank, but in no event less than 5 per cent of the total amount of notes issued, less the amount of gold or gold certificates held by the Federal Reserve agent as collateral security.

Federal Reserve notes are redeemable in gold on demand at the treasury department in Washington or in gold or lawful money at any Federal Reserve bank.

(3) *Gold held exclusively against Federal Reserve notes* $1,765,650,000

The sum of the first two items

(4) *Gold settlement fund with Federal Reserve Board* $417,440,000

[1] Part of this gold fund is lodged with the treasurer of the United States and part held in the vaults of the Reserve bank under the custody of the reserve agent. (See *Federal Reserve Bulletin*, July, 1926, pp. 467–78.)

This fund was established in May, 1915, for the purpose of effecting inter-Federal Reserve bank transfers and settlements.[2]

(5) *Gold and gold certificates held by banks* $758,129,000

This represents part of the vault cash held by the Reserve banks.

(6) *Total gold reserves* $2,941,219,000

The grand total of items 1, 2, 4, and 5. Gold imports and exports, changes in the volume of gold coin and gold certificates in circulation, fluctuations in the volume of gold held under earmarked account, the passage of gold from the arts into monetary use or from monetary use into the arts and the domestic production of gold, all combine to increase or decrease this item, directly or indirectly.

(7) *Reserves other than gold* $140,298,000

The Federal Reserve Act permits lawful money to be included in the reserves held against the deposit liabilities of the Federal Reserve banks. Hence this item comprises standard silver dollars, silver certificates, greenbacks, and treasury notes of 1890.

(8) *Total reserves* $3,081,517,000

This includes the total gold and lawful money holdings of the Federal Reserve banks.

(9) *Nonreserve cash* $79,932,000

This comprises the moneys held by the Federal Reserve banks, with the exception of Federal Reserve notes of other Reserve banks, not defined as lawful money. These include national bank notes, Federal Reserve bank notes, and subsidiary silver, nickels and cents. No part of this may be counted as reserve against either notes or deposits.

(10) *Bills discounted*

Secured by United States Government obligations	$ 89,421,000
Other bills discounted	161,977,000
Total bills discounted	$251,398,000

[2] For analysis of transfers through gold settlement fund, see Chaps. XV, XVI, and XVII.

This sum represents credit extended to member banks, and is subdivided into those bills that are secured by United States Government obligations and into other bills discounted. The first comprises the promissory notes of member banks secured by government obligations. These may have a life of not longer than fifteen days, though no limit is placed on the number of renewals permitted. The second includes promissory notes or bills of exchange of customers of member banks which have been endorsed by the member institution and rediscounted with the Reserve bank, and the fifteen-day promissory notes of member banks secured by commercial paper and bills of exchange eligible for rediscount of purchase.[3]

While at the present time the rates charged by the Reserve banks on the promissory notes of member banks secured by government obligations do not differ from the rate of rediscount on customers' paper, a difference in rate may exist and in fact has existed at one time or another in the history of the Federal Reserve system.

(11) *Bills bought in open market* $363,844,000

These include bankers' acceptances drawn in dollars or in foreign currencies, purchased outright or under resale agreement, (and a very small proportion of trade acceptances) secured from member and nonmember banks, dealers, and others under the provisions of Section 14 of the Federal Reserve Act. The rates of discount involved in the purchase of acceptances vary with the maturity of the paper and usually rule below rates of rediscount.[4]

(12) *United States Government securities*

Bonds	$163,785,000
Treasury notes	226,473,000
Certificates and bills	339,209,000
Total United States Government securities	$729,467,000

[3] See sections 13 and 13a of the Federal Reserve Act for legal provisions relative to eligibility of paper. For discussion of desirability of those provisions and of the acceptability of paper as distinguished from eligibility, see Vol. IV, Chap. I.

[4] See Vol. III, Chaps. XI, XII and XIII for further discussion.

Section 14 of the Federal Reserve Act not only gave the Federal Reserve banks power to purchase, under rules and regulations prescribed by the Federal Reserve Board, cable transfers, bankers' acceptances, and bills of exchange, with or without the endorsement of a member bank, but also conferred on them the right to buy and sell at home or abroad, obligations of the United States government.

Purchases of government securities are made either outright or under resale agreement. The latter method is employed in the assistance extended dealers in government securities.

Outright purchases may result (1) from temporary government financing at the quarterly tax payment periods; (2) for the purpose of offsetting gold movements; and (3) for the purpose of affecting the credit situation and of definitely easing rates of interest. Those that are bought to offset gold movements or to affect the credit situation are held in a special investment account, control over which is lodged with the Open-Market Policy Conference composed of the governors of the twelve Federal Reserve banks, acting under the supervision of the Federal Reserve Board.

Purchases and sales from the special investment account are made ordinarily through the Federal Reserve Bank of New York. Allotments of purchases are made to the various Federal Reserve banks in order to bring about a proportionate equalization of earning assets.

(13) *Other securities* $7,143,000

These consist of Federal land bank bonds, debentures of the Federal intermediate credit banks and "municipal" warrants that the Federal Reserve banks may purchase under rules and regulations formulated by the Federal Reserve Board. For the purpose of defraying expenses, a considerable body of "municipal" warrants was purchased in the first two years of the Federal Reserve system, which were disposed of in the early part of 1917 anticipatory of the entrance of the United States into the World War. Since that time only a negligible volume has been held. Federal land bank bonds and the debentures of the Federal intermediate credit banks constitute the bulk of the "other securities."

(14) *Total bills and securities* $1,351,852,000

These consist of the total of bills discounted, bills purchased, and United States government and other securities held, which comprise the so-called "earning assets" of the Federal Reserve banks.

Foreign loans on gold

(*Not on statement of December 31, 1930*)

This is an item which appears only rarely on the Federal Reserve statement, arising as it does from special transactions with foreign central banks. It may reflect a loan extended against the gold reserve of one central bank lodged with another or represent a loan extended against gold in transit. This latter type of transaction was described in *The New York Sun,* March 15, 1929:[5]

"Foreign loans on gold amounting to $7,562,000, appeared on the weekly statement of the Federal Reserve system yesterday. This item represents funds advanced to the Reichsbank in anticipation of gold which is now in transit to this country and which is expected to arrive next week. It is believed that the $2,500,000 gold recently released from earmark is possibly a part of the same transaction. The Federal Reserve Bank had no comment to make on the transaction, but the figures in the statement were so suggestive as to need no official elucidation."

(15) *Due from foreign banks* $704,000

This amount represents balances due from foreign central banks arising from current transactions.

(16) *Uncollected items* $584,783,000

This item must be studied in conjunction with the contra-liability item, "deferred availability items," both of which grow out of the collection system established by the Federal Reserve banks. The basic principle of this system as indicated previously is that member banks are not given immediate credit for checks and other "cash items" sent in for collection, but are given a deferred credit since from one to eight days are required to collect the items.

"Uncollected items" are nearly always larger than "deferred

[5] Page 47.

availability items," with the difference representing an extension of Federal Reserve credit to the market.[6]

"Uncollected items" include exchanges for the clearing house, transit items and certain miscellaneous cash items, while "deferred availability items" include government and other transit items. Prior to May 28, 1930, uncollected items included the Federal Reserve notes of other Federal Reserve banks, but on and subsequent to that date these were grouped under a separate item. The reason for this change was that while Federal Reserve notes of the other Reserve banks are uncollected items in so far as the holding bank is concerned, they were not regarded as an extension of Federal Reserve credit to the market.

There are a number of reasons, some of a more permanent and some of a more temporary character, accounting for the spread between "uncollected items" and "deferred availability items," or for what is commonly termed the Federal reserve float. One reason for the greater volume of "uncollected items" is that the time schedule as formulated is a bit generous and member banks in certain instances are given credit for checks before they are actually collected. Whole geographic areas are put on a certain

[6] On the statement for November 5, 1930, "deferred availability items" for the eleven Federal Reserve banks outside of New York were actually larger than "uncollected items." In a letter to the authors, Mr. H. V. Roelse, Manager, Reports Department, Federal Reserve Bank of New York, explained the reasons for this as follows:

"You are quite right that the situation with respect to deferred availability items and uncollected items outside of the New York district, which was indicated by the November 5 statement, was quite unusual.

"The answer, I believe, lies in the regulations which have been formulated regarding the collection of checks. Our own regulations provide that when, according to the usual schedule, items would be due for collection on a day that is a holiday in New York State, credit is not given until the following day. Our regulations also provide that, in the case of items drawn on localities other than those in which Federal Reserve banks or their branches are located, the time schedule followed is based on a given number of business days, rather than calendar days. The result is that, whenever a holiday intervenes between the time an item is presented for collection and the day on which it would normally be due for collection, the collection period is extended by one day.

"Since the week ended Nov. 5 included Election Day, which is a holiday in this state but not in all states, it is quite probable that some checks and other items were actually collected on Election Day in certain states, although credit was not given until the following day in the district where checks were presented, and also that the collection items in many parts of the country were collected on the following day (Wednesday), although, according to the regulations, an additional day was allowed for collection because of the holiday. Probably similar circumstances have been operative in many previous periods but have not been so apparent because the total amount of Federal Reserve 'float' was not so small as at present."

basis though actually it might take a longer time to collect checks at particular points. To make the schedule absolutely accurate would involve needless complexities.[7]

A circumstance operative in the New York reserve district is that the Federal Reserve Bank of New York, following earlier practices of the New York Clearing House, credits member banks after the lapse of one to two days for checks drawn on banks in the Eastern states, including banks in Maryland and Virginia, though payment is actually not received in some cases until after the lapse of three days. The New York Clearing House could collect such checks in the time allotted since the items were sent direct to the drawee banks, while the Reserve bank routes the checks via the Reserve bank of the particular district. By reason of the Clearing House precedent, no change is thought desirable or expedient. The float arising from this one circumstance runs from 10 to 15 millions of dollars a day and accounts for about one-half of the entire float at the New York Federal Reserve Bank. Incidentally, the Boston and Philadelphia Reserve banks follow the practice of New York in crediting items drawn on banks in Eastern states after a lapse of two days though a longer collection time is actually required. This practice has been opposed by Cleveland banks on the score that it has artificially diverted business to the banks of the Eastern Reserve districts.

There are other factors of a more random character which enter into the float account. For example, the New York Federal Reserve Bank gives immediate credit for all Clearing House items that arrive before 9 A. M., since these may ordinarily be made ready for the 10 A. M. clearance. Frequently, however, during dividend or income-tax payment periods, the checks arrive in such volume that it is physically impossible to prepare them for the 10 A. M. clearance. Even so, immediate credit is given on those arriving before 9 A. M. so as not to violate the agreement with the member banks. Furthermore if mails are delayed, due to lateness in train arrivals, immediate credit might be given items that

[7] *Letters to College Classes in Economics and Banking Discussing the Practical Operations of the Federal Reserve system,* issued by the Federal Reserve Bank of Richmond, p. 207.

would ordinarily have been sent through the Clearing House but which, under the circumstances, may not be collected until the following day.

The seasonal periodicity in the float of all Federal Reserve banks is depicted in the accompanying chart.[8] The effect of dividend payments, treasury tax payments and the volume of

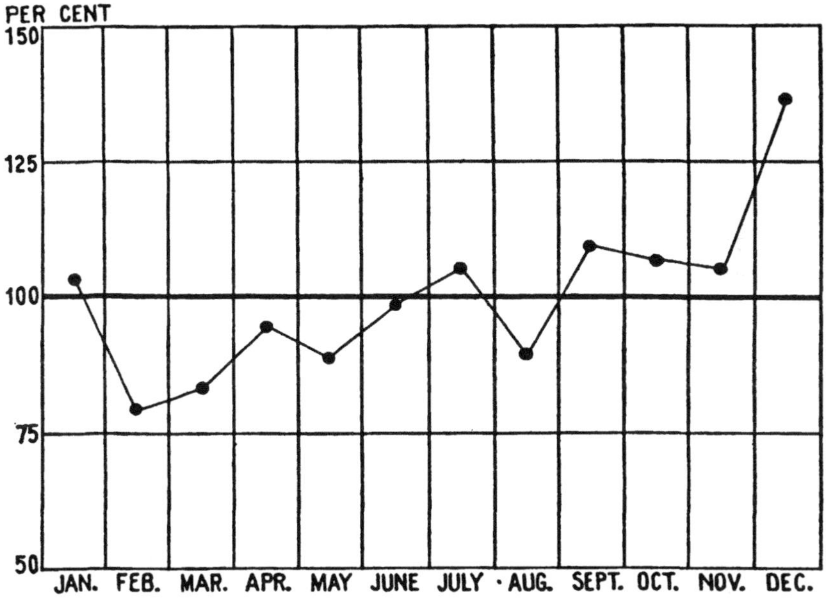

CHART 8. INDEX OF SEASONAL VARIATION IN THE FEDERAL RESERVE FLOAT.

checks around Christmas and the first of the year is depicted by the rise in the line at such times. These periodic movements have important correlative effects on member bank reserves, borrowings and money market tensions.

One significant tendency in recent years has been the steady decline taking place in the volume of the float. From 1922 through 1928 the annual rate of decline amounted to 7.6 per cent. Expressed in another fashion, the weekly averages in 1922 came to 96 millions of dollars and in 1928 to 55 millions of dollars.

[8] Source: *Federal Reserve Bulletin.* Index of seasonal variation based on monthly averages of weekly data, 1922–1928.

The reason for this lies in the improvements that have taken place in the time schedule and in the better facilities and means of clearance adopted. That this may be reduced still further is indicated in the annual report of the Federal Reserve Bank of Philadelphia for 1928:[9]

Before the establishment of the Federal Reserve system, many hundreds of millions of dollars of float was shown in the statements of the banks. This was recognized as an evil and the Federal Reserve system was expected to correct it. The method of collecting checks followed by the system known as its transit operations, has shortened the time in transit by sending checks to their destinations by the shortest routes and has reduced the risk and float by the daily telegraphic settlement of balances. It can be reduced further by the development of county and regional clearings on a broader scale and the more widespread practice of sending checks, payable in other districts, directly to those districts.

Under the direct sendings plan, an arrangement is entered into between the member bank and the Federal Reserve bank whereby the former may forward checks drawn on banks in other districts directly to the Reserve banks in those districts. At least one day of transit time is saved thereby. The checks do not come through this bank at all; the member bank simply advises us of the total amounts and destinations of the letters accompanying the checks which they have sent to other districts. More than three hundred banks in this district are now following this plan and it is urged that others avail themselves of it.

The majority of the checks handled by nearly all country banks are on banks comparatively nearby. In handling such checks through the usual channels, a period of three or more days is required before payment can be received. Country banks within a given area may enter into an agreement whereby they may send checks directly to one another by mail and, by daily advices of these sendings to the Reserve bank, have the balances resulting from these interchanges credited or debited to their reserve accounts one day later, thus saving at least two days. If any of the banks cooperating in such a clearing system are not members of the Federal Reserve system, the

[9] Pages 21–22.

balances of such banks can be settled through their city correspondents. In this district four county clearing systems, including 43 banks and 21 cities, are in operation outside of Philadelphia.

From time to time the suggestion is revived that the Reserve banks should give immediate credit for checks sent in by member banks for collection. On the basis of the Federal Reserve statement of December 31, 1930, the adoption of this suggestion would raise the member bank reserve account by 564 millions of dollars, if the Reserve banks were not to reduce their portfolio of government securities by an equal amount. Without such offsetting action on the part of the Reserve banks, the granting of immediate credit would make possible a very huge expansion in the superstructure of credit, not related to production or to the passing of goods from producer to consumer.

Rather an ingenious suggestion, advanced by Mr. Paul M. Warburg in his volumes, *The Federal Reserve System*,[10] is that the Reserve banks should give immediate credit for transit items but should at the same time charge interest on the time that the checks are being collected. Mr. Warburg would have the Reserve banks reduce their open-market holdings to offset the expansionist consequences and vary the rate of interest imposed on collection items so that they might protect themselves from being forced to carry a larger amount than desired and remain in constant touch with the market. This proposal would mean that the member banks would be constantly borrowing from the Reserve banks an amount equal to the checks in process of collection, at rates of interest fluctuating in accordance with Federal Reserve policy at the moment. An increase in rate might induce member banks to collect through correspondents with the possibility of a breakdown in the collection system of the Reserve banks. On the whole, perhaps the present method is to be preferred with the difference between "uncollected items" and the "deferred availability items" representing a noninterest-bearing extension of credit to the market. The Reserve banks have met with considerable suc-

[10] Vol. I, pp. 298–99.

cess in recent years in the reduction of the float and, if their success continues, the float may be reduced in time to a position of negligible importance.

(17) *Federal Reserve notes of other banks* $21,993,000

By the provisions of the Federal Reserve Act, one Reserve bank may not pay out the notes issued by another Reserve bank except upon the payment of a penalty tax of 10 per cent upon the face value of the notes paid out. The purpose of this provision was to force the issuing Reserve bank to face the constant test of redemption.

Notes fit for further circulation are sent home to the issuing Reserve bank and redeemed through the gold settlement fund. Notes unfit for further circulation are sent to Washington and are redeemed in the same fashion.

(18) *Bank premises* $57,843,000

This represents the buildings and equipment of all the Federal Reserve banks.

(19) *All other resources* $22,024,000

These comprise a miscellaneous group of items including claims on account of closed or suspended banks, overdrafts of member banks, premiums on securities owned, interest accrued, deferred charges, suspense accounts, etc.

(20) *Total assets* $5,200,648,000

LIABILITY ITEMS

(21) *Federal reserve notes in actual circulation* $1,663,538,000

Federal Reserve notes are government obligations and in addition constitute a first lien on the assets of the issuing Reserve bank. They are issued by the Federal Reserve Board through the Federal Reserve agent to the Federal Reserve bank in question. The Federal Reserve Board may reject a Reserve bank's application for Federal Reserve notes and, to the extent such application is granted, may charge a rate of interest on that portion of the volume of Federal Reserve notes not fully secured by gold. Not only those Federal Reserve notes which are in actual circulation but, in addition, those that are received from the Federal Reserve agent and held by the Reserve bank must be fully secured by gold, gold coin, gold certificates, discounted and purchased bills.

Though they constitute an important part of the whole, fluctuations in the amount of Federal Reserve notes in actual circulation are not an accurate index of changes in the total volume of money in circulation. The Reserve banks may meet a monetary demand not only by issuing Federal Reserve notes but also by paying out gold coin, gold certificates, silver coin, silver certificates, United States notes, etc., which are held in their gold and currency inventories.

Deposit liabilities

(22) *Member bank, reserve account* $2,470,583,000

This represents the legal reserves that member banks maintain against their own deposit liabilities.

(23) *Government deposits*[11] $18,819,000

The provisions of the Federal Reserve Act as it passed the House of Representatives (the Glass Bill) required the United States government to deposit all of its funds with the Federal Re-

[11] The amount of government deposits, as given on the statements of condition of the Federal Reserve banks and on the daily statement of the United States Treasury Department, do not always agree. The reason for this discrepancy was set forth in a letter under date of December 5, 1930, to the authors by Ogden L. Mills, then Undersecretary of the Treasury:

"The difference between the deposits of the United States Government in the Federal reserve banks, as shown on the two statements in question is due largely to the fact that the daily statement of the United States Treasury, for a given date, does not purport to be a final statement of the condition of all Treasury offices as of that date. It has not been found feasible to obtain wired reports daily from all offices on all items, so that the statement is in part based on mailed reports which bear dates other than that of the statement itself. The manner in which this statement is compiled is outlined on pages 2 and 3 of the inclosed pamphlet entitled, 'Periodical Publications of the Treasury Department, Revised to February 1, 1928, and Summary of Tabular Material in the Annual Reports of the Secretary of the Treasury from 1914 to 1927.' The difference referred to is greater during the period of the first two weeks of each month than during the remainder, owing to the heavy check payments made by disbursing officers and agencies of the Government from the last day of the preceding month to as late as about the 10th of the succeeding month, covering the monthly supply bills, pensions and other payments to veterans, transportation of the mails, personal services, etc. These payments involve charges to over twenty-five hundred active accounts of disbursing officers and the checks paid must be examined and cleared by the Treasurer as well as verification made of credits for the payments claimed in the Treasurer's account by the paying banks."

serve banks on which interest was to be paid at an amount fixed by the secretary of the treasury and the Federal Reserve Board. With the exception of deposits of the United States government, the Reserve banks were not to pay interest on deposit liabilities.

Inspired very largely by political rather than economic considerations, the Federal Reserve Act, as finally enacted, empowered the secretary of the treasury to make use of the Federal Reserve banks or of member banks as depositaries at his discretion. A further change was made in that no interest was to be paid by the Reserve banks on any deposit account.

Though motivated by political considerations, those who brought about this change in the Federal Reserve Act built much better than they realized. The entrance of the United States as a borrower in the money market, following the declaration of war, led to a very rapid growth in government deposits. If these had been transferred from commercial banks to the Reserve banks, the effect would have been most disturbing from the point of view of the money market, since member banks would have had to borrow from the Reserve banks an amount equal to the deposits transferred.[12] The reason is that a transfer of government deposits from member banks to the Reserve banks is accompanied by a decline in the member bank reserve account, since the Reserve bank simply credits the account of the United States government by the amount debited to member banks, which requires member banks to rediscount in order to replenish their depleted reserves, in the absence of other offsetting factors. The effect of this might have been quite as disastrous as was the insistence of Secretary Chase in the early days of the Civil War that banks pay for their war-loan subscriptions with specie. Through shifting accounts from member banks to the Reserve banks and vice versa, the United States government possesses a powerful weapon of credit control ancillary to those of the Reserve banks.

(24) *Foreign bank deposits* $5,761,000

These represent deposits of foreign banks, in the main of for-

[12] For a further discussion of this point, see Vol. IV, Chap. XIV.

eign central banks, arising from current transactions. Ordinarily these deposits do not exceed the amount appearing in this financial statement. In 1931, however, this was not true, and the deposits of foreign central banks grew to such sizeable proportions that they were a factor of great importance in the money market. Usually, amounts in excess of from 6 to 8 millions of dollars are placed in bankers' acceptances by the reserve banks for the account of the foreign central bank (see item 31 below). With guarantee of payment and repurchase, the Federal Reserve banks impose a charge for this service of 1/8 of one per cent per annum. In addition, without the imposition of such a charge, the Reserve banks stand ready to buy short-term government securities for the account of their foreign central bank correspondents. These the Reserve banks stand ready to repurchase or to sell in the market at the currently prevailing prices. However, the right is reserved by the Reserve banks to limit the amount of the acceptances and securities purchased for the account of any one central bank. Other services rendered by the Reserve banks for the account of their foreign central bank correspondents include: the safe-keeping of securities, the collection of checks and non-cash items, the payment of checks or drafts drawn on the Reserve banks, and the domestic transfer of funds by telegraph or draft. The accounts may be terminated at any time. All of these transactions are normally handled by the Federal Reserve Bank of New York, with the other Reserve banks sharing on a pro-rata basis in the amount of the deposits and in the acceptance guarantee.

(25) *Other deposits* $21,970,000

The bulk of this sum is made up of nonmember bank clearing accounts and, to a minor extent, of Federal Reserve officers' checks, Federal Reserve transfer and exchange drafts, and certain miscellaneous items such as deposits of the Federal intermediate credit banks.

(26) *Deferred availability items* $564,007,000

Discussed in connection with the analysis of "uncollected items."

(27) *Capital paid-in* $169,640,000

Member banks must subscribe for an amount of stock in their Federal Reserve bank equal to 6 per cent of their own capital and surplus. Only one-half of this amount has been called. Adjustments are made from time to time on the basis of the addition of new members, of insolvencies, liquidations, withdrawal of member institutions, and changes in the capital and surplus of member banks.

(28) *Surplus* $274,636,000

After the meeting of dividend requirements (6 per cent cumulative), the net earnings of each Reserve bank are carried to surplus account until this equals 100 per cent of subscribed capital (200 per cent of paid-in capital). Every year thereafter 10 per cent of net earnings is carried to surplus and the balance is paid to the United States government as a franchise tax. The secretary of the treasury, at his discretion, may use the amounts received to build up the gold reserve behind the greenbacks or to retire the public debt. By the end of 1930, the Federal Reserve banks had transferred $147,126,882 to the United States government, the bulk of which was paid from earnings accruing through 1920, 1921 and 1922.

Earnings vary considerably from year to year, and in their fluctuations exhibit an inverse relationship to holdings of United States securities by the Federal Reserve banks. The reason is that a sale of United States securities forces member banks to borrow from the Federal Reserve banks and at the higher rediscount rates imposed at the moment.

(29) *All other liabilities* $11,694,000

Undivided profits until the end of the calendar year, various reserves for self-insurance, for losses on account of failed and suspended banks, etc., accrued taxes, discounts on securities, suspense account and miscellaneous liabilities are included in this item.

Deflationary effects on increases in net worth

That increases in capital, surplus and net worth may have deflationary consequences may appear paradoxical. The reason is that a growth in these items directly or indirectly affects the member bank reserve account, and tends to force member institutions to increase their borrowings. At times this has been a factor of considerable importance.

(30) *Total liabilities* $5,200,648,000

MEMORANDA ITEMS

(31) *Contingent liability on bills purchased for foreign correspondents* $439,288,000

These are holdings of bankers' bills, which have received the endorsement or guarantee of the Federal Reserve banks and which are being held for the account of foreign central banks.[13]

(32) *Ratio of total reserves to total deposit and Federal Reserve note liabilities combined* ... 73.7 per cent

This represents the ratio of the total gold and lawful money holdings of the Federal Reserve banks to deposit and note liabilities combined.

"Free gold" [14]

The published reserve ratio of gold and lawful money holdings to note and deposit liabilities, which on this particular statement of condition amounted to 73.7 per cent, receives no recognition in the Federal Reserve Act and gives little inkling of the actual amount of the excess reserves of the Reserve banks or what has been termed "free gold." Paradoxically enough, the experience of the past has shown that the higher the reserve ratio, the lower usually is the amount of "free gold."

It is often assumed that the reserve banks are simply required to hold a gold and lawful money reserve of 35 per cent against deposit liabilities and a 40 per cent gold reserve against note liabili-

[13] For a further discussion, see Vol. III, Chap. XIII.

[14] In the preparation of this section, the authors were assisted by Messrs. Vladimir Kazakévich, Eric C. Vance and Geoffrey Crowther, graduate students at Columbia University. Reference should be made to the pioneer work of Dr. B. M. Anderson on the subject of "free gold." His studies are contained in *The Chase Economic Bulletin*, Sept. 29, 1930, entitled "The 'Free Gold' of the Federal Reserve System and the Cheap Money Policy."

ties, and that all specie held above these proportions represent excess reserves. This is a fallacy that is strongly entrenched and is given standing through the publication each week of the so-called reserve ratio. On the basis of the reserve ratio method of calculating "free gold," the excess reserves as of this particular date apparently amounted to $1,535,105,000,[15] whereas the actual amount of excess reserves or "free gold" was only $691,375,350. In other words, the reserve ratio overstated the situation by $843,729,650.

The smaller sum represents the true volume of excess reserves or "free gold," since it is computed strictly in accordance with the provisions of the Federal Reserve Act. These provide that the entire volume of Federal Reserve notes issued by the Federal Reserve agent to the local Federal Reserve bank must be fully secured, whether the Federal Reserve notes are in circulation or not. The collateral acceptable includes notes, drafts, or bills of exchange of the type that may be rediscounted for member banks or purchased in the open market, and gold and gold certificates.[16] Against Federal Reserve notes in actual circulation, a gold reserve of at least 40 per cent must be maintained. If deficiences occur, the reserve banks are taxed at progressive rates, and the rate of tax must be added to the rate of discount. A 5 per-cent redemption fund must be maintained on deposit with the treasury of the United States, to redeem such Federal reserve notes as are presented for redemption.

If the Federal Reserve banks do not hold in their portfolios sufficient eligible paper to provide a 60 per-cent cover, the difference must be met by an additional amount of gold. If, for

[15] Strangely enough, it is on this basis that the Federal Reserve Board itself computes the excess reserves of the system. (See *Annual Report of the Federal Reserve Board*, 1928, pp. 51–52.) The nearer the reserve ratio is to 40 per cent, the more closely would the excess reserves computed in this fashion equal the amount of "free gold."

[16] By the provisions of the so-called Glass-Steagall bill, enacted February 27, 1932, the Federal Reserve banks, with the approval of the Federal Reserve Board, were allowed to place the obligations of the United States, owned by the Federal Reserve banks, with the Federal Reserve agents as collateral security for Federal Reserve notes. This provision expires by limitation on March 3, 1933. While the amount of "free gold" was increased immediately through the enactment of this provision, it did not increase the potential maximum amount of "free gold." The Federal Reserve banks were still required to maintain a 40 per-cent gold reserve against Federal Reserve notes in circulation.

example, a Reserve bank is holding only 50 per cent as much eligible paper as it has issued in notes, it will be obliged to hold the remaining 50 per cent reserve in gold. It is for this reason that the amount of "free gold" varies inversely with the volume of eligible paper held by the Reserve banks until the amount of such paper has grown to 60 per cent of the amount of notes issued. After that point further increases in commercial paper will not affect the volume of "free gold," for the gold reserve is not permitted to fall below 40 per cent (except in the case of that amount of notes issued by the Federal Reserve agent to the Reserve bank, but not yet put into actual circulation).

In addition to the reserve against notes, the Reserve banks are required to maintain a 35 per-cent reserve against deposits, in gold or lawful money, the latter consisting of standard silver dollars, silver certificates, greenbacks and Treasury notes of 1890.

Using the consolidated statement for all Federal Reserve banks for December 31, 1930, to illustrate the method employed in computing the volume of "free gold," there was issued to the several Reserve banks as of that date $2,093,625,000 Federal Reserve notes.[17] Although only $1,663,538,000 were in actual circulation, the entire amount issued to the Federal Reserve banks is required by the statutes to be fully collateraled by gold or eligible paper. At that date bills discounted amounted to $251,-398,000 and bills bought to $363,844,000, a total of $615,242,000 of holdings of eligible commercial paper. This whole amount may be included in the security to be held behind the Reserve notes, since it does not exceed the permissible 60 per cent ratio. The difference between the holdings of commercial paper and the total amount of Federal Reserve notes issued to the banks, or $1,478,383,000, must be secured entirely by gold or gold certificates. In addition, a 5 per cent gold redemption fund is required against that amount of notes not fully secured by gold, which would amount to $30,762,100. To these two gold funds must be added a 35 per cent reserve, $880,996,550, consisting of gold

[17] This figure is not ordinarily published in the newspapers, but may be obtained from the mimeographed press release of the Federal Reserve Board which is reprinted in *The Commercial and Financial Chronicle.*

and lawful money to be held against total deposit liabilities. The following table indicates the amount of "free gold" possessed by the system.

Computation of the Volume of "Free Gold" Holdings
All Federal Reserve Banks

(As of December 31, 1930)

(1) Federal Reserve notes issued by Federal Reserve agents to Federal Reserve banks	$2,093,625,000
(2) Total of bills discounted and bills bought held by Federal Reserve banks [18]	615,242,000
(3) Gold cover required against Federal Reserve notes, *i.e.*, item (1) minus item (2)	1,478,383,000
(4) Gold redemption fund required against that portion of Federal Reserve notes not fully secured by gold and gold certificates	30,762,100
(5) Gold and lawful money reserves required against total desposit liabilities of Federal Reserve banks	880,996,550
(6) Total gold and lawful money reserves required, *i.e.*, items (3), (4) and (5)	2,390,141,650
(7) Total gold and lawful money holdings of the Federal Reserve banks	3,081,517,000
(8) Total gold and lawful money reserves required, *i.e.*, item (6)	2,390,141,650
(9) "Free Gold," *i.e.*, excess reserves above those required, item (7) minus item (8)	691,375,350

[18] The Federal Reserve banks do not lodge the full amount of their holdings of bills discounted and bills bought with the Federal Reserve agents. On this date the Reserve banks had actually placed with the Reserve agents $507,788,000 of eligible paper. The amount of "free gold" then would be reduced by $107,454,-000, the difference between the amount of bills discounted and bought held by the Reserve banks and that portion placed with the Reserve agents. The difference is due to the fact that the latter does not include: (1) acceptances purchased

With the system of regional banks established by the Federal Reserve Act, the reserve and the note issue provisions apply not to the system as a whole but to each Reserve bank. For this reason the amount of "free gold" should be calculated separately for each of the regional institutions. The results of such calculations reveal wide discrepancies existing among the banks of the different districts. The bulk of the "free gold" is usually held by the New York and Chicago Reserve Banks. In fact, the "free gold" holdings of these two banks constitute a much larger proportion of the total "free gold" of the system, than their gold and lawful money reserves bear to the total reserves of the system. The reason for this is that these two banks ordinarily hold a substantial volume of the bills discounted and bought by the twelve Reserve banks.

Although the excess reserves of one Reserve bank do not compensate for the deficit of another, in actual practice any Reserve bank which found itself deficient in "free gold" through the lack of a sufficient quantity of eligible paper could increase its holdings through the exchange of United States securities against the gold or acceptance holdings of other Reserve banks. An increase in either of these items, accompanied by a decrease in United States security holdings, would increase the volume of "free gold." The same result would take place if the acceptance holdings of one Reserve bank were exchanged for the gold of another, provided that the Reserve bank in need of gold held an amount of eligible paper greater than 60 per cent of the notes issued by the reserve agent to the bank.

The amount of "free gold" is a function of a number of variables. If reference is made to the table on page 130, it will be seen that it is affected by the total reserves of the Federal Reserve banks, by the volume of Federal Reserve notes held in the tills of the regional institutions, by the amount of eligible paper on hand, and by fluctuations in deposit liabilities.

---

abroad; (2) temporary items bought one day and sold the next; (3) agricultural paper of a maturity of over six months; (4) discounts at branches of Federal Reserve banks lacking an assistant Federal Reserve agent; (5) foreign trade acceptances not endorsed by a member bank. In this computation it is assumed that all eligible paper held is placed with the Reserve agents, so that the final result represents the maximum possible amount of "free gold."

The larger the total reserves of the Federal Reserve banks, the greater the amount of "free gold," if other factors remain the same. But of course other factors do not remain the same, and a change in total reserve might be accompanied by offsetting movements in other items, with the volume of "free gold" remaining unchanged.[19]

[19] See Beckhart, B. H., "The 'Free Gold' of the Reserve Banks and its Relation to Credit Policy," *The Annalist,* Jan. 16, 1931.

Chapter VII

THE FEDERAL RESERVE STATEMENT AS RELATED TO MEMBER BANK RESERVES—ANALYSIS OF STATEMENT

The preceding chapter was devoted to a description of the items appearing on the statement of condition of the Federal Reserve banks. Special consideration was given the meaning of the float account and the concept of "free gold." In this chapter an analysis will be made of the Federal Reserve statement, to give emphasis to some of the more important relationships.

From the point of view of the money market, if not indeed from the point of view of the entire credit economy, perhaps the two items of greatest significance in the Federal Reserve banks' statements are the member bank reserve account (item 22) on the liability side, and bills discounted (item 10) on the asset side. The first is important since it serves as the base for the superstructure of credit. Fluctuations in this item are tantamount to changes in the marginal supply of funds in the money market. Increases permit a multiple expansion in the superstructure of credit, granted the existence of a credit demand. Depending on forces of demand, the credit created may be employed in money market, commercial or investment use. Occasionally increases in the superstructure bring about changes in the base, but over longer periods the causal sequence is the opposite.[1] Decreases may lead to increases in

[1] The importance of the reserve account in the credit economy was sketched in the Report of the Federal Reserve Board for 1928 (pp. 7–8) in the following terms:
"In a period like the present, when the gold reserves of the country have been diminishd by more than 10 per cent through gold exports, while member bank credit has continued to expand, it is appropriate to define the character and extent of the Federal reserve system's responsibility for changes in credit conditions. The Federal reserve system is under obligation to make such use of its own lending power as will be, in the broadest sense, in the interests of the business of the country. Since the Reserve banks hold all the reserves of member banks and through credit policy can influence the rate of growth of these reserves, the Federal reserve system has a responsibility, within the limit of its powers, for the character of growth in the total volume of member bank credit. Increased loans and investments of member banks, regardless of the purpose for which the loan or

member bank borrowings, *i.e.*, in bills discounted, and fluctuations in bills discounted are important since they correlate closely with market rates of interest and give an indication of the plethora or scarcity of funds.

The consolidated statement

The activities of the interior Reserve banks frequently have a significance for the money market comparable to those of the New York Reserve Bank itself. For this reason use will first be made of a consolidated statement of condition. Purchases of securities and acceptances, for the most part, take place in New York City, with holdings of the interior Reserve banks representing later allocations. Even the discount operations of interior institutions may affect the New York market. A member bank in the interior may borrow to place funds on the call market or borrow to prevent the calling of funds from New York. If an interior member bank desires to repay loans to the local Reserve bank or to obtain currency it might do so through the calling of funds from New York, which might force banks there to rediscount with the Federal Reserve Bank of New York.

To illustrate the relationship of changes in items on the consolidated statement of condition of all Federal Reserve banks to money market fluctuations, use will be made of the statements of condition at the end of 1926 and 1927. This period witnessed a rapid increase in the open-market holdings of the Federal Reserve banks, which led to a growth in member bank reserve balances and in the volume of credit employed in the money market.

The member bank reserve account increased by 293 millions of dollars. On the basis of this increase in reserves, the loans and investments of all member banks increased by 2,605 millions of dollars; of all banks, by 3,405 millions of dollars; the deposits

investment is made, result in the creation of additional deposits. A growth in deposits, resulting from an increase in any class of loan or investment, in turn increases the reserve requirements of member banks and consequently their demand for Reserve bank credit. Every class of loan or investment, therefore, rests in the final analysis upon Reserve bank credit, which is the base of the entire credit structure, and excessive or too rapid growth in any field of credit, whether it be commerce, industry, agriculture or the trading in securities, is a matter of concern to the Federal Reserve system."

of all member banks increased by 1,587 millions of dollars; and of all banks, by 2,870 millions of dollars.

CONSOLIDATED STATEMENT OF ALL RESERVE BANKS *

(In millions of dollars)

Assets	*1926 Dec. 31*	*1927 Dec. 31*	*Change*
Gold with Federal Reserve agents	1,382	1,539	+ 157
Gold redemption fund with United States Treasury	67	57	− 10
Gold held exclusively against Federal Reserve notes	1,449	1,596	+ 147
Gold settlement fund with Federal Reserve Board	665	528	− 137
Gold and gold certificates held by banks:			
United States gold coin	116	111	− 5
Gold bullion and foreign coin	182	161	− 21
Gold certificates	407	337	− 70
Total gold reserves	2,819	2,733	− 86
Reserves other than gold	129	134	+ 5
Total reserves	2,948	2,867	− 81
Nonreserve cash	67	77	+ 10
Gold held abroad	....	....	.....
Bills discounted	637	582	− 55
Bills bought			
Outright	†	310	
Under resale agreement	†	82	
Total bills bought	381	392	+ 11
United States securities			
Bought outright	312	560	+ 248
Under resale agreement	3	57	+ 54
Total United States securities	315	617	+ 302
Other securities	3	1	− 2
Total bills and securities	1,335	1,591	+ 256
Due from foreign banks	1	1	(no change)
Reserve bank float ‡	45	63	+ 18
Total reserve bank credit outstanding	1,381	1,655	+ 274

* *Fourteenth Annual Report of the Federal Reserve Board,* 1927, pp. 64–65. This statement is in slightly more detail than those published in the newspapers.

† Not available.

‡ Uncollected items (exclusive of Federal Reserve notes of other Federal Reserve banks) in excess of deferred availability items.

CONSOLIDATED STATEMENT OF ALL RESERVE BANKS (CONTINUED)
(*In millions of dollars*)

Assets	*1926 Dec. 31*	*1927 Dec. 31*	*Change*
Federal reserve notes of other Federal Reserve banks	25	24	− 1
Bank premises	58	58	(no change)
All other resources	11	15	+ 4
Total resources	4,490	4,696	+ 197
Liabilities			
Federal reserve notes			
Held by other Federal Reserve banks	25	24	− 1
Outside Federal Reserve banks	1,826	1,766	− 60
Total notes in circulation	1,851	1,790	− 61
Deposits:			
Member bank reserve account	2,194	2,487	+ 293
Government	17	18	+ 1
Foreign bank	46	5	− 41
Other deposits	19	21	+ 2
Total deposits	2,276	2,531	+ 255
Capital paid in	125	132	+ 7
Surplus	229	233	+ 4
All other liabilities	9	8	− 1
Total liabilities	4,490	4,694	+ 195

On page 137 are grouped the changes in the items on the statement of condition that tended towards an increase in the member bank reserve account and those that tended towards a decrease. If from the total of those items which would bring about an increase in the member bank reserve account, are subtracted those that would induce a decrease, the difference amounts to 293 millions of dollars which is exactly equivalent to the actual increase in the reserve account. From an accounting point of view, no other result would be possible. An increase in a liability item, the member bank reserve account, must be accounted for by an increase in an asset item or by a decrease in another liability item.

The principal factor working in the direction of a decrease in the member bank reserve account was the decline amounting to 86 millions of dollars taking place in the total gold reserves of the Federal Reserve banks. Over the year the monetary gold stock

A SUMMARY OF FACTORS LEADING TO INCREASES AND DECREASES IN THE MEMBER BANK RESERVE ACCOUNT

AS COMPUTED FROM CHANGES IN THE FEDERAL RESERVE STATEMENTS FROM DECEMBER 31, 1926 TO DECEMBER 31, 1927

(In millions of dollars)

Items on Federal Reserve statement	*Leading to increases in member bank reserve account*	*Leading to decreases in member bank reserve account*
Asset Items		
Total gold reserves		−86
Reserves other than gold	+5	
Nonreserve cash	+10	
Bills discounted		−55
Bills bought	+11	
Total United States securities	+302	
Other securities		−2
Reserve bank float	+18	
Federal Reserve notes of other Reserve banks		−1
All other resources	+4	
Liability Items		
Federal Reserve notes in circulation	−61	
Government deposits		+1
Foreign bank deposits	−41	
Other deposits		+2
Capital paid in		+7
Surplus		+4
Other liabilities	−1	
Adjustment necessitated by failure of the financial statement expressed in round numbers to balance		+2
TOTAL	453	160

of the United States had declined by 113 millions of dollars. This would have brought about a decline in the gold reserves of the Federal Reserve banks of comparable proportions, had there not occurred a retirement amounting to 25 millions of dollars in the volume of gold coin and gold certificates in circulation which went to increase the gold reserves of the Federal Reserve banks.

The increase taking place in reserves other than gold, in nonreserve cash, and the decrease taking place in the volume of Federal Reserve notes in circulation, all of which reflected a reduction taking place in the volume of money in circulation, were factors tending towards an increase in the member bank reserve account. If to the total changes in these three items, amounting to 76 millions of dollars, is added the retirement from circulation of about 25 millions of dollars of gold coin and gold certificates, a gross reduction in the volume of money in circulation is indicated of 101 millions of dollars. To obtain the net reduction, which amounted to 92 millions of dollars, an adjustment would have to be made for changes in the volume of money held by the treasury department.[2]

The reduction in member bank borrowings (bills discounted) was a factor working in the direction of reduced reserve balances. The decline in this item was made possible by the increase in bills bought, and of United States securities held by the Federal Reserve banks. Together with the inflow of currency from circulation, these were large enough, not only to enable member banks to reduce borrowings in the face of gold exports, but to bring about a very substantial increase in member bank reserve balances. The increase in the open-market portfolio of the Reserve banks during 1927 was one phase, and the most important, of their cheap-money policy. Accompanying the decline in member bank borrowings, interest rates fell, and accompanying and resulting from the increase in member bank reserve balances, the total volume of credit rose rapidly. In response to the prevailing demand, this took the form largely of security loans and investments.

The increase of 18 millions of dollars in Federal Reserve bank float represented a temporary situation and one that would have but a transitory effect in the increase in member bank reserves. The growth of one million dollars in United States government deposits tended to reduce member bank reserves by that amount. As indicated earlier, the building up of government deposits at the Reserve banks has a deflationary effect in that, if other factors remain the same, member banks are compelled to borrow to

[2] See Riefler, *Money Rates and Money Markets in the United States,* Appendix II.

replenish their deficient reserves. The reduction of 41 millions of dollars in the deposits of foreign banks tended to increase member bank reserve balances, and the increase to the extent of 2 millions of dollars in the other deposits tended to reduce them. The increase in capital and surplus of 11 millions of dollars was a factor for tending towards the reduction of member bank reserves.[3]

By way of summary, it may be concluded that the increase in holdings in United States securities was responsible in large measure for the increase in member bank reserves. Both came to practically the same amount, with the other factors of increase and decrease offsetting one another.

The effect of Reserve bank open-market operations on the expansion of credit possesses potentially such great power that many students have concluded that purchases of securities should be made sparingly and only after searching deliberations.[4] To the layman, it might seem inconsequential whether the Reserve banks buy a few tens of millions of dollars worth of securities or not. If the market were affected simply by the quantity purchased, this would be true. But the funds released swell the member bank reserve account (unless used to reduce member bank borrowings, which would hardly be the case when bank rates are ruling at low figures) and on the basis of the enlarged reserve account credit expansion to a multiple extent may take place.[5] Once the superstructure of credit has expanded, deflation takes place only after painful and distressing liquidation. It is easy enough to expand credit during the stimulation and exhilaration of a boom. It is

[3] See pp. 126–27.

[4] Although no attempt is being made here to evaluate the economic effects of the open-market operations of the Reserve banks, it might not be out of place to insert at this point some remarks made by Dr. Miller of the Federal Reserve Board before the House Committee on Banking and Currency on April 30, 1928: "Let me add, Mr. Congressman, because it is a part of what I was saying, that in my opinion the importance of discount policy as an instrument of credit regulation shall be emphasized by the Federal reserve henceforth and an abridgement of open-market operations as a primary instrument of credit policy. I am of the opinion that open-market operations have been the cause of almost as much mischief in credit and economic situations as of good. I am inclined to think that as we get far enough away to review the history of the past four or five years in fuller perspective that conclusion will be justified." (*Hearings before the Committee on Banking and Currency,* House of Representatives, Seventieth Congress, First Session, on H. R. 11,806, pp. 125–26.)

[5] Unless the securities purchased simply offset gold exports or currency increases.

the retracing of the steps taken that is difficult and provocative of so much economic distress. While purchases of securities may lead to a multiple expansion in credit, later sales do not necessarily lead to a multiple contraction, but often simply to increased member bank borrowings. These will lead to higher rates of interest, particularly in the money market, and doubtless to a slackening in the rate of growth of bank credit, though not necessarily to a reduction in the total volume.

If the credit forced into the market by the Reserve banks in 1927 had served as the basis for an expansion in the volume of commercial loans, the operations in the open market would on the whole have been justified. An actual demand would have existed for the credit released. The situation is quite different where the credit released becomes the basis of an expansion in bank credit, essentially nonliquid and unstable in character, taking the form of security loans or investment purchases not related to savings. The classical doctrine of central banking, as exemplified in the case of the prewar Bank of England policies, was that a central bank should not force credit onto the markets but should simply stand ready to discount the paper presented of the quality and standards set by the practices of the particular central bank. Credit control was exercised through establishing standards of acceptability for the paper taken at rates fixed by the central bank.

It must be remembered, too, that the potency of the open-market operations of the reserve banks has been greatly enhanced in recent years by virtue of at least two considerations. These are the rapid absolute and relative growth in time deposits, which have enabled member banks to expand to a greater multiple on the basis of increases in reserve balances; and the tendency of currency in circulation up to 1930 to decline by a small amount absolutely, but relative to credit, in a precipitous fashion. This latter change meant that an expansion in open-market holdings will exert its full maximum effect on credit expansions, since no part need be segregated to provide for currency increases.

The Federal Reserve statements at the end of 1926 and 1927 were selected for purposes of illustrating the effect of open-market operations on member bank reserve balances and, as it happened, on the volume of credit utilized in the money market, in the form of brokers' loans, security loans to customers and investments. The sequence was from an expansion in open-market operations to an increase in member bank reserves, to the increase in nonliquid bank credit.

Change in Bank Credit Series from End of December, 1926 to the End of December, 1927

(In millions of dollars)

All Federal Reserve Banks	
Holdings of United States securities	+ 302
Member bank reserve balances	+ 293
All banks	
Loans and investments	+ 3,405
Deposits	+ 2,870
All member banks	
Loans and investments	+ 2,605
Deposits	+ 1,587
Reporting member banks	
Security loans *	+ 905
Investments *	+ 767
All other loans *	— 87
Bank loans to brokers *	+ 704

* Monthly averages of weekly data.

The security purchases increased initially the reserve balances of New York City member banks, enabled them to reduce their borrowings at the local reserve bank, brought about a lowering of money market rates of interest, and permitted an expansion in brokers' loans. This is ordinarily the experience with Federal Reserve credit policies. The money market responds first, and the effects are then diffused gradually over the country. Not only did the money market in 1927 first experience the taste of "cheap money," but so stimulated was it that it absorbed the larger part of the increase taking place in the credit superstructure.

An increase in credit forcing an increase in member bank reserves

In the previous example it was the increase in member bank reserves which was the effective cause in leading to an expansion in bank credit. This is the normal sequence over longer periods. The reverse sequence, an increase in member bank loans and the accompanying increase in deposit liabilities forcing an enlargement of reserves, was illustrated during the week of the stock market panic in October, 1929. Between October 23 and 30, the out-of-town banks and the "others" together withdrew 2,087 millions of dollars from the brokers' loan market. The calling of loans by the interior banks and by the "others" forced the New York City reporting member banks to increase their own loans to brokers. This was not required to the full amount of brokers' loans withdrawn, since there was considerable credit liquidation accompanying the drastic decline in stock prices. However, to take care of brokers' requirements for credit, the New York City reporting member banks increased their own loans to brokers by 992 millions of dollars. Their total loans and investments rose by 1,391 millions of dollars and demand deposits increased by 1,553 millions of dollars. There was no change in time deposits. In consequence of this increase in deposit liabilities, New York City member banks were forced to increase their reserve balances and did so to the extent of 243 millions of dollars. How this total was built up becomes apparent from an analysis of changes in the items on the statements of condition of the Federal Reserve Bank of New York for October 23 and 30. An increase of 246 millions of dollars is shown in member bank reserves, an amount 3 millions of dollars greater than the increase in the reserves of the New York City reporting member banks. The difference is due to the fact that the statement of condition of the New York Reserve Bank is affected by credit developments throughout the entire district and not alone by those in New York City, though these are usually predominating.

To group the items that tended in the direction of increased reserve balances, and those that tended in the direction of reduced balances:

A SUMMARY OF FACTORS LEADING TO INCREASES AND DECREASES IN THE MEMBER BANK RESERVE ACCOUNT

BETWEEN OCTOBER 23 AND 30, 1929

(In millions of dollars)

Items on statement of Federal Reserve Bank of New York	*Leading to increases in member bank reserve account*	*Leading to decreases in member bank reserve account*
Assets		
Total gold reserves	+ 10	
Reserves other than gold		− 2
Bills discounted	+ 139	
Bills bought		− 23
Total United States securities	+ 141	
Federal Reserve float *		− 1
All other resources	+ 1	
Liabilities		
Federal Reserve notes in circulation		+ 17
All other liabilities		+ 2
TOTAL	291	45

* Including the Federal Reserve notes of other Federal Reserve banks.

The increase in reserves required by the deposit expansion was made possible by purchases of United States securities on the part of the Federal Reserve Bank, and by member bank borrowings. The former represented the relief given the market by the Reserve Bank and the second a necessitous act on the part of the member banks. There were a few offsetting influences such as the decline in bills bought and the increased circulation of Federal Reserve notes. The decline in the acceptance holdings of the Federal Reserve banks reflected increased purchases on the part of those lenders who had formerly employed their funds on the call loan market. The increase in the amount of Federal Reserve notes in circulation represented an increase in vault cash held by the banks, as well as the usual end of the month and seasonal currency expansion.

Responsiveness of fluctuations in bills discounted

To bring about the necessary increase in their reserve account, member banks were forced to borrow as has been indicated, and they would have had to borrow nearly twice the amount they did had it not been for the purchase of securities by the Reserve Bank. As was indicated in a previous chapter, the member bank reserve account is usually maintained at or only slightly above the legal minimum. An increase in member bank deposits will force an expansion in member bank borrowings, in the absence of offsetting factors. Similarly, a reduction in member bank reserve balances due to sales of securities by the Reserve banks, exports of gold and currency expansions, will find expression, too, in increased borrowings. Whether the new level of borrowings will continue, depends on the permanency of the forces behind it and the willingness of banks to bring about, and the ability of the community to endure, a loan liquidation, paralleled by a deposit decline and a reduction in the required volume of member bank reserves. The amount released could be used to reduce borrowings and probably would be so used if the bank rate were maintained at a sufficiently high figure. Especially when the Federal Reserve banks are following a restrictive policy, borrowings are necessarily the responsive item on the Federal Reserve statement. For example, if the Reserve banks should decide, as a matter of policy, to dispose of their open-market holdings, this must be accompanied either by a decline in a liability item or by an increase in another asset item on the Federal Reserve statement. The liability items are relatively inelastic. They are conditioned by forces that would not be influenced immediately by the adoption of this policy. The volume of Federal Reserve notes in circulation, which is a part of the currency volume, assuming a stable level of prices and the absence of a hoarding demand, is determined by fluctuations in retail trade, employment, pay-roll totals, holiday demands, and agricultural needs. The other important liability item, the member bank reserve account, cannot decline since this is maintained at the minimum legal proportionate amount of the deposit liabilities of the member banks themselves.[6] Consequently as securities are sold or bills allowed to mature, member bank borrowings in the

[6] On this point the Federal Reserve Bank of Philadelphia in its 1928 report, (p. 16) made the following statement: "Under the federal reserve system well operated banks have found that they may, with perfect safety, work close to the limit of their reserves, depending on the reserve banks to care for the usual ups and downs of business and such emergencies as may occur." This practice, ac-

absence of offsetting factors [7] will rise, a decrease in one asset being offset by an increase in the only other asset that can possibly increase. Exports of gold will have the same effect unless they are offset by purchases of securities or bills by the Reserve banks. Once member bank borrowings have increased, their decline may be brought about only in the following ways:

(1) Through imports of gold

(2) Through a currency retirement

(3) Through purchases of bills and securities by the Reserve banks

(4) Through a loan liquidation, accompanied by a decline in deposits

The amount of member bank reserves released from the decline in deposits could then be used to pay off borrowings. Since the deposit liabilities of member banks are about 14 times as great as their deposit balances with the Reserve bank, there would be required a liquidation of $14 in deposits for every $1 of reserve funds released and available for reducing discounts.

The very sharp decline in member bank deposit totals through 1931, resulting from the liquidation taking place in credit, from the gold outflow and the hoarding of currency, did permit a substantial decline in member bank reserve balances. As between the end of 1930 and the end of 1931, member bank reserve balances fell by 510 millions of dollars.

(5) Through the sale of stock on the part of commercial banks and hence the conversion of deposits into capital liabilities. One dollar of reserve funds would be released for every 14 dollars of deposits converted.

(6) Through changes in various miscellaneous items on the Federal Reserve statement, such as an increase in the Federal Reserve float, a decline in government, foreign bank and other deposits, and a reduction in the capital, surplus, and in the other liabilities of the Reserve banks.

---

cording to Dr. Miller of the Federal Reserve Board, has released the banker from the constant sense of responsibility for his own condition. For Dr. Miller's testimony see p. 175, of *Hearings before the Committee on Banking and Currency*, House of Representatives, Seventieth Congress, First Session on H. R. 11,806.

[7] That is, an increase in the monetary gold stock.

In listing the various means of bringing about a decline in member bank borrowings, it is assumed that the funds acquired under (1), (2) or (3) will not be used simply to increase the member bank reserve account upon which a larger credit superstructure may be erected. The assumption is that they will be used to repay borrowings, and whether this is the case or not will depend in part on the discount rates in force at the Reserve banks. The amount of borrowing repayable under methods (4) and (5) relative to the liquidation or conversion needed would be small. Thus to repay loans of $100,000,000, member bank deposits would have to decline $1,400,000,000. There are limits to the loan liquidation which the business community may stand without disaster. There are equally effective limits to the conversion of deposit into stock liabilities. The dividends that may be paid on the enlarged capital structure and the willingness and ability of the community to convert the demand deposits standing to their credit into capital stock, are two limiting factors, among others that might be mentioned. This leaves the first three as the only means of effecting any substantial reduction in borrowings, unless credit liquidation is taking place on a substantial scale as in 1931.

As regards the items listed under (6), in the past twelve years the capital, surplus and undivided profits of the Federal Reserve banks have increased approximately 300 millions of dollars. It was indicated earlier in the chapter that an enlargement of their capital funds exerts a deflationary effect on the market. Either it must be offset by heavier rediscounts on the part of member banks or by factors that would otherwise have increased the member bank reserve account. A reduction in net worth through the payment of dividends from earnings or surplus, if accompanied by a reduction in member bank borrowings or an increase in member bank reserve balances, would be a factor working in the direction of lower interest rates and an expansion in the total volume of credit outstanding. Fluctuations in nonmember bank deposits with the Reserve banks excepting in 1931 and in the Federal Reserve float have exerted but temporary effects on member bank borrowings.

Separation of the more permanent from the more transitory factors

One advantage of the balance-sheet analysis is that the more permanent forces affecting member-bank borrowings may be separated from those of a more ephemeral character. That such is the case may be illustrated by the changes taking place in the consolidated statement of condition of all Federal Reserve banks between November 7 and 14, 1928. Member bank borrowings declined by 99 millions of dollars, which was accompanied by an increase in the member bank reserve account of 35 millions of dollars. The decline in borrowings was heralded with much acclaim in the press as an indication of a financial change for the better and a harbinger of lower interest rates. By setting up the accounting analysis, it is obvious that the decline in borrowings was due to a very considerable extent to an increase in the float account and therefore quite temporary in character.

A SUMMARY OF FACTORS LEADING TO INCREASES AND DECREASES IN MEMBER BANK BORROWINGS

BETWEEN NOVEMBER 7 AND 14, 1928

(In millions of dollars)

Items on consolidated statement of all Federal Reserve banks	*Leading to increases in borrowings*	*Leading to decreases in borrowings*
Asset items		
Total gold reserves		+ 16
Reserves other than gold		+ 3
Nonreserve cash		+ 9
Bills bought in open market		+ 25
United States government securities	− 1	
Federal Reserve float *		+ 57
All other resources		+ 1
Liabilities		
Federal Reserve notes in actual circulation		− 10
Member bank reserve account	+ 35	
Government deposits		− 10
Other deposits		− 4
TOTALS	36	135

* Including the Federal Reserve notes of other Federal Reserve banks.

The decline in borrowings would have been much greater had member banks not built up their reserve account by 35 millions of dollars. As it was, the leading factor in the decline was the rise in the float account, which usually increases around the first and middle of the month. The next most important factor was the increase in bill holdings, which reflected the policy of the Reserve banks in giving support to the bill market at that time, and which incidentally released funds making possible the speculative orgy that fall. The decline in the volume of Federal Reserve notes reflected simply the usual mid-November decrease preceding the heavy Christmas shopping demand.

Three statement analyses

To follow more completely the interactions of money market activities and Federal Reserve operations, changes in the statement of condition of the Federal Reserve Bank of New York must frequently be separated from those of the other Reserve banks. One reason is that the open-market policy of the system is reflected more accurately on the statements of the interior Reserve banks, while changes in the New York statement may be due to purely local and temporary influences. For example, fluctuations in holdings of United States securities on the consolidated statement might result from changes in resale agreements in New York. These reflect temporary money market requirements rather than a definite change in credit policies. The same would hold true in the case of acceptance holdings. Fluctuations in bill holdings of the Federal Reserve Bank of New York might result from changes in resale agreements, while an increase or decrease at the other eleven Reserve banks would more completely reflect changes in Federal Reserve policy. The reason is that bill holdings at the interior institutions, like security holdings, are for the most part held outright and represent allotments made by the Open-Market Policy Conference.

The separation of the statements also allows us to study the shifting of funds in and out of the money market, and their effect on Federal Reserve and member bank activities. This is illustrated, for example, by the changes in the Federal Reserve statements of September 25 and October 2, 1929:

CHANGES ON THE STATEMENTS OF CONDITION OF FEDERAL RESERVE BANKS BETWEEN SEPTEMBER 25 AND OCTOBER 2, 1929

(In thousands of dollars)

Asset items	*All Federal Reserve banks*	*Federal Reserve Bank of New York*	*Eleven other Reserve banks*
Total gold reserves	− 14,775	+ 94,490	− 109,265
Reserves other than gold	− 6,590	− 751	− 5,839
Nonreserve cash	− 7,598	− 4,320	− 3,278
Bills discounted	− 13,766	− 81,125	+ 67,359
Bills bought	+ 58,884	+ 13,123	+ 45,761
Total United States government securities	− 6,307	− 5,916	− 391
Other securities	− 50	− 150	+ 100
Due from foreign banks	+ 32	− 9	+ 41
Federal Reserve float	+ 28,554	+ 16,893	+ 11,661
Bank premises	+ 32	.....	+ 32
All other resources	− 247	− 250	+ 3
Liabilities			
Federal Reserve notes in actual circulation	+ 13,268	+ 9,167	+ 4,101
Member bank reserve account	+ 34,492	+ 27,288	+ 7,204
Government deposits	− 10,685	− 4,658	− 6,027
Foreign bank deposits	− 609	− 933	+ 324
Other deposits	+ 1,351	+ 1,441	− 90
Capital paid in	− 121	− 64	− 57
Surplus	.....	.....	.....
All other liabilities	+ 473	− 256	+ 729

It will be noted that member bank borrowings declined substantially at the Federal Reserve Bank of New York and rose by a large amount at the Reserve banks located elsewhere. The principal reason for the decline in New York was the increase which had taken place in total gold reserves, while the increase through the interior was occasioned largely by an opposite movement in reserves.

While the increase in gold reserves at New York was in part due to a small increase in the monetary stock of gold and in part to a substitution of Reserve notes and other forms of currency for gold certificates, it resulted in the main from a shifting of funds to New York. This movement was reflected in a gain of ownership amounting to 66 millions of dollars in the gold settlement fund on the part of the New York Reserve Bank, and the loss of an equal amount on the part of the interior institutions.

A SUMMARY OF FACTORS LEADING TO INCREASES AND DECREASES IN MEMBER BANK BORROWINGS

FEDERAL RESERVE BANK OF NEW YORK

BETWEEN SEPTEMBER 25 AND OCTOBER 2, 1929

(In thousands of dollars)

Items	*Leading to increases in borrowings*	*Leading to decreases in borrowings*
Asset items		
Total gold reserves		+ 94,490
Reserves other than gold	− 751	
Nonreserve cash	− 4,320	
Bills bought		+ 13,123
Total United States government securities	− 5,916	
Other securities	− 150	
Due from foreign banks	− 9	
Federal Reserve float		+ 16,893
All other resources	− 250	
Liabilities		
Federal Reserve notes in actual circulation	+ 9,167	
Member bank reserve account	+ 27,288	
Government deposits		− 4,658
Foreign bank deposits		− 933
Other deposits	+ 1,441	
Capital paid in		− 64
All other liabilities		− 256
TOTALS	49,292	130,417

Difference = 81,125 = decline in member bank borrowings

As would be expected, this particular gain was reflected in the statement of condition of the reporting member banks of New York City. Total deposits over the week reflected a gain of 165 millions of dollars, loans and investments an increase of 89 millions of dollars, while borrowing from the Federal Reserve Bank declined 84 millions of dollars.

Another fact disclosed by the three statement analysis is that a considerable portion of the increase in acceptance holdings, nearly

REPORTING MEMBER BANKS OF NEW YORK CITY CHANGES IN SELECTED ITEMS ON STATEMENT OF CONDITION

BETWEEN SEPTEMBER 25 AND OCTOBER 2, 1929

(In millions of dollars)

Items	*Change*
Total loans and investments	+ 89
Reserve with Federal Reserve Bank	+ 11
Net demand deposits	+ 149
Time deposits	+ 16
Due to banks	+ 78
Borrowings from Federal Reserve Bank	− 84
Brokers' loans	*Change*
For own account	+ 47
For account of out-of-town banks	− 50
For account of others	+ 47

78 per cent, took place at the interior Reserve banks. The increase reflected Federal Reserve policy of financing autumnal currency requirements, and not merely temporary assistance to the bill market in the form of resale agreements.

Summary

This section of the volume has been devoted to a discussion of member bank reserves and of the factors that induce increases or decreases. Separate chapters discussed the effect on member bank reserves of fluctuations in the monetary stock of gold, in the currency and in various items on the statement of condition of the Federal Reserve banks. The analysis of the Federal Reserve statement was left to the last inasmuch as it mirrors changes and shifts in the gold stock and in the currency volume. Not that the Federal Reserve banks occupy a passive rôle. Through their credit operations they may actively increase the volume of member bank reserves, or offset, within limits, the effect of changes in the gold stock and currency volume.

From the point of view of the money market, the discussion of member bank reserves and the factors bearing on them is essential. Member bank reserves, as indicated in the introductory section, directly or indirectly constitute the basis of credit employed in money market use and elsewhere. Increments and decrements are likely to affect the money market first. Increases may lead to the creation of a larger volume of credit, possibly at lower rates of interest. Decreases will induce increased member bank borrowings and may lead to rising rates of interest. In other words, changes in member bank reserves represent fluctuations in the marginal funds of the market.

PART THREE

THE CONCENTRATION OF FUNDS AND TRANSACTIONS IN THE NEW YORK MONEY MARKET WITH SPECIAL REFERENCE TO BANKERS' BALANCES

Chapter VIII

THE PROBLEM STATED AND THE CONDITION ANALYZED

Concentration of Funds in New York and Banking Reform

In a dramatic way the developments of the panic of 1907 demonstrated the evils inherent in the concentration of reserve funds in New York City. The concentration was due in the main to the nature of the New York money market, but also in part to the National Bank Act and to the banking statutes of the several states.[1] Control of the funds concentrated was not in the hands of a publicly established and regulated central bank, but had become vested through competitive forces in the hands of a group of large New York City banks. The social peril of a dominating financial center and the alleged withdrawal of funds from the farming West for speculation in the East furnished fuel for constantly burning issues. It would probably be no exaggeration to say that this problem in itself was sufficient to give impetus to the banking reform movement which eventually resulted in the establishment of the Federal Reserve system.

The problem of the concentration of funds was thoroughly discussed in the hearings on the Glass and Owen bills. Many of the statements made at that time are being repeated today and some of them will bear examination in the light of subsequent developments.

The problem of concentration had essentially a dual aspect. In the first place there was the *fact* of concentration which, it was alleged, consisted of drawing "capital" from productive employ-

[1] *Hearings before the Committee on Banking and Currency*, Sixty-third Congress, First Session, on H. R. 7837 (S. 2639), Vol. I, pp. 80–95, 227–29; Vol. III, pp. 2085 and 2089. (Hereafter referred to as *Senate Hearings on the Federal Reserve Act.*) See also *Hearings before a Subcommittee of the Committee on Banking and Currency,* Investigation of Financial and Monetary Conditions in the United States, Sixty-second Congress, Second Session, H. R. 429 and 504, pp. 1654–60. (Hereafter referred to as *Hearings of the Money Trust Investigation.*)

ment to speculative uses in Wall Street; [2] and in the second place there was the *problem* of concentration. The latter consisted essentially in the fact that the funds concentrated in the New York money market were periodically withdrawn, with resulting periodical credit stringencies, which on occasion developed into financial panics.[3]

The fact of concentration

The first aspect of the problem (the fact of concentration and its alleged drawing of "capital" from productive employment) is pictured in various parts of the hearings on the Federal Reserve Act, as well as in many popular writings. The following data were furnished by Mr. Samuel Untermeyer: [4]

Number of Out-of-Town Banks Depositing Funds in New York City Banks

Name of New York City bank	*Number of out-of-town bank depositors*
Bankers Trust Company	237
National Bank of Commerce	1,671
Chase National Bank	3,103
First National Bank	579
Guaranty Trust Company	182
Hanover National Bank	4,074
Liberty National Bank	312
Mechanics & Metals National Bank	1,010
National City Bank	1,889
National Park Bank	2,426
Total	15,483

It was brought out in the hearings that these banks had 60 per cent of the redeposits of all state and national banks of the coun-

[2] Gibbons, J. S., *Banks of New York and the Clearing House*, 10th ed. pp. 354–399.

[3] *Senate Hearings on the Federal Reserve Act*, Vol. I, pp. 95, 225, 510, 545, 600, 690, 960–62; Vol. II, pp. 973–75, 1347–49; Vol. III, pp. 2328–31 and 2699–2704.

[4] *Ibid.*, Vol. I, pp. 819–25.

try. Of the 111 banks and trust companies in New York City at that time, 30 held deposits of 19,015 banks. Such were the facts. The nature of the problem is illustrated also by Mr. Untermeyer's testimony when he said:

On the 1st of November, 1912 [sic], in the height of this last panic, the country banks had in 30 of the New York City banks $240,000,000, which the city banks were lending for them on the New York Stock Exchange, over and above the reserve of those banks—money that they had sent to New York to be loaned on the stock exchange by those 30 banks, in their own names; and of that amount 10 banks, to which I have referred, had $172,193,000 on that day belonging to their country correspondents loaned on the stock exchange, of moneys that did not form part of the reserves. This was independently of moneys that formed a part of the deposits of these country banks with the New York City banks; it was just money sent right on to be put into Wall Street, because of the high rates being paid for money then.[5]

And then he said, giving emphasis to the allegation that funds are withdrawn from productive enterprise to speculative Wall Street:

It was twice as much as these banks were lending in that way any 1st of November in any preceding year, yet the money was never more urgently needed at home.[6]

Another phase of this problem as it existed before the Federal Reserve system had to do with the loans extended by New York City banks. Statistics were presented by Mr. Alexander Gilbert, then president of the Market and Fulton National Bank of New York covering the distribution of loans and discounts granted by the 30 largest banks and trust companies, each of which had approximately $20,000,000 or more of loans and discounts, and all had together aggregate loans and discounts of $1,226,974,500 at the close of business, September 24, 1913.[7]

[5] *Senate Hearings on the Federal Reserve Act,* Vol. I, p. 825. Cf. *The Pujo Report,* (Report on Money Trust Investigation, Sixty-Second Congress, Third Session, House Report No. 1593), p. 159.

[6] *Senate Hearings on the Federal Reserve Act,* Vol. I, p. 825.

[7] *Ibid.,* Vol. III, pp. 2772–76.

Brokers' Loans

Loans made to Wall Street brokers for banks outside of the City of New York	$174,945,900
Loans made to Wall Street brokers for own account	$264,383,800

All Loans, Discounts and Advances Distributed Geographically

Made by New York City banks to borrowers in:	
Eastern states	$617,830,800
(Maine, New Hampshire, Vermont, Massachusetts, Rhode Island, Connecticut, New York, Pennsylvania, New Jersey, Maryland, District of Columbia and Delaware)	
Southern states	174,140,500
(Virginia, West Virginia, North Carolina, South Carolina, Georgia, Florida, Alabama, Mississippi, Louisiana, Kentucky, Tennessee, Texas and Arkansas)	
Western states	167,720,600
(Ohio, Indiana, Illinois, Michigan, Wisconsin, Minnesota, Iowa, Missouri, North Dakota, South Dakota, Nebraska, Kansas, Montana, Wyoming, Colorado, Oklahoma, New Mexico, Washington, Oregon, California, Idaho, Utah, Nevada and Arizona)	
Foreign countries	2,896,800
(Canada, etc.)	
Total of banks' loans, 30 New York City banks	$1,226,97[illegible],500

It is thus obvious that some reciprocal to the concentration of funds in New York City existed in the loans granted by New York City banks to banks and individuals throughout the entire country—nearly one-fourth of their total loans were extended to borrowers in the southern or western states. But on the other hand approximately one-third of all loans granted directly or indirectly by New York City banks at that time consisted in *loans to brokers—i.e.,* $175,000,000 in loans to brokers for the account of out-of-town banks, and $264,000,000 in loans to brokers for their own account. Over one-third of the brokers' loans directly represented funds from interior banks, and in addition, some part of the loans for own account *indirectly* represented funds from the interior banks in that they represented bankers' balances maintained with New York City banks. Professor Jeremiah W. Jenks stated in his testimony in the hearings on the Federal Reserve Act, that not only the large banks of New York City made such loans, but that the smaller banks throughout the country did likewise. They were in the habit of sending funds to New York and saying: "loan this for me on the call market at 6 per cent or 7 per cent or 8 per cent, if money is tight." Professor Jenks considered it a "bad thing for small country banks to speculate on the stock exchange on those call loans."[8] In addition there were the Canadian and other foreign funds that were attracted to the New York money market. In 1907 the banks in Canada were said to have had $82,000,000 loaned on call in New York City and the Bank of Japan, $60,000,000.[9]

The problem of the periodical withdrawal of concentrated funds

The second aspect of the problem concerns periodicities in the movement of funds concentrated in New York City.[10] While it is true that periodicities are fundamentally related to trade movements, the effects of such trade fluctuations on the money market are largely a banking problem and concerned for the most part with the technique of the banking system.[11] In the present study, this particular subject is treated under the topic of the ebb and flow of money market funds, since it is predominantly a

[8] *Senate Hearings on the Federal Reserve Act,* Vol. III, pp. 2624–25. He conceded that national banks were in part forced to do this since they were cut off from the very best local loans—real estate loans. Cf. *ibid.,* Vol. I, pp. 225–26 and 510.

[9] *Senate Hearings on the Federal Reserve Act,* Vol. I, p. 382.

[10] *Ibid.,* Vol. I, pp. 102–6 and 225–26.

[11] *Ibid.,* Testimony of Prof. O. M. W. Sprague, Vol. I, pp. 514–23. Cf. Kemmerer, E. W., *Seasonal Variations in the Relative Demand for Money and Capital in the United States,* National Monetary Commission, 1910.

movement rather than a form of concentration. At the time of the formation of the Federal Reserve system, however, it was regarded as a form of the concentration of funds—and the reasons which most bankers gave for this concentration of funds in the New York money market is typified by the testimony of Mr. George M. Reynolds, president of the Continental and Commercial National Bank of Chicago: [12]

Senator Nelson. . . . Is it not a fact that when money is plentiful in the interior of the country the country banks and the banks in the reserve cities send the money to New York, to the banks in New York, for the sake of getting their 2 per cent interest on deposits? The banks in New York, at that season of the year, in order to utilize that money and make that interest, instead of investing it in what I call commercial loans or commercial strictly they invest it in call loans on stock collateral on the stock exchange, in those gambling contracts; and there is where the money comes from to do that. And then, in the fall of the year when there is a demand for the money in order to move crops and so on, their money is tied up in those stock collaterals.

Now, would it not be safer to keep that money at home instead of getting that 2 per cent interest on it—would it not be better for the whole country?

Mr. Reynolds. I do not think, Senator, there is any question about that at all. That does not, however, change the force of my statement to the effect that it would reduce the income of the banks from their present status of a little over $10,000,000 a year, which must be borne at some place by somebody else. Now, if you want to ask whether, as a principle of economy, if it would be better to take that $10,000,000 and spread it in higher interest rates which the people would have to pay, that is another proposition.

Senator Nelson. Well, would it not be better, so far as the question of safety is concerned?

Mr. Reynolds. I do not think there is any question about that. Now, let me in the same connection make a statement as to how I regard this thing of the investment in the so-called stock exchange loans. If that money would be kept at home, Senator, and be invested by the local bankers in such loans as they can get over their counter,

[12] *Senate Hearings on the Federal Reserve Act,* Vol. I, pp. 225–26.

the liquidity of the assets of banks to that extent would be reduced, because I think you will agree that if the farmers of the country borrow this money and are called upon to pay it back before their crops have matured or before their live stock has been fattened for the market, it could only be done at a sacrifice.

Now, the whole tendency of sending money to New York for loans upon stock-exchange collateral is not because the banks of the West want to do it, but because, under existing conditions, it is the only place to which they can go and invest their money in a class of paper that can be collected immediately upon call.

Senator Nelson. Now, let me read you here from Mr. Sprague's report from the monetary commission upon the panic of 1907:

Among the many lessons which may be drawn from the study of the experience of the national banks during the crisis—

And then he goes over the crisis of 1873 and 1893, and then comes to this crisis—

The entire absence of liquidness and [sic] call loans, so far as the New York banks are concerned, is the most certain, and by no means the least important. And out of a total loan of $63,000,000 the call loan account was $54,000,000, and, furthermore, the time loans with collateral securities were stock exchange loans, to the extent of $4,000,000. The only kind of loan which was reduced at all was the ones of the variety of commercial loans, a time loan on paper with a single individual.

Now, during the panic the call loans were not reduced; it was the commercial loan which was reduced.

Mr. Reynolds. I agree with that as to the commercial loans. And in order that I may be understood clearly, let me state that it is a fact that the institution with which I am connected makes no loans in New York upon stock exchange collateral, either on call or on time, with the exception of very minor loans occasionally, where it is done for some particular purpose.

I might say that during the past six or seven years we have never had more than $1,000,000 or $2,000,000 loaned in New York at any one time against stock-exchange collaterals, very largely for the reason, first, that we cannot afford to; the rates are low. And secondly, for the reason that commercial banks in my city, almost uniformly, try to employ their money in commercial enterprises in an effort to develop the commercial and industrial enterprises of the communities from which we draw our money. . . .

Applied to normal times, the statement you have made is literally true, because the man who borrows money on stock-exchange collaterals in New York, and who wants to realize on them quickly, must depend on the ability of the borrower to reborrow that money immediately elsewhere or upon the sale of same. Now, if the condition is so bad that the banks of New York City are unable to extend the accommodation, the result is that there is a very violent break in the values of securities, and we are in the midst of a panic.

Banking theorists, testifying at the hearings, agreed with the logic of the bankers to the effect that in normal times the interior banks place funds on call in the brokers' loan market because of their realizability.[13] Professor O. M. W. Sprague said:

At the present time banks employ an undesirably large portion of their funds in stock-exchange loans, not because they have any particular preference for this sort of loan, not because they wish to give special consideration to those engaged in speculative activities, but because most bankers have been of the opinion that it was possible to liquidate stock-exchange loans more quickly than commercial loans.

One theory of considerable interest which attempted to explain the concentration of funds in the New York money market was brought out by Mr. William H. Allen, a merchant of Brooklyn, in the Senate hearings on the Federal Reserve Act.[14] Although his testimony is very confused, he maintained in general that after goods were shipped to the markets of the world, cash was not received in return in this country because the debits persistently amounted to more than the credits in the balance of international payments of the United States. The debts of the United States, for interest, dividends, expenditures of American tourists abroad, and immigrants' remittances, the cost of ocean freights, and other items, more than offset the cash claims for exports from the United States, year after year. The money in settlement of this overbalance of debts, he said, comes to New York from all parts of the country and finds its way into the foreign banks in New York; or the international banks that are controlled by Morgan, Kuhn Loeb

[13] *Senate Hearings on the Federal Reserve Act,* Vol. I, p. 498.
[14] *Ibid.,* Vol. I, pp. 375–82.

& Company, and other international houses. The bankers do not ship gold to Europe to pay this overbalance of debts, but they borrow on the other side to avert exports of gold. Part of this money which is thus held in New York is reinvested in loans, *i.e.*, loaned out in Wall Street and to other banks—and this "is the money that is concentrated in New York. Money that belongs to foreign bankers, and the West and the South never owned $1 of it. There are the $600,000,000 a year." Mr. Allen said further that the only reasonable explanation of the financial stringencies and the panic of 1907 were these foreign debts and the absorption of currency in the settlement of these debts. Little attention was paid at the time to this reference to the international balance of payments as a major factor in the concentration of funds in New York City; yet as a matter of fact it was important, as the present study, in a subsequent chapter on foreign concentration, shows.[15]

Remedies proposed to reduce concentration

Concerning remedies for the situation, it was quite generally agreed among experts that the thing to do was to reduce the motive for the concentration of funds in the call loan market *by making commercial paper more liquid,* so that it could compete in desirability with the call loan as a form of realizable asset for bank portfolios.[16] One method suggested was the establishment of a discount market.[17] Eliminating the payment of interest on deposits was not considered a solution, since it was recognized that the concentration of funds was not due to this fact alone. Mr. Reynolds in his testimony said that the balances would exist if no interest were paid, and Professor Sprague stated: [18]

You could abolish the interest upon reserves and yet New York would continue to be the center where the strain would be concen-

[15] *Infra,* Chap. XII. Cf. Feis, Herbert, *Europe: The World's Banker 1870–1914,* pp. 13–32, 74, 463–69; Hall, Ray, *Balance of International Payments of the United States, 1929,* pp. 52–62; *Senate Hearings on the Federal Reserve Act,* Vol. I, pp. 381–82.

[16] *Ibid.,* Vol. I, pp. 516–17.

[17] Warburg, Paul M., *Discount Systems of Europe,* National Monetary Commission, 1910.

[18] *Senate Hearings on the Federal Reserve Act* Vol. I, p. 510. (See also Vol. I of these studies.)

trated in emergencies, for outside banks would then lend direct in the New York Stock Exchange, as many of them do now.

It was generally agreed that the Federal Reserve system would provide the necessary means to reduce the concentration of funds in the New York money market. Jeremiah W. Jenks said:[19]

I think this bill, if put into effect, will to a very considerable extent turn investments, not only of New York banks, but other banks, away from call loans and stock-exchange loans into commercial loans up the State and elsewhere.

Professor O. M. W. Sprague, testified that the result of the Federal Reserve system would "unquestionably be that a somewhat smaller proportion of bank loans will be available to borrowers engaged in dealings in securities."[20] This would be in part due to the change in the relative liquidity of commercial paper contrasted with security loans, and in part to decentralization of reserves.[21] Mr. Samuel Untermeyer testified substantially to the same effect.[22]

On the other hand, the *Pujo Report* did not agree with this theory:[23]

The most effective way of keeping these funds at home, where they could perform their legitimate function of supplying the needs of trade and commerce in the section from which they are drawn, would be to limit the proportion of its resources that may be loaned by any bank on stock-exchange collateral.

Banks, like individuals, will use their money where it can be employed to the best advantage within legal limits. No currency system can or ever will be devised that will prevent that result.

Technological and financial forces in the concentration of funds

The apparent definitive nature of the concentration of funds indicated by the discussion above is not so clear as it might seem. This is discovered when the attempt is made to apply the test of

[19] *Ibid.*, Vol. III, p. 2624. [20] *Ibid.*, Vol. I, p. 498.
[21] *Ibid.*, Vol. I, pp. 510–11, 517–20. [22] *Ibid.*, Vol. I, p. 825.
[23] *Money Trust Investigation* (*Pujo Report*), 1913, pp. 158–59.

statistical measurement. The fact of the concentration of funds in the New York money market (the first aspect of the problem discussed above) is a broad economic problem touching upon the whole complex system of production and distribution, technological and financial. The system of technological distribution (*i.e.*, industry, trade, and commerce) in its relation to the concentration of funds is one phase of the problem and concerns itself with the rise of New York City as a great trading center and the resultant natural concentration there of trading funds. The system of financial distribution on the other hand (*i.e.*, security marketing, trading, and speculation) in its relation to the concentration of funds in the New York money market is another part of the same problem. Both should be kept in mind in any approach to the analysis of the facts, although unfortunately the statistical data are not entirely satisfactory for the proper separation of these two aspects of the problem. Before a statistical approach is attempted, some general considerations will be regarded briefly.

Reasons accounting for the concentration of funds in New York City

Trade in commodities has shown a natural tendency in the course of its development to become concentrated in places where it can be carried on most conveniently—hence the origin and evolution of towns. As further expansion took place, some towns became great trade centers, owing to advantages of location and transportation facilities, and for one to become the greatest of all was more or less a logical sequence. Trade in credit tended to develop along with trade in commodities and so the important commercial trading centers became money market centers. Consider the development of the Venetian cities, the Lombard bankers, the Hanseatic League of trading cities, and the financial centers of Antwerp, Amsterdam and London.[24] This is but a natural evolution. Early in the history of the United States, Boston, Philadelphia and Baltimore were important rivals of New York as trading and money market centers. With the completion of the Erie Canal, the trading advantage of New York City became

[24] Cf. Bagehot, Walter, *Lombard Street*, 14th ed., Chap. III.

more marked and its money market took the leadership from the others. With the growth of importance as a money market, New York developed specialized money market institutions which furnished facilities for credit transactions far surpassing similar organizations in any other part of the country.

In the course of the economic development of the United States, other commodity trading centers rose and, in the absence of established and convenient facilities, such trading centers would have developed important money markets; but because of the greater convenience and less expense involved, these new and growing commodity trading centers relied upon the developed money market institutions of New York City. It can only be surmised at what stage of development a commodity trading center such as Chicago will find it more convenient and cheaper to build up its own money market institutions than to rely upon those of New York City. Such may be said to be the evolutionary conception of the reason for the concentration of funds in New York City. This general explanation may be supplemented by citing a number of factors which have been mentioned from time to time as reasons for the concentration of funds in New York City.[25]

Demand for New York exchange

After the building of the Erie Canal, New York City developed as the leading center for the clearing of domestic trading transactions. In communication distance it was closer to the rapidly developing Ohio valley than Boston, Philadelphia or Baltimore. The state of New York had enacted comparatively sound banking and currency laws and the money and credit of New York City were therefore relatively stable. Even after the completion of the Pennsylvania system of canals, it was a practice to send certain goods from the Ohio valley to Philadelphia via the Erie Canal and New York City. Certain goods bound for Baltimore or Boston likewise passed through New York City.[26] New York became an entrepôt city and, with its relatively stable credit

[25] For a more complete historical discussion, see Vol. I of these studies.
[26] Harlow, A. F., *Old Towpaths*, pp. 128–32.

medium, became the center of domestic exchanges. Thus trading centers throughout the country tended to have balances in New York City banks in order to facilitate the clearing of transactions with one another. New York City also became the distributing center for the bulk of the foreign imports. Trading centers in the interior would remit for foreign purchases to New York City bankers and hence the financing of exports from New York logically followed. Even though a considerable portion of the exports from the interior moved physically down the Mississippi River and out through New Orleans, it was more convenient to finance these exports through New York City because of the tendency to accumulate funds there for the payment of imports. Thus New York City became the center of domestic exchange and foreign exchange. Added to the original superiority in this respect, it now possesses the additional advantage of a perfected organization and specialized institutions developed for the performance of such services. Putting it another way, these are the advantages of the momentum of an early start.

Secondary reserves in New York City

Interior banks came to look upon funds deposited in New York City banks as liquid by reason of the existence of an active money market and the consequent supposition that the funds could be withdrawn readily when required. This became even increasingly the case with the development of the call loan market.[27] In 1912 Mr. A. Piatt Andrew said of the call loan market: [28]

The lack of any provision in our system for mobilizing reserves, the lack of effective arrangements for liquefying commercial paper, and the absence of any source of flexibility in the banks' lending power unfortunately force the reserve city banks to keep large auxiliary reserves continually invested in call loans. The call-loan market, unsatisfactory as it is, furnishes to the banks of the country, under the present organization of banking, their only means of mobilizing their reserves, of liquefying their assets, and of securing

[27] Cf. Vol. I. Also *Senate Hearings on the Federal Reserve Act,* Vol. I, pp. 225, 498, 517–20.

[28] Senate Document No. 1003, Sixty-second Congress, Third Session, p. 13. Senate Documents, Vol. 24.

flexibility in their lending power—their only means of meeting strains and emergencies.

State and national laws long recognized the *status quo* and permitted country banks to keep part of their legal reserves on deposit in Reserve and Central Reserve cities.

Growth of securities market

In the third place, along with its growth as a commerical credit center, New York developed into a premier position for the marketing of securities and hence became the center for their sale and distribution. This caused the growth of the Stock Exchange organization and the development of the brokers' loan market, financed in part through the accumulated interior bankers' balances in New York City banks. The New York Stock Exchange organization maintains its leadership in security dealings for three reasons: (1) the great expense of building up such an organization, even if it were attempted in other large centers; (2) the fact that brokers' commissions are not so burdensome as to become a motive for the organization of new exchanges; (3) the fact that highly organized and expensive institutions, such as the corporate trust and agency services performed by the great New York trust companies,[29] have grown up in New York to facilitate the transfer as well as the original marketing of securities. In connection with the last reason, this leadership is guarded by the listing requirements of the New York Stock Exchange which require corporations desiring their stock listed to have a transfer agent and registrar *in New York City,* and listed bonds to have a trustee and paying agent *in New York City.* This hampers the growth of such specialized financial institutions in other centers.

Centralization of corporate control

Funds tend to be concentrated in New York City also because of the fact that the head offices of many of the largest and most important business corporations are located in or near New York

[29] Smith, James G., *The Development of Trust Companies in the United States,* Chaps. V and VII.

City, using New York City and its trust companies and banks as distributing centers for dividend payments on stocks and interest payments on bonds, for the accumulation of reserve funds for the amortization of bonded indebtedness and other large financial operations.

The services of New York correspondents

Finally, there is a concentration of funds in the New York money market due to the desire on the part of interior banks of the country to maintain "connections" with the money market center; among other reasons, to obtain services from those New York City banks in connection with the putting of the interior bank's funds on the brokers' loan market, or in connection with the possible desire of the interior bank to borrow from the New York City bank. These "connections" are necessary in order to obtain services for the interior bank's customers, principally when customers desire to make foreign remittances by buying foreign exchange through New York City banks, but also when its customers or the bank itself desire to buy or sell exchange on New York City.

Unit banking versus branch banking and concentration

It is probable that the unit banking system, with its lack of organization on a national scale and the impossibility of any plan for the mobilization of reserve strength of the country on an elastic basis, led to greater dependence upon the call loan market in New York City for realizable investments by interior banks, and hence to a greater concentration of funds in New York City. If a branch banking system had developed, it might be that larger banking centers would have developed in some of the other trading centers, such as Chicago, and the concentration of funds in New York City thereby made less essential to the maintenance of liquid portfolios by interior banks. However it might be argued that the growth of a branch banking system in this country would have resulted in powerful private central organizations in New York City where funds would not only be concentrated in fact, but the use of funds over the entire country virtually dictated by New York City banks.[30]

One of the outstanding aims of the Federal Reserve system was to mobilize the reserve strength of banks of the country. In accomplishing this, not a central bank, but a regional system of banking, was established. This might be likened to a federation of twelve money markets, one of which, to be sure, is the greatest in size though not necessarily in influence. This feature of the law was for the purpose of preventing a too great concentration of money market control. As Woodrow Wilson said:[31]

> No group of bankers anywhere can get control. No one part of the country can concentrate the advantage and conveniences of the system upon itself for its own selfish advantage. . . . I think we are justified in speaking of this as a democracy of credit.

This statement is attributed to Woodrow Wilson in a letter to Representative Underwood, sent prior to the opening of the Reserve banks. Certain interests wanted a great central bank but, as Beard says, the democracy feared such a financial power, with the result that the progressive political elements forced the banking interests to accept the plan of twelve Federal Reserve districts.[32]

Continued predominance of the New York money market

That the technological and financial forces involved in the rise of New York as a banking center and in the concentration of funds in the New York money market have not abated to any material extent, is brought out in the following charts. In these, comparison is made between the total deposits of the New York City banks, including bankers' balances, and total deposit liabilities in the rest of the country; and between the loans, discounts and investments of New York City banks and similar data for banks outside New York City. Chart 9 depicts the total de-

[30] Cf. *Hearings of the Money Trust Investigation*, pp. 1808–87, and 1959–87.

[31] Quoted from an article by the Honorable Pierre Jay, former Chairman of the Federal Reserve Bank of New York, entitled "Federal Reserve Operations and the New York Money Market," *Trust Companies Magazine*, March 1926, pp. 347–50.

[32] Cf. Beard, Charles A., *The American Leviathan*, pp. 364–65.

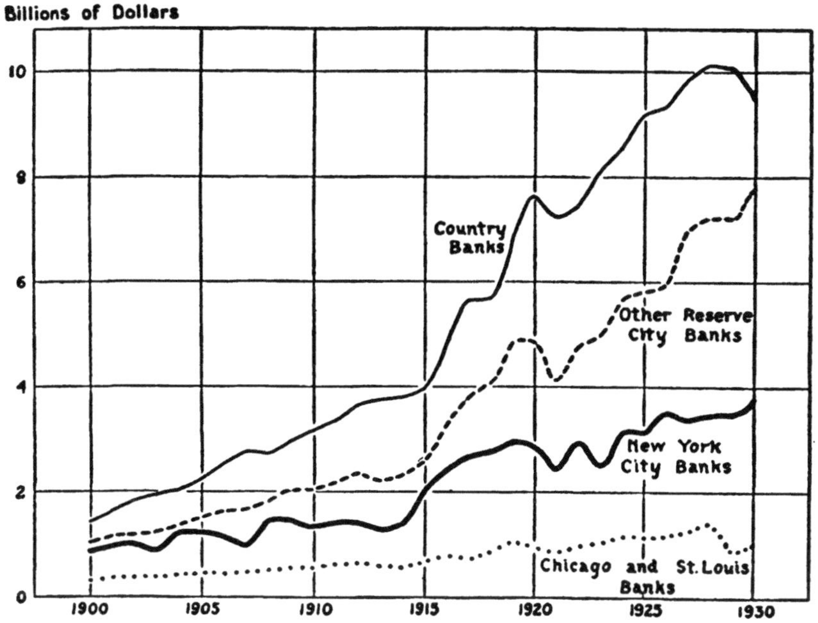

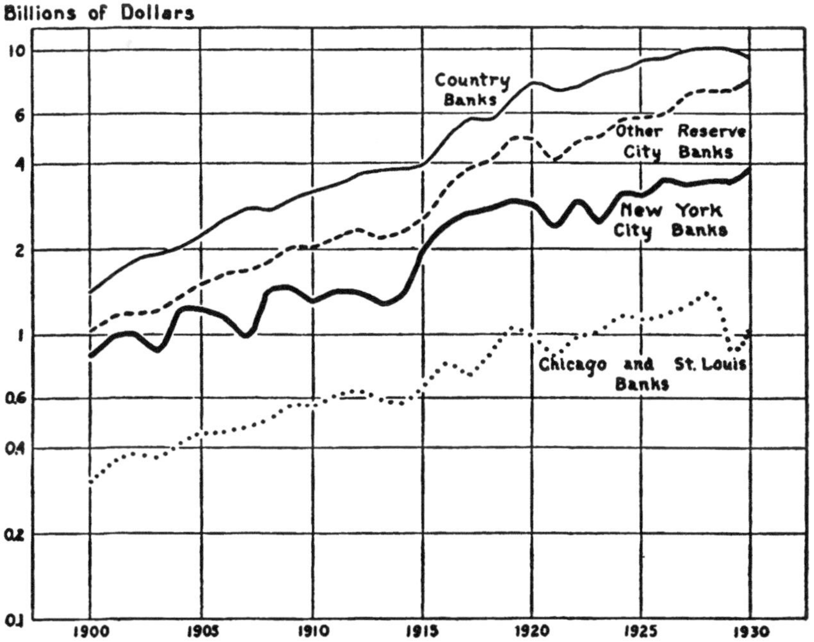

CHART 9. TOTAL DEPOSITS OF NATIONAL BANKS.

posits of national banks in New York City and outside New York City, for specified dates each year from 1900 to 1930. The data are plotted on an arithmetic scale to give a picture of the absolute amount of total deposits in each case; and on a ratio scale to indicate the rate of growth of the deposits in New York City banks, as compared with those outside.[33] Following are the equations of trend of these four series for the period 1913–1929:

Total deposits including bankers' balances but excluding government deposits:	*Equation of trend * 1913–1929*	*Annual per cent rate of growth*
New York City National banks	Log y = 0.02130x + 3.42145	5.0
Chicago and St. Louis National banks	Log y = 0.01911x + 2.96251	4.5
Other reserve city banks (national)	Log y = 0.03099x + 3.64980	7.4
Country banks (national)	Log y = 0.02862x + 3.83383	6.8

* Log of millions of dollars in each case, and origin at 1921.

It is thus seen that the rate of growth in the deposits of the New York City national banks has been somewhat less than the rate of growth in total deposits for the entire country, though in Chicago and St. Louis the rate of growth is even less than that experienced in New York City. Yet this difference in rate of growth is so small that the relative position of New York City has remained about the same during the period. Total deposits in New York City remain roughly three times as great as total deposits in St. Louis and Chicago combined.

In the interpretation of this series, the limitations of the data must be taken into consideration. It is possible for the con-

[33] Source: *Annual Reports of the Comptroller of the Currency.* The data for Chicago and St. Louis were taken together, because they were in this form until 1922. Since that time St. Louis has ceased to be a Central Reserve city. In the data here used the figures for St. Louis were deducted from "other reserve cities" and combined with the Chicago figures. Data at nearest call to Sept. 1 of each year.

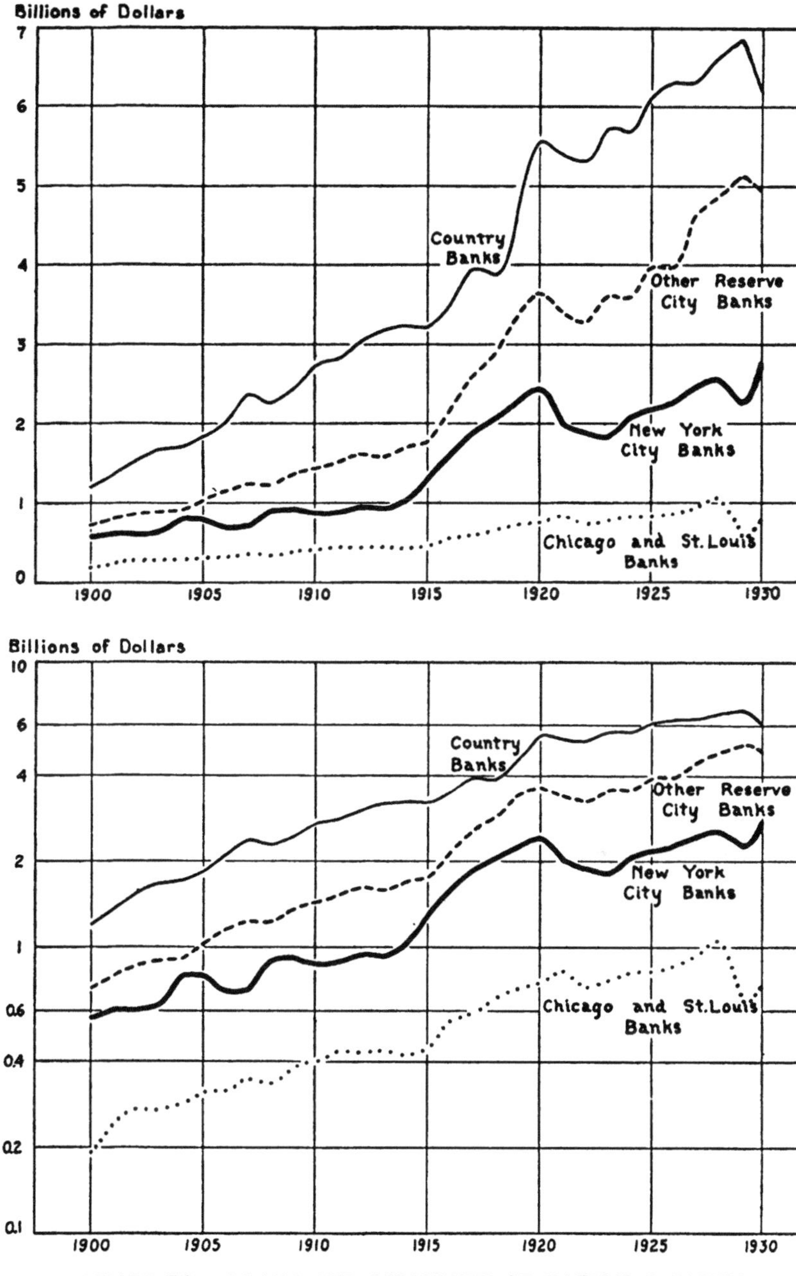

CHART 10. LOANS AND DISCOUNTS OF NATIONAL BANKS.

centration of loans in New York City to be increasing even though deposits remain the same or decline. Such divergence could be explained on the basis of an increasing volume of brokers' loans "for account of others" and for "out-of-town banks."[34] The series would be affected too by shifts from national banks to state banks and vice-versa. Many national banks in New York City, such as the National Bank of Commerce and the Chemical National Bank, have disappeared in recent years, owing to mergers or other causes. But so far as the above evidence is reliable, it may be concluded that approximately one-fifth of the total credit funds of the country (as reflected in total deposits) are on the books of the New York City banks with the exact amount fluctuating above or below this proportion according to the conditions at the moment influencing cyclical and seasonal changes. This proportion however has been gradually declining, owing to the more rapid growth of less settled parts of the country, and it will be noted that the decline was in evidence in national bank figures before the passage of the Federal Reserve Act.

Another approximation towards measuring the importance of New York as a credit center arises from a comparison of the loans and discounts of New York City national banks with the loans and discounts of national banks in other parts of the country. The accompanying Chart 10 is presented for this purpose. Again the data are plotted on an arithmetic, and on a ratio scale. It is seen that the New York City national banks occupy relatively about the same position with respect to total loans and discounts as they do with respect to total deposits; and the relative position of New York City national banks has been maintained throughout the period. There is no striking indication from the examination of either of these two series that the relative position of New York City has changed to a marked extent, barring important cyclical changes.

Chart 11 gives further substantiation, in comparing the investments of New York City national banks with those of banks outside.

[34] Cf. Anderson, Benjamin M., "Brokers' Loans and Bank Credit," *The Chase Economic Bulletin*, Oct. 1928.

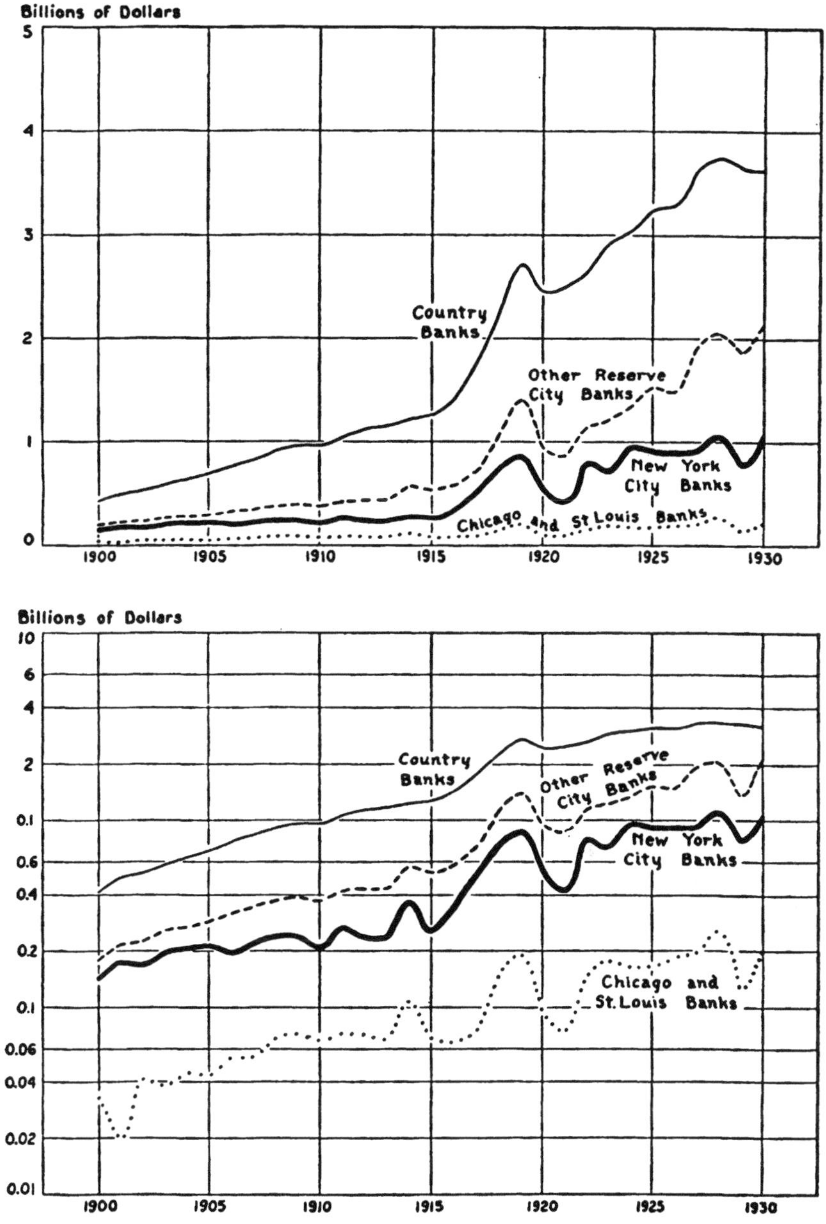

CHART II. TOTAL INVESTMENTS OF NATIONAL BANKS.

There is no clear indication of a change in general tendencies since the formation of the Federal Reserve system; but in order to check the conclusions drawn from national bank data, it is advisable to study data for a larger group of institutions. In other words, all member bank data in recent years constitute a

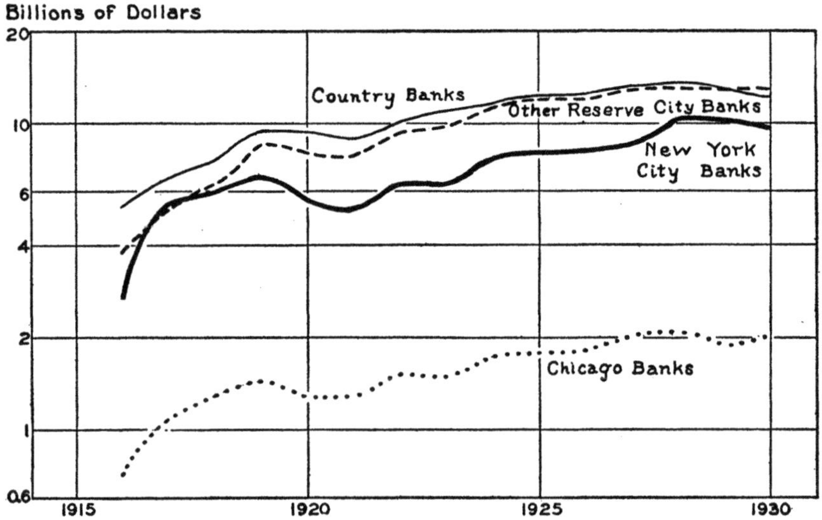

CHART 12. TOTAL DEPOSITS OF ALL MEMBER BANKS.

more complete series, and the conclusions reached may be tested by a brief survey of the available statistical material.

Total deposits of all member banks is presented in Chart 12 for the period 1916–1930; while Chart 13 depicts loans and discounts for the same period. The underlying data are presented also in tabular form. It will be noted that these data bear out the conclusions drawn from the study of national bank data. New York City deposits, loans and discounts approximate one-fifth of the total of the country, and the predominance of New York City is not only maintained throughout the period, but has increased as compared to Chicago and country member banks. This is further illustrated by the equations of trend of these four series for the period 1916–1930:

Total deposits in:	*Equations of trend* * *(1916–1930)*	*Annual per cent rate of growth*
New York City member banks .	Log y = 0.029050x + 0.832129	6.9
Chicago member banks	Log y = 0.025281x + 1.178081	6.0
Reserve city member banks . .	Log y = 0.033657x + 0.962614	8.1
Country member banks	Log y = 0.024784x + 1.005766	5.9

* Log of billions of dollars in each case, and origin at 1923 except for Chicago member banks, where the unit is log of hundreds of millions of dollars, and origin at 1923.

TOTAL DEPOSITS OF ALL MEMBER BANKS OF THE FEDERAL RESERVE SYSTEM *

(Central Reserve Cities, Reserve Cities and Country Banks)

DECEMBER 31, OF EACH YEAR

(In millions of dollars)

Year	*All member banks*	*Central Reserve city banks* †	*Other Reserve city banks*	*Country banks*
1916	12,661	3,598	3,756	5,307
1917	18,628	6,841	5,203	6,584
1918	21,457	7,542	6,331	7,584
1919	26,139	8,162	8,546	9,431
1920	24,220	6,886	7,980	9,353
1921	23,247	6,525	7,784	8,938
1922	27,288	7,886	9,348	10,053
1923	28,507	7,796	9,740	10,970
1924	32,384	9,484	11,281	11,619
1925	34,250	9,854	11,958	12,438
1926	34,528	9,952	12,029	12,548
1927	36,669	10,494	12,925	13,249
1928	39,075	12,465	13,044	13,566
1929	38,014	12,085	12,889	13,040
1930	37,117	11,736	13,029	12,351
1931	30,746	9,441	10,889	10,417

* Source: *Annual Reports of the Federal Reserve Board*, 1922–1929. Member Bank Call Reports.

† Beginning with 1919, St. Louis is included with other Reserve city banks.

From this study, the importance of New York City as the banking center of the United States is evident; also the continuation of such predominance since the establishment of the System seems to be clear.

The greater rate of growth, however, in deposits of other Reserve city banks (8.1 per cent as compared with 6.9 per cent per annum rate of growth of deposits in New York City member banks) has reduced by a small amount each year the large relative proportion of total deposits concentrated in New York City.

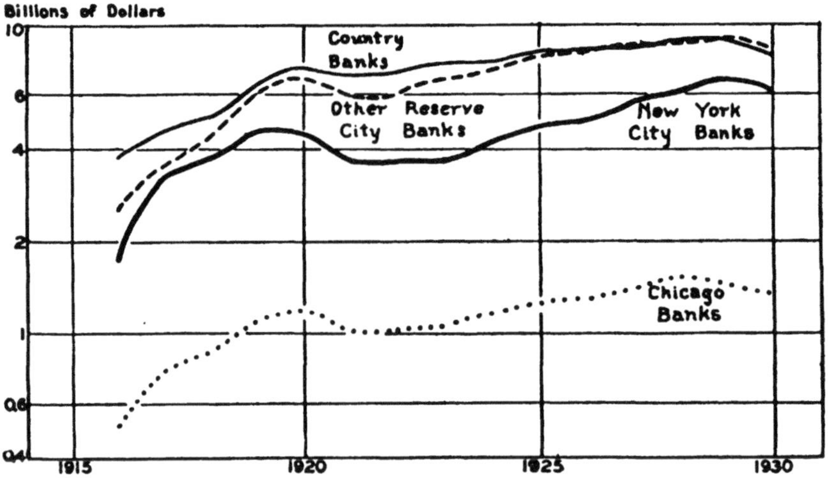

CHART 13. LOANS AND DISCOUNTS OF ALL MEMBER BANKS.

TOTAL DEPOSITS OF ALL MEMBER BANKS IN NEW YORK CITY AND CHICAGO

DECEMBER 31, OF EACH YEAR

(*In millions of dollars*)

Year	*New York City*	*Chicago*
1916	2,659	716
1917	5,434	1,068
1918	5,950	1,288
1919	6,723	1,439
1920	5,607	1,279
1921	5,248	1,277
1922	6,374	1,512
1923	6,305	1,491
1924	7,745	1,739
1925	8,068	1,786
1926	8,141	1,811
1927	8,485	2,009
1928	10,397	2,068
1929	10,206	1,879
1930	9,690	2,047
1931	7,817	1,624

LOANS AND DISCOUNTS OF ALL MEMBER BANKS OF THE FEDERAL RESERVE SYSTEM *

(Central Reserve Cities, Reserve Cities and Country Banks)

DECEMBER 31, OF EACH YEAR

(In millions of dollars)

Year	*All member banks*	*Central Reserve city banks*	*Other Reserve city banks*	*Country banks*
1916	8,714	2,411	2,571	3,731
1917 †	12,316	4,227	3,512	4,577
1918	14,224	4,800	4,350	5,075
1919	18,149	5,594 ‡	6,122	6,432
1920	19,555	5,631	6,653	7,271
1921	17,394	4,633	5,906	6,855
1922	17,930	4,691	6,224	7,015
1923	18,842	4,688	6,634	7,519
1924	19,933	5,359	7,106	7,467
1925	21,996	5,984	7,842	8,171
1926	22,652	6,181	8,165	8,305
1927	23,886	7,014	8,462	8,410
1928	25,155	7,537	8,702	8,915
1929	26,150	8,130	9,084	8,936
1930	23,870	7,491	8,379	8,001
1931	19,261	5,801	6,852	6,608

* Source: *Annual Reports of the Federal Reserve Board,* 1922–1929. Member Bank Call Reports.

† Beginning with 1917, excludes acceptances of other banks and bills of exchange or drafts sold with endorsement.

‡ Beginning with 1919, St. Louis is included with other Reserve city banks.

Summary

An analysis of the reasons for the fact of the concentration of funds in the New York money market leads clearly to the conclusion that on the whole it is one of the manifestations of economic growth and a reflection of the type of economic institutions in the United States. The question of the concentration of the *control* of credit constitutes a separate topic. In connection with this entire subject, there are really four topics to differentiate, and the relationships between them should be made clear. In the first place, there is the physical fact of the concentration of funds in the New York money market as a continuing thing, due to the position of New York City as an important entrepôt city and to other reasons above indicated. This concentration of funds will vary over a period of years in accordance with two general considerations: (1) the extent to which New York City is becoming relatively greater or relatively less important as an entrepôt city; and (2) changes in the banking and monetary system of the country.

In the second place, before the establishment of the Federal

LOANS AND DISCOUNTS OF ALL MEMBER BANKS IN NEW YORK CITY AND CHICAGO

DECEMBER 31, OF EACH YEAR

(In millions of dollars)

Year	*New York City*	*Chicago*
1916	1,735	501
1917 *	3,220	765
1918	3,701	867
1919	4,508	1,086
1920	4,454	1,177
1921	3,619	1,014
1922	3,663	1,028
1923	3,638	1,050
1924	4,202	1,157
1925	4,732	1,252
1926	4,895	1,286
1927	5,620	1,394
1928	6,018	1,519
1929	6,683	1,448
1930	6,147	1,344
1931	4,763	1,038

* Source: *Annual Reports of the Federal Reserve Board,* 1922–1929. Member Bank Call Reports.

Reserve system, there was a particularly marked seasonal concentration of funds in the New York money market—which was the cause or the effect, or merely a collateral feature in connection with, one of the outstanding defects of the National banking system which the Federal Reserve system aimed to correct.

In the third place there is a concentration of funds in the New York money market due to speculative activity in the stock market, the type of concentration which has given rise to the greatest concern.

Finally, there is the problem of the concentration of the control of bank credit. The concentration of the control of bank credit in New York City cannot be measured statistically, but it is a matter of common knowledge that the great financial interests of

New York City hold in their hands controlling lines leading to every important section of the country. Evidence to this effect was collected and analyzed by a United States congressional committee to investigate "the concentration of control of money and credit." [35] The whole subject of the concentration of the control of credit is more directly related to the long-term money market or the investment market and the monopoly problem in general, than to the short-term money market or the commercial credit market.

This chapter has served to disclose the conflicting opinions in the hearings on the Federal Reserve Act and in the *Pujo Report* as to the nature of the problem of the concentration of funds in the New York money market. The situation at the time of the formation of the Federal Reserve system has been briefly described, together with the expert interpretation of these conditions offered at that time and the predictions of these experts as to the effects of the proposed reforms.

It was found that many experts predicted that the Federal Reserve system would bring an end to the domination of the interior by Wall Street and it was freely claimed that there would be created a "democracy of banking" in the United States.

The dominant position of the New York money market was then studied statistically so far as it may be revealed by a comparison of the total deposits, loans, discounts, and investments in New York City banks, with the same items for banks in other parts of the United States. According to these data, there can be discerned no striking change in the relative position of New York City as a dominant financial center. However, the data used so far have obviously not exhausted the possibilities of inquiry, particularly in relation to such items as bankers' balances as distinct from total deposits. What has been given is in the nature of a summary; what is needed is a more detailed analysis of the facts. The task of the following chapters is to analyze what has happened under the Federal Reserve system, so far as the problem of concentration of funds in the New York money market is concerned.

[35] *Pujo Report*, 1913, pp. 131–33. Cf. *Hearings of the Money Trust In-*

Chapter IX

DIFFICULTIES OF STATISTICAL MEASUREMENT

By virtue of the reasons outlined in the preceding chapter, vast amounts of funds pass through the New York money market. From this it would normally follow that there must be a more or less continuous concentration of funds there, *i. e.*, a part of the flow being continuously *in* the New York money market. The whole of the flow may not be taken as a measure of the concentration of funds, although it might appear so, simply because the transactions are recorded on the books of New York City institutions.

Viewed in this manner, the concentration of funds in the New York money market may be defined as that portion available for money market use, whether at the expense of the rest of the country, or simply relative to the availability of funds in the rest of the country. Credit so utilized may originate from the Federal Reserve Bank of New York, from other parts of the country, or from foreign countries. It becomes for the moment a part of the funds of the money market in the form of loans or deposits. Not that the whole part remains, since as soon as some of the funds enter the New York money market, by the same contract they leave. It is this superficial view of concentration which is statistically measurable by such series as are available on brokers' loans, bankers' balances, acceptances, commercial paper, and various records of transactions of the New York money market. Concentration, viewed in this way, is really a continuous flow, of which at any moment a balance might theoretically be taken which would register a greater or less amount in the New York money market at that instant—greater if the flow towards the money market is greater, and less if the flow is less. This theoretical "real" concentration of funds in the New York money market might occur under the following conditions:

(1) Funds become more plentiful throughout the entire country, but still more plentiful in New York City than elsewhere;

(2) Funds remain just as plentiful throughout the entire country as before, but become more plentiful in New York City;

(3) Funds become less plentiful in some parts of the country and therefore relatively more plentiful in New York City;

(4) Funds become less plentiful in the entire country, including New York City, but still remain more plentiful in New York City in comparison with the rest of the country.

None of these aspects of "real" concentration are susceptible of exact statistical measurement, though often the statistics of superficial concentration are used as if they measured a real concentration of funds in the New York money market. When such statistics are used to measure the concentration of funds in the New York money market, there is further confusion which results from failure properly to analyze the nature of the data. For this reason, it may be well to consider the different forms of concentration.

Forms of concentration

Broadly speaking, there are three different forms of concentration in the New York money market:

(1) *Concentration of loans.* Concentration resulting from loans made in New York City by interior and foreign banks and corporations.

(2) *Concentration of transactions.* Concentration resulting from the use of the New York money market as a center of transactions in: (a) securities, (b) commercial paper, (c) acceptances.

(3) *Concentration of deposits.* Concentration resulting from the use of the New York banks as depositaries by out-of-town banks and corporations.[1]

In appropriate sections, statistical measures will be attempted of each of these forms of concentration so far as the data will permit. Since later chapters will discuss more fully the subject

[1] Reserves of nonmember banks are still deposited as under the old system.

of brokers' loans, commercial paper and acceptances, the primary purpose of the present part of the volume will be to deal in considerable detail with the subject of bankers' balances.

Concentration and the concept of "surplus bank credit"

Funds drawn for employment in the money market of New York City are frequently said to constitute the "surplus bank credit" of the country. By "surplus bank credit" the protagonists of this point of view have in mind that amount of available credit which is not absorbed by the customer-bank market.

Why the customer-bank market has not absorbed these funds is often a moot point of controversy and hence the term "surplus bank credit" will not be used in the present discussion as meaning funds "not *needed* by business," nor as meaning funds *"taken away* from legitimate business"; but merely in the technical sense of the definition above given.

The statistical measurement of the amount of "surplus bank credit" in the New York money market is complicated by the fact that it may be owned by (1) New York City banks, (2) interior banks, (3) individuals or large corporations, or (4) foreigners or foreign banks. The way in which "surplus bank credit" appears in statistical series depends upon these conditions of original ownership. Where it is owned originally by New York City banks it is likely to be sold first as Federal funds, and later put into the brokers' loan market, into commercial paper, acceptances, or bonds. Where it is originally owned by interior banks it is likely to take the form of increased bankers' balances in New York City banks and come into statistical being in the form of "due to banks and bankers" on the books of the New York City banks, which in turn might place the funds in one or another of the money market uses, but particularly in brokers' loans for own account. Thus brokers' loans for own account are in part a measure of the concentration in the New York money market of funds from the interior. However, the interior bank may request the New York City bank to put its funds directly into the brokers' loan market, into commercial paper, acceptances or bonds, the New York City bank acting as its agent. In this case the concentration of funds in the New York money market fails to be statistically expressed in bankers' balances, but appears in the series "loans to brokers for account of out-of-town banks," and also, of course, in the interior bank's security loans, or in holdings of commercial paper and securities if the funds are used for those purposes.

The "surplus bank credit" originally owned by corporations, individuals, investment trusts, foreign banks, etc.,[2] might take the form of an increase in the general deposits of New York City banks. In this case the statistical measure of concentration would be hopelessly intermixed with the general statistical series representing deposits in New York City banks—demand and time. The inference might be made that relatively larger deposits in New York City reflect a concentration of funds in the New York money market. Yet it is a paradox that a reduction in deposits in New York City banks may be the effect of an increased participation by corporations, individuals, investment trusts, etc., in the money market. New York City banks in the past fell into the practice of acting as agent in permitting large corporate or individual depositors to lend their surplus funds in the brokers' loan market. Such participation in the brokers' loan market by individual or corporate depositors manifested itself on the New York City bank's books as loans for account of "others," and might have resulted in a reduction of deposits in the New York City bank,[3] provided that the New York City bank was at such time not increasing its own participation.

Difficulties of statistical measurement of concentration

From the foregoing discussion of the forms of concentration and the ways in which these various forms are reflected in statistical data, it is obvious that there is great difficulty in obtaining any series which can be assumed to measure the concentration of funds in the New York money market. An exact statistical measurement of the concentration of such funds is quite out of the question. There are included in the general deposits of the New

[2] On the uses of foreign funds in the New York money market, see *infra*, pp. 244–60.

[3] Cf. *Annual Report of the Federal Reserve Board*, 1925, p. 15. See Vol. III, Chap. VI.

York City banks concentrated funds which cannot be separated from total deposits; there are concentrated funds in all three of the forms indicated above, some of which are measureable and some of which are not. In order to obtain an ideal statistical measure of the concentration of funds in the New York money market, it would be necessary, in the first place, to separate from the total deposits of New York City banks that part representing concentration from that part representing the needs of the community itself—obviously an impossible task. In the second place it would be necessary to separate the statistics of bankers' balances in New York City into several component parts: (1) that part which represents the normal continuing concentration due to the entrepôt function of New York City; (2) that part due to the deposit of reserves with New York City banks by nonmember interior banks; (3) that part of bankers' balances due to the deposits of reserves with New York City national banks by nonmember New York City banks and trust companies; and finally (4) that part representing deposits made by interior banks of "surplus bank credit" in order to earn the small amount of interest which is usually paid by New York City banks on such deposits. But even after this separation, assuming that it were possible, the item (4) would not completely measure the concentration of "surplus bank credit" in New York City, inasmuch as interior "surplus bank credit" is frequently loaned direct to brokers or invested in commercial paper, acceptances and securities. These limitations of the statistical information at hand should be kept in mind in the following attempt to measure the concentration of funds in the New York money market.

Concentration of loans—the brokers' loan market

The concentration of brokers' loans in New York City involves necessarily a concentration of transactions also, inasmuch as loans are transactions; and concentration in the brokers' loan market is due to the concentration of security transactions in New York City. Brokers' loans are classified as a "concentration of loans" because more than a mere transaction concentration is involved.

While brokers' loans represent a loan concentration in the New

York money market, they do not necessarily measure the concentration of *funds*.[4] The amount of concentrated funds represented is an indeterminant part of the whole—that part which remains for a time in the hands of speculators or stock market manipulators or pools in New York City. In general whenever a brokers' loan is made, the loan is used by the borrower to pay the seller of the

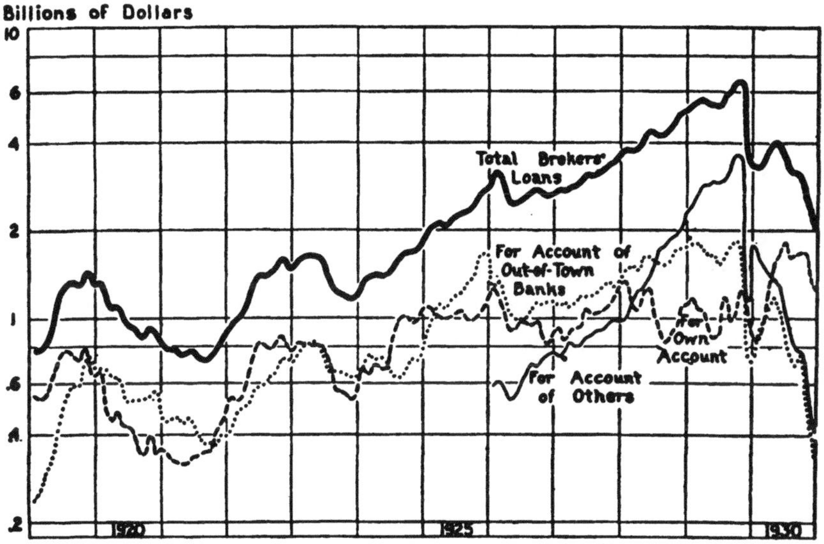

CHART 14. OPERATIONS IN THE SHORT-TERM MONEY MARKET—BROKERS' LOANS.

securities, and as soon as the seller receives payment, the funds are available for other uses, and in other parts of the country, though usually they are employed for further speculative activity. The ownership of the bank credit thus moves to the seller of the securities, and the liability for the indebtedness remains with the New York City borrower, the broker, though he shifts it by contract to the buyer of the securities. What remains in

[4] The funds of the money market are reflected in two ways on the aggregate bank statement of New York City banks, as follows: (1) on the asset side of the balance sheet, increases in the funds of the money market are reflected in increases in loans and discounts, or investments; while (2) on the liability side, such increases in the funds of the money market are reflected in increases in deposits or notes in circulation. The term *funds* of the money market refers to credit superstructure, the term *Reserve funds* to credit base.

New York City is the record of the loan, consisting of a claim by the broker against the property of his client. Such a procedure constitutes a dilution of the credit media of the country. To the extent that the dilution of credit takes place in the brokers' loan market, expansion for other types of commercial or business activity is curtailed unless there occurs an expansion in the cash basis of credit. The important aspect of brokers' loan concentration in New York is that it takes the form of mounting liabilities of security purchasers all over the country and abroad, to brokers in New York City. It is in this sense that brokers' loans constitute a concentration of loans in New York City in addition to being merely a concentration of transactions. It is this form of loan concentration which causes difficulties when liquidation is forced, as it is in every stock market panic or violent recession. Because of their obligations to "Wall Street," an enormous curtailment of purchasing power of individuals over the entire country takes place and trade is paralyzed. There is ushered in the usual period of depression, unemployment and the readjustment necessary for the next period of expansion.

As speculative activity rises, there is an increase in the flow of funds to and from the New York money market, with speculative manipulators and stock pools in New York City holding the funds longer. As the flow of funds through the New York money market increases at any time, so the balance in the market is greater. The statistical measure of this form of loan concentration in the New York money market is pictured in Chart 14, showing total brokers' loans, brokers' loans for own account, brokers' loans for account of out-of-town banks and brokers' loans for account of "others," 1919–1930.[5]

Loans for own account represent in part bank credit concentrated in the New York money market in the form of bankers' balances. That there is a close relationship between interior bankers' deposits in New York City and brokers' loans by New York City banks for their own account is indicated in Chart 15,

[5] The data used for this graph are the loans to brokers and dealers extended by reporting member banks of New York City, as published by the Federal Reserve Board.

which shows the data for bankers' balances and loans for own account as a percentage of computed trend and seasonal variation. It is seen that the major cyclical movements in bankers' balances in New York City correspond very closely to the major cyclical movements in loans to brokers by New York City banks for their

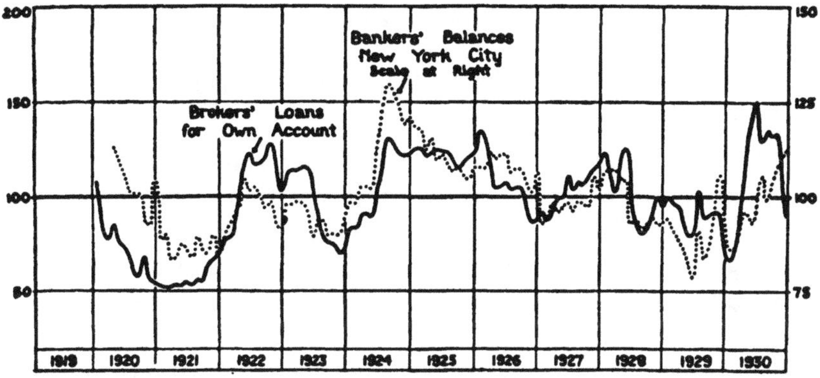

CHART 15. BANKERS' BALANCES AND BROKERS' LOANS FOR OWN ACCOUNT, NEW YORK CITY BANKS—CYCLICAL FLUCTUATIONS COMPARED

BOTH SCALES ARE IN PER CENT OF COMPUTED "NORMAL"—I.E. THE TREND AND SEASONAL VARIATIONS HAVE BEEN REMOVED.

own account. The cyclical movements in brokers' loans for own account may then be accounted for to some extent by similar cycles in bankers' balances in New York City. On the other hand, the growth in the volume of such loans cannot be so related, for the equation of trend in brokers' loans for own account is $y = 2.53x^2 + 54.2x + 734$ (origin at 1923), while the equation of trend in bankers' balances in New York City is $y = 9.36x + 983$ (origin at 1924), the latter showing a far less rapid growth than the former.[6]

The data on brokers' loans for account of "others" are not available prior to 1926. These were loans made to brokers by New York City banks (acting as agents only) for the account of individuals or corporations, investment trusts, foreign banks, etc. From the middle of 1928 to early in 1930, these were the most important of the various sources of loans to brokers.

[6] The equations of trend are in millions of dollars.

The brokers' loan statistics thus pictured in the chart show that the total volume of funds concentrated (as qualified by the above discussion of the meaning of the term) in the New York money market, for the purpose of margin trading in securities and, in smaller part to carry undigested securities, increased from about 750 millions of dollars in January 1919 to 6½ billions of dollars in October 1929, to fall sharply to 2 billions of dollars a year later.

Concentration of transactions—the commercial paper and acceptance markets

The commercial paper and the acceptance markets in New York City constitute a concentration of transactions. In New York City are located the largest commercial paper dealers in the country and the most active market in mercantile short-term credit. It is to these dealers that business men from all parts of the country resort, to sell their promissory notes in order to meet their credit needs. The dealers in turn sell these obligations to banks, wherever located, which are in possession of "surplus funds."

There has been a similar concentration of transactions in the case of the acceptance market. The bulk of the bills outstanding are those that have been accepted by New York banking houses. The important bill dealers are located in New York and the principal demand for acceptances has arisen from the Federal Reserve Bank of New York, buying for its own account, for the account of other reserve banks or for the account of foreign banks.

Series depicting the volume of commercial paper and acceptances outstanding are shown in the accompanying chart.[7] It will be noted that while acceptances outstanding have been increasing rapidly, the volume of commercial paper has declined over the entire period. There is no logical relationship between the fluctuations in these two lines. Bankers' acceptances arise mainly from foreign transactions and only a small portion of the decline in commercial paper could possibly be accounted for by the increase in acceptances.

It must not be supposed that the totals pictured on the chart represent a concentration of funds in New York. They represent

[7] Source of data: *Federal Reserve Bulletin.*

simply a concentration of transactions with the funds passing to and from New York depending on the location of the borrowing concerns and lending institutions.

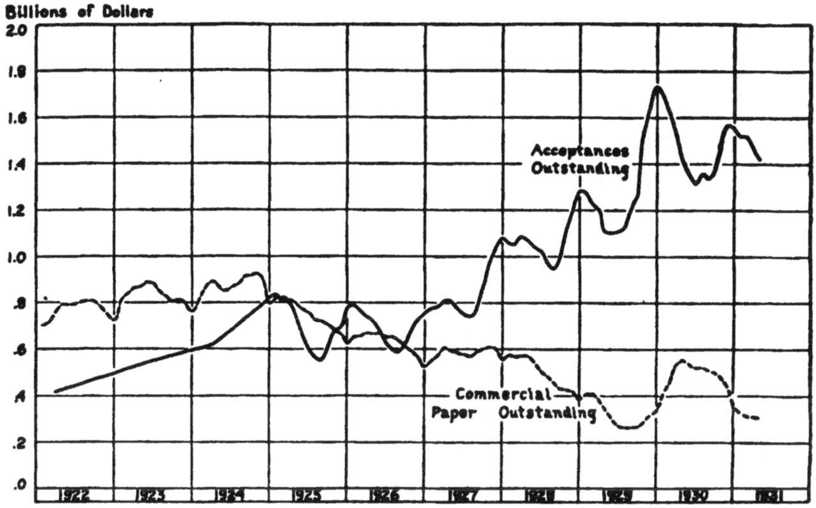

CHART 16. OPERATIONS IN THE SHORT-TERM COMMERCIAL MONEY MARKET.

Concentration of transactions—securities market

The securities markets in New York City constitute the trading centers for the exchange of ownership of enterprise and equities in debts, public and private, in this country and abroad. Vast sums of bank credit pass through the New York money market in the process of trading in the ownership of enterprise (by transfer of stock ownership), and trading in equities in debts, public and private (by transfers of bond ownership). Some conception of the volume of funds that changes ownership in this market is obtained by an analysis of the Chart 17 on page 193, showing operations in the long-term money market. The upper part presents annual data of total corporate issues, total capital issues, and the total volume of trading in securities on the New York Stock Exchange, estimated from published data. The lower portion pictures monthly data of total domestic issues and total foreign issues floated in the New York money market. The tremendous volume, measured in billions of dollars annually, of trading in the ownership of new enterprises, and in the purchase of equities in new corporate and government bond issues, is here visualized. Funds pass through the New York money market not only for the purchase and sale of ownership of new enterprises, and equities in new issues and refunding issues of securities; but also for the purpose of trading in existing securities. From the point of view of volume, the latter are far more important, as may be seen from the following table, and also in Chart 17.[8]

ESTIMATED ANNUAL TOTALS OF FUNDS PASSING THROUGH THE NEW YORK MONEY MARKET DUE TO OPERATIONS ON THE NEW YORK STOCK EXCHANGE INCLUDING BOND SALES

(In millions of dollars)

Year	*Bonds traded par*	*Shares traded*	*Total*
1911	890	9,652	10,542
1912	674	10,480	11,154
1913	501	5,893	6,394
1914	469	3,120	3,589
1915	956	12,802	13,758
1916	1,162	20,970	21,132
1917	1,052	13,690	14,742
1918	2,093	10,368	12,461
1919	3,772	26,292	30,064
1920	3,955	17,472	21,427
1921	3,505	11,115	14,620
1922	4,099	21,402	25,501
1923	2,754	19,908	22,662
1924	3,828	26,790	30,618
1925	3,398	54,240	57,638
1926	3,029	56,574	59,603
1927	3,322	92,320	95,642
1928	2,940	186,042	188,982
1929	3,020	267,919	270,939
1930	2,779	138,600	141,460
1931	3,075	72,100	75,175

[8] The volume of stock transactions is estimated by multiplying number of shares traded by the average of the yearly high and low prices of 50 stocks—*New York Times* averages. General sources of table: *New York Times,* Jan. 2, 1929, p. 35; *The Annalist,* Jan. 17, 1930, pp. 208, 218; Jan. 8, 1932, pp. 49–50; and *The Commercial and Financial Chronicle,* Jan. 11, 1930, p. 243.

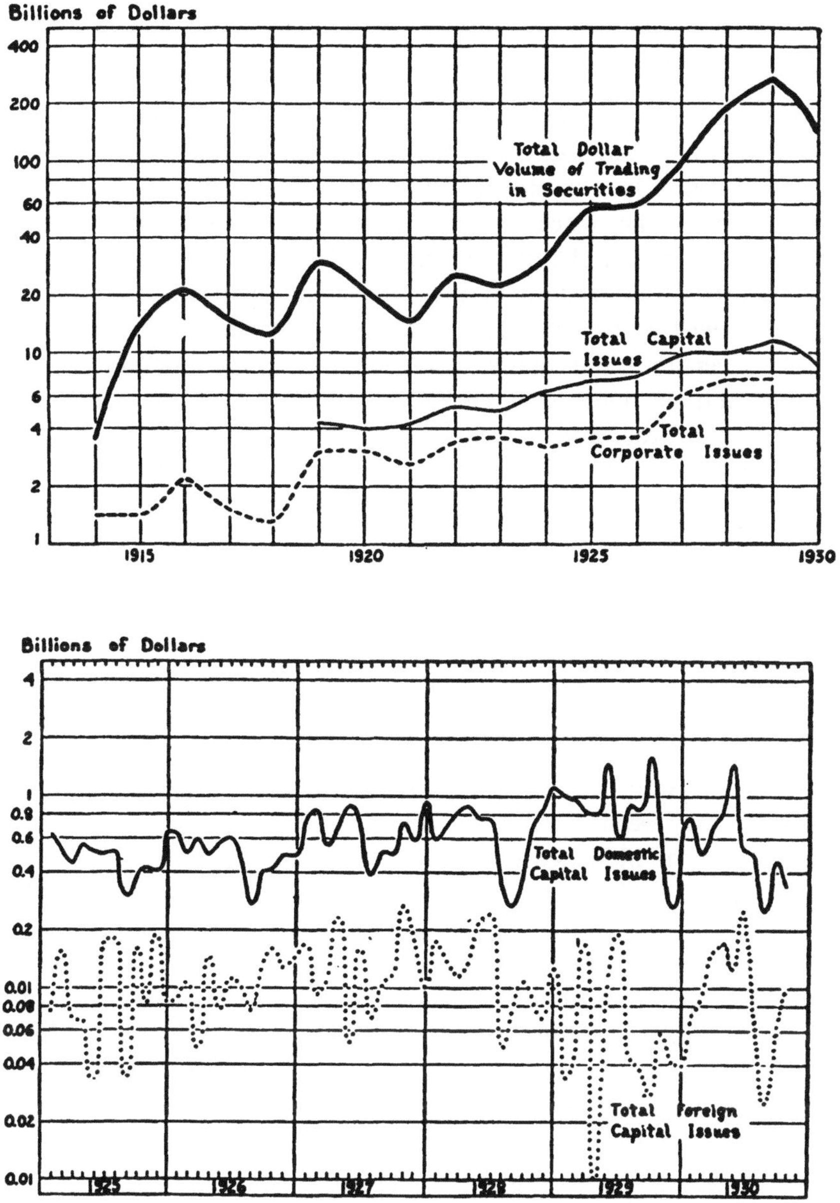

CHART 17. OPERATIONS IN THE LONG-TERM MONEY MARKET—SECURITY ISSUES AND TRADING.

Summary

The actual concentration of funds in the New York money market resulting from the concentration of loans and transactions, is almost entirely a matter of conjecture. In general, such concentration as takes place arises from the fact that it is an entrepôt city and the financial center of the United States for trading in commodities and trading in the permanent ownership of enterprise, as well as for speculation in such ownership. In the case of the acceptance, the commercial paper and capital markets, funds flow in and out, with New York City remaining the center for the recording of the transaction. There would be a more or less permanent concentration of funds in New York City to take care of the day-to-day operations of these markets, but the degree of actual concentration of funds in the New York money market from these causes is not to be measured by the volume of such transactions—it is only indicated or approximated to be some conjectured proportion of these sums. The same is true also of the brokers' loan market, except that in this case there results a concentration of non-liquid loan liabilities in the New York money market in addition to the concentration of transactions.

Concentration in the New York money market in the form of deposits may occur in the individual deposits of the New York City banks, as indicated in the discussion above; but the only directly measureable form of deposit concentration in the New York money market is the series "bankers' balances" in the New York City banks. Bankers' balances in New York City, and brokers' loans for account of out-of-town banks, and some portion of brokers' loans for account of "others," more nearly than any other statistical series supply indexes of the concentration of funds in the New York money market; yet even these are quite deficient as exact measures of concentration. They may be used merely as indicators of the degree of concentration. The degree to which bankers' balances may serve as a measure of concentration will be considered in the next chapter.

Chapter X

DEPOSIT CONCENTRATION

Interbank relationships [1]

Before the establishment of the Federal Reserve system, three significant reasons existed for the concentration of bankers' balances in New York City banks: (1) Deposit of bank reserves. The National Bank Act permitted interior national banks to deposit a portion of their legal reserves with approved national banks in reserve and central reserve cities. National banks in reserve cities could, in turn, deposit a proportion of their reserves in approved national banks in central reserve cities. Various state banking laws permitted state banks and trust companies to do likewise. At the present time, state banks and trust companies not members of the Federal Reserve system continue this practice. This is a concentration arising from the nature of the banking system. (2) The maintenance of deposits with correspondent reserve or central reserve city banks to facilitate domestic and foreign exchange operations. This represents a concentration of the normal continuing type due to requirements of trade. (3) Deposits of "surplus bank credit" on the part of interior banks with banks in reserve and central reserve cities, and particularly with those in New York City, to earn the 2 per cent or 3 per cent interest normally paid on such balances.

The amounts deposited were not earmarked for these three general purposes, but the funds which interior banks carried with reserve and central reserve city banks arose from these considerations,[2] and still do, except that member banks now keep their re-

[1] Cf. Watkins, L. L., *Bankers' Balances*. Mr. Watkins' book is a very complete statistical study of interbank relationships. The approach and conclusions vary somewhat from those of this study.

[2] As noted in the preceding chapter, bankers' balances do not reflect the total amount of "surplus bank credit" concentrated in New York City, because of the practice of making loans to brokers by interior banks through New York City banks as agents.

serves on deposit in the Federal Reserve bank of their district. Data regarding deposits maintained by banks are available in statistical form under the titles "due to banks and bankers" and "due from banks and bankers" classified by the location of the banks in central reserve cities, other reserve cities, and country banks. In this form the data will be used in the following analysis.

Meaning of Statistical Items, "Due to Banks" and "Due from Banks"

In this study primary interest lies in the significance of the "due to banks and bankers" as the item appears on the books of the New York City banks, though attention will be given to the subject in general, in order to see more clearly the relationships involved and the meaning of "due to banks" and "due from banks" as these items appear on the books of central reserve city, other reserve city, and country bank statements.

"Due to banks"

Items in bank statements, "due to banks," are essentially the same for all central reserve and reserve city banks in that they consist of the three forms of deposit concentration listed at the beginning of this chapter; but it is particularly true in the case of the New York City banks that the reported "due to banks" items include the concentrated funds from all parts of the interior. It is to be noted, however, that the "due to banks" item reported by the New York City banks also contain balances of New York City banks and trust companies, including the deposited reserves of non-member banks of the city. But in the main the funds deposited in New York City banks and appearing in the item "due to banks," consists of reserves and surplus bank credit of interior banks of the country, including other reserve city and country banks.

Quite different in fundamental character is the item "due to banks" reported by country banks, which consist in the main of interbank balances resulting from intercommunity or, to some small extent, foreign trade. On the books of a country bank this item includes due to other country banks as well as due to banks in reserve and central reserve cities.[3] It may also include borrowings by country banks from reserve or central reserve city banks, where such borrowing is from the country bank's "approved reserve agent" or its correspondent. This applies to the situation now, as well as before the Federal Reserve system.

"Due from banks"

The items in the bank statements called "due from banks" in general represent the contrabook entry to "due to banks." Reserve city banks' "due to banks" represent the obverse of the country banks' "due from banks." In the case of reserve and central reserve city banks, "due from banks" may include not only deposits in country banks and other reserve city banks, but also deposits abroad. Balances maintained with foreign institutions by the large New York City banks doing an extensive foreign banking business fluctuate widely and sometimes, in the case of individual banks, exceed the balances carried with interior domestic banks. Foreign balances maintained by New York City national banks on December 31, 1928, amounted in the aggregate to approximately $55,000,000. As of the same date national banks in other reserve cities had balances abroad of $35,000,000; and of this amount, the foreign bank balances of the Chicago banks accounted for $6,700,000. Deposits in interior domestic banks by New York City national banks at that time amounted to a little over $37,000,000; while Chicago national banks had $81,000,000 deposited with other domestic banks.[4]

The "due from banks" reported by country banks represents the "surplus bank credit" of the country banks maintained with banks in reserve and central reserve cities, as well as amounts to take care of exchange transactions. At the present time, nonmember country bank reserves, deposited in reserve or central reserve city banks, are also included in "due from banks" on the books of the country banks; but before 1917 the deposited reserves of member banks were separately reported under the title

[3] But some country banks carry deposited reserves of nonmember state banks; for example, the Newark banks in the state of New Jersey. Cf. Smith, James G., "Newark at the Crossroads," *Journal of Industry and Finance*, Nov., 1930, p. 13.
[4] *Abstract of Condition of National Banks*, No. 161.

"due from reserve agents." On December 31, 1928, the "due from banks" items reported by the country banks amounted to $816,000,000, while at the same time the deposits of country banks with foreign banks amounted to $1,863,000. New York City national banks at this time held deposits of $739,000,000 from other banks and trust companies in the United States.

"Due from banks," reported by other reserve city banks than New York City, are of a dual nature: on the one hand they represent deposits in correspondent country banks arising from exchange operations; and on the other hand they represent "surplus bank credit," or reserves (in the case of nonmember banks) on deposit in New York City banks. In the first respect they are similar to the same item on the books of New York City banks; while in the second respect they are similar to the "due from banks" items reported by country banks.

"Due to" and "due from" reserve agents

Published data on interbank deposits formerly included items entitled "due to" and "due from reserve agents." The essential nature of these items was that they represented the deposit of reserves of country banks in reserve city banks and the deposit of reserves of reserve city banks in central reserve city banks respectively. In addition, however, these items represented certain interbank relationships between depositing country banks and their reserve city reserve agents on the one hand, and between reserve city banks and their approved reserve agents in central reserve city banks on the other. For example, they represented amounts which were borrowed from national banks in New York City, Chicago or St. Louis, to replenish temporary deficiencies in reserves.[5] Before the establishment of the Federal Reserve system, it was the practice also for banks in reserve cities to send to country correspondents items for collection, remittances for which were, by agreement, not made immediately upon collection, but at a future time,

[5] This applied to the whole banking system before the Federal Reserve system. It still applies to nonmember banks and even member banks to some extent; but the items are no longer reported separately under this title "due to reserve agents," appearing merely as "due to banks." See Chap. XI, on the correspondent bank system.

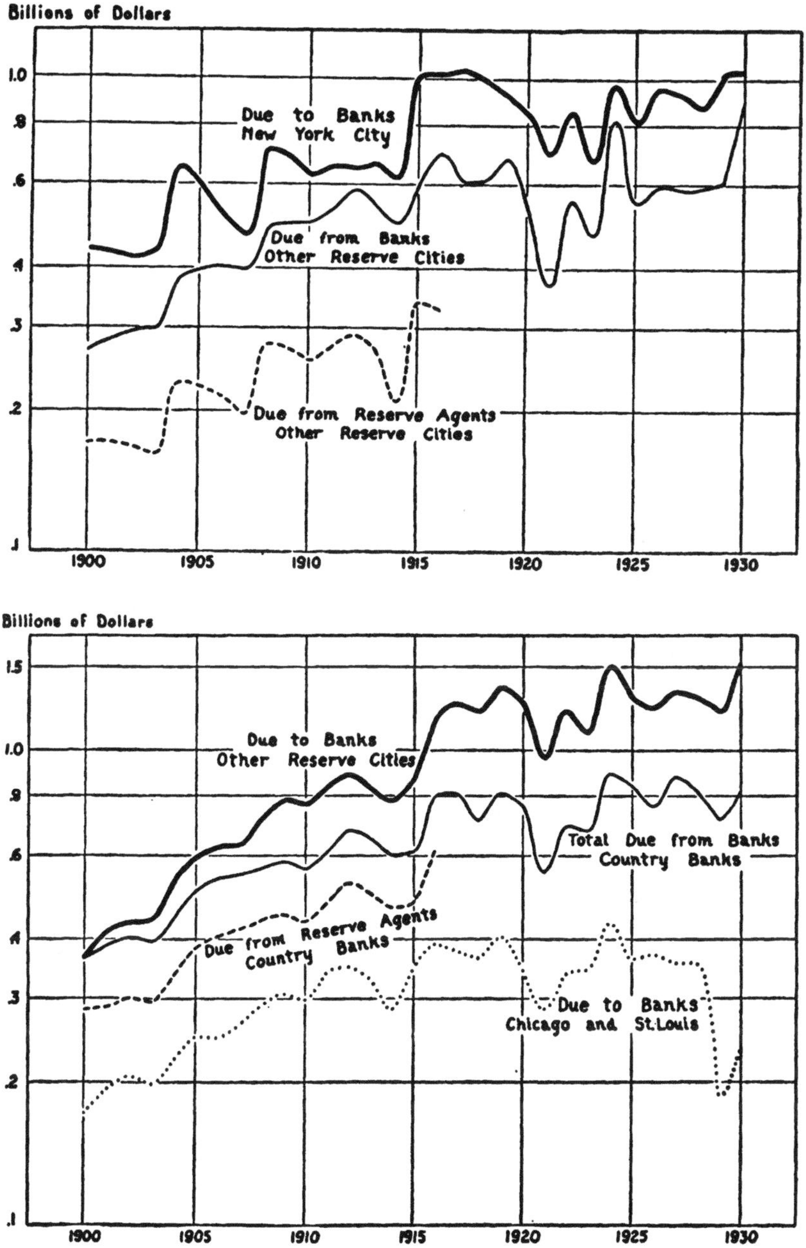

CHART 18. INTERBANK RELATIONSHIPS, NATIONAL BANKS.

perhaps at the end of the month. Reciprocal accounts were kept showing amounts "due from" and "due to" approved reserve agents, separately from the other "due from" and "due to" bank items. There were also occasions when the correspondent would overdraw its account with a reserve agent, creating a "due to" balance.[6] These practices are still followed by nonmember banks, but the items now appear under the general caption of "due to banks."

At the present time, so far as national banks are concerned, there is no such thing as an approved reserve agent, except in so far as the Federal Reserve banks may be so regarded. In many cases where nonmember banks carry deposits with member banks, those member banks may be designated "approved reserve agents" by the state bank commissioners.

Since 1917 all these various items "due to" and "due from" other banks (with the exception of "due to foreign banks"), appear under the title "due to" and "due from" banks in the statistics on the subject. The complex nature of bankers' balances in New York City should be kept in mind while they are being considered as a measure of deposit concentration in New York City.

Deposit Pyramiding in New York City

Up to this point, the discussion has been in the nature of an accounting description. Another phase of the subject is that which has come to be termed deposit pyramiding, the deposit of balances by country banks in reserve city banks, which in turn maintain balances with New York City banks. Chart 18 is presented as a study of these relationships:

(1) The item "due to banks" on the books of New York City national banks and "due from banks" on the books of other reserve city banks correlate positively;

(2) The item "due to banks" on the books of other reserve city national banks and "total due from banks" on the books of country banks correlate positively;

(3) The item "due to banks" on the books of Chicago and St. Louis national banks and "total due from banks" on the books of

[6] Letter from the comptroller of the currency, Feb. 16, 1929.

country banks correlate positively, with the exception of the extraordinary decline of the former in 1929.

This would seem to substantiate the pyramiding concept of deposits. Country banks evidently deposit funds in other reserve city banks or with banks in Chicago or St. Louis; and the other reserve city banks, in turn, deposit funds with New York City national banks. Country bankers' balances apparently have been more important in the case of national banks in Chicago and St. Louis than in the case of New York City national banks; in New York City, deposits by other reserve city banks are of greater importance, as the correlations indicated on the chart appear to demonstrate.

Deposit concentration in New York City measured by national bank data

In the study of deposit concentration use will first be made of national bank data, since they are available in a comparable form over a longer period of time. In Chart 19 (page 203), the relative importance of New York City national banks as depositaries for bankers' balances is depicted. From the chart it is apparent that the rate of growth of bankers' balances in country banks, as well as in other reserve city banks, has been more rapid over this period than the rate of growth of bankers' deposits in New York City, Chicago and St. Louis banks. This increase in bankers' balances in country and other reserve city banks probably pictures a natural development required to take care of interbank exchange relations accompanying the growth in domestic and foreign trade.

As would be expected, country banks hold the smallest amount of bankers' deposits. This continued true until 1925, when the bankers' balances of national banks in Chicago and St. Louis dropped sharply. New York City national banks usually hold about four times the amount of bankers' deposits held by all country banks, and about three times the amount held by the national banks of Chicago and St. Louis. Up to 1915 New York City alone was nearly as important a depositary for bankers' balances as all the other reserve cities combined. The equations of trend of these series, calculated for the years 1913–1929, are as follows:

Bankers' balances in national banks in:	*Equation of trend (In millions of dollars)* (Origin at 1921)	*Annual per cent rate of growth* *
New York City	$y = 5.1x + 899.8$	0.6
Chicago and St. Louis	$y = -2.9x + 341.5$	−0.8
Other reserve cities	$y = 25x + 1170$	2.1
Country banks	$y = 8.4x + 336.8$	2.5

* Annual rate of growth as a percentage of the year 1921.

The rate of growth is less in these series than that in the case of most banking series.[7] The trend is actually downward in the case of Chicago and St. Louis banks for the period 1913–1929.

The decline in bankers' balances in Chicago and St. Louis

An extraordinary decline has occurred in the volume of bankers' balances held by national banks in Chicago and St. Louis. The amount at the end of 1929 was only slightly greater than that held in 1900. Most of this decline occurred from December 31, 1928, to March 27, 1929.

TOTAL DEPOSITS AND BANKERS' BALANCES OF CHICAGO AND ST. LOUIS NATIONAL BANKS *

(In millions of dollars)

	Total deposits		*Bankers' balances*	
Date	*Chicago*	*St. Louis*	*Chicago*	*St. Louis*
Dec. 31, 1928	1,121	323	264	74
March 27, 1929	612	321	149	72
June 29, 1929	670	248	142	47
Oct. 4, 1929	686	217	145	44

* Compiled from *Abstract of Reports of Condition of National Banks.*

The decline shown in this table cannot be accounted for in Chicago by a decrease in the number of national banks, for the number actually increased in this period from 10 to 13. In St. Louis, on the contrary, the decline might be accounted for in this way, since the number of national banks decreased from 13 on December 31, 1928, to 8 on October 4, 1929.

[7] See Vol. IV, pp. 543–55.

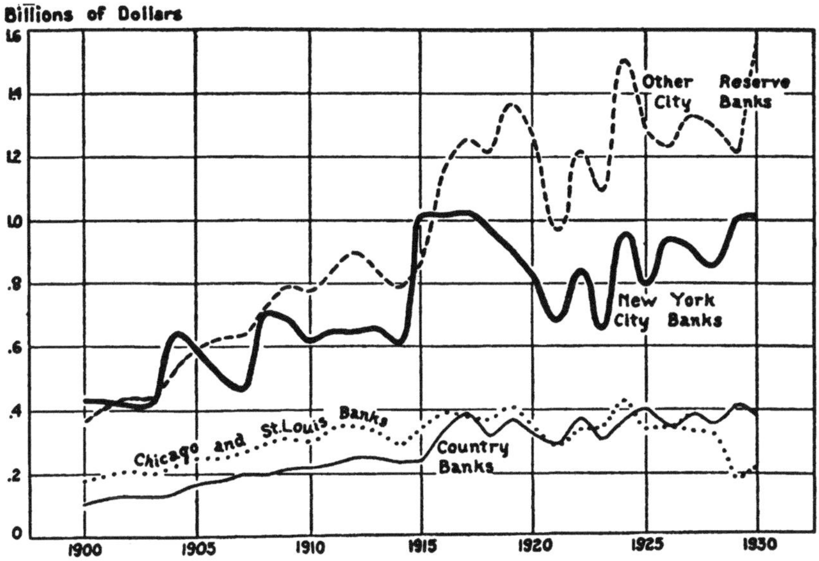

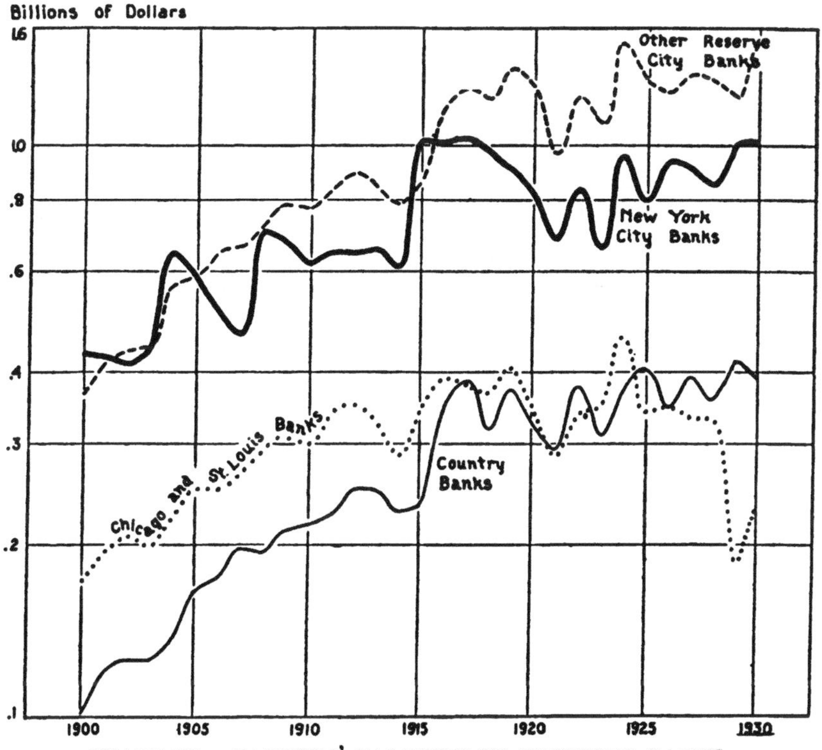

CHART 19. BANKERS' BALANCES IN NATIONAL BANKS.

The large decline in Chicago bankers' balances in 1929 might be an indication that country banks were transferring bank deposits from Chicago to New York City, either to be held as bankers' balances or to be placed on the brokers' loan market. The magnitude of the increase in bankers' balances in New York City from 1928 to 1929 (Chart 19) is about the same as the magnitude of the decrease in bankers' balances in Chicago during the same period.

Trend in bankers' balances—actual data

An analysis of national bank data on bankers' balances does not disclose any startling differences in trends before and since the organization of the Federal Reserve system, though the rate of growth in the series for the period since 1913 is somewhat less than the rate of growth in other banking statistics. If expectations had been realized, bankers' balances should have declined in absolute amount after the establishment of the Federal Reserve system. It would be expected that the decline would at least equal the amount of bank reserves deposited with reserve and central reserve city banks, and that there would be a tendency for bankers' balances to decline with the perfection of the Federal Reserve clearings and collection system. This latter fact may account for the fairly rapid decline in bankers' balances from 1917 to 1921, though this may also have reflected the depression of 1919–1921.

Bankers' balances relative to total deposits

It is the relative degree of concentration of funds in the New York money market in the form of bankers' balances which is significant, rather than the absolute amount.[8] The following Chart 20 compares the importance of bankers' balances of national banks in relation to their total deposits. The data pictured indicate that since the establishment of the Federal Reserve

[8] Bankers' balances in national banks in New York City in percentage of net demand and time deposits declined rapidly from about 55 per cent in 1913 to approximately 30 per cent in 1922–1925. See Burgess, W. R., *The Reserve Banks and the Money Market*, pp. 33, 318.

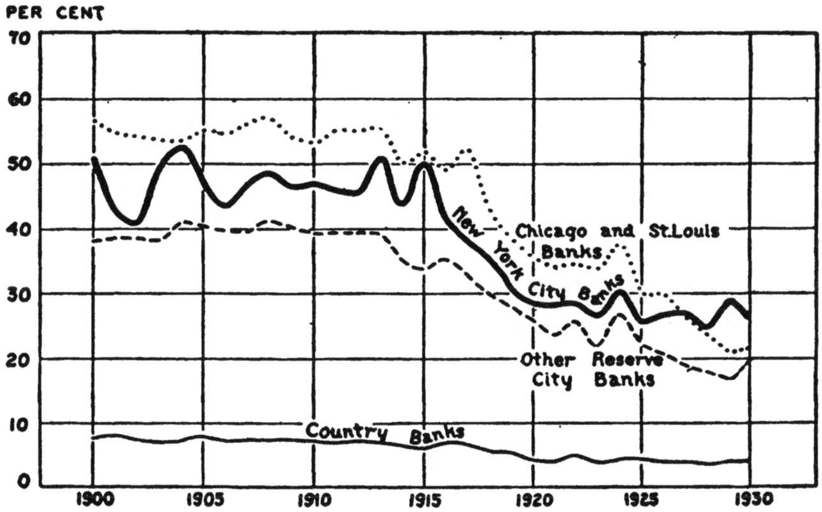

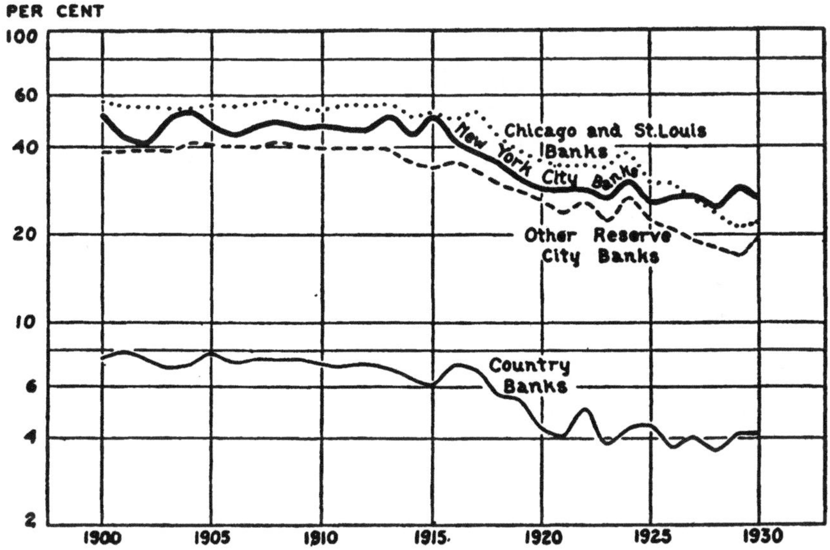

CHART 20. RATIO OF BANKERS' BALANCES TO TOTAL DEPOSITS, NATIONAL BANKS.

system there has been a steady decline in the proportion that bankers' balances bear to total deposits. This decline has taken place not only in New York City, but in other parts of the country as well. The ratio chart brings out the fact that the *relative* decline has been as great in the case of country banks as it is in the case of New York City, Chicago, St. Louis, and other reserve city banks. In New York City, however, as in other parts of the country, the decline has not been so rapid since 1925.

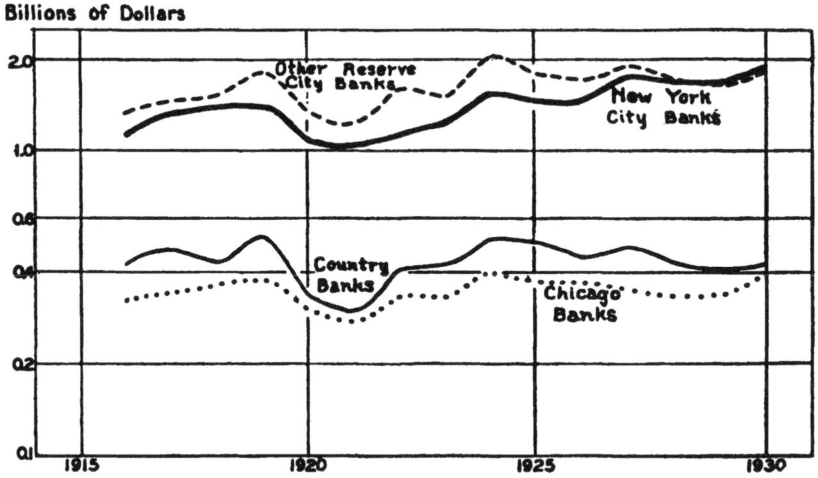

CHART 21. BANKERS' BALANCES IN ALL MEMBER BANKS.

Until recently the percentage that bankers' balances bear to total deposits has been greater in Chicago and St. Louis than in New York City, indicating that banks there, as measured by this criterion, have been fulfilling the functions of bankers' banks to a slightly greater relative extent than have New York banks.

Over the past fifteen years it is quite clear that the extent to which national banks are serving as bankers' banks has steadily declined. The most obvious reason is that national banks may no longer count inter-bank deposits as reserves. This tendency is due also in part to the increasing efficiency and utilization of the Federal Reserve clearing and collection system.

Deposit concentration in New York City measured by all member bank data

Inasmuch as the above conclusions are based upon a study of national bank data only, they need to be supplemented by similar data for state banks and trust companies and all member banks. The growth of the bankers' balances of all member banks in New

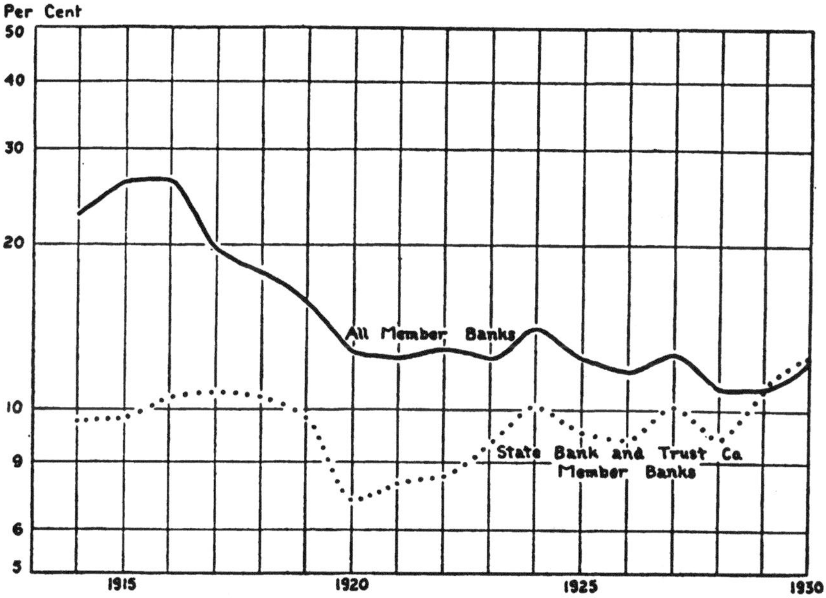

CHART 22. RATIO OF BANKERS' BALANCES TO TOTAL DEPOSITS, ALL MEMBER BANKS AND STATE BANK AND TRUST COMPANY MEMBERS.

York City, Chicago, in other reserve city banks, and in the country banks is shown in Chart 21, and the data are presented in tabular form on page 210.[9] It is apparent from the chart that the trend of growth in bankers' balances in New York City member banks is somewhat more rapid than the rate of growth in bankers' balances in other reserve city member banks. The importance of the New York money market as a point of concentration is thus certainly not decreasing in absolute amount, but even seems to be

[9] These data are not available prior to 1916.

increasing somewhat. It is to be noted that these results are somewhat in conflict with the conclusions arrived at in the study of national bank data alone; and the difference is to be accounted for by the inclusion of member state bank and trust company data.

From the table on page 210 it will be noted that state bank and trust company members of the Federal Reserve system have become relatively more important as receivers of bankers' balances than they were formerly; and that while bankers' balances of all member banks relative to total deposits have declined, this ratio in the case of state bank and trust company member banks shows no declining trend. This is shown also in Chart 22. At the end of 1914 the total of bankers' balances on deposit in member state banks and trust companies amounted to barely seven millions of dollars; while by the end of 1929 this amount had increased to over a billion and a half of dollars, and by the end of 1930 to over a billion and three-quarters. Holding less than one-tenth of the amount of total bankers' balances held with member banks in 1914, state bank and trust company members have increased their proportion of holdings of bankers' balances to more than one-third by the end of 1930. Until 1918 such increasing importance may have been due largely to the increase in numbers of state bank and trust company members of the Federal Reserve system. However, since 1920, as the table reveals, bankers' balances have grown relatively faster in the case of state bank and trust company members than have total deposits. While this may be due in part to mergers of national banks with state institutions, it is due in the main to the very rapid development of the trust companies as commercial banking institutions.[10]

At the end of 1929 bankers' balances with state bank and trust company members constituted approximately the same proportion (10.9 per cent) of total deposits, as did the bankers' balances of national banks. Since that time, the state bank and trust company member banks have more than held their own in the relative proportion of bankers' balances, as may be seen from the table.

[10] This is also clearly shown in the figures below on New York State banks. Cf. also Smith, J. G., *The Development of Trust Companies in the United States*, pp. 329–33 and 345–52.

Bankers' balances relative to total deposits—all member banks

In Chart 23, the change taking place in the bankers' balances of all member banks relative to total deposits during the period 1916–1930 is given.[11] It is to be noted that the rate of declining importance of bankers' balances is approximately the same for all classes of banks, except that in the case of all member banks in New York City the trend is somewhat less rapid. While in New York City bankers' balances are declining in importance relative

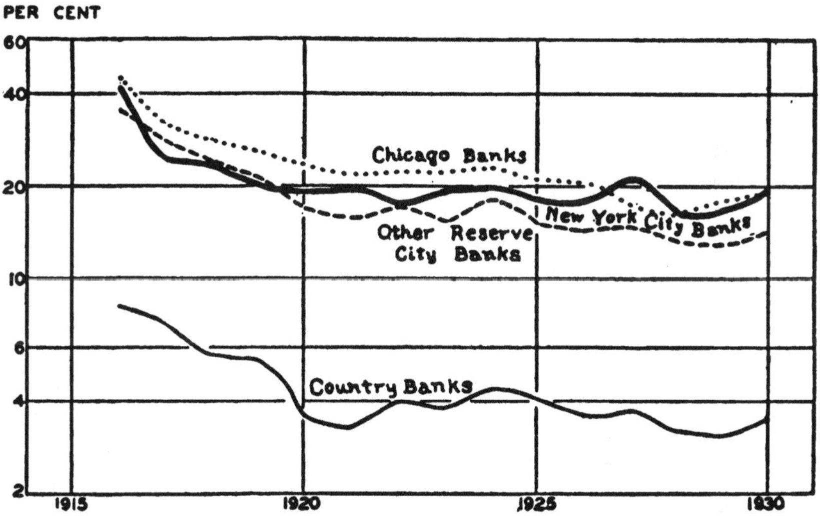

CHART 23. RATIO OF BANKERS' BALANCES TO TOTAL DEPOSITS, ALL MEMBER BANKS.

to total deposits, they are not declining according to these data, as rapidly, as is true in the rest of the country, though the difference in the rate of decline is not great.

Bankers' balances in New York City state banks and trust companies

The statement has been made, upon the basis of data examined,

[11] Source of data: *Annual Reports of the Federal Reserve Board,* and *Member Bank Call Reports.* Data given as of December 31 of each year. These data are not available in this classified form prior to 1916. Beginning in 1919, St. Louis is included with other reserve city banks.

that member state bank and trust companies throughout the country in recent years have become more important as depositaries of bankers' balances than have national banks. In New York City the same is true, for while national banks have shown a declining

TOTAL DEPOSITS RELATIVE TO BANKERS' BALANCES OF ALL MEMBER BANKS AND OF STATE BANK AND TRUST COMPANY MEMBER BANKS *

(In millions of dollars)

Year (December 31 of each year)	All member banks			State banks and trust companies		
	Total deposits	Bankers' balances	Percentage †	Total deposits	Bankers' balances	Percentage †
1914	8,305	1,876	22.6	73	7	9.5
1915	10,636	2,761	26.0	238	23	9.6
1916	12,661	3,303	26.1	400	41	10.4
1917	18,628	3,640	19.6	4,189	449	10.7
1918	21,457	3,794	17.7	6,003	629	10.5
1919	26,139	4,091	15.7	8,262	756	9.2
1920	24,220	3,062	12.6	7,932	539	6.8
1921	23,247	2,834	12.2	8,163	595	7.3
1922	27,288	3,453	12.7	9,859	726	7.5
1923	28,507	3,475	12.2	10,667	908	8.6
1924	32,384	4,504	13.9	12,372	1,236	10.1
1925	34,250	4,170	12.2	13,158	1,196	9.1
1926	34,528	4,003	11.6	13,656	1,203	8.8
1927	36,669	4,541	12.4	13,788	1,395	10.1
1928	39,075	4,192	10.7	14,734	1,300	8.8
1929	38,014	4,094	10.8	15,257	1,670	10.9
1930	37,117	4,557	12.3	14,197	1,758	12.4
1931	30,746	3,314	10.8	11,501	1,328	11.5

* Source of data: 1914–1922, *Annual Reports of the Federal Reserve Board,* 1924, p. 132 and 1926, p. 142; 1922–1927, from *Annual Reports of the Federal Reserve Board,* 1922–1927, approximately tables 79–85. *Annual Reports of the Federal Reserve Board,* 1929, pp. 103; 1930, p. 91; and *Member Bank Call Report, No. 54,* p. 6.

† Bankers' balances, divided by total deposits, times 100.

percentage of bankers' deposits to total deposits, state banks and trust companies in New York City (member and nonmember) have experienced a growth in bankers' deposits at about the same rate as the rate of growth in total deposits. This is shown in the table given on page 211, which contains data taken from the abstracts published by the New York state banking department.

TOTAL DEPOSITS AND BANKERS' DEPOSITS IN THE STATE BANKS AND TRUST COMPANIES OF NEW YORK CITY *

(In thousands of dollars)

Year (Autumn of each year)	Total deposits		Bankers' deposits	
	State banks	Trust companies	State banks	Trust companies
1917 . . .	542,132	2,150,958	45,066	316,872
1918 . . .	563,902	1,970,787	36,527	221,789
1922 . . .	891,862	2,025,825	33,281	206,360
1923 . . .	842,877	2,237,386	35,594	289,928
1924 . . .	969,724	2,882,556	39,824	435,379
1925 . . .	950,566	2,816,604	37,147	337,381
1926 . . .	1,360,521	2,993,940	77,331	382,372
1927 . . .	1,142,959	3,707,515	51,492	523,172
1928 . . .	878,950	3,845,869	31,302	463,241
1929 . . .	775,836	5,551,429	32,553	657,173

Year (Autumn of each year)	Total deposits of New York City state banks and trust companies	Bankers' deposits of New York City state banks and trust companies	Per cent of Bankers' deposits to total deposits
1917	2,693,090	361,938	13.4
1918	2,534,689	258,316	10.2
1922	2,917,687	239,641	8.2
1923	3,080,263	325,522	10.6
1924	3,852,280	475,203	12.3
1925	3,767,170	374,528	9.9
1926	4,354,461	459,703	10.6
1927	4,850,474	574,664	11.8
1928	4,724,819	494,543	10.5
1929	6,327,265	689,726	10.9

* *Abstracts of Condition,* published by the New York State Banking Department.

Concentration of bankers' balances in particular New York City banks

Not only is there a concentration of interior funds in the New York money market in a general sense, but the funds held are maintained with a few outstanding financial institutions. Chart 24 indicates how few are the really important recipients in New York City of funds from interior banks in the form of bankers' balances. At the end of 1929 of the 1,980 millions of dollars in bankers' balances in New York City, the Chase National Bank had 387 millions of dollars, or approximately 20 per cent; the National

City Bank had 329 millions of dollars; and the Guaranty Trust Company 215 millions of dollars. Six New York City banks held over 68 per cent of the interior funds in the New York money mar-

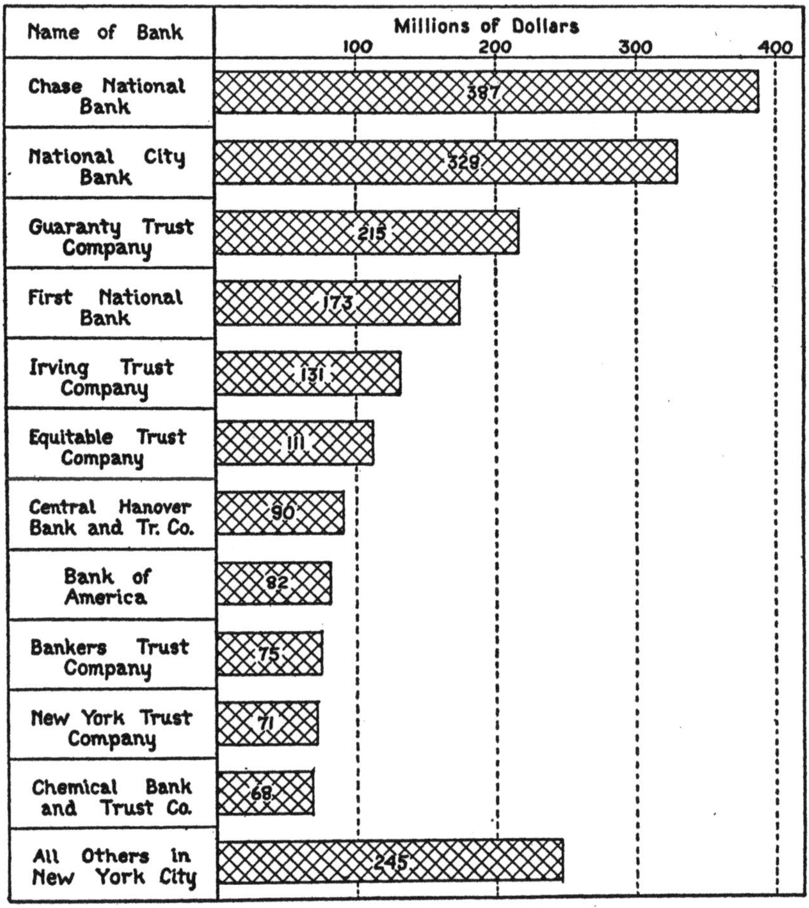

CHART 24. BANKERS' BALANCES CONCENTRATED IN SELECTED BANKS IN NEW YORK CITY.
DATA AS OF END OF 1929.

ket in the form of bankers' balances. Since that time, the Chase National Bank and the Equitable Trust Company have combined. Assuming that they hold the same proportionate amount together as they did separately, the present Chase National Bank would hold approximately one-fourth of the total of interior funds in the New York money market in the form of bankers' balances.

Geographical Distribution of Bankers' Balances in New York City

Further light is thrown upon the nature of the concentration of bankers' balances, and of the importance of New York as a banking center, through a study of the geographical location of the depositing banks. Such data are available in the reports of the comptroller of the currency for national banks for 1915, but not for any previous or subsequent date.[12] These figures are shown for selected cities in the table on page 214, and were used as a basis for Chart 25. From the chart, the predominant position of New York City in the matter of holding bankers' balances from banks in all sections of the country is apparent.

The national banks of the New England states (Maine, New Hampshire, Vermont, Massachusetts, Rhode Island and Connecticut) had on deposit in banks through the country a total of $226,000,000. Of this amount, 107 millions of dollars was on deposit with the New York City banks, 81 millions of dollars with Boston banks and 20 millions of dollars with Philadelphia banks. Approximately 47 per cent was thus deposited with New York City national banks, and 36 per cent with Boston national banks.

The national banks of the eastern states (New York, New Jersey, Pennsylvania, Delaware, Maryland and the District of Columbia) had on deposit in banks throughout the country a total of $879,000,000. Of this amount, 564 millions of dollars, or 64 per cent, was on deposit with New York City banks. Philadelphia banks held about 15 per cent, Chicago banks about 4 per cent, and Boston banks about 2 per cent.

The national banks in the southern states (Virginia, West Virginia, North Carolina, South Carolina, Georgia, Florida, Alabama, Mississippi, Louisiana, Texas, Arkansas, Kentucky and Tennessee) had on deposit in other banks throughout the country a total of $218,000,000. Of this amount, New York City national banks held 77 millions of dollars, or 35 per cent. St. Louis

[12] *Annual Report of the Comptroller of the Currency*, 1915, Vol. I, pp. 12–13.

DEPOSITS FOR CREDIT OF OTHER BANKS

HELD BY NATIONAL BANKS IN CENTRAL RESERVE AND RESERVE CITIES, AS OF NOVEMBER 10, 1915 *

(In thousands of dollars)

Deposits held by national banks in:	*Depositing national banks located in:*							
	New England states	*Eastern states*	*Southern states*	*Middle-western states*	*Western states*	*Pacific states*	*Total—All parts of the United States*	*Alaska ‡ and foreign countries*
New York City	106,942	563,768	76,585	219,321	28,640	72,322	1,067,579	105,548
Chicago	6,666	34,317	9,989	178,140	23,085	25,405	277,601	4,456
St. Louis	1,097	7,628	17,805	44,549	7,755	3,284	82,117	77
Boston	80,728	20,212	1,441	19,966	1,165	3,958	127,470	1,321
Philadelphia	19,932	132,485	9,688	26,525	960	3,670	193,259	1,856
Richmond	58	1,380	12,007	538			13,983	
Atlanta	324	395	3,281	109			4,109	15
Dallas		1	6,753 †	16	437	12	7,219	
Cleveland	200	4,005	748	39,924	166	527	45,570	1,090
Minneapolis		22	13	23,212	20,472	1,628	45,346	1,505
Kansas City		119	5,361	17,519	34,417	2,077	59,492	9
San Francisco	42	328	124	1,084	1,336	62,845	65,759	3,877
Other Reserve cities . .	10,437	114,053	74,095	144,200	74,980	59,515	477,285	4,018
TOTAL	226,426	878,713	217,890	715,103	193,413	235,243	2,466,789	123,772
Total held by national banks in Reserve cities, outside New York City	119,484	314,945	141,305	495,782	164,773	162,921	1,399,210	18,224

* Source: *Annual Report of the Comptroller of the Currency,* 1915, Vol. I, pp. 12–13.
† Houston national banks held $12,591,000 in Southern states.
‡ The amount deposited by Alaska national banks was $3;316,000.

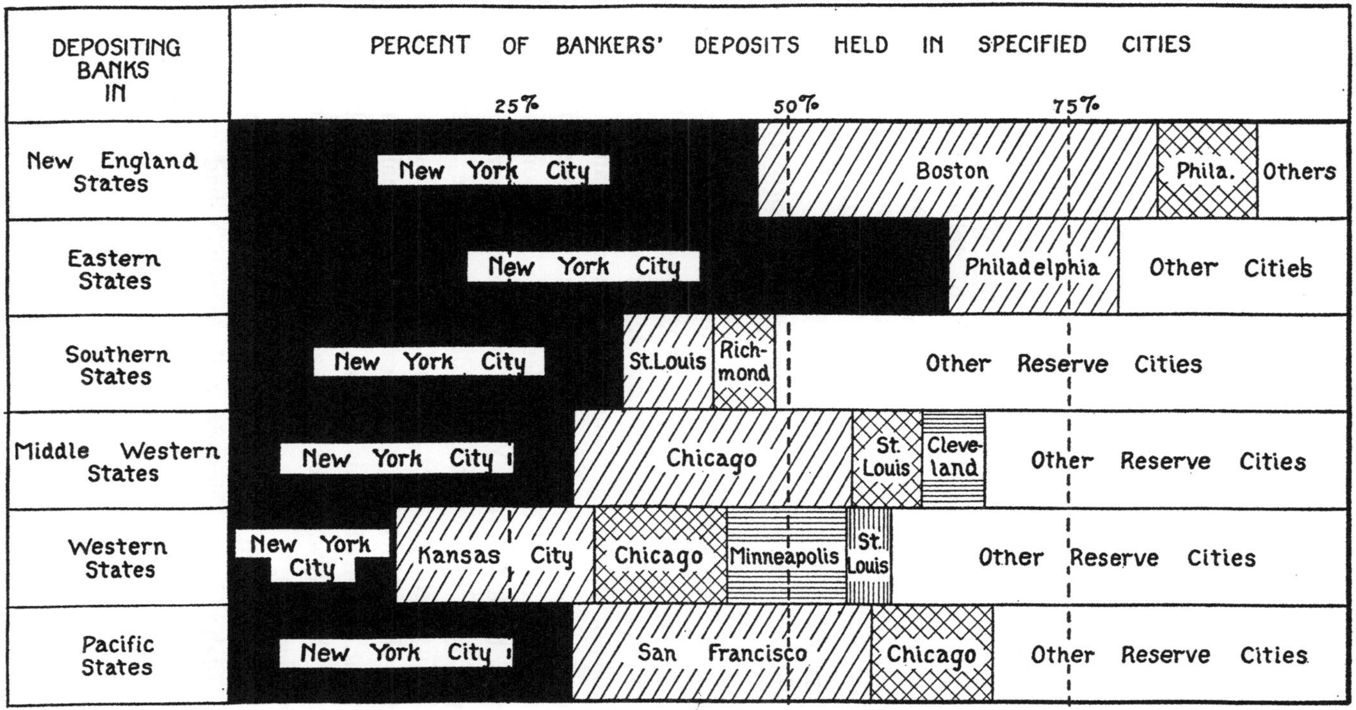

CHART 25. PROPORTION OF BANKERS' BALANCES CONCENTRATED IN NEW YORK CITY, IN COMPARISON TO OTHER RESERVE CITIES, NOVEMBER, 1915.

national banks held 18 millions of dollars, Richmond and Houston, 12 millions of dollars each, Chicago 10 millions of dollars, and Kansas City a little over 5 millions of dollars.

The national banks in the Middle West (Ohio, Indiana, Illinois, Michigan, Wisconsin, Minnesota, Iowa and Missouri) had on deposit in banks throughout the country $715,000,000. Of this amount 219 millions of dollars was held in New York City national banks, 178 millions of dollars in Chicago, 45 millions of dollars in St. Louis, 40 millions of dollars in Cleveland, 27 millions of dollars in Philadelphia, 23 millions of dollars in Minneapolis, and 17 millions of dollars in Kansas City. Thus New York City national banks held approximately 31 per cent of the bankers' deposits made by banks in the Middle West, with Chicago running a close second with 25 per cent.

The national banks in the western states (North Dakota, South Dakota, Nebraska, Kansas, Montana, Wyoming, Colorado, New Mexico and Oklahoma) had deposited in banks throughout the country on November 10, 1915, $193,000,000. Of this amount, 29 millions of dollars was held by New York City national banks, 34 millions of dollars by Kansas City national banks, 23 millions of dollars by Chicago national banks, 20 millions of dollars by Minneapolis national banks, and less than 8 millions of dollars by St. Louis banks. New York City national banks held about 14½ per cent of the bankers' deposits of the western states. Kansas City held a larger proportion of these bankers' deposits than did New York City, Kansas City national banks having 18 per cent. Thus for this section Kansas City was slightly more important than New York City as a center for the concentration of bankers' deposits.

National banks in the Pacific states (Washington, Oregon, California, Idaho, Utah, Nevada and Arizona) had on deposit in banks throughout the country a total of $235,000,000. Of this amount 72 millions of dollars was held by New York City national banks, 63 millions of dollars by San Francisco national banks, and 25 millions of dollars by Chicago banks. Thus New York City held about 31 per cent, San Francisco about 27 per cent, and Chicago about 10 per cent.

For the country as a whole, New York City held about 43 per cent, Chicago 11 per cent, Philadelphia about 8 per cent, and Boston about 5 per cent.

Banks in foreign countries had on deposit in national banks throughout the United States $124,000,000. Of this amount, $105,000,000 was held by New York City national banks, about $4,500,000 by Chicago banks and nearly $4,000,000 by San Francisco banks.

Chicago is considerably less important than New York City as a point of concentration, according to the analysis of these figures for the year 1915. Studies of the Bureau of Business Research of the College of Commerce and Business Administration of the University of Illinois [13] seem to indicate that this situation as a whole remains now about the same as it was in 1915, so far as the relative positions of New York City and Chicago are concerned.

Results of a questionnaire on bankers' balances at the end of 1928

Data giving the origin of bankers' deposits in New York City by sections of the country comparable to the 1915 figures given in the *Annual Report of the Comptroller of the Currency* for that year are not available; but by correspondence and interview similar data were obtained from six of the largest New York City banks and from six of the largest Chicago banks for the end of 1928. These figures are tabulated on page 218, with the 1915 figures of the comptroller for comparison.

So far as New York City banks are concerned, the most important single source of bankers' deposits is the eastern states. On November 10, 1915, total bankers' deposits in New York City national banks amounted to $1,068,000,000, of which $563,800,000, or over 50 per cent came from banks in the Eastern states. The second largest contributor to bankers' balances with New York City banks was the mid-western section of states whose banks had $219,300,000 on deposit in New York City national banks on that date. Banks in the New England states had $106,-

[13] Bulletin 21, *An Analysis of Bankers' Balances in Chicago, 1928*, especially pp. 11-17; and Bulletin 17, *Chicago as a Money Market*, 1928.

900,000 on deposit in New York City banks. From the table of data below, it is clear that the amount of concentration of funds in the New York money market from the New England states was less in 1928 than in 1915, both absolutely and relatively. Similarly the concentration of funds in the New York money market

BANKERS' DEPOSITS WITH NEW YORK CITY BANKS

(In thousands of dollars)

Location of depositing banks	*Deposits held in New York City banks to the credit of other banks*			
	November 10, 1915		*End of 1928**	
	Amounts	*Percentage*	*Amounts*	*Percentage*
New England states . . .	106,942	10.0	33,120	6.5
Eastern states	563,768	52.8	211,220	41.4
Southern states	76,585	7.2	82,922	16.3
Middle western states . .	219,321	20.5	124,437	24.4
Western states	28,640	2.7	22,715	4.5
Pacific states	72,322	6.8	35,787	7.0
Total, United States . .	1,067,579	100	510,202	100

* The 1928 data were secured from a representative group of banks, which held approximately 50 per cent of total bankers' balances in New York City member banks.

from the Eastern states was less absolutely and relatively. But by way of contrast, the concentration of funds in the New York money market from the southern states was more than twice as great as it was in 1915, and from the western states it was nearly twice as great. Concentration from the middle western states and the Pacific states was slightly greater than in 1915.

According to these data, in 1928 there was relatively greater concentration of funds in the New York money market in the form of bankers' deposits from the South and the West than in 1915. While it is true that the 1928 figures include only 50 per cent of the bankers' balances held with New York City banks, the data are presented in the belief that they are representative. The proof of this lies in the circumstance that the results are reasonably in accord with other known facts. Bankers' balances from rapidly developing sections of the country would be expected to increase more rapidly than bankers' balances from more slowly developing sections. The very rapid growth of manufacturing in the South and Middle West, in comparison with a relatively less rapid growth in the eastern and New England states would be a causative factor and is clearly reflected in the statistics of the manufacturing census. It may be concluded with reasonable assurance that in the aggregate there was approximately as much geographic concentration of funds in the New York money market by means of bankers' balances in 1928 as there was in 1915. The operation of the Federal Reserve system has brought very little in the way of an absolute decline of concentration in this form. But relatively the amount of concentration in the New York money market in 1928 is less than in 1915, since bankers' balances have become less important as compared to total deposits.

Results of the analysis of the bankers' balances in Chicago are similar in some respects to those of the New York City figures as may be seen from the table on page 220. As for New York City, so also for Chicago, an absolute and relative decline of deposits from banks in the New England states and the eastern states has taken place. There was a relative and absolute increase in deposits from banks in southern and middle western states, allowance being made for the fact that the 1928 figures here given represent approximately 50 per cent of total bankers' deposits held in 1928. Also there was a relative and an absolute decrease in concentration of funds in Chicago from western and Pacific states.

There are a number of points that should be noted in a comparison of New York City and Chicago. In the first place, in 1915 New York City banks held 3.8 times as large a volume of bankers' deposits as did Chicago; at the end of 1928, New York City member banks held 3.8 times as large a volume of bankers' deposits as did Chicago.[14] In the second place, New York City has become more important as a depositary of funds for the interior of the coun-

[14] "Due to banks," New York City reporting member banks, Nov. 28, 1928, came to $1,183,288,000. "Due to banks," Chicago reporting member banks, Nov. 28, 1928, came to $314,131,000. *Federal Reserve Bulletin,* Dec. 1928, p. 875.

try, the far West, and particularly the South, while it has become somewhat less important relatively as a depositary of funds for banks in New England and in the eastern states. This relative decline is due to the natural growth of the South and West. Chicago, on the other hand, has become more important as a depositary of bank funds in the contiguous territory, and relatively less important as a depositary of funds from banks in other parts of the country. During this period, therefore, New York City has become more predominantly than before, a financial center for the country as a whole, whereas Chicago has tended to become more and more a specialized financial center for the Middle West alone.

BANKERS' DEPOSITS WITH CHICAGO BANKS

(In thousands of dollars)

Location of depositing banks	Deposits held in Chicago banks to the credit of other banks			
	November 10, 1915		End of 1928 *	
	Amounts	Per cent	Amounts	Per cent
New England states . . .	6,666	2.4	1,824	1.2
Eastern states	34,317	12.4	8,391	5.4
Southern states	9,989	3.6	7,148	4.6
Middle western states . .	178,140	64.2	119,154	77.2
Western states	23,085	8.3	9,085	5.9
Pacific states	25,405	9.2	8,656	5.6
Total, United States . .	277,601	100	154,258	100

* The 1928 data are from a group of representative banks, which hold approximately 50 per cent of total bankers' balances in Chicago member banks.

Dispersion of bankers' balances since the Federal Reserve system

While it is true that New York City has become, relative to Chicago, more important as a point of concentration of bankers' balances since 1915, it is also true that the reserve cities as a whole are relatively less important. In 1915, of the total of bankers' balances in national banks in the United States, 73.4 per cent were in national banks in the twelve Federal bank cities; while in 1928 this proportion had fallen to 58.8 per cent. Though the reserve function of bankers' balances had been largely removed, the "normally continuing" part, was growing, that part due to domestic sectional trade and international trade. The following table is presented to show the changes taking place from 1915 to 1928.

PROPORTION OF BANKERS' BALANCES HELD BY BANKS IN FEDERAL RESERVE BANK CITIES *

(In millions of dollars)

Banks in:	*November 10, 1915*		*End of 1928*			
	National banks		*National banks*		*All member banks*	
	Amount	*Per cent of total*	*Amount*	*Per cent of total*	*Amount*	*Per cent of total*
Boston	127.5	6.4	90.2	5.9	112.4	4.9
New York City	1,067.6	53.6	739.0	48.3	1,213.0	52.7
Philadelphia . .	193.3	9.7	149.1	9.7	177.6	7.7
Cleveland . . .	45.6	2.3	6.1	0.4	60.7	2.6
Richmond . . .	14.0	0.7	11.0	0.7	24.9	1.1
Atlanta	4.1	0.2	18.1	1.2	18.3	0.8
Chicago	277.6	13.9	238.8	15.6	328.4	14.3
Minneapolis . .	45.3	2.3	49.6	3.2	49.6	2.2
St. Louis . . .	82.1	4.1	67.7	4.4	81.8	3.6
Kansas City . .	59.5	3.0	52.0	3.4	84.8	3.7
Dallas	7.2	0.4	36.8	2.4	36.8	1.6
San Francisco .	65.8	3.3	71.7	4.7	112.2	4.9
TOTAL	1,989.6	100.0	1,530.1	100.0	2,300.5	100.0
Total in the United States .	2,709.6		2,596.9		3,649.0	
Per cent total in Federal Reserve bank cities is to total in the United States	73.4		58.8		63.0	

* Source of data: *Annual Report of the Comptroller of the Currency*, 1915, Vol. I, pp. 12–13; *Abstract of Condition of National Banks*, No. 161, p. 7; and *Member Bank Call Report No. 42*, pp. 2 and 14.

It is evident that a dispersion of bankers' balances has occurred, not only through distributing bankers' balances in various of the Federal Reserve bank cities, but also through the fact that other reserve cities have become more important points of concentration and have increased slightly in a relative sense as money market centers. Certainly it cannot be maintained that this has been entirely due to the Federal Reserve system—it may have been due to the natural process of growth and the consequent increase in relative importance of new banking centers. Bankers' balances held in the other reserve cities may be similar to those in Chicago in that they consist of deposits from banks in adjacent sections. From this table, Chicago apparently was relatively more important as a point of concentration in 1928 than in 1915; but in the last section it was seen that this growth in Chicago bankers' balances is largely from its own territory and Chicago is less important as a point of concentration of bankers' balances from the whole of the United States.[15]

Bankers' Deposit Concentration Partially Offset by Interbank Loans

The true situation regarding the degree of concentration of bankers' balances in New York City may not be judged from a study of bankers' balances alone, by reason of the fact that this deposit concentration is partially offset by loans made by New York City banks to the interior banks as well as to individuals and to corporations in the interior of the country. In other words, the commercial banks, of New York City particularly but in other places also, perform the function of bankers' banks.

The accompanying table, showing the extent to which banks in the Federal Reserve cities make loans to banks as well as to individuals and to corporations, gives a picture of the extent to which commercial banks act as bankers' banks. These data are for national banks only and are available in such comprehensive form only for the date indicated. Loans made by national banks to other banks, as distinct from loans made to individuals and to

[15] Cf. University of Illinois Bulletin No. 33, Bureau of Business Research, *The Banking Structure of the Seventh Federal Reserve District*, 1931.

corporations, were a surprisingly insignificant item in the case of the New York City banks, amounting to $87,000,000 out of a total of $1,580,000,000. The national banks of Kansas

LOANS MADE BY NATIONAL BANKS CLASSIFIED BY TYPE OF BORROWER *

NOVEMBER 10, 1915

(In thousands of dollars)

Lending national banks in:	*Loans made to:*				
	Banks	*Individuals, corporations, etc.*	*Others, including foreign borrowers*	*Securities purchased from banks with resale agreement*	*Total*
New York City	87,104	1,384,039	108,421	703	1,580,268
Chicago	24,278	343,066	8,109	1,441	376,894
St. Louis . . .	15,123	74,452	7,160	137	96,872
Boston	7,192	234,199	1,629	206	243,226
Philadelphia . .	8,346	241,650	18,085		268,082
Richmond . . .	2,532	34,338	39		36,908
Atlanta	2,505	25,246	80	30	27,861
Dallas	1,856	22,310	224	28	24,417
Cleveland . . .	1,416	58,883	9,652	68	70,019
Minneapolis . .	5,507	58,229	7,498		71,234
Kansas City . .	25,836	44,533	5,044	27	75,440
San Francisco .	2,796	100,014	3,483		106,293
Other Reserve cities	61,604	829,900	29,878	1,596	922,978
TOTAL . .	246,095	3,450,859	199,302 †	4,236	3,900,492

* Source of data: *Annual Report of the Comptroller of the Currency*, 1915, Vol. I, pp. 15–16.

† Includes $89,000,000 loaned in foreign countries and $1,000,000 loaned in Alaska.

City and St. Louis played a far more important rôle as bankers' banks, relatively speaking, than did the national banks of New York City. Of total loans amounting to $75,000,000 by Kansas City national banks, $26,000,000, or over one-third, were loans to other banks. Of total loans of $97,000,000 by St. Louis national banks, $15,000,000, or about 14 per cent, were loans to other banks. With the rediscount privilege under the Federal Reserve system, it would be expected that these banks would occupy a less prominent position as bankers' banks. There are no published data upon which to base a general conclusion in this respect; but through inquiry data were obtained for a representative group of Kansas City banks as of December 31, 1928. These banks on that date had total loans and discounts of $65,712,000, and of that amount only $6,880,000 consisted of direct or indirect loans to banks and bankers. This is less than 10 per cent, as compared to over 33⅓ per cent in 1915.[16] At the end of 1928 a representative group of the largest New York City banks had aggregate loans of $2,246,159,000; and of these $232,994,000 were loans to other banks. In other words, 10.4 per cent of the loans of these banks represented credit extended to other banks. In November, 1915, loans to other banks by New York City national banks constituted 5.6 per cent of total loans. Thus in 1928 New York City banks were exercising the functions of bankers' banks to even a greater extent than they were in 1915, assuming the figures and general economic conditions to be comparable. At the end of 1928 a representative group of the largest Chicago banks had aggregate loans of $633,965,000, and of this amount $18,088,000 or 2.9 per cent, were loans to other banks. In November, 1915, loans to other banks by Chicago national banks constituted 6.8 per cent of total loans.[17] As further evidence to the effect that the bankers' bank function of interbank loaning is still being very largely performed by banks other than the Federal Reserve banks, total bills payable and rediscounts of national banks of the United States, as of December 31, 1928 amounted to $785,309,000. Of this amount, $81,818,000 represented borrowing from banks other than the Federal Reserve banks, total rediscounts with the Federal Reserve banks being $178,294,000

[16] Correspondence with Mr. M. L. McClure, Federal Reserve Agent, Federal Reserve Bank of Kansas City.

[17] Approximately 10 per cent of the rediscounts of New Jersey national banks and 20 per cent of the bills payable of New Jersey national banks represents borrowing from banks other than the Federal Reserve Bank. Smith, J. G., "New Jersey Banking in 1928," *Journal of Industry and Finance*, May 1929, p. 7.

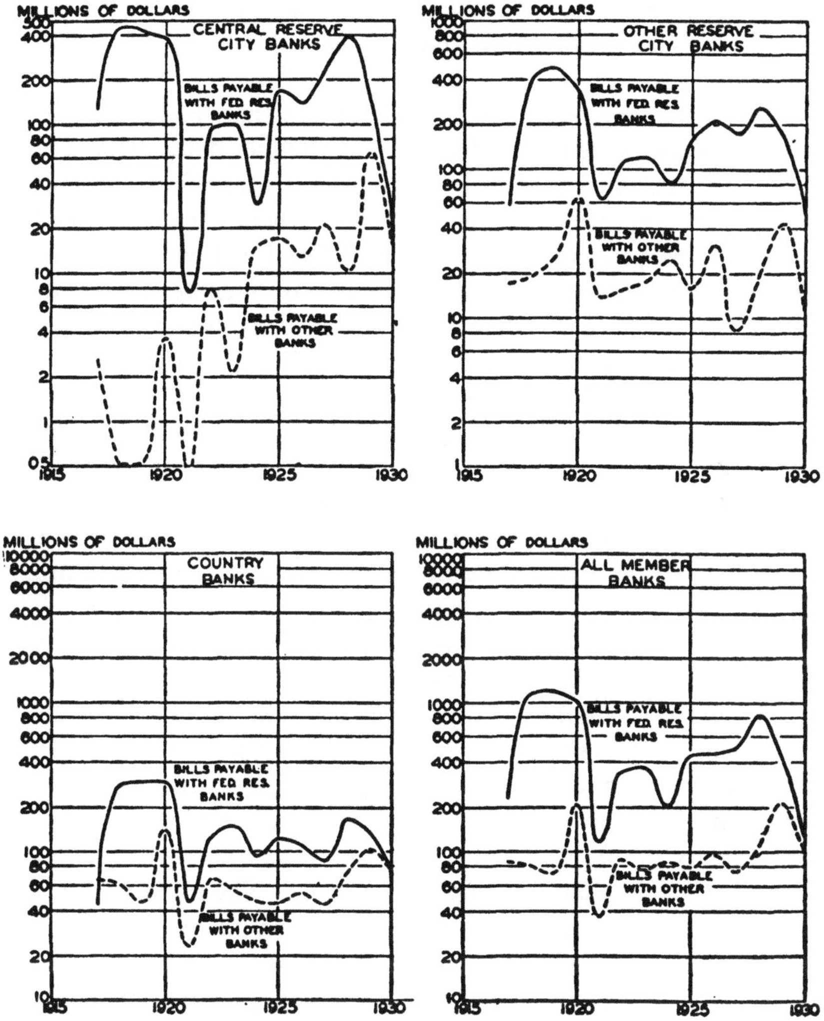

CHART 26. BORROWINGS FROM FEDERAL RESERVE BANKS COMPARED WITH BORROWINGS FROM OTHER BANKS.

and total bills payable to Federal Reserve banks being $525,197,000. Close to 25 per cent of the bills payable by *country* national banks are payable, not to Federal Reserve banks, but to other banks.[18]

[18] *Abstract of Condition of National Banks,* No. 161, p. 8.

In order further to illustrate the continued importance of interbank borrowing from others than Federal Reserve banks, data on borrowings by all member banks from Federal Reserve banks compared to their borrowings from others than Federal Reserve banks are presented in Chart 26.[19] These data demonstrate clearly the thesis of the above discussion, to the effect that banks continue to perform services for each other, even for member banks, which properly form a part of the functions of a central bank. As the chart shows, borrowings of member banks from others than the Federal Reserve banks are considerable in amount, not only by the country banks, but also by Reserve and Central Reserve city banks. In fact, the volume of borrowings by Central Reserve city member banks from others than Federal Reserve banks has increased at a more rapid rate over the period of years from 1920–1930 than have borrowings from Federal Reserve banks. At the end of 1930 the borrowings of central reserve city member banks from others than Federal Reserve banks amounted to nearly as much as the borrowings from the Federal Reserve banks. The development of the Federal funds market is reflected statisically in the item "bills payable to others than the Federal Reserve bank." [20]

At certain times the borrowings from others than Federal Reserve banks have shown an inverse correlation with borrowings from Federal Reserve banks. For example, while borrowings from Federal Reserve banks by central reserve city member banks was rapidly declining during 1924, interbank borrowings rapidly increased. This happened again in 1929. The same tendency is evident also in the case of other reserve city member banks. In the case of country banks, on the other hand, borrowings from others than Federal Reserve banks are positively correlated throughout the period with borrowings from the Federal Reserve banks. But country member bank borrowings from others than Federal Reserve banks constitute a very important proportion of total borrowings of this type of bank. It should be pointed out

[19] These data were obtained from the Division of Research and Statistics of the Federal Reserve Board. Beginning in 1919, St. Louis is included in other reserve city banks.

[20] See dotted curve of the chart, showing the rise in bills payable to others than the Federal Reserve banks by central Reserve city member banks. Also, on Federal funds in general, see *supra*, pp. 40–48.

LOANS MADE BY NATIONAL BANKS IN SELECTED CITIES ACCORDING TO GEOGRAPHICAL LOCATION OF THE BORROWERS *

NOVEMBER 10, 1915

(In thousands of dollars)

Loans made to borrowers located in:

Loans made by national banks in:	*New England states*	*Eastern states*	*Southern states*	*Middle-western states*	*Western states*	*Pacific states*	*Total—All parts of the United States*	*Alaska and foreign countries*
New York City . . .	69,294	1,140,679	131,321	127,863	14,754	16,109	1,500,020	80,248
Chicago	11,116	30,765	22,562	288,969	14,044	7,846	375,302	1,592
St. Louis	986	2,770	18,117	69,820	4,769	359	96,822	50
Boston	168,357	33,345	8,307	24,353	2,257	1,655	238,273	4,953
Philadelphia	7,625	218,607	18,762	19,021	1,311	1,697	267,023	1,058
Richmond		417	36,438	54			36,908	
Atlanta		40	27,420	326	75		27,861	
Dallas		121	24,041	82	148	26	24,417	
Cleveland	496	3,903	682	65,501	361	42	69,996	34
Minneapolis		208	125	63,115	7,141	382	70,973	261
Kansas City	110	416	8,781	40,699	25,028	397	75,431	9
San Francisco	190	1,433	424	2,366	360	100,659	105,432	860
Other Reserve cities .	4,276	236,364	182,296	264,248	112,471	120,903	921,548	1,421
TOTAL	262,450	1,669,068	479,276	966,417	182,719	250,075	3,810,006	90,486
Total loans made by banks in Reserve cities outside New York City	193,146	528,389	347,955	838,554	167,965	233,966	2,309,986	10,238

* Source of data: *Annual Report of the Comptroller of the Currency*, 1915, Vol. I, pp. 18–19.

that while borrowings from Federal Reserve banks result in a rise in total member bank reserves, borrowings from others than Federal Reserve banks do not have this effect, although they may increase the reserve balance of the borrowing bank at the expense of the reserve balance of the lending bank.[21]

Geographical location of borrowers from commercial banks in Federal Reserve cities

While the New York City national banks in 1915 were making loans to individuals, corporations and banks in all sections of the country, these were not so important, relatively speaking, as the concentration of bankers' balances. This is shown by a comparison of data on deposit concentration and the table on page 227 showing the geographical distribution of loans.

Individuals, corporations and banks in New England borrowed $262,000,000, of which $69,000,000 was loaned by New York City national banks, $168,000,000 by Boston national banks and $11,000,000 by Chicago national banks. Customers in eastern states were borrowing $1,669,000,000 from national banks, of which $1,141,000,000 was loaned by New York City national banks, $219,000,000 by Philadelphia national banks, $33,000,000 by Boston national banks and $31,000,000 by Chicago national banks. Borrowers in the southern states borrowed $479,000,000 from national banks, of which $131,000,000 was loaned by New York City national banks, $36,000,000 by Richmond national banks, $27,000,000 by Atlanta national banks, $24,000,000 by Dallas national banks, $23,000,000 by Chicago national banks, and $18,000,000 each, by St. Louis and Kansas City national banks. Borrowers in the middle western States borrowed $966,000,000, of which $289,000,000 was loaned by Chicago national banks, $128,000,000 by New York City national banks, $70,000,000 by St. Louis national banks, $65,000,000 by Cleveland national banks, $63,000,000 by Minneapolis national banks, $41,000,000 by Kansas City national banks, $24,000,000 by Boston national

[21] The reasons for such continued importance of interbank borrowing other than from Federal Reserve banks are brought out in the chapter following, on the correspondent bank system.

banks and $19,000,000 by Philadelphia national banks. Borrowers in the western states borrowed $183,000,000 of which $25,000,000 was loaned by Kansas City national banks, $15,000,000 by New York City national banks, $14,000,000 by Chicago national banks, $7,000,000 by Minneapolis national banks and $5,000,000 by St. Louis national banks. Borrowers in the Pacific states borrowed $250,000,000 of which $101,000,000 was loaned by San Francisco national banks, $16,000,000 by New York City national banks, $8,000,000 by Chicago national banks, and about $1,600,000 by Philadelphia and Boston national banks respectively. Approximately 60 per cent of the $90,000,000 loaned to foreign borrowers was loaned by New York City national banks.

Analysis of "due from banks" as a measure of concentration of bankers' balances in New York City

The analysis in this chapter has been based on the assumption that the best approach to a measure of the importance of New York City as a depositary of interior bank funds was through a study of the "due-to-banks" data reported by New York City banks. It was found upon examination that the "due from banks" reported both by country banks and by other reserve city banks contained elements which had little bearing on the problem.

Beginning February, 1931, the "due from bank" data have been "purified" by the Division of Research and Statistics of the Federal Reserve Board. The data are for all member banks and represent the amounts due from New York City banks reported by member banks outside New York City.

They support the contention that the "due from bank" data, as reported by other reserve city and country banks, are of little value in an historical study of concentration of funds in the New York money market. The total reported "due from banks in the United States" by all member banks on December 31, 1930, was $2,455,948,000.[22] The portion of this reported by New York City member banks was $146,940,000,[23] leaving $2,309,008,000

[22] *Federal Reserve Bulletin*, March, 1931, pp. 176–77.
[23] *Member Bank Call Report*, No. 50, p. 12.

"due from banks" reported by member banks outside New York City. Of this amount, only a little over one-fourth was due from banks in New York City—*i.e.*, $641,271,000, as shown in the table below, based on the data compiled by the Federal Reserve Board:[24]

NEW YORK BALANCES OF MEMBER BANKS OUTSIDE NEW YORK CITY

AMOUNTS DUE FROM BANKS IN NEW YORK CITY AS REPORTED BY MEMBER BANKS IN THE FEDERAL RESERVE DISTRICT SPECIFIED

(In thousands of dollars)

Federal Reserve district	*December 31, 1928*	*December 31, 1929*	*December 31, 1930*
Boston	48,227	82,262	77,082
New York *	70,991	72,538	92,706
Philadelphia	43,812	41,553	45,703
Cleveland	55,529	41,210	62,796
Richmond	23,268	23,111	27,064
Atlanta	29,119	28,182	34,777
Chicago	83,164	62,965	116,899
St. Louis	20,734	18,303	33,112
Minneapolis	18,686	16,154	23,814
Kansas City	29,582	27,972	33,487
Dallas	26,887	27,781	25,012
San Francisco	59,787	77,076	68,819
TOTAL	509,786	519,107	641,271

* Due from banks in New York City as reported by member banks located in the New York district but outside New York City.

Even when the data on "due from banks" are purified, as they are in this table, to represent only those funds concentrated in New York City, they are still of less value as a measure of concentration than the "due to banks" as reported by New York City banks. On December 31, 1930, New York City member banks reported $1,350,113,000 as "due to other banks in the United States" as compared to the above figure of $641,271,000 reported by interior member banks as "due from banks in New York City." The difference between these two figures is accounted for in the main by the fact that the "due to banks" reported by the New York City member banks includes due to nonmember as well as due to member interior banks and hence gives a more complete

[24] *Federal Reserve Bulletin,* March, 1931, p. 140.

measure of funds concentrated in New York City. The part of New York City bankers' balances due to nonmember banks is a very important part, as the above analysis shows. At the same time, it should be remembered that the "due to banks" reported by New York city member banks include amounts due to other banks in New York City; but this is a relatively small amount.[25]

Summary

The concentration of funds in New York City from the interior in the form of bankers' balances continues to exist under the Federal Reserve system to a degree but little less than was the case prior to the establishment of this system. Concentration continues in this form for the threefold purposes of (1) maintaining balances in New York City correspondent banks to facilitate exchange transactions, and to have a "connection" in New York City for certain important purposes more fully discussed in the next chapter; (2) maintaining a depositary for surplus credit; and (3) maintaining a depositary for bank reserves of the interior nonmember banks.

From an examination of data for national banks, for all member banks, for state banks and trust companies, members and nonmembers, the conclusions reached were: (1) that New York City is just as important a point of concentration of bankers' balances relative to other centers as it was before the Federal Reserve system, and slightly more so; but (2) that concentration in the form of bankers' balances relative to total deposits is less important than it was before the Federal Reserve system in all sections of the country; and (3) that member state banks and trust companies, however, have shown a growth in bankers' balances approximately at the same rate as the growth taking place in their total deposits. Within New York City, itself, it was found that the concentration of bankers' balances is in the hands of a certain few large financial institutions.

The geographical sources of bankers' balances in New York City were then analyzed so far as it was possible with the data

[25] "Bills payable to others than the Federal Reserve bank" is a separate and additional item.

available and by the questionnaire method. It was found that the New York money market is a major point of concentration of funds from all parts of the country and that even where a certain section of the country has its own money market, a major relative proportion of its bankers' balances are sent to New York. The conclusion seemed to be justified that the New York money market is increasing in importance as the nationally predominant money market. While regionally important money markets are developing, these disclose no tendency to encroach upon the function of the New York money market as a *national* financial center.

The situation with respect to interbank borrowing other than from Federal Reserve banks was examined and it was found that even member banks resort to such borrowing in spite of the presumed privileges of membership in the Federal Reserve system. These facts were a clear indication of the continued predominant existence of the bankers' bank function exercised by the large financial institutions of New York City, and will be the subject of further discussion in the next chapter.

An important part of the analysis in this chapter consisted of an investigation into the nature of the items, "due to banks" and "due from banks," as they are reported by the banks in central reserve city, other reserve city, and country, banks. This study led on the one hand to a statistical and graphic presentation of deposit pyramiding in New York City, and on the other hand to the conclusion that the "due to banks" reported by New York City banks constitutes a better measure of concentration of bankers' balances in New York City than the "due from banks" reported by country banks and other reserve city banks.

Chapter XI

REASONS FOR DEPOSIT CONCENTRATION—THE CORRESPONDENT BANK SYSTEM

Natural evolution of the correspondent bank system

The evolution of the correspondent bank system has been described as one arising from the forces of competition and natural trade developments to take care of interbank relationships, particularly between different communities. Banks in every city or town in the United States have what are called correspondent banks in larger trading centers, with which they maintain a minimum required balance in return for certain services. Before the establishment of the Federal Reserve banks, the debit and credit balances created by intercommunity trade between the banks of the small communities and the banks of the larger trading centers, and also between the several minor communities themselves, were settled through the correspondent bank system entirely. This included the clearing of checks and the handling of drafts and collection items. The establishment of the Federal Reserve clearing system has for the most part taken over the function of the clearing of checks from the correspondent bank system, and now such checks are very largely settled through the Federal Reserve banks by means of the clearing mechanism in operation. The relative decline in the importance of bankers' balances which has been disclosed (*i.e.*, relative to total deposits) is fundamentally accounted for by the fact that the Federal Reserve clearing system has been steadily taking over more and more of that part of the function previously performed by bankers' balances and the correspondent bank system.

In the course of the development of the correspondent bank system, certain practices arose involving the routing of checks, the existence of the "float," and the resulting deceptive appearance of bank reserves which placed the correspondent bank system in ill repute. As a part of the program of banking reform inaugurated by the Federal Reserve system, there was contemplated the elimination of the necessity of the correspondent bank system. This was to be accomplished through the centralization of reserves in the regional banks (the Federal Reserve banks) and through the establishment of a Federal clearing system. A remarkably efficient system has been created by law and administrative mandates to take care of the clearing of checks between banks of different communities and for the transfer of funds between communities through the gold settlement fund. Yet the correspondent bank system continues to exist, as the figures so clearly testify. This mechanism of the correspondent bank system for taking care of interbank relationships evolved through natural forces and has not been entirely displaced by the system created by law. There are two important reasons for the continued existence of the correspondent bank system: (1) some of the functions meant to be absorbed by the Federal Reserve clearing system are, contrary to expectation, still performed better by the old system; and (2) some of the functions which are performed by the correspondent bank system have not been assumed by the Federal Reserve system, and probably never will be.[1]

Survival of check clearing through correspondent banks

While the Federal Reserve clearing system was established to take care of the intercommunity clearance of checks, much of this work is still handled, and more conveniently, by correspondent banks. To take a specific case, here is a check drawn on the First National Bank of Princeton payable to A. V. Manning and Sons in Trenton. It happens that A. V. Manning and Sons bank with the Trenton Banking Company, which is a correspondent bank of the First National Bank of Princeton. The check was deposited in the Trenton Banking Company and credited to the account of A. V. Manning and Sons, debited to the account of the First National Bank of Princeton and never entered the Federal

[1] Cf. in general, Tippetts, C. S., *State Banks and the Federal Reserve System*, pp. 65–102. Watkins, L. I., *Bankers' Balances*, pp. 356–86.

Reserve clearing system, since the clearance was more simply and quickly accomplished by interbank debits and credits. Again, here is a check drawn on the First National Bank of Princeton payable to H. M. Voorhees and Brothers, Trenton. H. M. Voorhees and Brothers deposited the check in the Broad Street National Bank of Trenton, whose correspondent bank in Princeton is the Princeton Bank and Trust Company. The Broad Street National Bank credited H. M. Voorhees and Brothers' account and debited the account of the Princeton Bank and Trust Company, which in turn presented the check for payment in Princeton at the First National Bank. Checks drawn on a Princeton Bank (in the Philadelphia Reserve District) cashed in New York City may not go through the Federal Reserve clearing system if it happens that they are cashed at the New York City correspondent of the Princeton bank; and the clearing of checks through the correspondent system in preference to the Federal clearing system may cross Federal Reserve district lines even between distant places. For example, a check drawn on the First National Bank of Princeton payable to the American Economic Association was cashed by the American Economic Association at the State Bank and Trust Company of Evanston, Illinois, which endorsed it and sent it to its correspondent bank in Philadelphia, the Philadelphia-Girard National Bank. The Philadelphia-Girard National Bank endorsed it and sent it to its Princeton correspondent bank, the Princeton Bank and Trust Company, which endorsed it and presented it for payment to the First National Bank of Princeton. It apparently never went through the Federal clearing system. Again, a check made payable to the Baltimore and Ohio Railroad Company was cashed at the Philadelphia National Bank, which sent it directly to the Princeton Bank and Trust Company, and the latter presented it for payment at the First National Bank of Princeton. A check made payable to the Review of Reviews Corporation was cashed at the Putnam Trust Company of Greenwich, Connecticut, and it was sent by them to the Philadelphia-Girard National Bank, and by them to the Princeton Bank and Trust Company, which presented it for payment at the First National Bank of Princeton. All of the above examples are checks drawn in the course of the years

1927–1929. The following are a number of interesting examples of checks drawn in the year 1930. A check drawn on the First National Bank of Princeton, cashed at the First National Bank in Denver, Colorado, went through the Continental Illinois Bank and Trust Company of Chicago and the Guaranty Trust Company of New York before reaching the Federal Reserve Bank of Philadelphia. A check similarly drawn and cashed in Denver, Colorado, went direct to the Denver branch of the Federal Reserve Bank of Kansas City and thence to the Federal Reserve Bank of Philadelphia. A check similarly drawn and cashed in Denver, after passing through four banks in Denver, finally went to the Chase National Bank of New York and thence to the Federal Reserve Bank of Philadelphia to be cleared on the First National Bank of Princeton. A check payable to the United States Chamber of Commerce, went from the Washington Loan and Trust Company to the Marine Trust Company of Buffalo before finding its way to the Federal Reserve Bank of Philadelphia for clearance on the First National Bank of Princeton. By way of summary, it may be said (1) that a check paid by a bank which is a correspondent of the payee bank may not go through the clearing system, and (2) a check paid by a nonmember bank may be cleared through the correspondent bank system rather than the Federal Reserve clearing system, and certainly will be if the nonmember banks does not remit at par.

Furthermore, it must be remembered that the Federal Reserve districts as arranged under the Act are to some extent artificially delineated. The following is a statement from a resident of New York City:

> I usually spend my week-ends in New Haven, Connecticut, and have occasion while there to pay bills with checks on a New York bank. If these checks are cleared through the Federal Reserve clearing system, they must be sent from New Haven to the Boston Federal Reserve Bank, then back to the New York Federal Reserve Bank and through the clearing house here to the bank in which my account is kept. This process takes so long that usually the New Haven bank receiving my New York checks sends them to its correspondent bank in New York which puts them directly through the New York

Clearing House. The point is, of course, that most of Connecticut should really be included in the territory of the New York Reserve Bank, but artificially has been assigned to the Boston district.[2]

No matter what the delineations of the districts, there would be instances of this sort.

Other cases where the correspondent system, instead of the Federal clearing system, performs the clearing function are those dealing with checks difficult to collect, such as those which may require legal proceedings.[3] A correspondent bank will perform this service for its bank clientèle, whereas the Federal Reserve bank in such an eventuality will merely return the check as uncollectable.

Numerous banks, particularly the country banks in the Northwest and the South, have had their names withdrawn from the Federal reserve "par" list and are exacting a collection charge. Such checks are cleared through the correspondent bank system. Below are some statements quoted from bankers on this subject:

> The check and draft collection system of the Federal Reserve system does not cover all the country and also in some sections Federal Reserve service does not give quick service on unpaid items.
>
> . . .
>
> In some cases the collection of items on certain points can be handled more economically by a correspondent bank. For example I know of certain New York banks that will handle items without charge, giving immediate credit to some of their correspondent banks.

With reference to the handling of items for collection, a nonmember bank said, as a reason for not joining the system: "The collection of our items is taken care of just as well by our correspondents." While it is true that nonmember banks may apply and be admitted to the clearing services of the Federal Reserve clearing system, for the most part the clearing functions for nonmember banks are performed by the correspondent bank system.

[2] Letter from J. Edward Meeker, economist of the New York Stock Exchange, Jan. 24, 1929.

[3] The discussion here and following is based upon correspondence with bankers in New York City, New Jersey, Chicago, and St. Louis; and upon interviews with bankers in New York City.

Reserve function of the correspondent bank system

The correspondent bank system performs the function of reserve depositaries for nonmember bank reserves, as it did for all banks before the Federal Reserve system. Nonmember state banks and trust companies of New York State alone had on deposit with "approved reserve agents" nearly $104,000,000 in December, 1929.[4] Nonmember trust companies had on deposit with "approved reserve agents" over $84,000,000 in December, 1929. The nonmember trust companies of New York county had $42,000,000 so deposited in 1928, and $44,000,000 in December, 1929. Many nonmember banks are reluctant to join the Federal Reserve system because they now receive interest varying upwards to 3 per cent on these deposited reserves, whereas if they joined the system they would receive no interest on their reserves deposited with the Federal Reserve bank. It is thus apparent that a considerable portion of the bankers' balances still consist of deposited reserves.

Interbank borrowing and the correspondent system

Many assumed that with the establishment of the Federal Reserve system interior banks would no longer have need to borrow from their New York City correspondents. Perhaps this was envisaged as one of the desirable eventualities by those who framed the Federal Reserve Act. On the contrary, however, it is far from complete realization, and essentially so for two reasons: (1) borrowing from the Federal Reserve bank may be accomplished only in certain legally defined ways, *i.e.*, on discount of eligible paper, or short-term borrowing against government securities; and (2) borrowing from correspondent banks is frequently more convenient.

Concerning the first reason, nonmember banks, of course, cannot borrow from the Federal Reserve banks, and member banks may borrow only through rediscounting eligible paper or against government securities. Borrowings against other types of

[4] *Abstract of Condition of New York State Banks and Trust Companies*, New York State Banking Department.

securities are not permitted by law. On these, the correspondent bank system offers a means of obtaining credit. The following are some statements from bankers on this point:

We are large investors in bonds of the savings bank class which we use in case we wish to borrow money from our New York correspondents. This we could not do with the Federal Reserve bank.

. . .

The bills receivable of many banks do not come within the Federal Reserve requirements, due to the nature of the bank's business. At the same time, the notes receivable are equally as good if not safer than those supported by financial statements.

. . .

Many banks carry as a secondary reserve, underlying bonds of first class railroads and first class utilities, which cannot be used as collateral at the Federal Reserve bank.

Country member banks, on December 31, 1929, had investments of $3,172,380,000 in "other bonds, stocks and securities" which were not eligible for borrowing on at the Federal Reserve bank, as against $1,266,750,000 invested in government securities. All member banks had $5,920,921,000 invested in "other bonds, stocks and securities," on December 31, 1929, as against $3,862,968,000 investments in government securities.[5] Of the total loans of all member banks on June 30, 1928, about $4,650,000,000 (or 13.3 per cent of total loans and investments) was reported as eligible for rediscount at Federal Reserve banks.[6]

It is evident from the above data that interior banks maintain bankers' balances in New York City and other reserve cities for the purpose of being able to borrow from the city correspondent banks when necessary. Loans to banks by New York City member banks amounted to $410,000,000 on December 31, 1929.[7] The New York City banks usually require that borrowing interior banks keep a minimum balance equal to about 20 per cent of the bank's borrowings. When the interior bank is not borrowing,

[5] *Federal Reserve Bulletin*, Dec. 1928, p. 884, *Member Bank Call Report*, Nos. 42, 46.

[6] *Federal Reserve Bulletin*, Dec. 1928, p. 882.

[7] *Member Bank Call Report*, No. 46, p. 3.

no minimum is set, but they are expected to maintain a sufficient balance to pay for the services rendered by the New York City bank. There is no exactness of the *quid pro quo* calculated in connection with the services rendered any one bank—correspondent banking is considered advantageous to the New York City bank in general and in addition to the profits immediately involved. The percentage for the minimum balance changes from time to time in accordance with the competitive situation.

Safe-keeping and custodianship services and the correspondent bank system

The New York Federal Reserve Bank carries custodianship accounts only for its own members, *i.e.,* member banks located in New York state, northern New Jersey and Fairfield County, Connecticut. Furthermore, the custody services of the Federal Reserve Bank of New York is confined to bonds owned by the member bank. In contrast to this, the New York City banks as correspondents under custodian service for member and nonmember banks in the New York Federal Reserve district and for member and nonmember banks all over the country, will take care of securities, either for the correspondent bank itself, or of customers of correspondent banks. Interior banks frequently desire to keep their securities in New York City in safe-keeping for two reasons: (1) to have them there in case they wish to borrow on them —they will thus be immediately available as collateral for credit when needed; and (2) to have them in New York City in case they wish to dispose of them—funds will thus be immediately available for transfer by telephone or telegraphic order. In connection with the safe-keeping service, New York City banks not only take care of the securities, attending to the matter of collecting interest coupons and watching for called bonds but will, at the request of the correspondent bank, study their portfolio with a view to giving investment advice.

This arrangement allows for the greatest convenience in case the correspondent bank wishes to borrow from the New York bank, since the loan may be negotiated by telephone in a few minutes. Borrowing from the Federal Reserve bank entails the collection of the right amount of eligible paper from the bank's portfolio of loans and discounts.[8] Where banks keep government securities in safe-keeping with the Federal Reserve banks, the same convenience in this respect is, of course, obtained.

Investment services and the correspondent bank system

The New York City banks perform a variety of investment services for their correspondent banks which serve as a powerful motive for the continuation of that system and for the maintenance of bankers' balances. The vast files of credit information in the large New York City banks are available to interior correspondent banks. New York City banks take orders to buy or sell securities for the interior bank, having them executed through their own broker. The New York City banks give interior correspondent banks participation in new security issues, participation in domestic acceptance credits, will buy for the interior bank commercial paper and acceptances. The New York banks' services in the purchase of unlisted securities is particularly desirable to the interior banks. Interior banks prefer to deal through a New York correspondent bank, rather than directly through a broker.

Finally, the New York bank will place funds for the account of the interior bank on the call loan market, *i.e.*, brokers' loans. These are highly realizable from the point of view of the interior institution and at times rates are higher than rates on other types of liquid bank investments, such as acceptances and commercial paper.

The utilization of this service performed by the New York banks for interior banks is obviously reflected in the size of the item "loans for account of correspondents" or "loans for account of out-of-town banks."

Correspondent bank system and the payment of interest on balances

Banks ordinarily keep available an amount of "working reserve" in excess of the legal reserve on deposit at the Federal

[8] On Dec. 31, 1929, country member banks had bills payable to Federal Reserve banks $137,000,000, as against bills payable to others of $105,000,000. *Member Bank Call Report*, No. 46, p. 3.

Reserve bank. A small part of this "working reserve" consists of cash in the bank's own vaults, but there is an additional amount kept with correspondents in various cities, the accounts being so placed as in the judgment of the correspondent best to suit its convenience. It is probable that in the case of some part of the funds in excess of reserve requirements deposited by member banks with city correspondents, the payment of interest on balances is a leading inducement.[9] As a matter of fact, this inducement has been of such importance that in some cases it has kept banks from joining the Federal Reserve system. One banker wrote:

> We have not joined the Federal Reserve system because it would cost us about $90,000 a year to do so. This is about the amount we are now receiving by way of interest upon our reserve which we deposit with our New York correspondents, which are members of the Federal Reserve system.

Interior member banks pare their deposits with the Federal Reserve bank to the minimum, since these yield no interest, and maintain their surplus funds with their New York correspondent. To some extent, interior banks place funds on time deposit to obtain a still higher rate of return.

Correspondent bank system and foreign exchange

While it is true that an interior bank could buy foreign exchange from New York banks and pay with a Federal Reserve check, it is more convenient to have a balance with the New York bank furnishing the foreign exchange in order that charges may be made directly into that balance instead of waiting for remittances. The interior bank is thereby enabled to render more prompt and efficient service to its customers. The importance of this motive for keeping balances in New York correspondent banks by interior banks may be better appreciated when it is realized that in the year 1927, for example, there were transactions in foreign exchange in excess of 4.4 billions of dollars to pay for

[9] Correspondence with comptroller of the currency, Feb. 16, 1929.

merchandise imports, over 600 millions of dollars for tourist expenditures, close to 300 millions of dollars in interest payments to foreigners on their investments made in this country, 241 millions of dollars for immigrant remittances, over 1½ billions of dollars to pay for foreign securities purchased in this country, and over 600 millions of dollars worth of American securities bought back from foreigners.[10]

Summary

This chapter is, in a sense, an explanation of the statistical picture presented in the preceding chapters on concentration. It has served to explain why the correspondent bank system continues to exist as an important feature of banking practice in this country. While some of the functions formerly performed by the correspondent bank system have been taken over by the mechanism created by the Federal Reserve system, there is still left sufficient justification for the continued existence of the correspondent bank system. This is accounted for only in part by the need for such services by nonmember banks; for it has been seen that interior member banks also have need of the services of a New York correspondent, in addition to their Federal Reserve bank connections.

[10] Hall, Ray, "The Balance of International Payments of the United States, in 1927," *Bureau of Foreign and Domestic Commerce*, pp. vi–vii.

Chapter XII

FOREIGN FUNDS

Reasons for foreign funds' concentration

Broadly speaking, foreign funds tend to be concentrated in the New York money market for four fundamental reasons: (1) those growing out of commodity trading with foreigners by the people of the United States; (2) those growing out of security trading with foreigners; (3) those growing out of travel and immigration; and (4) those growing out of miscellaneous international exchange transactions, gold movements, and the newer monetary standards.[1]

In the first place, the maintenance of deposits by foreigners in New York City is necessitated by foreign trade in commodities and services. Foreigners buying commodities or services from people in this country arrange payment through mutual banking connections, and foreigners who sell commodities to persons in this country receive payment through an increase in the first instance in funds to their credit in New York City, or, indirectly, through an increase in the New York City balance to the credit of the foreign bank with which the foreign merchant deals. In other words, it is because New York City serves very generally as the foreign exchange market in the trade relationships between traders in this country and foreign traders that the existence of foreign trade in commodities and services results in a continuous flow of funds through the New York money market, which requires foreign banks to maintain deposit balances there for the convenience of their own customers abroad.

The New York money market is employed also by foreigners who wish to buy American securities, either directly, if the for-

[1] Cf. *The Annalist*, Jan. 27, 1928, pp. 216–17. Feis, Herbert, "Our Foreign Investment Position: An Analysis of Recent Capital Movements," *The Annalist, Feb.*

eigner has a bank account of his own in a New York City bank, or indirectly through the foreigner's own bank which, in turn, has a balance in New York City bank against which it may draw for the purchases desired by the foreign bank's client. A foreigner who wishes to sell securities in the New York money market will receive payment through an increase in his balance in his New York City bank, in the first instance, if he has such an account, or through an increase in his balance in his own bank, which, in turn, has received a credit to its balance with its New York City correspondent.

A foreign corporation which wishes to borrow capital in the American market will arrange through a New York banking firm to "float" its securities through the mechanism of the New York money market—and upon the marketing of its securities will receive an increase in its New York City balance, or in its balance in its own foreign bank, which in turn has received a credit to its balance with the New York City bank. Inasmuch as New York City constitutes the security trading market in the United States and the center for the distribution of new security issues, foreign dealings in American securities and American dealings in foreign securities, including new issues and purchases and sales of old issues, results in a continuous flow of funds through the New York money market and a consequent balance of foreign funds at any given time in the New York money market.

In any case, where there is the desire on the part of foreigners to make payments to people in the United States, or on the part of individuals in this country to make payments to individuals abroad or to convert funds into foreign money which they intend to spend while touring abroad, there is created the necessity for interbank relationships between New York City banks and foreign banks through which these conversions of funds and transfers can be made. These interbank relationships are evidenced by foreign deposit balances with New York City banks, and also by deposit balances of New York City banks abroad.

24, 1928, pp. 366–67. *Commercial and Financial Chronicle,* Feb. 16, 1929, pp. 927–57. Burgess, R. W., "The Money Market in 1929," *Review of Economic Statistics,* Feb. 1930, pp. 15–20.

Deposit balances in New York money market due to limited gold exchange standard

Foreign funds tend to be concentrated in the New York money market by reason of the fact that the New York money market has grown to be an important international deposit center since the World War. The principles of the "limited" gold exchange standard were widely adopted. Before the War, to adopt the gold exchange standard was a mark of financial weakness or instability, and, though this is still true to a certain extent, its adoption since the War came to be looked upon more as a means of economizing the world's supply of monetary gold, and of avoiding the expense of international movements of gold in the form of express and interest costs.[2] In other words, foreign central banks have maintained credits, very largely in New York City, in the form of liquid assets which can be realized upon immediately if necessary to stabilize exchange rates and to maintain parity between their currency and that of other gold standard countries. These foreign central bank balances are not only maintained with the Federal Reserve banks,[3] but to a very great extent also with the New York City commercial banks. In June, 1927, the Federal Reserve Board estimated that as much as $1,000,000,000 of the operating reserves of foreign central banks was in the form of dollar exchange. The following is quoted from the *Federal Reserve Bulletin* of June, 1927:[4]

> Of the total holdings of foreign assets by central banks, a considerable proportion is held in the United States. While there is no way to determine this proportion precisely, there is reason to believe that it is large, and that perhaps as much as $1,000,000,000 of the operating reserves of foreign central banks is in the form of dollar exchange.

[2] In July, 1927, liquid foreign assets of thirty central banks amounted to $1,900,000,000. Anderson, B. M. *Some Major Forces in the International Money Market.* See also, on the desirability of having foreign funds invested in the New York money market, the testimony of Governor Strong in the Strong Bill Hearings, *Hearings before the Committee on Banking and Currency,* House of Representatives, Sixty-ninth Congress, First Session, on H. R. 7895, Part I, (1926), p. 452.

[3] Foreign deposits in Federal Reserve banks are prorated among the twelve Federal Reserve banks according to capital and surplus. *Annual Report of the Federal Reserve Bank of Philadelphia,* 1926, p. 13.

[4] Pages 392–93.

In view of the strong reserve position of the Federal Reserve banks and of the American policy of placing no legal or practical restrictions on gold withdrawals, so that balances with banks in the United States are convertible at any time into exportable gold, dollar exchange is considered throughout the world as equivalent to gold. To build up the volume of dollar exchange at their command has been the policy of many central banks, which find it safe, convenient, and profitable to keep a portion of their reserves productively employed in the United States, rather than to keep them unproductive in the form of gold in vault.

Other reasons for the concentration of foreign funds in New York City

In addition, the New York banks perform the services for foreigners already described in connection with the making of loans in the brokers' loan market, in the purchase of short-term securities, commercial paper and acceptances for foreign account.[5]

Gold movements, limited gold exchange standard, and the New York money market as a center of international finance

Only to a minor extent may the foreign balances with New York banks be considered as the results of importations of gold or currency. For the most part the balances were built up in a manner that does not add to the basic funds of the money market.[6] Some of the balances were the result of security flotations, often for the purpose of currency stabilization. Thus a nation desirous of relating the external value of its currency to the dollar might float bonds through one of the larger investment houses in New York and leave the whole or a part of the proceeds on deposit. This deposit account would be drawn upon as needed through the operation of the gold exchange standard. Still another means in which these balances were built up is through what has since

[5] Dr. B. M. Anderson comments in the following very interesting way on this situation: "Through the device, therefore, of letting gold in one country function as if it were simultaneously in several countries, a vast expansion of credit has been taking place throughout the world, and very especially in the United States." *Some Major Forces in the International Money Market.*

[6] Cf. Schacht, Hjalmar, "The Money Markets before and after the War," *Harvard Business Review,* Jan. 1931, pp. 129–39.

been termed the "repatriation of capital."[7] What is meant here can best be illustrated by referring to the case of France. In 1926 the French franc dropped precipitately. There had developed a "flight of capital" from the franc owing to the disturbed political situation and the apparent hopelessness of the tangle of French finances. The peasants and *bourgeoisie* were converting their paper francs into dollars and the newly stabilized pound sterling. As this was done the movement became a cumulative one, the franc fell at a rate exceeded only by such declines as those experienced by the Russian ruble and the German mark. The flight from the franc, the conversion of francs into other currencies, and the consequent rise in deposit balances in England and the United States, and in dollar and pound securities forced the external value of the franc below its internal value. Foreigners were thus enabled to get more and more francs for their own money, and hence the products and services of France with less of their own products and services. Through sales of their currency the French built up foreign balances, which were further augmented by French exporters leaving those balances abroad which had accumulated from their export business. After the coalition cabinet had been established in 1926 and confidence strengthened, the French who had purchased foreign currencies or accumulated foreign balances, disposed of them to the Bank of France which thus came into possession of large balances in foreign countries and particularly in the United States.

International bank balances are created by the underlying economic factors described above and once created are employed as a governor or balance wheel to reduce exchange rate fluctuations. Speaking from the point of view of the international trade relationships of the United States, a credit item may be regarded as one which tends to increase the balances of American banks abroad or to decrease the balance carried by foreigners in American banks; and a debit item as one which tends to reduce the foreign bank balances of Americans or to increase the deposits of foreigners in banks in this country. If credits are consistently larger than debits, our deposits in foreign banks increase, and deposits of foreigners in

[7] Cf. *Supra*, Chap. IV

our banks decline. Foreign exchange rates accordingly fall, while dollar exchange in foreign markets rises to a premium. It might eventually become profitable for foreign banks to ship gold to the United States to increase balances in order to sell more dollar exchange at the high rates, and for American banks to accept gold in payment of their excessive balances of low-priced foreign funds. Similar correctives operate simultaneously through fluctuations in money rates and, less promptly, through changes in capital exports and imports, and in security and commodity prices.[8]

Statistical measurement of the factors in foreign concentration of funds in the New York money market

It would be highly desirable at least theoretically to have the statistics of foreign funds in the New York money market segregated as to the various reasons for their creation as outlined above, particularly into: (1) foreign funds in the New York money market due to the trade in commodities and services; (2) foreign funds in the New York money market due to trade in securities and issues of new securities; (3) foreign funds arising from miscellaneous causes; and (4) foreign funds, largely of foreign central banks, due to the use of the gold exchange standard in the maintenance of international exchange relationships. Not only are data not available in such form, but in fact adequate aggregate data are not available. The following analysis is therefore an attempt to present existing data and to weigh their significance as measures of the concentration of foreign funds in the New York money market.

Evidence of the movement of funds through the New York money market to take care of foreign trade in commodities and services is contained in the figures showing the volume of foreign trade, tourist expenditures, immigrant remittances, and the other invisible items of foreign trade. Such data do not, of course, show the amount of concentration of foreign funds in the New York money market; but rather give a statistical approximation of the *raison d'être* of such concentration. Statistics of the

[8] *The Guaranty Survey*, July 29, 1929, p. 5.

volume of foreign securities owned in this country are similarly indicative. All member banks in the United States owned $726,-400,000 of foreign securities on June 30, 1928, and on December 31, 1930, this item amounted to $714,928,000. Of this amount, on June 30, 1928, $420,600,000 were owned by country banks and on December 31, 1930, $382,317,000 were owned by country banks. On December 31, 1931, country member banks held $280,516,000 in foreign securities out of a total of $540,072,000 held by all member banks. Purchases and sales of these securities by country banks involve the movement of funds through the New York money market, as few country banks have foreign accounts.[9] Further indicative figures of reasons for concentration of foreign funds in the New York money market are the data for foreign capital issues in this country:[10]

TOTAL NEW FOREIGN CAPITAL ISSUES IN THE UNITED STATES DURING THE YEARS SPECIFIED

(In millions of dollars)

Year	*Corporate issues*	*Government issues*	*Total*
1920	178.2	344.3	522.5
1921	121.3	455.3	577.5
1922	127.4	632.4	759.8
1923	67.1	293.0	360.2
1924	317.8	927.0	1,244.8
1925	516.0	791.4	1,307.3
1926	725.8	623.9	1,349.8
1927	812.3	912.4	1,724.7
1928	887.6	689.2	1,576.8
1929	649.8	130.1	779.9
1930	516.2	619.6	1,135.8
1931	217.8	50.4	268.2

The annual data in the above table are based upon figures compiled by *The Commercial and Financial Chronicle,* and differ somewhat from the figures compiled by the Federal Reserve Bank of New York. For 1928 the total foreign capital issues, accord-

[9] *Federal Reserve Bulletin,* Dec. 1928, p. 882. Cf. *Annual Report of the Federal Reserve Board,* 1927, p. 111; and *Member Bank Call Report,* No. 50, p. 5; and No. 54, p. 5.

[10] *Statistical Abstract of the United States,* 1928, pp. 309–9; 1929, p. 315; 1930, p. 313; and *The Commercial and Financial Chronicle,* Jan. 17, 1931 and Jan. 16, 1932.

ing to the data of the Federal Reserve Bank of New York, amounted to $1,251,000,000, as compared to the $1,576,800,000 in the table. In 1929 the figures of the Federal Reserve Bank of New York give a total of only $671,000,000, and in 1930 the Federal Reserve Bank of New York total was $905,000,000.[11]

These data, together with the figures on the visible and invisible items in the foreign trade balance, give the background of economic information which constitutes the reason for the fact that foreign funds and transactions tend to be concentrated in the New York money market.

The statistical measurement of concentration of foreign funds—Federal Reserve bank data

There are a number of sources of data measuring in part the volume of foreign funds in the New York money market. First, there are statistics of the funds deposited by foreign central banks with the Federal Reserve banks. Not all of these funds are with the Federal Reserve Bank of New York, since bookkeeping allotments are made to the other Federal Reserve banks. There deposits appear, therefore, on the books of all twelve of the Federal Reserve banks, but are available at New York to the foreign central bank. During 1930 the foreign central bank deposits in Federal Reserve banks ranged from about 5½ millions to 7 millions of dollars. These accounts are simply the unused foreign balances maintained with the Federal Reserve banks and are naturally kept at a minimum, since the foreign owner of the funds desires to have his American funds profitably invested in bills or government securities at all times.

The real measure of the concentration of foreign central bank funds in the New York money market, so far as Federal Reserve bank data are concerned, is the amount of purchases in the form of acceptances and government securities. Data of the amount of foreign central bank purchases of government securities are not available, but the amount of bills purchased by the Federal Reserve banks as agent for foreign central banks are shown on their

[11] *Federal Reserve Bulletin*, April, 1931, p. 192. The data appearing in the *Bulletin* do not include refunding issues.

weekly statement of condition under the title "Contingent liability on bills purchased for foreign correspondents by Federal Reserve Banks." Chart 27 is the total of the two series mentioned above, and represents the total concentration of foreign central bank funds in the New York money market so far as Federal Reserve data are available. The amount of concentration of

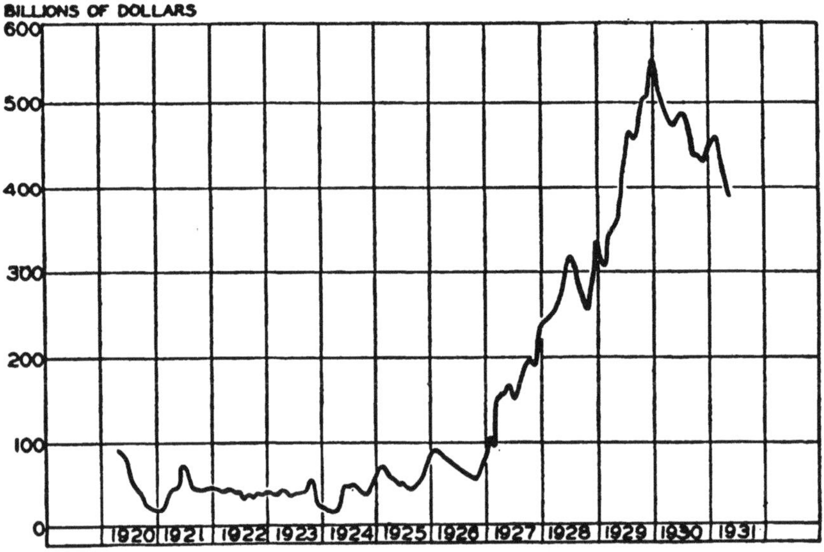

CHART 27. FOREIGN FUNDS IN THE NEW YORK MONEY MARKET—FEDERAL RESERVE BANK DATA.

"CONTINGENT LIABILITY ON BILLS PURCHASED FOR FOREIGN CORRESPONDENTS BY FEDERAL RESERVE BANKS" PLUS DEPOSITS IN FEDERAL RESERVE BANKS OF FOREIGN CENTRAL BANKS.

foreign funds in New York has shown a rapid increase since the beginning of 1927; but to some extent this increase has been offset by a decline in government securities owned by foreign central banks.[12]

The statistical measurement of the concentration of foreign funds—commercial bank data

In addition to the funds of the central banks, foreign commercial banks have funds in the New York money market and

[12] Source of data: *Annual Reports of the Federal Reserve Board. Federal Reserve Bulletin.* See also discussion, pp. 256–60.

also foreign central banks have funds with New York commercial banks. Some clue to the amount of these is conveyed by the total amount of foreign balances carried with all member banks in various cities. These are given in the following table, as of December 31, for the four years 1928, 1929, 1930 and 1931. Foreign bank balances in all member banks amounted on December 31, 1930, to about $634,927,000, of which nearly 87 per cent is with member banks in New York City.[13] In 1929 this percentage was 86.2 and in 1928 it was 87.9.

FOREIGN BANKERS' FUNDS DEPOSITED IN THE UNITED STATES

ALL MEMBER BANKS

(In thousands of dollars)

All member banks located in:	*Foreign deposits in all member banks of specified cities, Dec. 31*			
	1928	*1929*	*1930*	*1931*
New York City . . .	477,799	496,917	551,238	368,740
Boston	25,765	18,769	20,585	12,007
San Francisco . . .	10,328	10,544	14,841	6,976
Chicago	9,089	26,533	26,094	32,179
Philadelphia	3,355	3,737	4,011	2,114
New Orleans	2,182	2,326	1,980	1,415
Los Angeles	2,121	1,853	1,926	1,002
Cleveland	2,002	2,701	2,024	1,103
Detroit	1,991	1,805	2,500	1,169
Seattle	863	889	1,312	696
Pittsburgh	718	2,272	848	396
Minneapolis	690	900	509	693
Buffalo	689	997	1,785	1,241
St. Louis	384	400	312	173
Other reserve cities *	2,947	2,289	3,031	1,694
Country Banks . . .	2,350	2,832	1,931	2,142
TOTAL	543,273	576,664	634,927	433,740

* Less those included in the table separately.

Growing importance of foreign funds, indicated by national bank data

In order to obtain a picture of the changing relative importance of foreign deposits in this country since 1915, it is necessary to

[13] *Member Bank Call Reports.* Cf. *Federal Reserve Bulletin*, July, 1927, p. 465.

resort to national bank figures. In relation to total bankers' balances, foreign bankers' balances in the national banks of all Reserve cities were in 1930 more than twice as important as in 1915.[14]

Bankers' Balances in All Reserve Cities—National Banks

Date	*Domestic*	*Foreign*
Nov. 10, 1915	$2,466,788,500	$123,772,188
Dec. 31, 1928	2,241,190,000	289,223,000
Dec. 31, 1929	1,838,769,000	236,882,000
Dec. 31, 1930	2,055,069,000	303,257,000
Dec. 31, 1931	1,490,369,000	181,777,000

And this growing importance of foreign funds is still more marked in the case of the New York City national banks:

Bankers' Balances in New York City National Banks

Date	*Domestic*	*Foreign*
Nov. 10, 1915	$1,067,579,000	$105,548,000
Dec. 31, 1928	738,958,000	241,437,000
Dec. 31, 1929	507,662,000	194,269,000
Dec. 31, 1930	570,580,000	251,990,000
Dec. 31, 1931	413,859,000	146,123,000

Foreign bankers' balances with New York City national banks increased from an amount equal to but 10 per cent of domestic bankers' balances in 1915 to over 38 per cent on December 31, 1929; 44 per cent on December 31, 1930. The proportion fell to 35 per cent on December 31, 1931.

For the past few years data have been published on foreign *time* deposits in American commercial banks. It is to be noted that these amounts are in addition to the data given above on foreign bankers' deposits with banks in this country.[15] The following table presents these figures for all member banks: [16]

[14] *Annual Report of the Comptroller of the Currency,* 1915, Vol. I, pp. 12–13. *Abstract of Condition of National Banks,* No. 161, p. 7; No. 165, p. 9; No. 169, p. 9. These figures are not comparable with all member bank data given above.

[15] Correspondence with the Federal Reserve Board and with the Comptroller of the Currency, Jan., 1931. Also see *Member Bank Call Report,* No. 54, p. 5.

[16] *Member Bank Call Reports,* No. 50, p. 5; and No. 54, p. 5. Cf. *Federal Reserve Bulletin,* Dec., 1929, p. 828. These figures were first published separately in June, 1929. See *Member Bank Call Report,* No. 50, p. 3.

TIME DEPOSITS OF BANKS IN FOREIGN COUNTRIES WITH COMMERCIAL BANKS IN THE UNITED STATES

(Data as of end of each year; in thousands of dollars)

All member banks in:	*1929*	*1930*	*1931*
New York City	133,197	182,313	21,299
Chicago	7,050	23,000	1,000
Other Reserve city banks	13,675	32,268	3,821
Country banks	87	.....	5
TOTAL	154,009	237,581	26,125

Thus to measure the foreign deposit concentration of funds in the New York money market, at the end of 1930, there should be added to the $551,238,000 of deposits with New York City member banks on the part of foreign banks, the $182,313,000 of time deposits, making a total of $733,551,000. By the end of 1931, however, this large total had declined by about 50 per cent; namely, to $390,039,000. These figures do not include time deposits by foreign individuals, firms or corporations other than banks.

Foreign deposits other than by foreign banks

In addition to the deposits with New York City banks by foreign bankers, there are those of foreign corporations and individuals which aggregate, according to reliable sources, an amount nearly as large as the deposits of foreign banks. In the case of six of the large New York City banks, holding about 50 per cent of all bankers' balances in New York City, at the end of 1928 total deposits on the part of foreigners amounted to $488,305,000, of which $273,781,800 was due to foreign banks and $214,523,200 was due to foreigners other than banks.[17] There are no published data of deposits in New York City to the credit of foreign corporations, firms and individuals other than banks. The data on foreign funds in the United States published by the comptroller for national banks and the Federal Reserve Board for member banks include only balances in New York City to the credit of foreign banks, and to branches of United States banks abroad, in the case of the Federal Reserve Board figures.

[17] Data obtained by correspondence and interviews.

The statistical measurement of foreign concentration —studies of the Department of Commerce

The most satisfactory measure of the concentration of short-term foreign funds in the United States as a whole is now available in "The Balance of International Payments of the United States" prepared under the direction of the Bureau of Foreign and Domestic Commerce. These data do not constitute a complete enumeration, but are an adequate and representative sampling of the whole. They do not give the data for New York City alone, but for the United States as a whole. The statistics published are based upon a questionnaire, returns on which were received from 188 leading financial institutions transacting foreign business, including the twelve Federal Reserve banks, all large private

SHORT-TERM CAPITAL MOVEMENTS OF THE AMERICAN MONEY MARKET *

(In millions of dollars)

Item	*Dec. 31, 1929*	*Dec. 31, 1930*	*Dec. 31, 1931*	*Increase or decrease, 1931*
Due from foreigners †				
1. Deposits	210	294	125	− 169
2. Advances and overdrafts . .	205	212	279	+ 67
3. Short-term investments ‡ . .	40	94	57	− 37
4. Other short-term loans . . .	278	323	310	− 13
5. Outstanding liabilities on unmatured bills drawn under credits granted by American banks to foreigners and accepted by American banks	884	879	521	− 358
Total short-term funds due from abroad	1,617	1,802	1,292	− 510
Due to foreigners				
6. Deposits	1,662	1,640	1,022	− 618
7. Advances and overdrafts . .	27	36	33	− 3

* Source of data: Finance and Investment Division of the Bureau of Foreign and Domestic Commerce, Department of Commerce, Washington, D. C., June, 1932, revised data.

† The foreign branch of an American bank is a foreigner; an American branch of a foreign bank is an American.

‡ Including undiscounted American-drawn acceptances held for collection by foreign banks.

SHORT-TERM CAPITAL MOVEMENTS OF THE AMERICAN MONEY MARKET—Continued

Item	*Dec. 31, 1929*	*Dec. 31, 1930*	*Dec. 31, 1931*	*Increase or decrease, 1931*
8. Investments:				
Acceptances	865	702	265	− 437
Treasury bills	62	86	39	− 47
All other §	281	168	51	− 117
9. Undiscounted foreign-drawn acceptances held for collection by American banks . .	105	90	38	− 52
10. Outstanding liabilities on unmatured bills drawn under credits granted by foreign banks to Americans and accepted by foreign banks . .	35	15	14	− 1
Total short-term funds due to foreigners	3,037	2,737	1,462	− 1,275

§ Almost entirely in brokers' loans.

bankers in New York, foreign banking agencies in this country, and the largest investment trusts. The above table is compiled from this publication.

As may be seen from this table, the net outflow of short-term capital from America to abroad during 1930 amounted to $485,-000,000; including the decrease of accounts due to foreigners by $300,000,000 and the increase of accounts due from foreigners by $185,000,000. Similarly, during 1931 the net outflow of short-term capital amounted to $765,000,000. The decrease during 1931 in accounts due to foreigners amounted to $1,275,000,000, but this was offset by a decrease in accounts due from foreigners by $510,000,000.

According to the analysis of the Department of Commerce for about six years prior to 1928 short-term foreign funds in the American money market increased, and this increase of short-term foreign funds in this country has been an important offset to our heavy long-term credits to foreigners, constituting in effect a backwash from these exports of long-term capital. "Of our net short-term indebtedness to foreigners of $1,864,000,000 on January 1, 1928, hardly half could have existed six years earlier."

The increases in foreign short-term funds in this country since 1921 are attributed to "flights of capital" from depreciating currencies, the growth of an American bill market, the internationalizing of the dollar, and the large increase in our international turnover. Central banks have judged this to be the safest gold-standard market in which to keep their foreign exchange holdings. Foreign long-term borrowers from America build up large sums of dollar exchange needed to meet their dividend, sinking-fund, and bond-redemption maturities.[18]

Information given under the title of "due from foreigners" is not of primary interest here, since these data represent "concentration of American short-term funds abroad"; but they serve to emphasize the tremendous relative importance of foreign concentration in this country and reveal the net balance in the concentration of foreign funds in this country. At the end of 1927 the net concentration of foreign short-term funds came to $1,864,-196,000; at the end of 1928 to $1,638,094,000; at the end of 1929 to $1,420,000,000; at the end of 1930 to $935,000,000; but at the end of 1931 the net had declined to only $170,000,000. It must be noted that over half the aggregate of the "due from" banks item in foreign countries is due from branches of American banks abroad.[19]

Of particular interest in connection with the concentration of funds in the New York money market, is the section of the above table on "Foreign funds 'put out' (in the American market)," listed as item 8 in the table. On the following page is a brief summary of the data on foreign concentration derived from these figures.[20]

Comparing the amount of funds put into acceptances with that shown in the table of purchases of bills for foreign correspondents by Federal Reserve banks, it is seen that the Federal Reserve banks apparently purchase about half of the bills procured on behalf of foreigners in this country. At the end of 1927 the volume of bills purchased for foreign correspondents by Federal Reserve

[18] Concerning recent large withdrawals, see Vol. IV, pp. 163–65.

[19] *Member Bank Call Report,* No. 42. *Abstract of Condition of National Banks,* No. 161. Letter from the Federal Reserve Board, July 8, 1929.

[20] Such data are gathered regularly by the Federal Reserve Bank of New York, but are not made public.

banks amounted to $229,000,000, whereas total bills purchased for foreign correspondents by all banks in this country (including the Federal Reserve banks) amounted to about $406,000,000. By the end of 1929 the amount purchased for foreign account by the Federal Reserve banks had increased to $548,000,000, and by all banks in this country to $891,132,000. Increases of foreign funds put into the acceptance market from 1927 to

CONCENTRATION OF SHORT-TERM FOREIGN FUNDS IN THE UNITED STATES

(In millions of dollars)

Year Dec. 31	Total deposits and short-term investments	Deposits	Foreign funds "put out" in the money market			Total foreign funds "put out"
			Acceptances	Brokers' loans	Treasury certificates	
1925 . .	1,394	1,106				288
1926 . .	1,862	1,443				419
1927 . .	2,890	1,938	406	101	444	952
1928 . .	2,644	1,580	565	333	166	1,064
1929 . .	2,870	1,662	865	281	62	1,208
1930 . .	2,596	1,640	702	168	86	956
1931 . .	1,377	1,022	265	51	39	355

1929, and in the brokers' loan market for 1927 to 1928, were accompanied by a decline from 1927 to 1929 from over $444,000,000 to about $62,000,000 in the amount of foreign funds put into treasury certificates. This was due very largely to the extension of tax exemption to acceptances.

Loans to brokers in New York City for foreign account increased from $101,362,000 at the end of 1927 to nearly $333,000,000 at the end of 1928. At the end of 1929 they declined to about $281,000,000. It is suggested that, since these figures are for the end of the year, there may be considerable drawing down of brokers' loans for window-dressing purposes. However, as far as published data reveal, the proportion of foreign funds in the brokers' loan market is not large. It is not large compared to total brokers' loans, constituting about 2 per cent of total brokers' loans in 1927; 5 per cent in 1928 and 6.7 per cent in 1929. The amount of foreign funds in the brokers' loan market is small, too, compared to total foreign funds in this country, constituting 11.5 per cent in 1928, 9.3 per cent in 1929, 6.1 per cent in 1930 and 3.5 per cent in 1931.[21]

Summary

The increase in the concentration of foreign funds in the New York money market during the years 1924–1930 was due mainly to three factors: (1) the increasing volume of international trade financed in the United States; (2) the entrance in a very substantial way of the New York money market into the category of a world money market; and (3) the deposit and use in the open market of foreign central bank funds, particularly in the acceptance market.

Not only is the foreign trade of the United States financed through the New York money market, but to a considerable extent trade between other countries as well is so financed. At the same time there has been an increase in the foreign concentration of funds in New York, as the New York money market has come to be a depositary of short-term funds by foreign central banks which have adopted in part or in whole the principles of the gold exchange standard, as this existed up to the time of the wide-spread abandonment of the gold standard in 1931.

[21] For an account of Canadian funds in the brokers' loan market, see Vol. III, Chap. VI.

CHAPTER XIII

PERIODIC VARIATIONS IN BANKERS' BALANCES AND SOME GENERAL CONCLUSIONS

Seasonal Variation in Bankers' Balances 1900–1916 and 1920–1928 Compared

Up to this point, the material presented on the subject of the concentration of funds in the New York money market has dealt with the magnitude of such concentration, particularly as reflected in bankers' balances. In this chapter the attempt will be made to analyze more closely the nature of the problems involved, such as the periodicity of bankers' balances, and the relationship of bankers' balances to business activity and to bank reserves.

Indexes of seasonal variation have been calculated from the comptroller's call data on the "due to banks" items of national banks from selected cities for the period 1900–1916, in order to compare the results so obtained with the index of seasonal variation obtained by an analysis of the reporting member bank data for 1920–1928. These are shown in Chart 28. It was found that wherever the seasonal variation is well defined for the earlier period it corresponds closely to that for the recent period, not only as to time of variation but also as to relative magnitude of fluctuations. This is especially true in the case of seasonal variations in Richmond and Atlanta as compared with those of Savannah; and in Minneapolis and Dallas for each period. In Boston, New York City, and Philadelphia, where the seasonal variation was not well defined from 1900 to 1916, nor from 1920 to 1928, there is considerable difference in the timing of the seasonal variations. This may be due to fluctuations of sampling, and may indicate that there is nothing but a fortuitous seasonal variation in these cities, or that seasonal influences have changed.

The seasonal variation in New York City bankers' balances

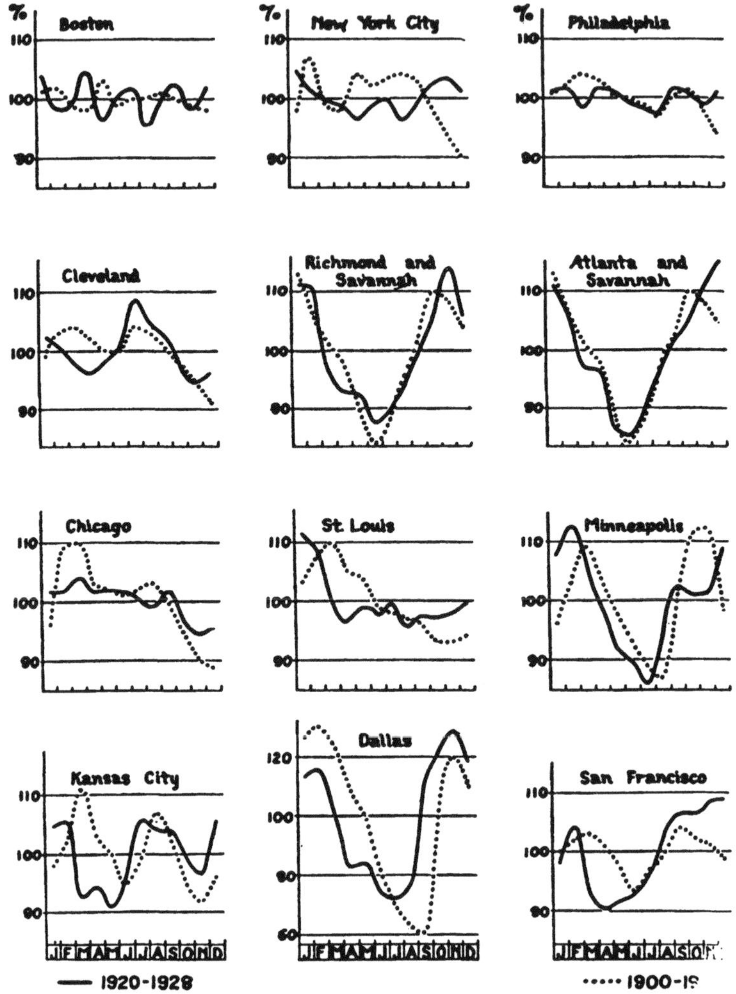

CHART 28. SEASONAL VARIATIONS IN BANKERS' BALANCES: IN NATIONAL BANKS IN SELECTED CITIES, 1900–1916, AND IN REPORTING MEMBER BANKS, 1920–1928.

before the Federal Reserve system was only moderately well defined, as the scatter diagram shown in Chart 29 indicates. In Chicago, on the other hand, the index of seasonal variations is clearly consistent and well defined.[1] To give emphasis to this

[1] The method used for the calculation of these indexes of seasonal variation was to take a five-call moving total of the data published in the *Annual Reports of the*

point, scatter diagrams are shown in Chart 30 illustrating the well defined nature of the seasonal variation in bankers' balances in Dallas for the period 1920–1928 as compared to the poorly defined seasonal variation in New York City bankers' balances.[2]

Seasonal variations in bankers' balances in New York City cover a range of only 3.3 per cent above the average in December to 3.7 per cent below the average, in May, the high and low points respectively. This represents an approximate seasonal net flow of $66,000,000 to New York City in the form of bankers' balances from the low to the high point of the year. Practically the same seasonal relationship in bankers' balances existed before the Federal Reserve system, so far as range of variation is concerned. However, the consistent drawing down of New York City bankers' balances in the fall of the year, which was so clearly evident in the earlier perior, is not evident in the index of seasonal variation in bankers' balances in New York City for the period 1920–1928.

Relationship Between Bankers' Balances and Business Activity

General considerations

In discussing the relationship between bankers' balances and business activity, it is necessary to keep in mind the fact that bankers' balances not only serve to facilitate intercommunity and foreign trade, but that they also serve as "reservoirs" of "surplus bank credit" and of reserves. The theory underlying the normal continuing type of bankers' balances may be stated somewhat as

Comptroller of the Currency, dividing the original call data by this five-call moving total centered at the third call, and expressing the result in a percentage figure. These percentages of the five-call moving total are plotted at a point on the graph corresponding to the actual date of the call. Thus this method does not assume that each call occurred at the same date each year but places the call data at that part of the year to which it properly belongs in the scatter diagram. The median line of calls is then drawn in by inspection, and from points taken from this median line the monthly index of seasonal variation is calculated.

[2] The method used was to divide the raw data by a twelve-months' moving total centered at the seventh month, expressing the result as a per cent, and plotting these percentage results on the graph. The median is then found by count for each month and the index of seasonal variation calculated from that, by expressing the medians as a percentage of their own average.

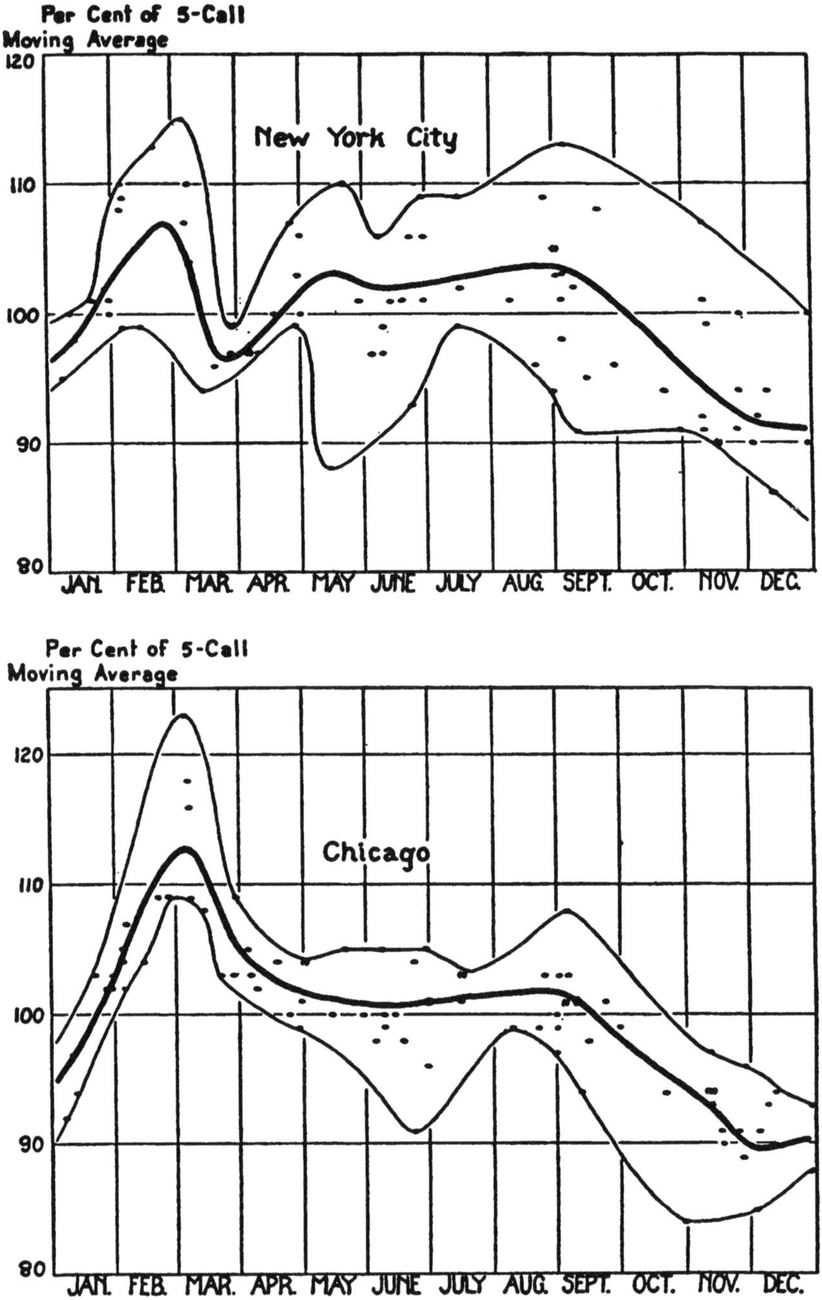

CHART 29. SCATTER DIAGRAMS SHOWING SEASONAL VARIATIONS IN BANKERS' BALANCES IN NEW YORK CITY AND CHICAGO, 1900–1916.

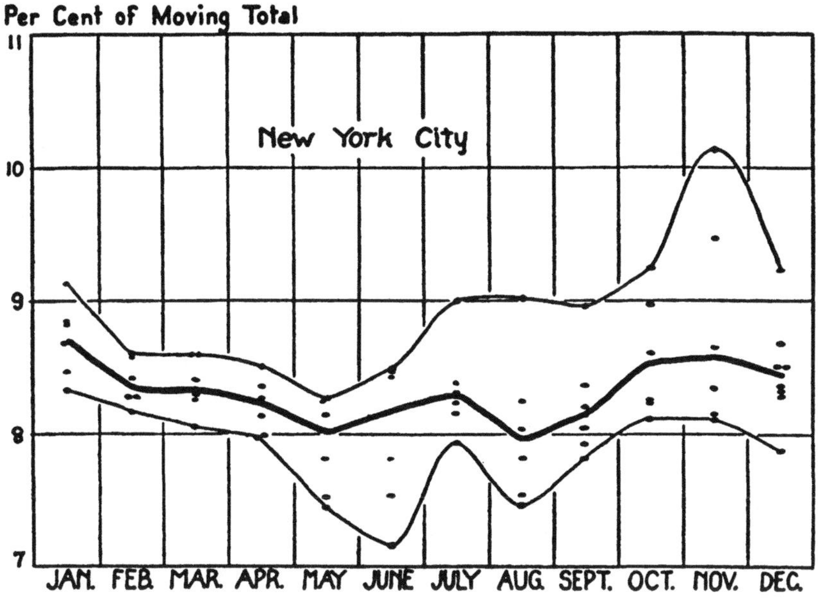

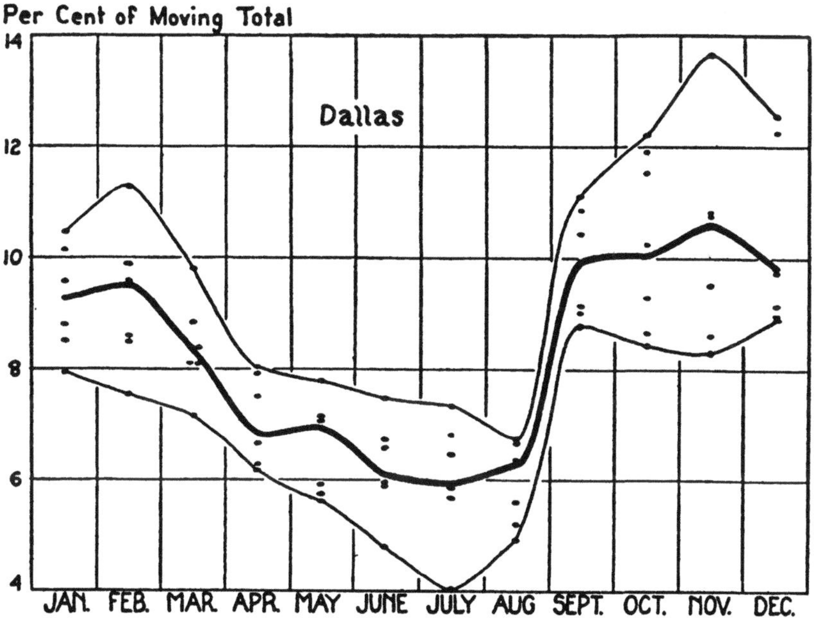

CHART 30. SCATTER DIAGRAMS SHOWING SEASONAL VARIATIONS IN BANKERS' BALANCES IN NEW YORK CITY AND DALLAS, 1920–1928.

follows: As the trade of a community increases over a period of time, the loans and investments and deposits of banks must increase in proportion, or in the absence of such an increase prices must decline. Commercial bank deposits perform the function of a clearing house of equities in the purchasing power of a given community. In a similar way, bankers' deposits very largely serve this purpose between communities. Traders in one community receive claims upon the purchasing power of persons in a distant community in the form of checks and the accumulation of such individual trades between communities results in the creation of debit or credit balances between the banks of the two communities, just as trade within a given community shifts balances between local banks. The balances between banks within a community are ordinarily settled daily through a clearing house, or through some clearing arrangement. Making due allowance for the decline in the proportion of intercommunity clearing performed by bankers' balances, by virtue of the Federal Reserve clearing system the amount of such balances would still tend to reflect fluctuations in intercommunity trade, *i.e.*, trade in commodities, securities and services. So far as commodity trade is concerned, this would consist mostly of wholesale transactions or export trade, although some retail trade would be included, *i.e.*, purchases from mail-order houses. But for the most part it would be expected that bankers' balances of this type would have a positive correlation in seasonal and cyclical movements with wholesale and export trade.

An attempt will be made to discover to what extent this type of relationship between bankers' balances and business activity exists, in so far as seasonal variations are concerned.

Measurement of seasonal variations

Chart 31 presents by Federal Reserve cities the relationship existing between seasonal variations in bankers' balances and business activity. Taking bank debits as a reasonable measure of trade activity,[3] it is to be noted that seasonal variations in bankers'

[3] Ada M. Matthews and A. Ross Eckler's study entitled "Regional Business Conditions: A Study of Bank Debits," *Harvard Review of Economic Statistics*, Aug., 1928, pp. 140–55. Cf. *Federal Reserve Bulletin*, July, 1924, p. 555.

balances correlate positively, not negatively, with the district indexes of business activity. It is also to be noted from the scales

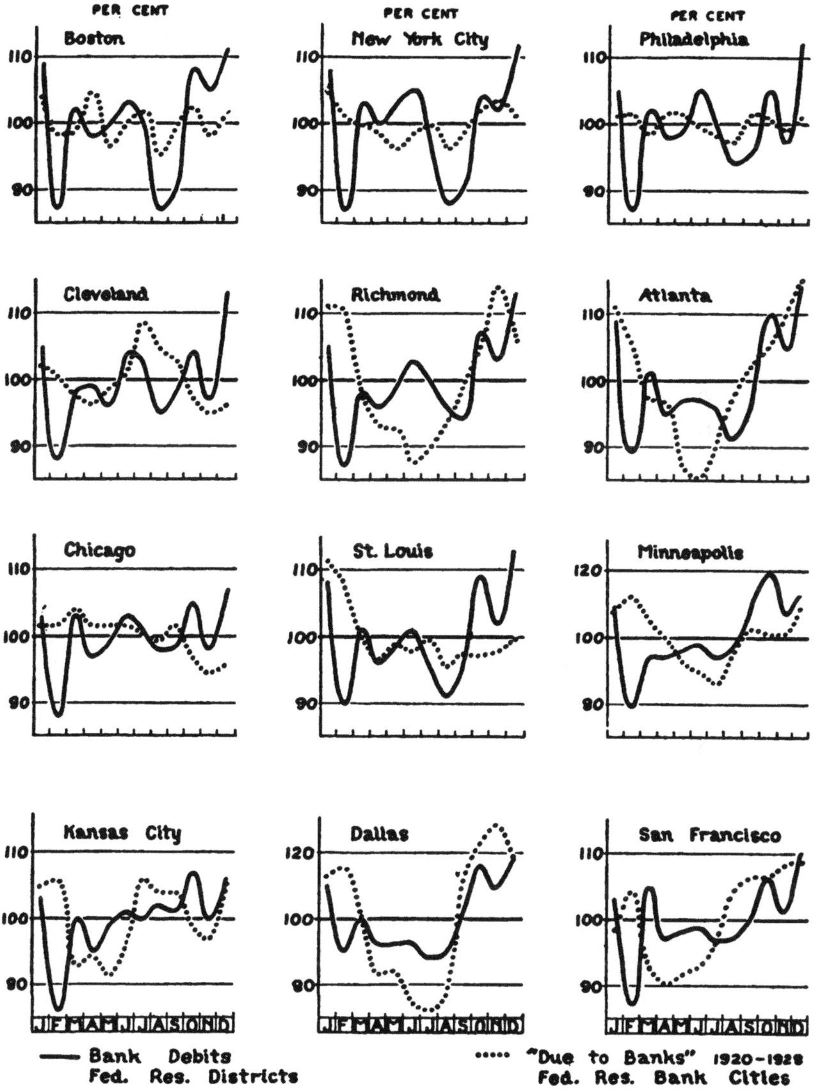

CHART 31. SEASONAL VARIATIONS IN BANKERS' BALANCES AND IN BANK DEBITS BY FEDERAL RESERVE DISTRICTS.

that the range of seasonal variation is slight in Boston, New York City, and Philadelphia; but in Richmond, Atlanta, Minneapolis, and Dallas, the range is relatively wide. In Cleveland, Chicago, St. Louis, Kansas City, and San Francisco, there is a moderately wide range of seasonal variation.

This may be due to the fact that old and well developed communities, with great diversity of interests in industry and commerce, tend to have such a large volume and complexity of trade with other communities, that fluctuations with any one of the communities are insignificant in comparison to the total; or that the seasonal fluctuations tend to be so varied that the whole of that community's trade reflects no seasonal variation owing to the compensating influences of a large number of different seasonally variable trade relationships. Such seems to be the case in the Federal Reserve cities of Boston, New York, and Philadelphia. But in new communities, or in communities which have some predominant specialty, fluctuations in bankers' balances are largely influenced by intercommunity trading in that special product. For example, this is true of the Federal Reserve cities of Richmond, Atlanta, Minneapolis, St. Louis, Kansas City, Dallas, and to some extent, San Francisco, Chicago, and Cleveland.

It seems to be fairly well established, as far as seasonal fluctuations are concerned, that bankers' balances increase with seasonal increases of trade and decrease with seasonal decreases in trade and that wherever the seasonal variations are marked and well defined, as in Richmond and Dallas, bankers' balances are reflective of an increase in credit arising from a larger volume of intercommunity or foreign trade.

However it is apparent that some other influence is present in the case of such centers as New York, Boston, Philadelphia, Cleveland, and Chicago. As stated above, this may be due to the fact that there is a cancellation of seasonal trade influences; but it is probably also due to the fact that in such centers bankers' balances perform other functions, and this is particularly true of New York City.

Bankers' balances in New York City compared to business activity—seasonal fluctuations

The relationship disclosed in the preceding sections between the seasonal variations of bankers' balances and business activity would be presumed to exist only if bankers' balances were used solely for the purpose indicated, namely, the taking care of the

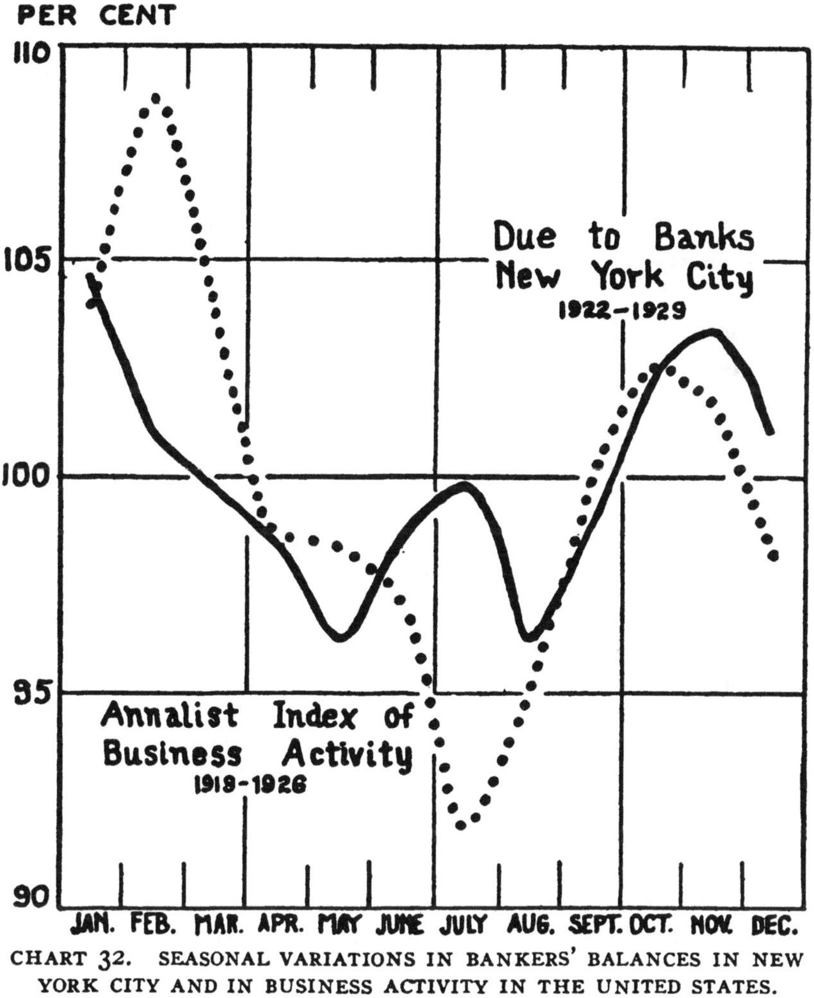

CHART 32. SEASONAL VARIATIONS IN BANKERS' BALANCES IN NEW YORK CITY AND IN BUSINESS ACTIVITY IN THE UNITED STATES.

exchange transactions of ordinary intercommunity and foreign trade. To carry this idea further, Chart 32 is presented to show the relationship between the index of seasonal variation in New York City bankers' balance (1920–1928) and the index of seasonal variation in business activity for the entire country.[4] Comparison between the index of seasonal variation in New York City bankers' balances and the seasonal variation in business activity discloses no precise relationship throughout the whole year. Even so the major seasonal decline in business activity from February to July is paralleled in part by the major seasonal decline in New York City bankers' balances from January to May. The major seasonal rise in general business activity takes place from July to October and this is paralleled in part by the major seasonal upswing in New York City bankers' balances from August to November. Therefore, so far as any relationship is disclosed between the seasonal variation in New York City bankers' balances and business activity, increases of the one seem to go with increases of the other and vice versa.

While it is true that the index of seasonal variation in New York City bankers' balances is not well defined, the relationship shown would seem to indicate that bankers' balances in New York City for the period 1920–1928 did not serve, seasonally at least, as a reservoir for interior "surplus funds" as distinguished from those required in trade financing, although the tendency of bankers' balances in New York City to correlate inversely with business activity was noted in the *Federal Reserve Bulletin.*[5] And again, it appears from the *Annual Report of the Federal Reserve Board* that [6]

> the increasing business activity and credit demands of the country were reflected first in the withdrawal of balances by banks in the interior from their New York correspondents. The amounts due to other banks by reporting member banks in New York City show a downward trend throughout the latter half of the year. It is largely these withdrawals of funds from the large banks in New York City that have caused the recent increased borrowings from the New York reserve bank by these metropolitan banks. This movement of funds from the financial center is partly seasonal in character and is often an early indication of the revival of loan activity in the interior.

[4] This index was computed by taking the medians of the seasonal variations of the separate series entering into *The Annalist* index of business activity.

[5] *Federal Reserve Bulletin,* December, 1924, p. 904.

[6] *Annual Report of the Federal Reserve Board,* 1922, p. 12.

This statement of the Federal Reserve Board is cautious and may not be taken as the expression of a generalization; but attention should be called to the fact that such a decline in bankers' balances may have no relationship whatever to an interior move-

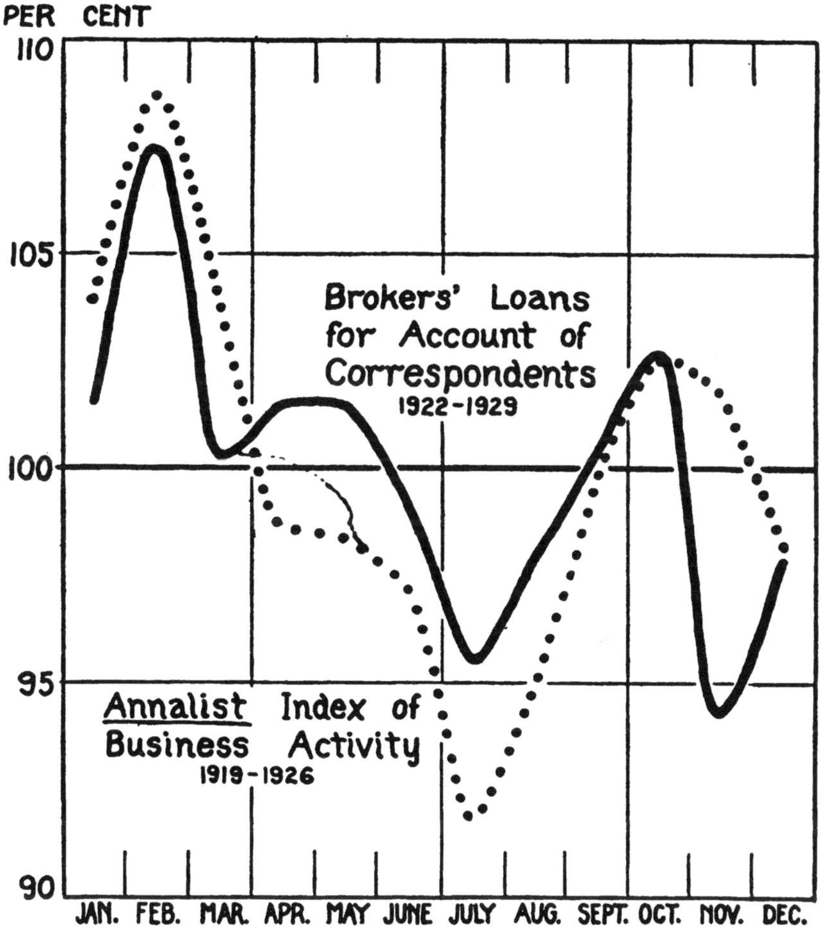

CHART 33. SEASONAL VARIATIONS IN BUSINESS ACTIVITY AND IN BROKERS' LOANS FOR ACCOUNT OF CORRESPONDENTS.

ment of funds, for (1) the decline in bankers' balances may be due to the drawing down of their New York City balances by interior banks and the placing of the funds in the brokers' loan market; and (2) the decline in bankers' balances may be due to a general decline in trade activity, and hence a decline in the exchange need for such balances.[7] Bankers' balances have statistical characteristics so far as seasonal variations are concerned, therefore, which make them a very poor measure of an interior *movement* of funds.

Similarly, the seasonal variation in business activity is compared in Chart 33 to the seasonal variation in brokers' loans for the account of correspondents, 1922–1929. Here again, there appears to be no tendency for the volume of interior funds placed in the New York money market to be in the nature of "surplus" bank credit. The seasonal increases and decreases in both series are similar, indicating that at times of seasonal increases in business activity more, rather than less, interior money is loaned directly in the New York money market in the form of brokers' loans.

Cyclical variations in business activity and New York City bankers' balances compared

No attempt has been made to relate cycles in bankers' balances in other Federal Reserve cities with indexes of business activity in the respective Federal Reserve districts, partly because of the lack of readily available regional indexes of business activity, and also because the subject of particular interest in this study is the relationship of New York City bankers' balances to business activity. In order to test the relationship of bankers' balances in New York City and trade activity, the seasonal variation and trend in New York City "due to banks" were removed from the data and an index of computed "normal" was obtained. This is shown in Chart 34, with the *Annalist Index of Business Activity* from which the influences of seasonal variation and trend have already been removed. With the exception of the years 1920–1921, there is a marked inverse relationship between the two series. Superficially viewed, this seems to substantiate the hypothesis often adduced, that in periods of business recession funds flow to the New York money market in the form of bankers' balances, while in times of increasing business activity bank-

[7] See also Andrew, A, Piatt, "Some Facts and Figures Relating to the Money Trust Inquiry," *Senate Document No. 1003, Sixty-second Congress, Third Session*, p. 12.

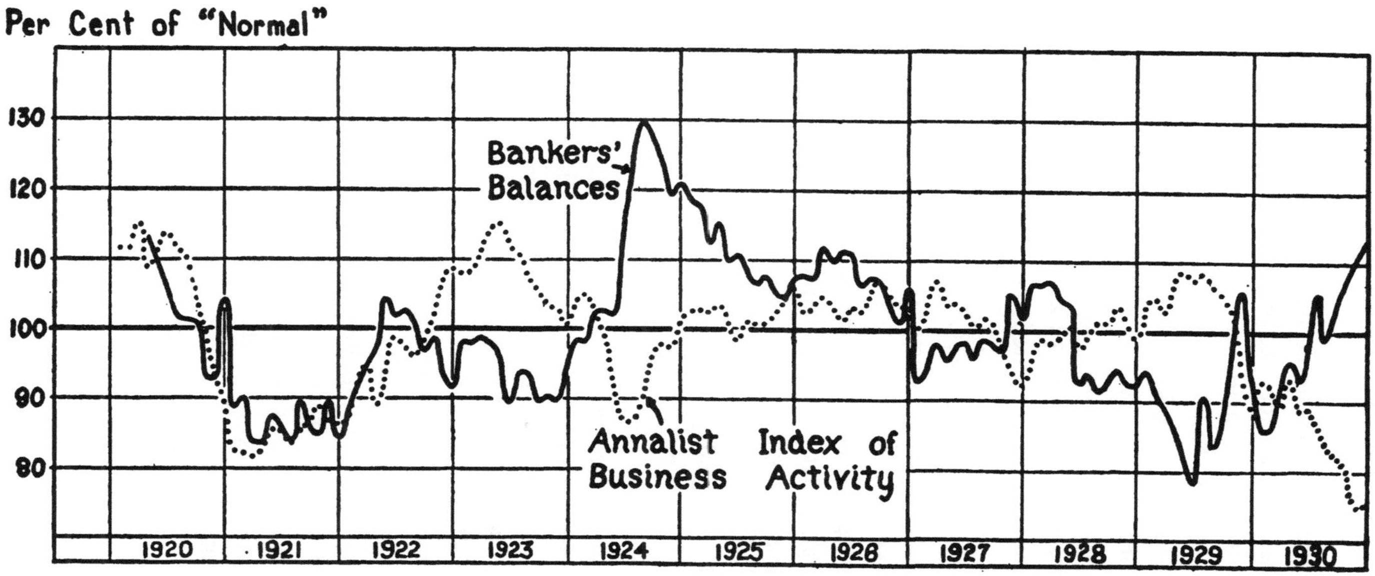

CHART 34. CYCLICAL FLUCTUATIONS IN BANKERS' BALANCES IN NEW YORK CITY AND IN THE BUSINESS ACTIVITY OF THE UNITED STATES.

ers' balances tend to decline. However it cannot be presumed that, because bankers' balances in New York City are declining, funds are necessarily moving to the interior. They may be shifting from bankers' balances to brokers' loans "for account of out-of-town banks."

In order to study the relationship between bankers' balances and brokers' loans for account of out-of-town banks, the series are presented in Chart 35 as a percentage of computed "normal" with the similarly treated data of the call loan rate. In 1920–1921 a positive correlation is disclosed, but from 1922 to date the cyclical fluctuations in the series seem to offer convincing demonstration of a tendency for interior banks to shift their funds from bankers' balances to the brokers' loan market in periods of increasing business activity and vice versa. It seems clear from this graph that cycles in bankers' balances and the call loan rate are inversely correlated. In other words, as the call loan rate rises, bankers' balances tend to decline, the funds being transferred presumably from bankers' balances to call loans and vice versa.[8] This negative relationship between bankers' balances and brokers' loans for account of out-of-town banks is according to expectation, because it is known that shifts of funds are made by interior banks from balances with New York City banks to the brokers' loan market and vice versa, depending largely upon the call loan rate. In 1924, owing to low call loan rates, there was a shift from call loans to bankers' balances, while in 1925 there was an inverse shift. In 1928–1929 there was some shifting from bankers' balances to call loans, although at that time call loans were being held down somewhat by Federal Reserve "moral suasion" policy. In 1930 there was a marked decline in demand in brokers' loans with a resulting great decline in the call loan rate, and New York City bankers' balances rose. It should be pointed out that this relationship also obscures the worth of bankers' balances as a measure of the interior flow of funds, as to cyclical variation, just as was found to be the case in relation to seasonal variations.

[8] Cf. *Annual Report of the Federal Reserve Bank of San Francisco*, 1930, p. 8.

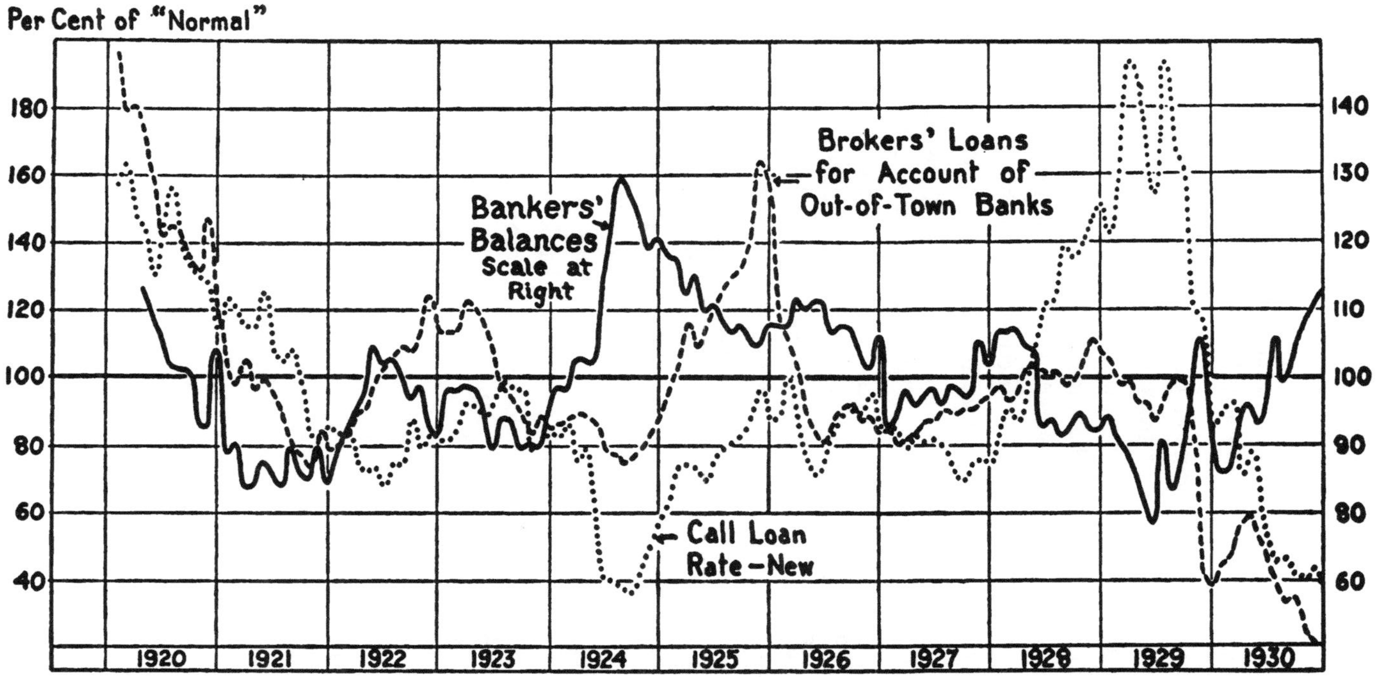

CHART 35. CYCLICAL FLUCTUATIONS IN BANKERS' BALANCES IN NEW YORK CITY, IN LOANS TO BROKERS FOR ACCOUNT OF OUT-OF-TOWN BANKS, AND IN THE CALL LOAN RATE.

Statistical evidence of importance of bankers' balances as reserve deposits for nonmember banks

Before the establishment of the Federal Reserve system, approximately one-half of bankers' balances were constituted of reserve funds,[9] and it is a reasonable estimate that approximately 20 per cent of bankers' balances in New York City at the present time represent the deposited reserves of nonmember banks.[10] Chart 36 depicts cyclical fluctuations in bankers' balances in New York City, compared with these in the reserve deposits with the Federal Reserve banks of the reporting member banks outside of New York City. The chart reflects a considerable degree of correlation in the cyclical fluctuations of these two series. The conclusion seems to be evident that fluctuations in the volume of bankers' balances in New York City are largely influenced by the deposit there of the reserves of nonmember interior banks. The graphic comparison is between bankers' balances and the reserve deposits of member banks, while the inference drawn is with reference to nonmember banks; but it would seem to follow for this reason: The interior nonmember banks keeping reserve deposits in New York City banks would be banks in cities such as the 140 cities from which member banks report under the caption "reporting member banks of leading cities" outside New York City. And it is probable that interior nonmember bank reserves deposited in New York City would tend to have the same type of cyclical fluctuation as the reserve deposits of reporting member banks with their respective Federal Reserve banks.

Furthermore, as Chart 37 on page 279 shows, the seasonal movement in these two series is closely correlated which is further substantiation of our thesis. The general character of the seasonal variation corresponds closely to that of currency demand or retail trade, and not to the agricultural seasonal movement which is apparent, however, in fluctuations in bankers' balances on deposit with Chicago banks.

[9] Watkins, L. L., *Bankers' Balances*, pp. 76–80.

[10] Since about 40 per cent of the banking resources of the country are in nonmember banks. Cf. Tippetts, C. S., *State Banks and the Federal Reserve System*, pp. 148–51.

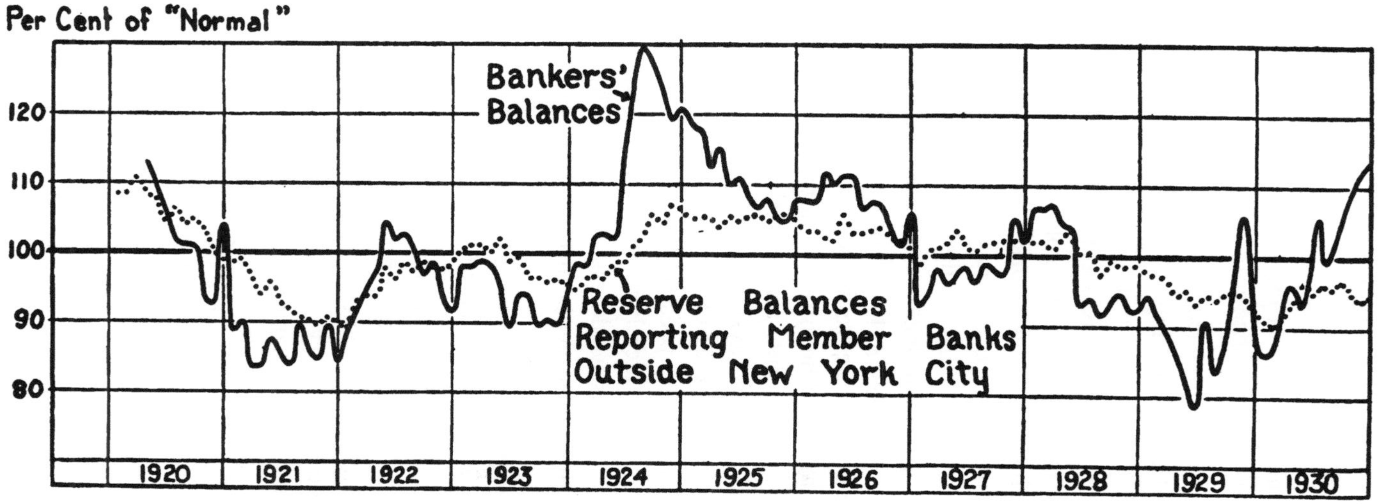

CHART 36. CYCLICAL FLUCTUATIONS IN BANKERS' BALANCES IN NEW YORK CITY AND IN THE RESERVE BALANCES OF REPORTING MEMBER BANKS OUTSIDE NEW YORK CITY.

Inherent weakness in present credit structure due to the correspondent banking system

Under the Federal Reserve system, even more than under the old national banking system, deposits with commercial banks permit a multiple pyramiding of credit. The reserve pyramiding before the Federal Reserve system had as its ultimate reserve the 25 per cent reserves in gold or lawful money (essentially gold) maintained in New York City banks. To the extent that deposits in New York City commercial banks comprise reserves of interior nonmember banks today, the ultimate reserve consists of the 35 per cent legal minimum requirement of gold or lawful money underlying the deposits of New York City banks with the Federal Reserve bank. The reserve deposit of New York banks against the interior nonmember bank's deposited reserves is but 13 per cent, and not the 25 per cent required before the Federal Reserve system.[11]

The existence of extensive pyramiding continues as an essential weakness in the present banking structure, arising in part from the extent to which bankers' balances still serve as reserves. Particularly is this weakness aggravated by the growth of non-liquid loans and investments in the portfolio of the banking system.

Summary of origins of, and reasons for the concentration of, domestic bankers' balances

Ever since New York became a dominant commercial center, interior banks have remitted funds in order to build up or to maintain their balances. As early as the 1830's, as indicated in Volume I, country bank balances had attained appreciable proportions. The demand of interior merchants for New York funds, with which to pay for their purchases of commodities, and the necessity on the part of country banks of providing means for the redemption of their bank notes in an important commer-

[11] The pyramiding possibilities, therefore, of $100 (in gold or reserve bank credit), when a New York City member bank's deposits are counted as reserves for an interior bank, are 100 (100/35 × 100/13 × 100/10), or $21,976 in the case of a reserve city nonmember bank; in the case of a country bank it would be 100 (100/35 × 100/13 × 100/7), or $31,395.

cial center, were among the many reasons for this early practice of keeping bankers' balances in New York City. The balances were not in the nature of merely seasonal surpluses; to maintain

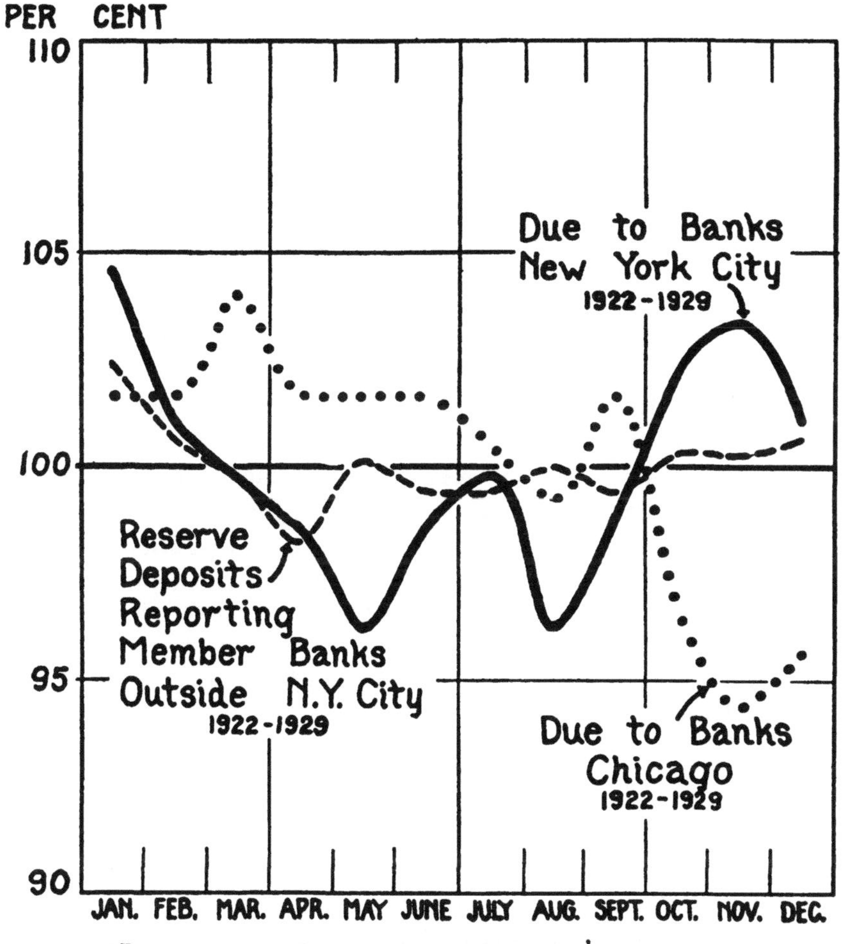

CHART 37. SEASONAL VARIATIONS IN BANKERS' BALANCES IN NEW YORK CITY, IN CHICAGO, AND SEASONAL VARIATIONS IN RESERVE BALANCES OF REPORTING MEMBER BANKS OUTSIDE NEW YORK CITY.

this thesis historically would be to ignore the more permanent elements among the forces that brought funds to New York. The payment of interest on bankers' balances on the part of certain New York City banks had little to do with the aggregate concentration of such funds in the city, though it did determine with which of the banks they would be deposited. Trade currents, financing methods, and the requirements of a basis for intercommunity clearing of checks and bank notes, were among the more basic forces.

The framers of the National Bank Act gave legal recognition to the practice of maintaining balances in New York. The amount of balances allowed to be counted was largely determined by actual practice at the time. A statistical presentation of the practice then is contained in Volume I, which reveals that the pyramiding of reserves, for which the Act has often been blamed, was not its creature but an already existing *status quo* that led to the particular provisions.

During more recent years, and down to the present time, the basic reasons for the concentration of bankers' balances remain fundamentally the same. In summary, balances are maintained that interior banks may sell New York exchange, may meet the demand for foreign exchange, may buy and sell securities, may place funds on the call market, and may be in a position to borrow from their New York correspondents on collateral not acceptable at the Federal Reserve banks.

Failure to realize fully the expected effects of the Federal Reserve system

The fears of the commercial bankers that the Reserve Act would cut into the absolute volume of bankers' deposits in New York City have not been realized.[12] The absolute amount of bankers' balances has increased in the past fifteen years in New York City, although at a low rate per annum on the average; and the relative amount has declined appreciably. This was shown in the charts in the preceding chapters.

In recent years foreign balances have become an increasingly important factor in the New York money market. The reëstablishment of the gold standard in the United States earlier than in

[12] Willis, H. P., and Steiner, W. H., *Federal Reserve Banking Practice.* Willis, H. P., *The Federal Reserve System.* Watkins, L. L., *Bankers' Balances*, pp. 43–63. Conway, Thomas, Jr., and E. M. Patterson, *The Operation of the New Bank Act*, p. 318.

other belligerent nations, following the Armistice, and the predominant position held by the United States in fiancing the world's capital needs, have been responsible for the concentration of foreign short-term funds in New York. On long-term account the United States is a creditor (exclusive of war debts to the United States and also exclusive of investments in foreign missionary and educational institutions) to the extent of over 15,000 millions of dollars, and correlatively has been a heavy debtor on short-term account.[13] The foreign funds in New York have been maintained partly to finance foreign trade and partly to stabilize foreign exchange rates.

The Federal Reserve system and the correspondent bank system

The payment of interest still has little to do, directly at least, with the maintenance of these balances, although the payment of interest in some cases may influence state banks and trust companies to remain outside the Federal Reserve system and in that indirect way make the aggregate of bankers' balances in New York City larger than otherwise would be the case. The effect of the Federal Reserve system has been to reduce the amount of these balances relatively but not absolutely. Such balances must be maintained, since the Reserve banks are unable to supply all the services required by the interior banks. To a certain extent, therefore, it may be said that the correspondent bank system supplements the Federal Reserve system, and strengthens or extends the control of the Federal Reserve system over the credit structure of the country as a whole, for member banks in central and reserve cities largely act as bankers' banks and these banks are peculiarly subject to the credit policies adopted by the system. In a sense the Federal Reserve system has aided the maintenance of the correspondent bank system for, through the use of the Federal Reserve clearing system, the city banks have been able to improve and to diminish the cost of the services they offer correspondent banks in the way of clearances and the collection of items.[14] Interbank borrowing in the correspondent bank system

[13] United States Department of Commerce, *The Balance of International Payments of the United States for 1930*, p. 35.
[14] Cf. Watkins, L. L., *Bankers' Balances*, pp. 151–204.

supplements the bankers' bank functions of the Federal Reserve banks. Before the establishment of the Federal Reserve system, the correspondent bank system existed as an unregulated system of concentration of funds in New York City; under the Federal Reserve system, this concentration continues in somewhat smaller relative, but none the less important, volume.

The making of commercial paper more liquid by the rediscounting privilege has strengthened the credit structure, but it has not removed the fundamental economic causes of concentration in general, as was expected by bank reformers, nor has it specifically reduced the attractiveness of security collateral loans as a form of bank investment. The correspondent bank system tends to imperil further this situation, through its close relationship to the brokers' loan market but, at the same time, the useful functions of the correspondent bank system cannot be denied, particularly as a supplement to the Federal Reserve system in binding together the banks of the United States in a unified system of banking and in performing for country banks essential services to the profitable existence of such banks—services which the Federal Reserve system will not perform. Some have argued that the solution of this problem is that offered by the *Pujo Report,* namely, to "limit the proportion of its resources that may be loaned by any bank on stock-exchange collateral."

The fact of concentration divorced from the problem of concentration by the Federal Reserve system

The fact of the concentration of funds and transactions of the country in the New York money market has not been materially changed since the Federal Reserve Act, but the entire aspect of the situation is different because there is now a measure of centralized control over the large banks which serve as bankers' banks for the interior nonmember banks and for interior member banks when the latter require services not available at their Federal Reserve bank. Owing to more efficient clearings and collection systems for the bulk of such items and to an efficient mobilization of reserves and an efficient device for the movement of funds, the volume of concentration of bankers' balances in the

New York money market is less, relative to total deposits, and less, relative to total volume of transactions, than it was before the establishment of the Federal Reserve system. While other large banking centers have developed as concentration points, serving limited areas, the New York banking group has become even more national and international in scope of service. Such a tendency will no doubt continue in the future, with the country dividing itself into marketing areas along competitive lines and corresponding financial areas, each with its own predominant center; but with New York City as the predominant center for the country as a whole in relationships between (1) more widely separated parts of this country, and even more particularly (2) between all parts of this country and other countries. The rising volume of foreign trade of the United States, the exports of capital, and the increasing volume of the concentration of foreign short-term funds in the New York money market, attest to the importance of this second factor as a cause for the continued concentration of funds and transactions in the New York money market.

As stated in Chapter VIII above, the problem of concentration consisted in the difficulties attendant upon the withdrawal of funds from the New York money market for the periodical requirements of the interior banking structure of the country. In other words, the problem in the past has been to withdraw supposedly highly liquid funds out of the short-term or call money market when needed by the interior, without demoralizing and undermining the credit structure of the entire country. This problem, though existing in a different form, has been divorced from its former relationship with bankers' balances by the fact that seasonal requirements may be met within Federal Reserve districts by use of Federal Reserve bank credit. The result is a better synchronization of credit supply and demand, making it possible for the different seasonal influences in various parts of the country to cancel each other the more easily.

PART FOUR

THE EBB AND FLOW OF MONEY MARKET FUNDS

Chapter XIV

SOME GENERAL CONSIDERATIONS

Relationship between concentration of funds in the New York money market and the ebb and flow of money market funds

The concentration of funds in the New York money market at any given moment may be likened to a balance sheet item, which is related directly to the *movement* of funds, which in turn may be likened to a profit and loss item. The two subjects must be considered together in a study of the money market involving an analysis of different aspects—the balance sheet aspect, and the profit and loss aspect, of money market funds.

It is the purpose of this and the following chapters to discuss the forces that add to or detract from the funds of the money market, to attempt a statistical measurement of the ebb and flow (the movement of funds out of and into the New York money market), and to show in what fashion this statistical measurement is modified by the increments and decrements in those funds which are due to Federal Reserve policy. An attempt will be made to measure statistically the total net movement of funds into and out of the New York money market over a period of years, taking into account (1) the movement between New York and the remainder of the United States, (2) the movement between New York and foreign countries, and (3) increases and decreases of funds in the New York money market due to an expansion or contraction of money in circulation and of Federal Reserve bank credit.

The economic characteristics of the twelve Federal Reserve districts

The forces affecting the movement of funds into and out of the New York money market (geographical movement) may be better understood after a brief survey of the economic characteristics of the twelve Federal Reserve districts. In the table on page 289, certain data pertaining to the economic character of each of the twelve Federal Reserve districts are given, including loans and investments, land area, population and the agricultural and

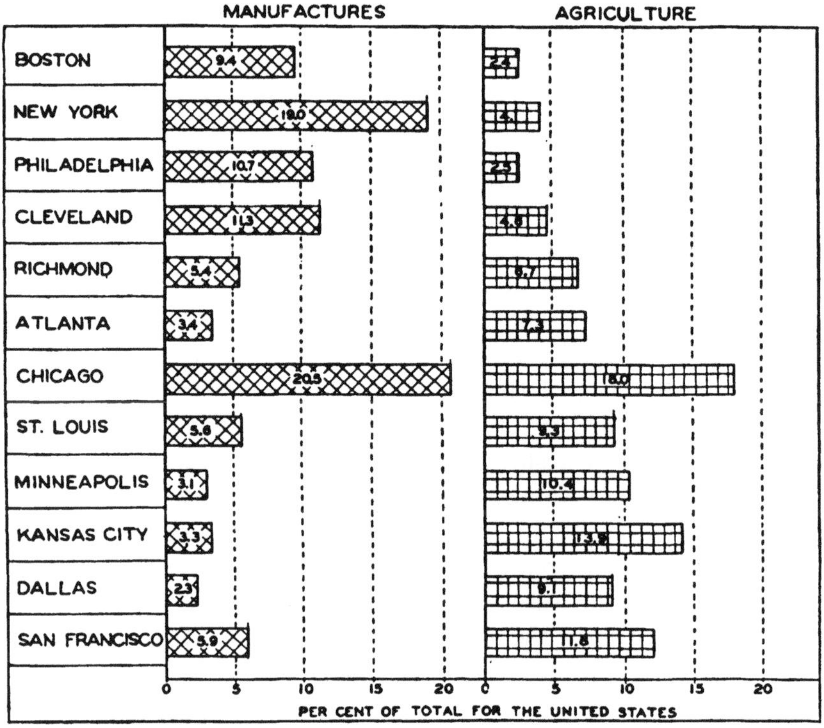

CHART 38. ECONOMIC CHARACTERISTICS OF THE TWELVE FEDERAL RESERVE DISTRICTS.

manufacturing production of each district. These data are also shown in percentage form, and Chart 38 brings out the contrast between the predominantly industrial and the predominantly agricultural districts.

Boston.—Cotton, woolen and worsted goods manufacturing constituted approximately one-fourth of all the manufacturing business of the Boston district, according to the Census of Manufactures of 1927. The total manufacturing products

lines of manufacture, each of which contributed over $3,000,000 to the New England income.

Philadelphia.—The Federal Reserve district of Philadelphia [2] includes the eastern two-thirds of Pennsylvania, the southern half of New Jersey and all of Delaware. The most important products of Pennsylvania are iron and steel, but the bulk of these are manufactured in and around Pittsburgh, which is in the Cleveland district. Other important industries of Pennsylvania include silk manufactures (in which it is the leading state), petroleum refining, cane sugar refining, the manufacturing of cigars and cigarettes, clothing, electrical machinery, knit goods, leather tanning, pottery, chemicals and other diversified products. It is a district of miscellaneous industries and the total value of manufactured products of the district for 1927 was probably about $7,000,000,000. In agriculture this district is unimportant.

Cleveland.—The Federal Reserve district of Cleveland includes the state of Ohio, the western third of Pennsylvania, a small part of West Virginia and the eastern third of Kentucky. It thus includes within its borders the great eastern steel center, including the steel industries of Pittsburgh. Steel industry ranks first in this district, with motors second and rubber tires and tubes third. In agriculture Ohio is important in the production of dairy cattle, beet sugar and winter wheat. Kentucky is important in the production of tobacco.

Richmond.—The Federal Reserve district of Richmond includes the states of Maryland, most of West Virginia, Virginia, North Carolina and South Carolina. In Maryland the principal manufactures are in connection with canning and preserving, glass, iron and steel, petroleum refining, tin ware, slaughtering and meat packing, fertilizers, and shirts. In Virginia, North Carolina and South Carolina the principal manufacturing industry is textiles (cotton), constituting roughly a third of the value of all products. Others of importance are cigars and cigarettes, lumber and timber products, knitted goods, furniture and ferti-

[2] The Federal Reserve district of New York is considered later. See *infra.* pp. 295–308.

lizers. In agriculture Maryland is important in the production of strawberries and apples. Virginia is important in the production of apples and tobacco. North Carolina ranks high in the production of cotton and tobacco. West Virginia is important in the production of coal. The total manufactures of this district in 1927 probably amounted to about $3,500,000,000. The district is in a transitional stage from one of agricultural importance to one of industrial importance, but is still relatively more important as an agricultural district. Its agricultural products constituted in 1928 roughly 6.7 per cent of the total for the United States, while its industry comprised about 5.4 per cent. This district produced in 1929 nearly one-half of the tobacco crop of the United States. Of 14,828,000 bales of cotton produced in the United States in 1929, the Richmond district accounted for 1,625,000 bales.[3]

Atlanta.—The Federal Reserve district of Atlanta includes the states of Georgia, Florida, Alabama, the eastern two-thirds of Tennessee, the southern half of Mississippi, and the southern part of Louisiana. The important manufactures located in this district are iron and steel in Alabama, cotton goods in Alabama and Georgia, the petroleum refining of Louisiana, and the grain-mill and food products of Tennessee. The total production of industry in the Atlanta district in 1927 was about $2,225,000,000. While the industries are diversified, outstanding among them are (1) the lumber industry; (2) the iron and steel industry; (3) tobacco, cotton goods and petroleum. The total value of agricultural cash crops of this district is estimated to have been $737,000,000 in 1928, a little more than 7.3 per cent of that for the entire United States. While this district is of prime importance both in tobacco and cotton production, it is relatively more important in cotton production. In this it is second only to the Dallas district.

Chicago.—The Federal Reserve district of Chicago includes the states of Michigan and Iowa, the southern half of Wisconsin, the northern half of Illinois and the northern two-thirds of Indiana. The industrial output of 1927 included iron and steel

[3] *Federal Reserve Bulletin,* Jan., 1931, p. 25.

products, motor production, slaughtering, butter, and cheese, as the principal items, aggregating over $12,000,000,000, or approximately one-fifth of the total for the United States. In agriculture the Chicago district is the principal producer of corn, producing 879,380 bushels in 1929 out of a total of 2,614,132 bushels produced in the United States.

St. Louis.—The Federal Reserve district of St. Louis includes Arkansas, most of Missouri, the southern half of Illinois, the western two-thirds of Kentucky, the southern third of Indiana, the western third of Tennessee and the northern half of Mississippi. The industrial output includes lumber products, cottonseed oil, petroleum, slaughtering, boots and shoes and other commodities of less importance, aggregating in 1927 about $3,662,000,000. The total value of the crops of the district is estimated to have been $933,000,000 in 1928. The district is of outstanding importance in the production of cotton and tobacco, ranking as second largest producer of tobacco and the third largest of cotton. It is the third largest corn-producing Federal Reserve district.[4]

Minneapolis.—The Minneapolis district includes the states of Minnesota, North Dakota, South Dakota, most of Montana and the northern part of Wisconsin. The industrial output of the district in 1927 amounted to approximately $2,000,000,000, comprising flour, feed and grain products, slaughtering, butter, cheese, and lumber products. Outstanding industries are flour, feed and grain products, and butter, cheese and other dairy products. The total value of farm products of this district is estimated to have been $1,044,000,000 in 1928, or over one-tenth of the value of all farm products of the United States. This district produces more than two-thirds of the spring wheat grown in the United States. In 1929 the Minneapolis district produced 177,398,000 bushels of spring wheat as contrasted with the yield of the entire United States of 232,963,000 bushels. The district is the second largest producer of oats, and it is the leading Federal Reserve district in the production of potatoes, accounting for nearly one-seventh of the potatoes grown in the United States.

[4] *Federal Reserve Bulletin,* Jan., 1929, p. 26; Jan., 1931, p. 25.

Kansas City.—The Kansas City district includes the states of Nebraska, Kansas, Wyoming, Colorado, the northern two-fifths of New Mexico, most of Oklahoma and a small strip of Missouri. In 1927 the total industrial output of the district amounted to about $2,170,000,000, the principal industries being slaughtering, petroleum and grain-mill products. This district is far more important, relatively speaking, agriculturally than industrially. The total value of agricultural cash crops of the district in 1928 is estimated to have been $1,393,000,000 or about one-seventh of that of the United States. It is the most important winter wheat-producing district, producing in 1929 over two-fifths of the winter wheat grown in this country.

Dallas.—The Dallas district includes the State of Texas, the southern three-fifths of New Mexico, a small part of Oklahoma, and the northern part of Louisiana. The industrial output of the district in 1927 aggregated about $1,513,000,000, of which probably 40 per cent consisted of petroleum and its products, the rest consisting of cottonseed oil and slaughtering products. The value of the agricultural cash crops in 1928 aggregated approximately $915,000,000. This district is the outstanding cotton producing Federal Reserve district, accounting for over 40 per cent of the crop. While Texas is still of great importance in the production of beef cattle, the far greater relative importance of cotton and petroleum production in this district now overshadows the cattle industry. Supremacy in livestock production is now in the Kansas City district.

San Francisco.—The San Francisco district includes the states of California, Oregon, Washington, Idaho, Utah, Nevada and most of Arizona. The industrial output of the district in 1927 is estimated to have been about $3,851,000,000, of which the most important items were lumber and its products, petroleum refining, and smelting, including copper and lead. The total value of agricultural crops is estimated at $,1,183,000,000 for the year 1928. The San Francisco district is the third most important wheat-producing Federal Reserve district, and it is the largest producer of fruits and nuts.

Forces affecting the movement of funds into and out of the New York money market

The forces which affect the movement of funds in and out of the New York money market may be thought of as comprising New York's balance of payments with the rest of the country and the rest of the world. According to such analogy, the various forces which bring about an ebb and flow of money market funds may be summarized as follows: ebb and flow of funds caused by (1) trade in commodities; (2) trade in securities; (3) trade in the equities of enterprise and claims against enterprise and governments; (4) distribution of earnings of enterprise in the form of interest and dividends; (5) government fiscal operations; (6) financial operations maintaining market equilibrium; (7) miscellaneous items.

Ebb and flow of funds of the New York money market resulting from trade in commodities

New York City is the clearing center for the settlement of commercial transactions between other parts of the United States and foreign countries, as well as between New York City and foreign countries. The total imports of merchandise into the United States amounted in 1929 to $4,400,000,000 and in 1930 to $3,061,000,000; while total exports of merchandise from the United States amounted in 1929 to $5,241,000,000 and in 1930 to $3,843,000,000.[5] In addition, the other items which are considered as "commodity" trade included in 1930 silver imports of $43,000,000; silver exports to $54,000,000; bunker coal and oil sales to foreign vessels $44,000,000; bunker coal and oil sales to our own vessels in foreign ports $10,000,000; sales of vessels to United States from foreigners $3,000,000; and sales of vessels to foreigners $3,000,000. In the course of this movement of merchandise into the United States from foreign countries, there

[5] All data concerning the international balance of payments of the United States have been taken from "The Balance of International Payments of the United States in 1929 and 1930," *Bureau of Foreign and Domestic Commerce,* Washington, D. C.

is necessarily set into motion a return flow of funds in payment. One might visualize pipe lines extending to all parts of the United States and converging in New York City, where they again diverge and spread out to carry the flow of funds to the original sellers of the foreign goods. Thus imports of merchandise are the first factor to cause a flow of funds to the New York money market and, in turn, from the New York money market. Similarly in the case of the exports of commodities from persons and firms over the United States to foreign countries, there is necessarily set into motion a return movement of funds in payment for those goods, and a system of pipe lines again converging in New York may be visualized; and these diverge from New York City to the various parts of the interior of this country where the original seller of the exports is located. Where these pipe lines converge in New York City there is a "reservoir of funds"—the pipe lines carrying funds out of the country flow into the same reservoir as those which carry funds into the country—and this reservoir is the foreign exchange market.

In addition the relationship between New York and the rest of the United States in commodity trade brings about a movement of funds into and out of the New York money market. The New York Federal Reserve district, containing as it does approximately 13.1 per cent of the entire population of the United States in less than 2 per cent of the total area, is perhaps the greatest market in the world for finished goods and food products. Many of the manufactured products consumed are made and sold within the district, but many of these and most of the food products are purchased from without the New York district. The total value of the manufactured products of the United States in 1927 amounted to approximately $62,700,000,000, while the total value of manufactured products of the New York district amounted in the same year to approximately $12,388,000,000.[6]

In contrast with this large proportion of the manufactures of

[6] Estimated from data in "Statistics for Industries, States and Cities," *Census of Manufactures, 1927*. So far as the analysis in the present chapter is concerned, it is believed that the 1929–1930 Federal statistics will show practically the same results. These later figures were not available when this study was made.

the United States attributable to the New York district, it produced in 1929 less than 1 per cent of the corn yield of the United States, a little over 2 per cent of the yield of oats, less than one-tenth of 1 per cent of the yield of spring wheat, less than 7 per cent of the hay, and only a little over 8 per cent of the total yield of white potatoes of the United States.[7] The value of live stock in New York and New Jersey (part of course in Philadelphia district) combined in 1925 amounted to about $195,000,000, compared to a total for the United States of $4,858,389,000; but the value of dairy products of these two states in 1924 amounted to over 10 per cent of the value of dairy products of the United States. In 1924 the value of all crops of New York and New Jersey amounted to about $205,000,000, compared to a total of $7,473,000,000 for the United States.[8] Only in the case of dairy products, of most vegetables and fruits (with the exception of citrus fruits), does this area produce in proportion to population. It is obvious therefore that the difference between population and food production constitutes the first fundamental basis for trade in commodities between the New York district and the rest of the country.[9] New York buys agricultural products and sells services and manufactured goods. Also New York buys building materials largely from outside the Federal Reserve district. There are many manufactured products which, owing to a geographical division of labor, New York does not produce in great quantity—for instance, the textile industry in New England and the South, the automobile industry of Cleveland and Detroit, the iron and steel industries of Pennsylvania, Ohio, Illinois and Alabama, the pottery industries of southern New Jersey and Pennsylvania, West Virginia, Ohio and Illinois, all find their principal markets centered around New York. Some of the heavy industries formerly located close to New York have migrated to less expensive sites, but still have their principal market

[7] From data in *The Federal Reserve Bulletin,* Dec., 1928, p. 846; Jan., 1931, p. 25.

[8] *Census of Agriculture,* 1925.

[9] In 1926, of a total of 899,431 car-lot shipments of sixteen fruits and vegetables, 125,253 were unloaded in New York. *Crops and Markets,* June, 1927, p. 221, United States Department of Agriculture.

in New York City.[10] This centralized market in New York City for many manufactured products exists not only because of the large consumer market but since, as a derivative of that, buyers for consumer markets in all parts of country make their inquiries to a very large extent through dealers and brokers in New York City.

Ebb and flow of funds due to trade in services

In the same manner, a flow of funds is set into motion where the object traded is a service rather than a commodity. During 1930 services bought and sold in foreign trade included such items as unrecorded parcel-post shipments estimated at $20,000,000 paid and $20,000,000 received; repairs and tonnage dues paid by foreigners to Americans, $46,000,000, and paid by Americans to foreigners $31,000,000; freight payments by foreigners to Americans $155,000,000, and freight payments by Americans to foreigners, $251,000,000; insurance transactions paid by foreigners to Americans, $70,000,000, and insurance transactions paid by Americans to foreigners $70,000,000; advertising paid by foreigners to Americans $4,000,000, and advertising abroad, paid by Americans to foreigners, $45,000,000; and cablegrams, radiograms and telephone services paid by foreigners to Americans, $21,000,000, and paid by Americans to foreigners, $15,000,000.

No estimates exist of the volume of the trade in services between New York City and the rest of the country, but it is certain that the amounts would be large, particularly in connection with the services of insurance companies and of the other financial institutions of the New York money market, such as investment banks in connection with underwriting operations, trust companies for personal and corporate trusts, and brokerage fees arising from security trading. The fees earned by New York City banks during 1929 for investing in the brokers' loan market for out-of-town banks and for the "others" aggregated in the neighborhood of $75,000,000. The head offices of most large cor-

[10] *Regional Plan of New York and Its Environs,* especially Vol. IA, "The Tobacco Industries," p. 49; "The Wood Industries," p. 51; "The Chemical Industries," pp. 48–49; "The Printing Industry," and "The Metal Industry," pp. 17–37; Vol. VI, pp. 189–90; Vol. IB, "Food Manufacturing Industries," pp. 44–47.

porations are in New York City, and there also is the center of credit intelligence, both business and financial. The payments by national corporations, not only for the services of financial institutions, but for the use of space in New York City, must be a very substantial sum. In 1929 income from services rendered by the New York City banks and trust companies in stock transfers and corporate trust deeds must have aggregated between \$100,000,000 and \$200,000,000; and fees for participation in underwriting schemes is, of course, a large but incalculable amount.

Ebb and flow of funds due to trade in the equities of enterprise and claims on enterprise and governments

A flow of funds into and out of the New York money market is brought about similarly by reason of the fact that it is the center for trading in securities for the United States, both of domestic and foreign issue. It is the center for trading in the ownership of important American enterprises, and indeed of world enterprise to a certain degree. On the New York Stock Exchange the ownership of enterprise is bought and sold in shares, passing from the hands of buyers in one state to sellers in other states or even in foreign countries. There is a constant flow of funds into and out of the money market to take care of these transactions. Similarly claims against enterprises or governments in the form of bonds are traded in on the New York money market for buyers and sellers all over the world. Credit is obtained from, or extended to, other parts of the world through the New York money market—investment of new capital by Americans abroad flows out, and investment of new capital by foreigners in this country flows in, through the New York money market.

In the case of foreign securities, the importance of the flow of funds through the New York money market may be visualized by quoting the Department of Commerce figures for the balance of payments of the United States for 1929 and 1930. New foreign securities publicly offered here amounted at par in 1928 to \$1,484,000,000; in 1929 to \$696,000,000, and in 1930 to \$1,082,-

000,000; new direct investments abroad were made by Americans aggregating in 1928, $378,000,000; in 1929, $335,000,000 and in 1930, $253,000,000; and foreign stocks and bonds were bought from foreigners in small lots aggregating in 1928, $556,-000,000; in 1929, $578,000,000 and in 1930, $360,000,000; redemption and sinking fund payments to foreigners amounted in 1928 to $70,000,000; in 1929 to $77,000,000 and in 1930 to $77,000,000; and American stocks and bonds bought back from foreigners amounted in 1928 to $1,015,000,000; in 1929 to $1,-078,000,000 and in 1930 to $833,000,000. This caused a flow of funds from all parts of this country (wherever the final purchasers were located) into New York and then a flow of the funds out of New York to the foreign sellers of the securities. On the other hand a tremendous return flow of invested funds took place. American stocks and bonds sold to foreigners aggregated $1,503,000,000 in 1928, $1,585,000,000 in 1929 and $941,000,000 in 1930; new direct investments by foreigners in this country amounted to $70,000,000 in 1928, $31,000,000 in 1929, and $19,000,000 in 1930; foreign stocks and bonds resold by owners in this country to foreigners abroad amounted to $451,000,000 in 1928, $449,000,000 in 1929, and $806,000,000 in 1930; resales to foreigners of direct investments amounted to $50,-000,000 in 1928, $58,000,000 in 1929, and $51,000,000 in 1930; and bond redemption and sinking fund payments received from foreigners amounted to $361,000,000 in 1928, $276,000,000 in 1929, and $250,000,000 in 1930. These caused a flow of funds from foreigners to the New York money market and thence a flow of funds out of New York to the original sellers of the securities wherever located in the United States.

In the case of domestic trade in securities, there are no available published data, but in a previous chapter it was estimated that during 1928 there was a total trade in old issues amounting to close to $190,000,000,000, of this amount $2,940,000,000 being in bonds and $186,000,000,000 in stocks. In this connection it should be noted that most of the trading in bonds is on an "over the counter" basis, and much is handled through the bond departments of banks and trust companies and other financial institutions. Some considerable portion of this trading would merely be between two parties located in the New York market, and in that case there would be no flow of funds into and out of the money market; but to the extent that one or both of the traders (*i. e.*, the original buyer or the original seller, not the brokers) are located outside of the New York money market, a flow of funds into and out of New York is set in motion.[11]

Ebb and flow of funds due to the fact that New York is the center for the distribution of the earnings of enterprises and for payment of interest claims

The paying agencies of most large American corporations and of foreign governments borrowing from this country are located in New York City, this being an important part of the corporate trust and agency services performed by the highly organized New York City trust departments of banks and trust companies. When interest on bonds is due, or dividends are to be paid, there is a flow of funds to New York to build up balances for these payments, and when payments are actually made there is a flow of funds out of New York to all parts of the country, wherever the recipients of the payments are located. Americans received in interest and dividends on forign investments $817,000,000 in 1928, $876,000,000 in 1929, and $826,000,000 in 1930; while payments to foreigners on their investments in this country aggregated $252,000,000 in 1928, $270,000,000 in 1929, and $237,000,000 in 1930. Domestic industrial, railroad and traction company company dividends in 1929 amounted to between 2¾ and 3 billions of dollars.[12]

Ebb and flow of funds due to miscellaneous items

A number of miscellaneous items of trade bring about in the aggregate a large movement of funds which it is difficult to classify under the above categories. During 1928 tourist ex-

[11] Dr. W. R. Burgess, from a position of close vantage of money market forces, has reached the tentative conclusion that New York gains on investment and loses on commercial transactions. Logically this would be so, as it is the center for investment in new enterprise and expansion of old, the funds thus collected being used 'for commercial purposes" as they flow out of New York.

[12] *Babson's Desk Chart.*

penditures by Americans in Canada, Mexico and abroad amounted to $804,000,000, in 1929 to $868,000,000, and in 1930 to $811,-000,000; while tourist expenditures by foreigners in this country amounted to $163,000,000 in 1928, $183,000,000 in 1929, and $171,000,000 in 1930; in 1930 immigrant remittances from this country to foreigners amounted to $199,000,000, and remittances by Americans abroad to persons in this country to $33,000,000; missionary and charitable contributions abroad by Americans amounted in 1930 to $49,000,000; imports of Canadian electric power amounted to $4,000,000 in 1930; foreign subscriptions to the American press amounted to $5,000,000 and American subscriptions to the foreign press amounted to $3,000,000; moving picture royalties paid by Americans amounted to $6,000,000, paid to Americans by foreigners to $50,000,000; and patents, copyright sales and royalties amounted to about $15,000,000 each way.

Miscellaneous items of a similar nature can be readily visualized as between the New York money market and the rest of the country, but no figures or estimates are available of such domestic transactions.

Ebb and flow of funds due to government operations

In the case of foreign relations, there is a large movement of funds through the New York money market in connection with foreign government operations. First of all there are the war debt receipts, which in 1928 amounted to $210,000,000, in 1929 to $212,000,000, and in 1930 to $241,000,000, these including war debt receipts on account of interest and principal. This causes a flow of funds into the New York money market from abroad, whence it is dispersed in accordance with treasury operations. Other United States government receipts from abroad amounted to $53,000,000 in 1928, $60,000,000 in 1929, and $46,-000,000 in 1930; while United States government payments abroad amounted to $113,000,000 in 1928, $157,000,000 in 1929, and $127,000,000 in 1930.

In connection with domestic operations of the United States government, there are the tax receipts, interest payments, disbursements, treasury sales and redemptions of short-term certificates, and treasury redemptions of long-term government bonds. During the fiscal year 1929 the total ordinary receipts of the treasury department amounted to $4,033,200,000, and during 1930 to $4,177,900,000. The receipts from individual or personal income taxes amounted to $1,019,000,000 in 1929, and to $1,060,900,000 in 1930. Of the internal revenue receipts in 1930 of $3,040,145,733, there was collected in the state of New York $928,955,021, while over $123,948,441 was collected in the state of New Jersey, the bulk of whose population is in the New York district. Thus more than 30 per cent of the national revenue was collected in the New York district and, as collected, represented funds drawn out of the New York money market. In addition, the treasury sold during the fiscal year of 1930, $3,201,-562,000 of certificates of indebtedness, which sum likewise represents funds withdrawn from the money market. On the other hand the treasury made large disbursements: in 1930 expenditures chargeable against ordinary receipts, $3,994,000,000; $3,578,967,700 in certificates of indebtedness were redeemed; $830,000,000 in Liberty Loan bonds and long-term government debt including treasury notes was redeemed; and $658,602,155 was paid out in interest.[13] Normally the operations of the United States treasury counterbalance withdrawals from (government receipts) and additions to (government expenditures) the funds of the money market. To the extent that the treasury department accumulates balances larger than needed in the New York money market and balances in other parts of the country are drawn down for government expenditures, it is necessary for the treasury to transfer funds out of New York to these other parts of the country. Conversely, when the treasury needs funds to meet expenditures, interest payments or redemption operations in New York, the funds are transferred to New York from other parts of the country. The latter tends to be the case more often than the former, *i. e.*, the bulk of treasury transfers are to New York from other parts of the country. The treasury operations thus cause an ebb and flow of funds of the money market.

[13] *Annual Report of the United States Treasury*, 1930, pp. 3, 637, 690, 1025.

Ebb and flow of funds due to the financial operations tending to maintain money market equilibrium and stability

The above forces which cause an ebb and flow of funds of the New York money market would tend, in the long run, to balance each other, just as in the long run there is a true balance of international payments; but during intervals of more or less duration of time there is a tendency for the forces causing an ebb of funds from the New York money market to overbalance the forces causing a flow of funds into the New York money market. To meet this situation, the natural forces of competition, as well as deliberate policies on the part of the central banks of the world, have created a highly flexible force which acts as an "evener" or equilibrating force in the ebb and flow of funds. The natural forces of competition operate to this end through the interest rate if funds tend to ebb from the New York money market more rapidly than they flow into it, rates tend to rise, and as the interest rates rise, interior banks find it profitable to transfer funds to New York to take advantage of the higher rates. Of similar equilibrating nature are the operations of foreign central banks in the New York money market through the Federal Reserve bank or commercial banks as agents, described in a previous chapter. Foreign shipments and receipts of gold and currency also serve as eveners on certain occasions.[14] Among domestic financial relations of this sort are bankers' balances in New York City, brokers' loans, loans by New York City banks to interior correspondents, and sales of commercial paper and acceptances. The competitive capitalistic financial operations do not always properly perform the function of stabilizer in the money market, and at times even serve to augment instability. Such was the case in some of the financial panics in the history of the United States and this was also evident in the stock-market boom of 1928–1929, with the accompanying inflation in the brokers' loan market. In normal times, however, even brokers' loans to a certain extent perform the evener function

[14] Cf. *Federal Reserve Bulletin*, June, 1927, p. 393, on the effect of foreign central bank dollar balances in New York banks.

for commercial banks throughout the country and for the New York money market. When competitive capitalistic financial operations fail in this function, the Federal Reserve system is theoretically supposed to furnish the needed stabilizing influence.

Effects of foreign and domestic movements of money market funds contrasted

The prominent position of the City of New York as a center of commerce, trade, industry and finance gives rise then to a constant demand for and supply of New York funds in all parts of the United States and of the world. New York City, with its financial institutions, stands as a financial intermediary between various parts of the United States, and between all parts of the United States and abroad.[15]

A domestic demand for New York dollars will ordinarily augment the funds in the money market, though this is not necessarily the case with a foreign demand. The domestic demand for and purchase of New York dollars, expressing itself through changes in the ownership of the gold settlement fund and through an increase in the reserve account of member banks in New York, will lead to an increase in the volume of funds in the market. For example, assuming that the "A" corporation of St. Louis wishes to increase its account with a New York national bank by one million dollars, it would make its wishes known to its St. Louis bank, say the St. Louis National Bank, which would charge the deposit account of the corporation. This bank would then request the Federal Reserve Bank of St. Louis to charge its reserve account and to wire the Federal Reserve Bank of New York that one million dollars are to be credited to the New York National Bank's reserve deposit for the account of the "A" corporation. The bookkeeping results of the transaction so far may be summarized as follows:

(1) The deposit account of the "A" corporation with the St. Louis National Bank is reduced by $1,000,000.

(2) The reserve account of the St. Louis National Bank with its Reserve bank is reduced to $1,000,000. Incidentally this

[15] Cf. Chap. VIII, *supra*, pp. 165–81.

might force the St. Louis National Bank to borrow from the Reserve Bank in order to bring its reserve up to the legal minimum.

(3) The account of the New York National Bank with the Federal Reserve Bank of New York is increased $1,000,000. If this addition were to bring its account above the legal minimum, the excess would be available for lending wherever a demand for credit might exist; or the excess might be used to liquidate some of the bank's borrowings from the Reserve Bank.

(4) The account of the "A" corporation with the New York National Bank is increased by $1,000,000.

(5) Against this increase in deposit liabilities of $1,000,000 on its books, the New York National Bank needs a reserve deposit increase with the Federal Reserve Bank of New York of only $130,000; so that the net increase in its reserve deposit comes to $870,000. Therefore, as indicated in (3) above, it can use a part of this transfer of Federal funds either for further expansion of credit, or to pay off some of its existing indebtedness to the Reserve Bank or it may sell it in the Federal funds market.

The evening of the day that the transaction had taken place, the New York Reserve Bank would gain and the St. Louis Reserve Bank would lose $1,000,000 in the gold settlement fund. The fact that a demand for New York dollars expresses itself through changes of ownership in the gold settlement fund, without involving the shipment of currency, has had two important results. First, it has led to an elimination of those domestic rates of exchange that were quoted daily prior to the establishment of the fund as between New York City and the other leading commercial centers. Secondly, a domestic demand for New York dollars will actually increase the funds in the money market unless the interior banks should meet the demand for New York dollars by drawing on their bank balances in New York, or unless the interior banks make the transfer to New York through the correspondent bank system rather than through the Federal Reserve system, or unless there are counteractive forces at work, e. g., if the New York member bank elects to pay off indebtedness at the Reserve Bank in preference to expanding on the larger reserves created by the transfer of Federal funds.

Contrary to the domestic situation, a foreign demand for and purchase of New York dollars will not add to the funds of the money market, unless it should take the form of or result in:

(1) Shipments of gold or of American currency to New York;

(2) A release of gold earmarked at the Federal Reserve Bank of New York for the account of some foreign correspondent;

(3) An increase in the volume of gold earmarked abroad for the account of the New York Reserve Bank;

(4) A decline in the deposit accounts of foreign banks with the Federal Reserve Bank of New York.

The last case requires further elaboration: Let us assume that the Bank of England has an account with the Federal Reserve Bank of New York, against which it is selling dollar exchange to British commercial banks desirous of putting funds on the brokers' loan market. This operation would augment the funds of the money market through releasing Federal Reserve credit and would have an effect identical with an equivalent amount of open-market purchases. The released Reserve bank credit would go to increase the reserve account of some member bank. The situation would be quite different if the Bank of England were selling cable transfers or drafts on a commercial bank in New York. This operation would increase the reserve account of some bank, but at the expense of the bank on which the cable transfers or drafts were being sold, so that the total volume of reserve funds would remain unchanged.

A foreign demand for and purchase of New York dollars without expressing itself in one of the four ways described above, normally would not affect the funds of the market. During 1928 the New York papers referred to the heavy buying of dollars in London, stimulated by the differential in interest rates, as an inflow of foreign funds with the implication that the total volume of loanable funds was increased thereby. Actually the demand for dollars, leading at times to a decline in sterling exchange rates to the gold export point, meant simply a transfer in ownership of dollar balances. Those owning dollars arising from commerce, the sale of securities, etc., were able to dispose of them on a rising market so that the net result of the operations was simply to effect a transfer of title. It is true that the sale of dollar balances might have led to a transfer of credit as within the United States from the commercial to the speculative or from the investment to the speculative markets, but it did not lead to any net increase either in the volume of loanable funds in the aggregate or of the cash basis.

Summary

In this chapter the general nature of the ebb and flow of funds of the New York money market has been related to the economic characteristics of the various Federal Reserve districts. It was pointed out that differences in economic comparative advantages inherent in the nature of various parts of the country lead to trade in commodities, services, and securities. An earlier chapter brought out the fact that these trading relationships center very largely in the New York money market, in so far as the financing of such intersectional trade is concerned. The forces affecting the movement of funds through the New York money market are summarized in New York's balance of payments with the rest of the country and in the balance of payments between this and foreign countries.

In addition to the flow of funds due to trading in commodities and securities, there is the flow of funds resulting from payment for services rendered by New York City financial institutions, and the flow of funds through the New York money market due to the financial operations of the United States government.

Finally it was noted that, from the point of view of the money market, domestic transfers of funds to New York are far more important than a similar movement of foreign funds. A domestic transfer of funds through the gold settlement fund is in the form of Federal funds, while foreign transfers usually take the form of changes of ownership of bank deposits, with no resulting addition to the cash basis of the money market. The conditions under which foreign transfers of funds affect the cash basis of the money market were summarized.

Chapter XV

STATISTICAL MEASUREMENT OF THE FLOW OF FUNDS—ESTIMATION AND ANALYSIS

An estimate of the total flow of funds through the New York money market

With full appreciation of the hazards involved, owing to lack of sufficient data, an attempt will be made to estimate the total flow of funds through the New York money market. While this procedure cannot consist in a precise presentation of facts, it will serve at least to help visualize the magnitude of the ebb and flow.

The estimate will be divided into two parts: the first based upon the balance of international payments, upon the assumption that all these payments pass through the New York money market; and the second based upon the ebb and flow of funds as between New York and the rest of the United States, the purely domestic ebb and flow of funds. An important statistical defect in the method used is that duplications are involved, in that much of the domestic flow of funds between New York and the rest of the country arises from foreign trade, but this difficulty is unavoidable. A minor defect is the assumption that all items entering into the balance of international payments pass through the New York money market, though this probably very closely reflects the truth.[1]

An estimate of the flow of funds through the New York money market due to international economic relations is given in the table on page 310.

There are no data upon which to base a similar analysis of the movement of funds between New York and the rest of this coun-

[1] Andrew, A. Piatt, *Financial Diagrams,* Sixty-first Congress, Second Session, Senate Doc. 509, Plate 18, National Monetary Commission. Also see Young, Allyn A., *An Analysis of Bank Statistics for the United States.*

try, arising from purely domestic transactions. Data are lacking of the trade in commodities and services between New York and the rest of the country. The total volume of security trading for 1929 was estimated in the preceding section on the con-

ESTIMATE OF FLOW OF FUNDS THROUGH THE NEW YORK MONEY MARKET DUE TO INTERNATIONAL ECONOMIC RELATIONSHIPS

DURING THE YEAR 1929 *

Cause of ebb and flow of funds	*Flow of funds to New York from the interior and ebb of funds from New York to foreigners*	*Flow of funds to New York from foreigners and ebb of funds from New York to the interior*
I Trade in commodities	$4,756,000,000	$5,490,000,000
II Trade in services (including short-term interest and commissions)	452,000,000	450,000,000
III Trade in securities	2,791,000,000	2,405,000,000
IV Distribution of dividends and interest from New York . .	270,000,000	876,000,000
V Miscellaneous items	1,163,000,000	294,000,000
VI Government operations . . .	157,000,000	272,000,000
VII Financial operations—equilibrating forces	1,849,000,000 †	3,332,000,000
TOTALS	11,438,000,000	13,119,000,000

* Based upon *The Balance of International Payments of the United States in 1929*, Department of Commerce.

† These include pure cash items and short-term capital obligations. These items are not strictly comparable to the others in the table, as the short-term capital obligations are taken as the balance of short-term obligations outstanding as of December 31, 1929, instead of the flow of short-term funds during the year. For this reason, the two sides do not balance. The total flow of short-term funds is not available. The flow of short-term funds to New York from abroad does not flow from New York to the interior of the United States directly, but is added in the first instance to the funds of the New York money market. Cf. *The Balance of International Payments of the United States in 1929*, pp. 56–58.

centration of funds, but an incalculable portion of this total represents transactions between speculators and investors located in New York City, and that portion would not cause a movement of funds between New York and the rest of the country. On the financial side, the total dividend and interest payments by American enterprise during 1929 amounted to $7,122,000,000;

and during 1930, to $8,347,200,000.[2] Miscellaneous items, such as tourists' expenditures, freight receipts, etc., are not calculable as between New York and the rest of the country, although casual observation would indicate a very large volume of flow of funds arising from these sources. Treasury operations, causing an ebb and flow of funds in the New York money market during 1928, aggregated $4,235,000,000;[3] in 1929, $3,393,000,000; and in 1930, $4,399,000,000. The financial operations of banks, including the volume of funds flowing to New York in the form of bankers' balances or funds to be invested in the short-term money markets and the countermovement of funds back to the interior is unobtainable, the net result alone being reflected in figures giving the volume of bankers' balances and volume of brokers' loans, commercial paper, acceptances outstanding, etc.

A rough estimate of the total domestic flow of funds due to all causes during 1928, 1929 and 1930 may be made by studying the total of all operations of the Federal Reserve Bank of New York for these years. For the year 1928 these transactions aggregated $209,532,000,000; for 1929, $261,860,000,000; and for 1930, $235,897,100,000. They may be classified somewhat as presented in the table on page 312.

This assumes that the entire movement of funds between New York and the rest of the country passes through the New York Federal Reserve Bank, by reason of the operations of the gold settlement fund and the Federal Reserve clearing system. This assumption probably underestimates the actual ebb and flow. This would seem to be the case, judging from total clearings of the New York Clearing House, which for the year 1928 amounted to $391,727,000,000; for 1929, to $477,242,000,000; and for 1930, to $347,109,000,000.[4] A large part of this total, of course, would consist of local settlements within the New York area.

[2] Standard Statistics, *Statistical Bulletin*, "Base Book Issue, 1930–1931," p. 48; June, 1931, p. 15.

[3] This figure includes United States government coupons paid and United States security issues, redemptions and exchanges; but does not include the treasury transfers of funds between the New York district and other districts. *Annual Report of the Federal Reserve Board*, 1928, p. 157; 1929, p. 145; 1930, p. 153.

[4] *The Commercial and Financial Chronicle*, Jan. 5, 1929, p. 73; Jan. 10, 1931, p. 260.

In the second place, the inadequacy of Federal Reserve bank operations in indicating the total ebb and flow of funds between the New York money market and the rest of the country would be inferred from the facts disclosed in the chapter on the correspondent bank system. A large volume of funds are handled through the correspondent bank system without affecting Federal

ESTIMATED DOMESTIC EBB AND FLOW OF FUNDS OF THE NEW YORK MONEY MARKET AS REFLECTED IN FEDERAL RESERVE BANK OPERATIONS *

Ebb and flow of funds due to:	*Total amount of ebb and flow of funds*		
	1928	*1929*	*1930*
(1) Trade in commodities, services, securities and miscellaneous items	$172,446,000,000 †	$225,889,000,000 †	$217,310,500,000
(2) Treasury operations	5,260,000,000 †	4,263,000,000 †	5,637,600,000
(3) Equilibrating forces—Federal Reserve bank credit and currency flow	31,826,000,000	31,708,000,000	12,949,000,000

* *Annual Report of the Federal Reserve Board* for 1928, p. 157; 1929, p. 145; 1930, p. 153.

† Of the $67,426,000,000 "transfers of funds" in 1929, it is estimated that $870,000,000 were government transfers. See "inter-reserve bank transfers" of table 75, *Annual Report of the Federal Reserve Board*, 1929, p. 147. Of the $55,470,000,000 "transferred funds" in 1928, it is estimated that $1,025,000,000 were government transfers. See "inter-reserve bank transfers" of table 79, *Annual Report of the Federal Reserve Board*, 1928, p. 159; 1930, pp. 153, 155.

Reserve operations. For example, a bank in Chicago receives in the course of ordinary business a check for $25,000 drawn on a New York City bank. If the check were cleared through the Federal Reserve clearing system, it would enter into the total of the operations of the Federal Reserve Bank of New York. However, if the Chicago bank desires to build up its balance with its New York City correspondent by that amount (or by an amount consisting of that check plus a number of others) the Chicago bank will save time and interest by merely sending the check direct to its New York correspondent for credit to its account. In such case the check or checks would never go through the Federal

Reserve clearing system and would not enter into the total operations of the Federal Reserve Bank of New York. An incalculable but large amount of the domestic movement of funds to and from the New York money market takes place in this way. Furthermore a large corporation which carries balances with both a New York City bank and a Chicago bank may require funds in New York to take care of dividend or interest payments or sinking fund operations. The transfer could take place by correspondence, wire or telephone between the two institutions, if correspondent banks; and such transfers would not enter into the total of operations of the Federal Reserve clearing system.

It may be concluded that the significance of the estimates in the above tables, then, lies simply in their indication of the size of the ebb and flow of funds of the New York money market through the course of a year; and that the actual total amounts are considerably larger than the data presented. A further significant fact is the revelation that the total ebb and flow of funds of the New York money market due to domestic economic relationships is vastly greater than the ebb and flow of funds due to foreign trade relationships. The total ebb and flow of funds of the New York market due to foreign trade relationships during 1929 amounted to approximately $24,000,000,000, whereas the ebb and flow of funds due to domestic economic relationships in that year amounted to at least ten times as much, or $262,000,000,000. This is about the ratio of the domestic to the foreign trade of the United States.

Total ebb and flow of funds of the New York money market distinguished from net ebb and flow

Complete statistics concerning the total ebb and flow of funds of the New York money market are unobtainable, largely by reason of lack of data relating to domestic trade in commodities, services, securities, and miscellaneous items. The mechanism for the accomplishment of such movements is not under control, statistically speaking, and all facts are not included in the published data. It was possible simply to give some impression of the vast quantity of such movements in the aggregate.

Measurement, however, of the *net* ebb and flow of funds is possible, though of great complexity. The total movement of funds, whatever it may be, results, in a certain *net* movement of reserve funds between the New York district and each of the other eleven Federal Reserve districts of the country, and this net movement of Reserve funds is reflected in gold settlement fund operations. For brief periods of time, the ebb and flow of funds through the correspondent banking system might give rise to a small percentage of error in such *net* ebb and flow, and the required net flow of Reserve funds from New York to a given district might for a time be suspended by an expansion of Reserve bank credit in the latter district; but, on the whole and over longer periods, the net ebb and flow of funds would be accurately and ultimately reflected in gold settlement fund data.

Net movement and gold reserves

The net movement of funds through the gold settlement fund results in a change of ownership of actual gold reserves. While total daily settlements and interdistrict transfers through the gold settlement fund represent the movement hither and yon of commercial investment or speculative credit, the net result of these transfers and settlements is a transfer of gold reserves. This situation is explained by the fact that the balance of any Federal Reserve bank in the fund is counted as part of its gold reserves. The fund serves the triple rôle of (1) a clearing fund of bank credit; (2) a clearing fund of Reserve bank credit (where and when inter-Federal Reserve bank rediscounting takes place, and when other Federal Reserve banks remit to New York for open-market purchases of securities and bills); and (3) a clearing fund for gold reserves.

The reserves of the respective Federal Reserve banks are increased or decreased by the amount of the net increase or net decrease in ownership in their gold settlement fund accounts. The balance of each Federal Reserve bank is *in gold,* and this results from the *total* debits and credits. A study of the *net* movement involves, therefore, a study of specie reserves and Reserve bank credit, in contrast with the preceding series of chapters on the concentration of funds of the money market, which dealt with the superstructure of bank credit.

The net ebb and flow is in the nature of an equilibrating movement akin to the movement of gold in international trade, and it is through the mechanism of the gold settlement fund that the gold reserves of the country are distributed among the twelve Federal Reserve districts in accordance with the economic relationships of various parts of the country, just as gold is distributed in international trade among gold standard nations.[5] The net movement of funds through the gold settlement fund also serves to distribute throughout the country the gold which flows into this country because of international trade relationships; and conversely, through the gold settlement fund, gold is gathered in the New York money market at such times as it is needed for export, due to foreign economic relationships.

Inasmuch as the net movement of funds through the gold settlement fund results from the total ebb and flow of funds between Federal Reserve districts, it is probable that certain conclusions concerning the total ebb and flow of funds may be drawn from an analysis of the net movement.

Gold reserves mobilized in Federal Reserve banks

Nearly all of the gold of the country, outside of that with the Treasury Department, is held under the control of the Federal Reserve banks. There is a relatively small amount in the hands of the general public, and some in the vaults of member and nonmember banks. The amount in circulation, however, is negligible. For this reason, changes in the gold reserves of the different Federal Reserve banks result from: (1) imports, exports, and earmarking operations; (2) inter-Reserve-bank transfers; (3) transfers from or to the United States government. The third includes the gold produced domestically.

Foreign gold movements

The New York money market is the center for the collection and distribution of gold movements due to imports and ex-

[5] Cf. *Annual Report of the Federal Reserve Bank of Boston*, 1927, p. 9.

ports. When foreign gold bullion or gold coin is imported into the New York customs district it may go, as indicated in a previous chapter, to the Federal Reserve bank or to the assay office.[6] In the latter case the assay office issues to the consignee a gold bullion check in return for the gold, which then becomes the property of the United States treasury. The gold bullion check, which is a treasury check, would be cashed by the consignee and eventually would be paid by the Federal Reserve Bank of New York. The Federal Reserve Bank of New York might do one of two things with this treasury check: either present it to the United States treasury for credit on gold settlement fund account; or present the gold bullion check to the assay office and receive gold certificates. Since 1920, it has normally been the case that the Federal Reserve bank simply has debited the treasury account by the amount of the check and the treasury has deposited gold in the gold settlement fund to credit of the Federal Reserve Bank of New York. In either case, the gold reserves of the Federal Reserve Bank of New York are increased, and the gold may then be distributed throughout the entire country by means of debits and credits through the gold settlement fund, in accordance with existing trade and other economic relationships. Conversely, an export movement of gold initially affects the gold reserves of the New York Federal Reserve Bank. The reserves of the Federal Reserve Bank of New York might then be replenished by movement from the interior in accordance with trade or other relationships which, in the aggregate, induced the gold exports.

Domestic gold movements

Trade between districts, as well as foreign trade, induces interdistrict changes in gold reserves. For example, assuming that someone in New York buys merchandise from Chicago and remits by check drawn on his bank in New York, the Chicago bank may deposit the check with the Federal Reserve Bank of Chicago for collection, which will send the check by mail to the New York Federal Reserve Bank. The New York Federal Reserve Bank,

[6] See Chap. IV.

in receiving the check, enters it on its books in the account "Due to the Federal Reserve Bank of Chicago" and immediately sends it through the New York clearing house, so that the canceled check finally reaches the drawee bank in New York. At the end of the day, the New York Federal Reserve Bank sends a wire to Washington giving the total amount "Due to the Federal Reserve Bank of Chicago" which is the sum of all similar items plus the results of transfers by wire. In Washington, the New York Federal Reserve Bank receives a debit in the gold settlement fund and the Chicago Federal Reserve Bank receives a credit. Thus through this particular transaction and millions like it, funds move to and from the New York and Chicago districts, and in the same way to other districts throughout the country. Transfers of funds by wire, between the New York money market and various parts of the country, arising from commercial transactions, security transactions and other causes, produce the same movement of funds through the gold settlement fund, excepting, of course, in those cases in which checks are settled or transfers by wire made through the correspondent bank system instead of through the Federal Reserve system.

Transfers of funds between the Federal Reserve banks themselves, as distinguished from the movement of funds between member banks and customers of member banks, take place when one Federal Reserve bank "rediscounts" with another Federal Reserve bank, or when any of the other eleven Federal Reserve banks remit funds to the Federal Reserve Bank of New York to be invested in the acceptance market or in government securities, or when withdrawals are made from such investments. The primary purpose of inter-Federal Reserve bank rediscounting is to "move" reserves from a district with a strong reserve ratio to a district with a low reserve ratio. The bank accommodated receives the proceeds as a credit in the gold settlement fund. For example, the gold reserves of the Federal Reserve banks on October 29, 1920, were affected by the fact that there was a total of interdistrict accommodation amounting to $260,440,000 distributed as indicated in the table on the following page.

[7] *Federal Reserve Bulletin,* April, 1922, p. 402.

Since March 22, 1922, there has been no interdistrict accommodation. In the course of the liquidation of the inter-Federal Reserve bank rediscounts, reserve funds flowed back again to the districts from which they were originally derived, or were counterbalanced by commercial or other transactions between districts.

A similar movement in gold reserves takes place when interior Federal Reserve banks participate in the open-market operations of the Federal Reserve Bank of New York according to allotments arranged by the Open Market Policy Conference. The paper is actually held in the vaults of the Federal Reserve Bank of New York as custodian, but the amount of participation in open-market purchases is debited to the gold settlement fund account of the respective Federal Reserve banks.

VOLUME OF INTER-FEDERAL RESERVE BANK REDISCOUNTING, OCTOBER 29, 1920

Grantor banks		*Grantee banks*	
Boston	$84,396,000	New York	$61,362,000
Philadelphia	37,201,000	Richmond	14,275,000
Cleveland	138,750,000	Atlanta	36,122,000
San Francisco	93,000	Chicago	7,050,000
		St. Louis	37,305,000
		Minneapolis	26,603,000
		Kansas City	44,895,000
		Dallas	32,828,000
TOTAL	$260,440,000		$260,440,000

The interdistrict movement of Federal Reserve notes is another cause for changes in ownership of gold reserves. When the notes of a Reserve bank find their way into circulation in districts other than those in which they were issued, they are returned to the issuing Federal Reserve bank, resulting in a gold movement from the Reserve banks issuing the notes to the Federal Reserve bank in which these "foreign" notes were deposited. If it were true that the volume of foreign Federal Reserve notes deposited with a Federal Reserve bank equaled the volume of its notes deposited with other Federal Reserve banks, there would be no net gold movement caused by these note transactions. But the amounts do not balance and frequently vary greatly. A large number of people, for instance, come to New York for business or pleasure and spend money there in the form of the Federal Reserve notes of their home districts. These notes are deposited by hotel or storekeepers with their banks which, in turn, deposit them with the New York Federal Reserve Bank. In this way the New York Federal Reserve Bank always has a large volume of the Federal Reserve notes of other Reserve banks in its possession. These foreign Federal Reserve notes are redeemed either by presentation to the issuing Federal Reserve bank or to the treasury department.[8] The fact that the New York Federal Reserve Bank continuously returns more notes to other districts than it receives from them is reflected in the statistical data presented later.[9]

In addition to the movement of gold reserves due to the above causes, the fiscal operations of the United States government result in interdistrict gold movements.[10] The principal fiscal operations of the United States government resulting in such movements are the issue and redemption of treasury certificates and notes, the payment of interest on outstanding obligations, and the collection of income and corporation taxes. In New York, redemptions far exceed allotments.[11] Certificates issued in other districts drift to New York, the financial center of the country, and are redeemed there at maturity. None of the other districts show a material excess of redemptions over allotments, and most of them reflect larger allotments than redemptions. Tax collections in New York fall relatively far below the proportion of certificate allotments and redemptions. For example, nearly 50 per cent of the tax certificates maturing in 1921 were redeemed in New York, while only about 27 per cent of income and excess profits taxes were collected in that district. On the other hand, in the Boston, Richmond, and Atlanta districts tax receipts constitute materially larger proportions of the total for the country than do certificate redemptions. In other districts the differences are less pronounced. As a consequence, on income-tax

[8] For further discussion, see Chap. V.

[9] See also *Federal Reserve Bulletin*, April, 1922, pp. 402–3.

[10] *Ibid.* Cf. *Annual Report of the Federal Reserve Bank of New York, 1927*, pp. 18–19.

[11] *Federal Reserve Bulletin*, April, 1922, pp. 400–3.

dates and for a few days following, the government lacks sufficient funds in New York to pay for maturing certificates and consequently issues to the Federal Reserve Bank of New York special certificates to cover the deficit. As income-tax funds are collected, the government transfers funds to New York, to be used to retire the special certificates. Transfers of gold to New York on government account from nearly every part of the country during the ten days following income-tax dates are exceedingly heavy. On the other hand, it is in New York that most of the payments on government contracts are made. Funds thus made available are distributed when corporations send out dividend and interest checks or supply working funds for plants and branches in other parts of the country. Statistically this is reflected in the fact that New York gains through transfers and loses through clearings. This situation is reflected in the statistical presentation which follows in subsequent chapters.[12]

In general, about two-thirds of every issue of United States government securities, especially the short-term issues, find their way to New York by maturity date. This results not only from the large proportion of banking assets in New York, but also from the custodian services performed by New York banks for correspondent banks and individuals all over the country. By way of contrast, the proportion of Federal income taxes collected in the New York district is about one-third of the total for the country. Consequently treasury disbursements to redeem maturing obligations regularly exceed receipts within the New York Federal Reserve district at tax periods, and the balance is met, as indicated above, by transferring a part of the proceeds of tax collections in other districts to New York. To replace the funds transferred by the treasury, commercial banks in other districts withdraw funds from New York after each tax period, which funds represent a consummation of trading or funding transactions —either receipts from a part of the retirement of matured government securities, securities sold, interest and dividends received or proceeds from merchandise exported and financed through New York.

[12] Cf. *Annual Report of the Federal Reserve Bank of New York*, 1927, pp. 18–19.

Summary

The attempt was first made in this chapter to present an approximation of the total ebb and flow of funds of the money market. The data available permitted only a general approximation to the total ebb and flow. In consequence the possibility of obtaining a relatively exact picture of the *net* ebb and flow of funds was advanced as an alternative method of analysis. Some of the complexities of available statistical material on the net movement of New York money market funds were discussed, in relation to the fundamental economic characteristics of such series.

This led to a discussion of the nature of gold movements between the New York money market and abroad, as well as to a discussion of the nature of the movement of funds in domestic exchange through the gold settlement fund. It was pointed out that the New York money market is the center for the distribution of gold throughout the United States, and a point of assembly for gold exports. The nature of the items entering into domestic transfers of funds through the gold settlement fund was discussed and it was indicated that statistical measurements of net movements, as this chapter envisages, are related to movements of reserve funds, or the cash basis, in contrast to the discussion in the preceding part of this book, on the concentration of money-market funds which had to do with the superstructure of bank credit. This difference is due to the nature of the data available in the respective fields of study.

CHAPTER XVI

STATISTICAL MEASUREMENT OF AGGREGATE NET MOVEMENT

In previous chapters it was indicated that it is impossible to measure accurately the total ebb and flow of the funds of the money market and that the net movement which takes place is essentially one of reserve funds. The movement of reserve funds into and out of the money market for purposes of study may be subdivided into three main parts: (1) changes in the international ownership of gold;[1] (2) changes in the ownership of gold as between the various Federal Reserve districts, which take place through the mechanism of the gold settlement fund; and (3) the movement of Reserve funds into and out of the money market due to the activities of the Federal Reserve banks, including payments and receipts of currency. The subsequent statistical analysis will consist of a study of these three classes of movements of reserve funds.

Changes in Credit Base—United States

Gold movements

The accompanying tables give the net movement of gold into and out of the United States by months since the beginning of 1915. In the first table, the net movement is given while in the second table the cumulative movement, with the cumulation beginning from January 1, 1914, is shown. These figures take into account not only the "visible" gold movement, but the "invisible" as well, *i. e.*, earmarking operations, since it is total changes in the *ownership* of gold which affects the credit base. Actual imports and exports of gold, without taking into account changes in the own-

[1] This would normally include a study of international movements of United States currency.

NET MOVEMENT OF GOLD TO AND FROM THE UNITED STATES

VISIBLE NET IMPORTS AND NET EXPORTS (—), CORRECTED BY NET CHANGES IN EARMARKED GOLD AND FOR GOLD HELD ABROAD BY FEDERAL RESERVE BANKS *

(In millions of dollars)

Month	*1915*	*1916*	*1917*	*1918*	*1919*	*1920*
January	6.2	4.8	38.2	0.7	− 1.3	− 42.4
February	11.7	− 7.7	81.7	− 2.5	0.8	− 40.4
March	24.7	− 3.4	121.6	− 0.9	6.8	− 31.3
April	15.4	− 7.6	15.4	− 0.8	9.7	0.9
May	29.9	15.4	− 5.4	3.0	− 0.9	7.0
June	49.5	113.9	42.7	20.9	− 56.8	19.5
July	15.1	52.4	− 42.1	− 9.4	− 52.8	− 5.1
August	60.5	29.4	− 28.0	− 4.2	53.5	− 11.6
September	40.0	85.3	− 27.3	− 0.2	2.6	21.0
October	76.7	90.4	− 7.0	− 0.7	− 90.0	79.8
November	57.3	20.6	− 4.3	− 1.1	− 73.7	31.4
December	33.5	130.5	12.5	0.2	− 39.6	14.1

Month	*1921*	*1922*	*1923*	*1924*	*1925*	*1926*
January	20.7	25.7	22.7	44.9	− 69.3	10.2
February	39.6	27.0	11.3	35.2	− 48.4	10.6
March	86.6	32.5	5.6	31.1	− 24.6	16.2
April	79.1	10.7	9.5	43.5	2.1	− 4.8
May	57.1	5.6	45.3	41.5	11.7	− 6.4
June	39.8	11.4	18.9	26.9	2.8	15.0
July	65.5	42.3	25.9	15.9	1.9	18.8
August	84.2	18.1	30.7	7.8	11.5	1.4
September	73.6	23.1	27.4	− 11.2	− 1.8	− 9.5
October	47.5	1.8	26.5	− 1.4	25.6	7.7
November	50.7	14.7	39.0	12.7	− 11.9	1.5
December	29.5	21.7	31.9	− 30.9	− 0.8	10.8

Month	*1927*	*1928*	*1929*	*1930*	*1931*	*1932*
January	63.9	− 8.3	− 17.8	4.5	46.3	− 49.6
February	23.1	− 8.3	25.5	60.0	18.6	− 64.2
March	9.3	− 59.1	32.3	68.5	28.6	33.6
April	10.9	− 45.4	71.7	66.2	42.0	− 29.0p
May	− 46.8	− 108.3	39.7	25.5	53.6	
June	8.8	− 49.9	22.7	15.9	156.1	
July	− 2.8	− 2.9	12.7	− 22.6	− 10.2	
August	2.6	6.7	17.4	− 19.6	41.5	
September	− 20.5	− 0.7	11.0	6.5	− 258.5	
October	− 33.6	15.5	13.0	20.3	− 445.3	
November	− 93.2	− 18.3	− 22.2	33.1	117.7	
December	− 75.9	7.5	− 86.4	17.5	34.0	

Preliminary. See *Federal Reserve Bulletin*, May, 1932, p. 294.

* Compiled from *Annual Reports of the Federal Reserve Board*, 1927, p. 79; 1928, pp. 88–90; 1929, pp. 82–83; 1930, pp. 68–69. *Federal Reserve Bulletin*, June, 1931, p. 307 and May, 1932, p. 294.

CUMULATED NET MOVEMENT IN THE OWNERSHIP OF GOLD TO AND FROM THE UNITED STATES

CUMULATION BEGINS JANUARY 1, 1914 *

(In millions of dollars)

Month	*1915*	*1916*	*1917*	*1918*	*1919*	*1920*
January	− 159.0	260.1	817.6	978.1	981.1	698.3
February	− 147.4	252.4	899.3	975.6	981.9	657.9
March	− 122.7	249.0	1,020.9	974.7	988.7	626.6
April	− 107.3	241.5	1,036.3	973.9	998.4	627.5
May	− 77.4	256.9	1,030.9	976.9	997.5	634.5
June	− 27.9	370.8	1,073.6	997.8	940.7	654.0
July	− 12.8	423.2	1,031.5	988.4	887.9	648.9
August	47.7	452.5	1,003.5	984.2	941.4	637.3
September	87.7	537.8	976.2	984.0	944.0	658.3
October	164.5	628.2	969.2	983.3	854.0	738.1
November	221.8	648.9	964.9	982.2	780.3	769.5
December	255.3	779.4	977.4	982.4	740.7	783.6

Month	*1921*	*1922*	*1923*	*1924*	*1925*	*1926*
January	804.3	1,483.2	1,714.8	2,031.7	2,133.5	2,111.8
February	843.9	1,510.2	1,726.1	2,066.9	2,085.1	2,122.4
March	930.5	1,542.7	1,731.7	2,098.0	2,060.5	2,138.6
April	1,009.6	1,553.4	1,741.2	2,141.5	2,062.6	2,133.8
May	1,066.7	1,559.0	1,786.5	2,183.0	2,074.3	2,127.4
June	1,106.5	1,570.4	1,805.4	2,209.9	2,077.1	2,142.4
July	1,172.0	1,612.7	1,831.3	2,225.8	2,079.0	2,161.2
August	1,256.2	1,630.8	1,862.0	2,233.6	2,090.5	2,162.6
September	1,329.8	1,653.9	1,889.4	2,222.4	2,088.7	2,153.1
October	1,377.3	1,655.7	1,915.9	2,221.0	2,114.3	2,160.8
November	1,428.0	1,670.4	1,954.9	2,233.7	2,102.4	2,162.3
December	1,457.5	1,692.1	1,986.8	2,202.8	2,101.6	2,173.1

Month	*1927*	*1928*	*1929*	*1930*	*1931*	*1932*
January	2,237.0	2,010.6	1,729.6	1,871.5	2,189.7	1,917.6
February	2,260.1	2,002.3	1,755.1	1,931.5	2,207.7	1,853.4
March	2,269.4	1,943.2	1,787.4	2,000.0	2,236.3	1,887.0
April	2,280.3	1,897.8	1,859.1	2,066.2	2,278.3	1,858.0p
May	2,233.5	1,789.5	1,898.8	2,091.7	2,331.9	
June	2,242.3	1,739.6	1,921.5	2,107.6	2,488.0	
July	2,239.5	1,736.7	1,934.2	2,085.0	2,477.8	
August	2,242.1	1,743.4	1,951.6	2,065.4	2,519.3	
September	2,221.6	1,742.7	1,962.6	2,071.9	2,260.8	
October	2,188.0	1,758.2	1,975.6	2,092.2	1,815.5	
November	2,094.8	1,739.9	1,953.4	2,125.3	1,933.2	
December	2,018.9	1,747.4	1,867.0	2,142.8	1,967.2	

Preliminary. See table on p. 323.

* Cumulated net movement in 1914 was — 165.2.

ership of gold brought about by earmarking operations, are no longer significant as a measure of the movement of reserves in international exchange. Central banks of many countries, on some form of the gold standard, are permitted to count as specie reserves not only the gold actually held in vault, but also gold owned by them but physically held in custody in some other country. This is called "earmarked" gold, inasmuch as it is segregated and marked in such a manner as to indicate that the identical coins or bars designated are the foreign bank's property and altogether subject to its disposal. Such gold earmarked by the Federal Reserve Bank of New York as agent for a foreign central bank ceases to be a part of the gold reserves of the Federal Reserve Bank of New York just as if it were physically shipped abroad. Similarly, the Federal Reserve Bank of New York has sometimes had gold held abroad, earmarked as its property, instead of having the gold shipped to New York. Therefore any change in gold earmarked for foreign account, during a given month, must be counted as a part of the net movement. Gold released from earmarked account is usually exported, and when this is the case it must be counted as a deduction from the exports of that period in which it was released.[2]

Other factors affecting the credit base

Changes in the monetary stock of gold must be supplemented by further analyses. The reason is that the effect which gold movements have upon the credit base depends on: (1) whether or not increases in the monetary gold stock are drawn on to increase the volume of money in circulation, in the form of gold coins or gold certificates; and (2) whether or not the gold movement is offset or supplemented by changes in the volume of Federal Reserve bank credit, corrected for Federal Reserve note circulation.

In order to depict the net movement of Reserve funds used

[2] United States Department of Commerce, *The Balance of International Payments of the United States in 1928*, pp. 52–53. Cf. *Federal Reserve Bulletin*, Dec., 1927, p. 801.

as reserve base and not for circulation purposes, Chart 39 is inserted. There are shown cumulated since 1919: (1) the net movement of gold to and from the United States, compared with the net movement of total Federal Reserve bank credit outstanding; (2) the net movement of gold to and from the United States, corrected for that part which has gone into circulation, compared to the cumulated movement of Federal Reserve bank credit corrected for Federal Reserve note circulation; and (3) the cumulated net movement in the credit base, which is the sum of (1) and (2) above; *i. e.*, the movement of gold affecting the credit market plus (algebraically) the movement of Federal Reserve bank credit affecting the credit market. The curve on this graph labeled "member bank reserves" portrays the cumulated net changes in the total reserve deposits of all member banks. Presumably the cumulated movement in the total credit base—gold affecting the credit market plus Federal Reserve credit affecting the credit market—should correlate closely with the movement of total member bank reserves.[3] It is to be noted that this is true for every year with the exception of 1922, when member bank reserves moved in the opposite direction (increased) from that followed by the movement of the net credit base, which caused the two lines to diverge. Both series increased during 1924, but with member bank reserves rising faster than the net credit base, which caused the two lines to diverge somewhat further apart. Aside from these two years, however, there is a close parallelism throughout the period.

The validity of the method used above in calculating the credit base may be checked by use of another formula. The total monetary gold stock of the United States, plus Federal Reserve credit outstanding, minus money in circulation, should give a series approximating fluctuations in the credit base. Such calculations are presented in Chart 40 on page 328, along with the series presented in the previous chart giving changes in the credit base as first calculated. The result shows a striking degree of positive

[3] Except for changes in treasury currency (other than gold certificates, which have been taken into consideration) and for the unexpended capital funds of the Federal Reserve banks. Changes in treasury currency may account for the divergence in 1922, particularly the operations in connection with the Pittman Act.

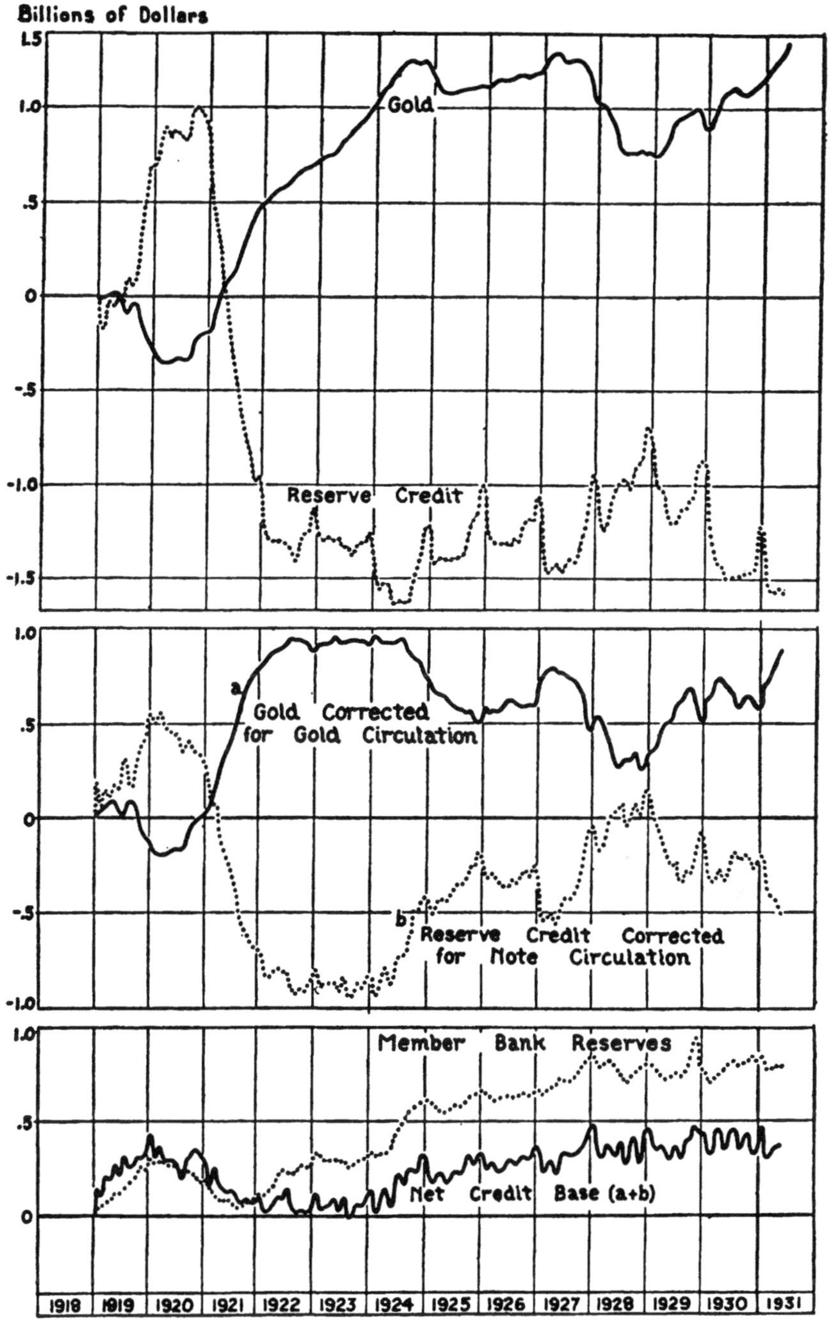

CHART 39. FACTORS AFFECTING THE NET CREDIT BASE, MOVEMENT OF GOLD AND FEDERAL RESERVE CREDIT, UNITED STATES.

correlation and affords a check on the accuracy of the first method.

Changes in Net Credit Base—New York Money Market[4]

Gold movements—foreign transactions

Of considerably greater difficulty is the presentation of a similar study for the New York money market as distinct from

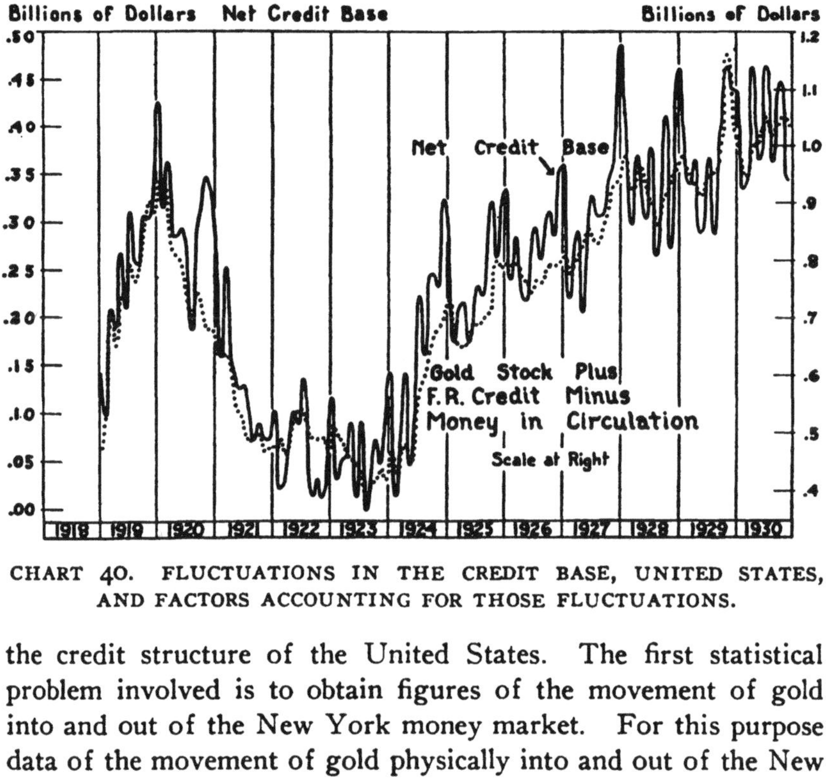

CHART 40. FLUCTUATIONS IN THE CREDIT BASE, UNITED STATES, AND FACTORS ACCOUNTING FOR THOSE FLUCTUATIONS.

the credit structure of the United States. The first statistical problem involved is to obtain figures of the movement of gold into and out of the New York money market. For this purpose data of the movement of gold physically into and out of the New York money market (net visible gold imports and exports of the New York, Buffalo and St. Lawrence customs districts) are used and these data are then corrected for earmarking operations. Gold which arrives in customs districts outside of the New York

[4] The data used in this section embrace the New York Federal Reserve district, not simply the money market; but the money market factors and forces predominate in the district, and that is the only form in which data are available for use in such a study as is here attempted.

NET MOVEMENT OF GOLD TO AND FROM THE NEW YORK MONEY MARKET IN INTERNATIONAL EXCHANGE *

VISIBLE NET IMPORTS AND NET EXPORTS (—) (BUFFALO, ST. LAWRENCE AND NEW YORK CUSTOMS DISTRICTS); CORRECTED BY NET CHANGE IN EARMARKED GOLD, AND ALSO CORRECTED FOR GOLD HELD ABROAD BY THE FEDERAL RESERVE BANK OF NEW YORK

(In millions of dollars)

Month	*1914*	*1915*	*1916*	*1917*	*1918*	*1919*
January	2.15	2.45	5.70	40.74	2.16	— 1.30
February	— 6.98	9.17	— 5.63	86.01	— 1.41	— 1.69
March	4.25	18.71	— 4.07	114.21	0.70	4.05
April	2.15	9.95	— 3.71	22.77	1.14	4.41
May	—15.76	25.24	20.97	32.36	4.03	— 0.90
June	—45.53	45.64	113.60	92.28	22.57	—34.30
July	—32.16	8.79	32.20	5.69	— 7.61	—23.15
August	—16.13	9.35	30.81	1.07	— 1.94	93.63
September	—19.79	8.13	84.89	—10.43	0.04	24.94
October	—41.81	59.97	88.83	— 5.98	0.30	—51.06
November	—11.54	46.58	23.14	— 2.69	0.63	—35.13
December	1.43	33.54	128.91	13.32	0.28	—18.64

Month	*1920*	*1921*	*1922*	*1923*	*1924*	*1925*
January	—13.94	20.92	22.61	21.49	43.66	—63.15
February	—25.34	32.08	24.51	11.70	31.65	—32.29
March	—21.08	100.96	32.24	4.83	30.66	—22.24
April	11.09	78.65	9.20	8.31	39.35	3.59
May	— 1.95	50.45	3.99	43.60	38.08	10.38
June	10.58	39.15	11.31	18.19	24.45	5.92
July	8.86	59.77	41.38	23.80	14.37	2.58
August	7.55	81.43	17.17	30.71	6.61	11.23
September	36.13	74.35	21.90	26.44	—12.06	— 1.08
October	104.46	52.24	1.07	24.32	— 0.96	24.07
November	49.16	50.31	13.28	37.85	12.76	—14.83
December	39.38	28.17	20.29	30.77	—31.41	— 4.91

Month	*1926*	*1927*	*1928*	*1929*	*1930*	*1931*
January	9.51	60.66	— 8.07	— 18.11	3.69	43.76
February	7.36	16.42	— 7.64	24.39	16.94	15.07
March	17.19	0.20	— 59.69	32.02	22.78	24.12
April	— 5.81	4.50	— 44.59	72.11	43.25	29.71
May	— 7.95	— 52.69	—108.07	38.76	7.06	51.32
June	1.80	3.57	— 48.68	21.35	5.83	148.16
July	0.99	— 2.98	— 2.12	10.48	— 30.15	— 15.03
August	— 8.94	2.09	6.65	15.03	— 34.04	11.86
September	— 23.72	— 30.85	— 1.16	10.10	— 0.92	—264.17
October	— 0.07	— 34.15	14.06	5.05	3.39	—475.57
November	— 14.01	— 92.98	— 19.26	— 23.51	14.98	35.47
December	1.20	— 74.99	7.39	— 88.37	15.82	— 38.14

* Compiled from: *Monthly Summary of Foreign and Domestic Commerce, passim.* Data on earmarked gold contained in the *Annual Report of the Federal Reserve Board,* 1928, p. 88. *Federal Reserve Bulletin,* June 1931, p. 307. Gold

CUMULATED NET MOVEMENT IN THE OWNERSHIP OF GOLD TO AND FROM THE NEW YORK MONEY MARKET IN INTERNATIONAL EXCHANGE

(In millions of dollars)

(Cumulation begins January 1, 1914. Derived from preceding table.)

Month	*1914*	*1915*	*1916*	*1917*	*1918*	*1919*
January	2.15	−177.27	103.50	654.18	1,004.95	1,022.38
February	− 4.83	−168.10	97.87	740.19	1,003.54	1,020.69
March	− 0.58	−149.39	93.80	854.40	1,004.24	1,024.74
April	1.57	−139.44	90.09	877.17	1,005.38	1,029.15
May	− 14.19	−114.20	111.06	909.53	1,009.41	1,028.25
June	− 59.72	− 68.56	224.66	1,001.81	1,031.98	993.95
July	− 91.88	− 59.77	256.86	1,007.50	1,024.37	970.80
August	−108.01	− 50.42	287.67	1,008.57	1,022.43	1,064.43
September	−127.80	− 42.29	372.56	998.14	1,022.47	1,089.37
October	−169.61	17.68	461.39	992.16	1,022.77	1,038.31
November	−181.15	64.26	484.53	989.47	1,023.40	1,003.18
December	−179.72	97.80	613.44	1,002.79	1,023.68	984.54
Month	*1920*	*1921*	*1922*	*1923*	*1924*	*1925*
January	970.60	1,210.36	1,880.53	2,108.36	2,412.54	2,502.89
February	945.26	1,242.44	1,905.04	2,120.06	2,444.19	2,470.60
March	924.18	1,343.40	1,937.28	2,124.89	2,474.85	2,448.36
April	935.27	1,422.05	1,946.48	2,133.20	2,514.20	2,451.95
May	933.32	1,472.50	1,950.47	2,176.80	2,552.28	2,462.33
June	943.90	1,511.65	1,961.78	2,194.99	2,576.73	2,468.25
July	952.76	1,571.42	2,003.16	2,218.79	2,591.10	2,470.83
August	960.31	1,652.85	2,020.33	2,249.50	2,597.71	2,482.06
September	996.44	1,727.20	2,042.23	2,275.94	2,585.65	2,480.98
October	1,100.90	1,779.44	2,043.30	2,300.26	2,584.69	2,505.05
November	1,150.06	1,829.75	2,056.58	2,338.11	2,597.45	2,490.22
December	1,189.44	1,857.92	2,086.87	2,368.88	2,566.04	2,485.31
Month	*1926*	*1927*	*1928*	*1929*	*1930*	*1931*
January	2,494.82	2,523.52	2,253.59	1,972.37	2,093.47	2,202.17
February	2,502.18	2,539.94	2,245.95	1,996.76	2,110.41	2,217.24
March	2,519.37	2,540.14	2,186.26	2,028.78	2,133.19	2,241.36
April	2,513.56	2,544.64	2,141.67	2,100.89	2,176.44	2,271.07
May	2,505.61	2,491.95	2,033.60	2,139.65	2,183.50	2,322.39
June	2,507.41	2,495.52	1,984.92	2,161.00	2,189.33	2,470.55
July	2,508.40	2,492.54	1,982.80	2,171.48	2,159.18	2,455.52
August	2,499.46	2,494.63	1,989.45	2,186.51	2,125.14	2,467.38
September	2,475.74	2,463.78	1,988.29	2,196.61	2,124.22	2,203.21
October	2,475.67	2,429.63	2,002.35	2,201.66	2,127.61	1,727.64
November	2,461.66	2,336.65	1,983.09	2,178.15	2,142.59	1,763.11
December	2,462.86	2,261.66	1,990.48	2,089.78	2,158.41	1,724.97

holdings abroad compiled from *Federal Reserve Bulletins, passim,* condition statements. Cf. *Monthly Review of Credit and Business Conditions,* Federal Reserve Bank of New York, Jan., 1928, p. 1.

Federal Reserve district reaches the New York money market, if at all, through the gold settlement fund, which will be considered later. Data on gold movements of the New York money market are presented in the tables on pages 329–30, showing the net movement by months since 1914 and the cumulated movement from the beginning of 1919 of gold movements into and out of the New York money market due to foreign transactions, *i. e.*, visible net imports and exports of gold to and from the New York Federal Reserve district, corrected for earmarking operations and for changes in the volume of gold held abroad by the Federal Reserve Bank of New York.

Gold movements—domestic transactions

The movement of gold into and out of the New York money market, as measured by net imports and exports, constitutes only a partial measure of the whole of the net movement. In addition there is the movement on domestic account through the operations of the gold settlement fund. These are presented in tables on pages 333–35, giving net and cumulative movements of gold to and from the New York money market and the interior of the country since the beginning of 1919.

The gold settlement fund data appearing in these tables are given as if on a monthly basis, although the figures are not so published. The data as published overlap from about the middle of one month to the middle of the next. This makes the gold settlement fund data slightly non-synchronous with the other data presented, but this is unavoidable. The gold settlement fund data include commercial transits and settlements, government transfers and Federal Reserve note clearings. This movement of funds to and from the New York money market through the gold settlement fund, added algebraically to the foreign gold movement, to and from New York, described above, gives the total movement of the ownership of gold to and from the New York money market.

The trend and cyclical variations in the movement of gold to and from the New York money market is better depicted over the period of time studied by cumulating the monthly net movements. The cumulated movement of gold to and from New York due to international exchange is shown in Chart 41, along with the cumulated movement of gold to and from the United States, and the cumulated movement of gold through the gold settlement fund to and from the New York money market. The graph is carried back simply to the beginning of 1919, inasmuch

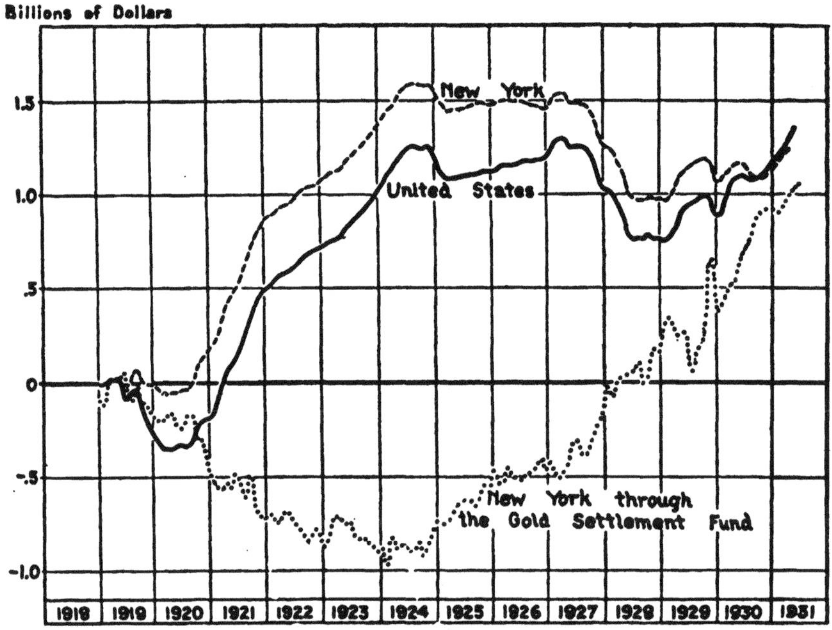

CHART 41. CUMULATED MOVEMENT OF GOLD, NEW YORK, FOREIGN AND DOMESTIC, COMPARED WITH GOLD MOVEMENTS FOR THE UNITED STATES.

as earlier gold settlement fund data are not considered suitable for this analysis.

Examination of the tables and Chart 41 discloses certain periods in the cumulated movement of gold on foreign account: (1) the period of loss of gold by the New York money market from January to November, 1914, followed by; (2) a period of gain, wiping out the loss of the previous period and continuing with minor outward movement periods until October, 1919; (3) from October, 1919, until March, 1920, there was a rapid outward movement of gold from the New York money market on for-

NET MOVEMENT IN THE OWNERSHIP OF GOLD INTO AND OUT OF THE NEW YORK MONEY MARKET IN DOMESTIC EXCHANGE

THE NET INCREASES OR NET DECREASES (—) OF FUNDS IN NEW YORK AS A RESULT OF TRANSACTIONS THROUGH THE GOLD SETTLEMENT FUND, INCLUDING GOVERNMENT TRANSFERS, TRANSIT CLEARINGS AND FEDERAL RESERVE NOTE CLEARINGS *

(In thousands of dollars)

Month	*1919*	*1920*	*1921*	*1922*	*1923*
January	−103,963	− 40,879	−121,123	14,569	− 98,475
February	− 28,848	6,613	− 31,080	− 1,422	67,179
March	134,122	− 8,665	− 26,766	− 56,158	97,080
April	5,092	36,212	41,291	30,579	1,737
May	− 3,181	− 12,069	− 32,775	46,351	− 45,441
June	51,708	− 63,231	93,790	− 47,622	12,684
July	−105,684	− 11,354	− 73,166	− 25,853	− 69,599
August	− 61,391	76,818	− 76,722	− 26,394	− 19,058
September	81,139	− 2,351	38,857	− 57,550	13,173
October	− 90,581	−139,874	− 75,970	− 16,518	− 35,704
November	2,726	9,665	− 45,108	69,444	− 2,490
December	− 46,915	− 87,914	− 4,839	568	− 40,584
TOTAL	−165,776	−237,029	−313,611	− 70,006	−119,498

Month	*1924*	*1925*	*1926*	*1927*	*1928*
January	25,671	64,623	86,609	46,200	136,878
February	− 97,132	− 18,659	− 84,476	− 48,197	− 45,212
March	150,747	− 4,716	10,414	− 37,623	90,769
April	− 65,806	41,683	87,101	48,317	29,244
May	19,706	54,299	− 47,495	40,327	4,352
June	16,670	29,528	6,141	98,552	6,012
July	− 53,249	1,233	− 30,274	347	38,721
August	3,468	17,712	55,997	− 86,344	18,529
September	56,927	− 54,432	− 13,919	27,660	−118,670
October	− 96,731	73,356	41,106	69,828	62,741
November	90,533	57,371	33,715	71,545	126,012
December	51,799	− 22,784	− 52,441	61,808	− 17,621
TOTAL	102,603	239,214	92,478	292,420	331,755

* Tabulation from the *Federal Reserve Bulletin* and the *Weekly Statement of the Gold Settlement Fund Transactions,* issued by the Federal Reserve Board. The data include the movement of reserve credit in interbank rediscounting, 1919–1921 inclusive, and open-market operations.

NET MOVEMENT IN THE OWNERSHIP OF GOLD INTO AND OUT OF THE NEW YORK MONEY MARKET IN DOMESTIC EXCHANGE (CONTINUED)

THE NET INCREASES OR NET DECREASES (—) OF FUNDS IN NEW YORK AS A RESULT OF TRANSACTIONS THROUGH THE GOLD SETTLEMENT FUND, INCLUDING GOVERNMENT TRANSFERS, TRANSIT CLEARINGS AND FEDERAL RESERVE NOTE CLEARINGS *

(In thousands of dollars)

Month	*1929*	*1930*	*1931*	*1932*	
January	137,406	40,358	5,658	69,357	
February	45,993	52,882	— 28,172	65,781	
March	— 28,078	47,257	22,908	— 52,198	
April	— 72,090	21,481	— 64,828	29,879	
May	25,267	91,551	44,776	8,100	
June	— 34,447	66,433	27,477	279,529	
July	—186,217	34,209	20,583		
August	133,329	66,895	— 7,782		
September	27,835	72,903	31,968		
October	149,167	34,760	529,301		
November	165,029	26,708	— 5,495		
December	—141,326	— 4,186	— 40,470		
TOTAL	221,868	551,251	535,924		

eign account, followed by; (4) a long period of inward movement lasting until August, 1924; (5) from August, 1924, until April, 1927, when there was little sustained trend in either direction; but (6) beginning with April, 1927, and continuing throughout 1927 and 1928, there was a distinct outward movement of gold from New York on foreign account which was followed (7) by an inward movement of large proportions, which, with the exception of the end of 1929, continued without interruption, to September, 1931. These correspond to the periods, already described, of the movement of gold, into and out of the country as a whole, on foreign account.[5]

Federal Reserve bank credit

The data considered so far have to do with the net movement in and out of the New York money market of *primary reserves,* that is the gold reserves of the Federal Reserve Bank of New York.

[5] See Chap. IV.

CUMULATED NET MOVEMENT OF THE OWNERSHIP OF GOLD TO AND FROM THE NEW YORK MONEY MARKET IN DOMESTIC EXCHANGE THROUGH THE GOLD SETTLEMENT FUND

CUMULATION BEGINS JANUARY 1, 1919*

(In thousands of dollars)

Month	*1919*	*1920*	*1921*	*1922*	*1923*
January	− 103,963	− 206,655	− 523,928	− 701,847	− 884,897
February	− 132,811	− 200,042	− 555,008	− 703,269	− 817,718
March	1,311	− 208,707	− 581,774	− 759,427	− 720,638
April	6,403	− 172,495	− 540,483	− 728,848	− 718,901
May	3,222	− 184,564	− 573,258	− 682,497	− 764,342
June	54,930	− 247,795	− 479,468	− 730,119	− 751,658
July	− 50,754	− 259,149	− 552,634	− 755,972	− 821,257
August	− 112,145	− 182,331	− 629,356	− 782,366	− 840,315
September	− 31,006	− 184,682	− 590,499	− 839,916	− 827,142
October	− 121,587	− 324,556	− 666,469	− 856,434	− 862,846
November	− 118,861	− 314,891	− 711,577	− 786,990	− 865,336
December	− 165,776	− 402,805	− 716,416	− 786,422	− 905,920
Month	*1924*	*1925*	*1926*	*1927*	*1928*
January	− 880,249	− 738,694	− 477,494	− 425,425	− 42,327
February	− 977,381	− 757,353	− 561,970	− 473,622	− 87,539
March	− 826,634	− 762,069	− 551,556	− 511,245	3,230
April	− 892,440	− 720,386	− 464,455	− 462,928	32,474
May	− 872,734	− 666,087	− 511,950	− 422,601	36,826
June	− 856,064	− 636,559	− 505,809	− 324,049	42,838
July	− 909,313	− 635,326	− 536,083	− 323,702	81,559
August	− 905,845	− 617,614	− 480,086	− 410,046	100,088
September	− 848,918	− 672,046	− 494,005	− 382,386	− 18,582
October	− 945,649	− 598,690	− 452,899	− 312,558	44,159
November	− 855,116	− 541,319	− 419,184	− 241,013	170,171
December	− 803,317	− 564,103	− 471,625	− 179,205	152,550
Month	*1929*	*1930*	*1931*	*1932*	
January	289,956	414,876	931,427	1,531,050	
February	335,949	467,758	903,255	1,596,831	
March	307,871	515,015	926,163	1,544,633	
April	235,781	536,496	861,335	1,574,512	
May	261,048	628,047	906,111	1,582,612	
June	226,601	694,480	933,588		
July	40,384	728,689	954,171		
August	173,713	795,584	946,389		
September	201,548	868,487	978,357		
October	350,715	903,247	1,507,658		
November	515,744	929,955	1,502,163		
December	374,418	925,769	1,461,693		

* Derived from preceding table.

From the point of view of member banks and the money market, an important addition to these data is necessary, since member banks interchangeably use as reserves, primary reserves or Federal Reserve bank credit. In other words, member bank reserves equal primary reserves plus Federal Reserve bank credit. In this analysis the important consideration is the net movement of funds *affecting the money market;* and, so far as the money market is concerned, the net movement of gold and net movement of Federal Reserve credit are homogeneous—each may be used as member bank reserves. The gold movement data, then, do not represent the sole source of increase in the funds of the money market. They represent only the *external* gains to the New York money market, and to this there must be added algebraically the net *internal* gains or losses resulting from variations in the earning assets of the Federal Reserve Bank of New York, together with changes in certain of the other items on its financial statement, and increases or decreases in the New York money market of the Reserve credit of other Federal Reserve banks and in certain instances of foreign central banks.

While it is true that from the point of view of logical treatment of money market fluctuations, the two types of movements (first, gold or primary reserves and, second, Reserve bank credit) should be studied separately, yet they are closely bound together, in that fluctuations in the one may be provocative of counter or offsetting fluctuations in the other, and that fluctuations in the one may be completely counteracted by the influence of fluctuations in the other. For example, an external gain typified by gold imports would enable member banks, if they so desired, to repay borrowings at the Federal Reserve Bank of New York. If such were the case, the gain to the money market from external sources would be nullified by the loss internally. Similarly, an external drain in the form of gold exports or gold losses to New York through the gold settlement fund might be offset through increases in borrowings from the Federal Reserve banks, or through the open-market operations of the Reserve banks.[6]

[6] Cf. Analysis developed in Chap. VII.

Method of calculating Federal Reserve bank credit outstanding in the New York money market

The Federal Reserve Board publishes a series intended to represent the volume of reserve credit outstanding in the entire country,[7] but does not give estimates of that portion of the total which is in the New York money market. The following are the items which should be aggregated to measure the net movement of Reserve bank credit as affecting the New York money market:

(1) Bills discounted by the Federal Reserve Bank of New York.

(2) Acceptances, United States securities and other securities purchased by all twelve Federal Reserve banks—the open-market operations of any Federal Reserve bank result in the movement of Reserve credit into and out of the New York money market, since practically all such purchases are localized there. The allotment of these purchases to another district is reflected in gold settlement fund data, *i. e.,* the New York Federal Reserve Bank gains in the gold settlement fund.

(3) Foreign loans on gold and due from foreign banks for all twelve Federal Reserve banks constitutes a movement of reserve funds into and out of the New York money market, since increases or decreases of these items result in a movement of funds through the foreign exchange market of New York and constitute an ebb and flow of Reserve credit into and out of the New York money market. If this Reserve credit then moves to other parts of the country, it will be reflected in the gold settlement fund data.

(4) Reserve bank float of the Federal Reserve Bank of New York.

Up to this point the basis of calculation is similar to that of the Federal Reserve Board in its calculation of Reserve credit for the system as a whole, and to this should be added algebraically:

(5) Changes in the capital, surplus and other liabilities of the Federal Reserve Bank of New York. As these increase, there is a corresponding decrease in Reserve credit in the money market and vice versa; and

[7] *Annual Report of the Federal Reserve Board,* 1928, pp. 47–49; 1929, pp. 45–70.

(6) Changes in government, foreign bank and other deposits of the Federal Reserve Bank of New York. Increase in these causes a corresponding decrease in Reserve credit in the market, and vice versa.

When changes in the latter two are combined algebraically with the changes in Reserve credit outstanding obtained under (1),

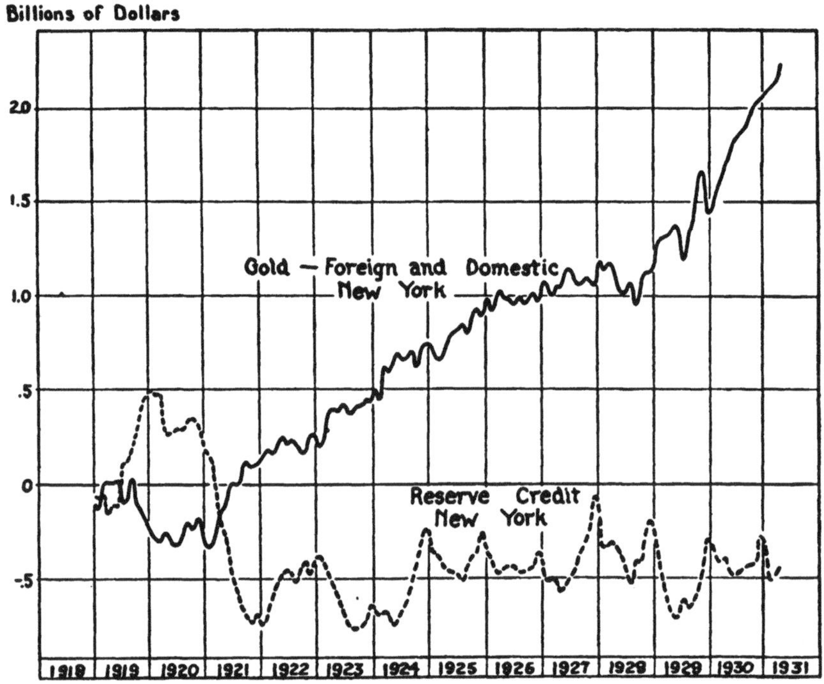

CHART 42. CUMULATED MOVEMENT OF RESERVE CREDIT AND GOLD TO AND FROM THE NEW YORK MONEY MARKET.

THE GOLD CURVE ON THIS CHART IS THE ALGEBRAIC SUM OF THE TWO NEW YORK CURVES ON CHART 41, PAGE 332.

(2), (3) and (4) above, the resulting figures represent the total movement of Reserve bank credit into and out of the New York money market, though not necessarily the net movement of reserve funds inasmuch as gold movements and currency must be taken into account. These data are presented in the following tables and are shown in cumulated form in Chart 42 along with the total cumulated gold movement to and from the New York money market, due to foreign and domestic transactions.

TOTAL AMOUNT OF FEDERAL RESERVE BANK CREDIT IN THE NEW YORK MONEY MARKET BY MONTHS *

(*Monthly averages of daily data; in millions of dollars*)

Month	*1914*	*1915*	*1916*	*1917*	*1918*	*1919*
January		9.33	63.4	195.1	688.5	1,226.2
February		16.80	79.6	197.2	707.0	1,243.8
March		28.76	104.6	181.3	878.4	1,267.9
April		37.10	127.3	226.2	901.0	1,149.3
May		40.04	147.5	263.6	838.2	1,212.1
June		30.19	143.7	386.0	843.6	1,194.9
July		32.33	162.3	342.4	736.0	1,399.5
August		41.40	164.6	283.2	778.2	1,376.6
September		46.71	160.5	332.4	993.4	1,411.4
October		50.63	164.7	490.2	1,222.9	1,484.9
November	2.76	51.25	167.8	677.3	1,223.2	1,647.0
December	1.72	49.88	194.1	691.2	1,288.5	1,721.7
Month	*1920*	*1921*	*1922*	*1923*	*1924*	*1925*
January	1,765.9	1,406.5	508.5	852.6	557.2	903.1
February	1,762.8	1,388.5	567.4	808.9	543.3	878.3
March	1,744.9	1,237.8	635.9	774.8	568.9	856.5
April	1,572.7	1.039.7	693.2	709.2	550.1	795.1
May	1,536.9	951.6	767.3	662.9	484.1	778.3
June	1,546.7	799.9	788.9	565.9	528.8	772.1
July	1,540.8	698.4	783.4	515.6	577.9	749.2
August	1,553.3	656.0	725.2	484.8	619.4	736.8
September	1,606.6	575.6	777.1	492.8	732.2	802.3
October	1,619.1	530.9	820.1	490.8	831.9	856.0
November	1,603.5	511.9	770.1	526.5	916.4	887.7
December	1,559.7	567.7	842.2	600.1	1,023.2	978.9
Month	*1926*	*1927*	*1928*	*1929*	*1930*	*1931*
January	885.0	793.4	1,054.2	975.1	942.1	921.4
February	849.5	717.7	898.2	808.7	859.9	759.3
March	773.1	724.9	901.7	722.8	861.3	777.5
April	769.1	733.1	939.7	617.9	879.0	826.4
May	796.6	681.1	917.2	560.4	789.9	790.0
June	798.1	718.8	868.3	562.3	788.9	780.5
July	807.5	757.8	801.1	666.6	802.5	801.1
August	783.8	782.2	725.1	612.8	817.5	926.0
September	787.9	884.0	839.4	659.8	844.2	1,076.3
October	791.0	933.1	927.4	698.2	844.3	1,620.1
November	808.4	1,044.9	972.5	807.5	842.6	1,455.3
December	891.5	1,174.8	1,072.2	989.8	1,006.3	1,332.2

* Derived from Table 1, pp. 47–49 and Table 72, p. 143, *Annual Report of the Federal Reserve Board*, 1928, substituting in place of rediscounts of all twelve Federal Reserve banks those of the New York Federal Reserve Bank, and for total float that of the New York Federal Reserve Bank. Float of the Federal Reserve Bank of New York is not available previous to 1927; so it was estimated to be .40 per cent of total float of the system. Float is not available at all before 1917.

FIRST APPROXIMATION TO NET MOVEMENT OF RESERVE BANK CREDIT INTO AND OUT OF THE NEW YORK MONEY MARKET *

(Monthly averages of daily data; in millions of dollars)

Month	*1914*	*1915*	*1916*	*1917*	*1918*	*1919*
January		7.6	13.5	1.0	−2.7	−62.3
February		7.5	16.3	2.1	18.6	17.6
March		12.0	24.9	−15.9	171.4	24.1
April		8.3	22.7	44.9	22.6	−118.6
May		2.9	20.2	37.4	−62.8	62.8
June		−9.8	−3.8	122.4	5.3	−17.2
July		2.1	18.6	−43.6	−107.6	204.6
August		9.1	2.3	−59.2	42.2	−22.9
September		5.3	−4.1	49.2	215.2	34.8
October		3.9	4.2	157.8	229.5	73.5
November	2.8	0.6	3.1	187.1	0.3	162.1
December	−1.0	−1.4	26.3	13.9	65.3	74.7

Month	*1920*	*1921*	*1922*	*1923*	*1924*	*1925*
January	44.2	−153.2	−59.2	10.4	−42.9	−120.1
February	−3.1	−18.0	58.9	−43.7	−13.9	−24.8
March	−17.9	−150.7	68.5	−34.1	25.6	−21.8
April	−172.2	−198.1	57.3	−65.6	−18.8	−61.4
May	−35.8	−88.1	74.1	−46.4	−65.9	−16.8
June	9.8	−151.7	21.6	−97.0	44.6	−6.2
July	−5.9	−101.5	−5.5	−50.2	49.1	−22.9
August	12.5	−42.4	−58.2	−30.8	41.6	−12.4
September	53.3	−80.4	51.9	8.0	112.7	65.5
October	12.5	−44.7	43.0	−2.0	99.8	53.7
November	−15.6	−19.0	−50.0	35.6	84.5	31.7
December	−43.8	55.8	72.1	73.6	106.8	91.2

Month	*1926*	*1927*	*1928*	*1929*	*1930*	*1931*
January	−93.9	−98.1	−120.6	−97.1	−47.7	−84.9
February	−35.5	−75.7	−156.0	−166.4	−82.2	−162.1
March	−76.5	7.2	3.5	−85.9	1.4	18.2
April	−3.9	8.2	38.0	−104.9	17.7	48.9
May	27.4	−52.1	−22.5	−57.5	−89.1	−36.4
June	1.6	37.7	−48.9	1.9	−1.0	−9.5
July	9.4	39.0	−67.2	104.3	13.6	20.6
August	−23.8	24.4	−75.9	−53.8	15.0	124.9
September	4.1	101.9	114.2	47.0	26.7	150.3
October	3.2	49.1	88.0	38.4	0.1	543.8
November	17.4	111.8	45.1	109.3	−1.7	−164.8
December	83.2	129.9	99.7	182.3	163.7	−123.1

* Estimated from the amount of Reserve bank credit outstanding in the New York money market. Reserve bank credit outstanding in the New York money market calculated as the sum of discounts of the Federal Reserve Bank of New York, the open-market portfolio of the entire Federal Reserve system, foreign loans on gold, due from foreign banks and Federal Reserve bank float of the Federal Reserve Bank of New York.

FINAL APPROXIMATION OF THE NET MOVEMENT OF RESERVE BANK CREDIT INTO AND OUT OF THE NEW YORK MONEY MARKET *

(*Monthly averages of daily data; in millions of dollars*)

Month	*1919*	*1920*	*1921*	*1922*	*1923*
January	− 64.8	34.4	− 120.0	− 66.3	16.7
February	− 7.5	− 21.5	− 33.4	53.9	− 51.1
March	17.1	1.6	− 151.2	93.1	− 41.6
April	− 114.5	− 174.4	− 195.6	53.2	− 65.2
May	61.7	− 38.5	− 73.8	64.9	− 46.5
June	− 12.5	18.0	− 146.8	31.9	− 97.7
July	226.3	5.1	− 102.1	− 2.9	− 42.6
August	14.1	− 2.7	− 46.3	− 61.4	− 30.8
September	38.5	52.5	− 85.8	52.7	1.8
October	61.8	15.2	− 42.8	50.5	4.3
November	149.0	− 19.8	− 17.4	− 64.4	34.5
December	93.3	− 47.6	44.7	82.1	77.1

Month	*1924*	*1925*	*1926*	*1927*	*1928*
January	− 48.3	− 131.3	− 87.7	− 93.5	− 122.5
February	− 5.4	− 16.4	− 37.4	− 72.5	− 159.5
March	21.7	− 9.2	− 72.6	2.2	3.8
April	− 25.9	− 61.9	− 6.6	9.5	37.2
May	− 56.1	− 17.3	26.7	− 66.4	− 25.2
June	45.4	− 7.4	4.5	41.6	− 48.8
July	45.4	− 20.3	7.7	44.4	− 70.9
August	31.4	− 13.0	− 27.3	26.9	− 78.7
September	118.8	65.4	− 7.9	100.0	114.9
October	97.2	48.0	12.5	45.3	87.3
November	88.6	25.9	15.5	112.9	39.7
December	98.4	97.5	89.5	138.5	98.9

Month	*1929*	*1930*	*1931*	*1932*	
January	− 98.4	− 44.9	− 87.6	− 120.5	
February	− 166.5	− 73.6	− 154.1	− 115.1	
March	− 93.7	− 3.8	16.6		
April	− 108.8	20.2	49.2		
May	− 55.7	− 86.7	− 35.7		
June	− 0.1	− 4.9	3.2		
July	104.2	12.5	27.5		
August	− 55.8	11.8	168.6		
September	34.2	26.5	156.1		
October	46.7	0.6	531.4		
November	102.8	1.8	− 178.2		
December	184.4	159.0	− 136.2		

* Table on page 340, corrected for changes in Reserve credit due to changes in capital, surplus and other liabilities of the Federal Reserve Bank of New York; and also for changes in Government, foreign bank and other deposits of the Federal Reserve Bank of New York.

Statistical correction of data for currency movements

In the previous tables there have been presented statistical measurements of the movement of primary reserves (gold) into and out of the New York money market, and statistical measurements of the secondary reserves (Reserve bank credit) into and out of the New York money market. Still another factor must be considered, and that is the part of the gold movement and Reserve bank credit movement which expresses itself in the form of currency fluctuations. In order to obtain that amount of gold movement which affects the market, the net amount must be corrected for that portion which takes the form of circulating gold coins or gold certificates; and similarly Reserve bank credit must be corrected for changes in the circulation of the Federal Reserve notes of the Federal Reserve Bank of New York. If the inflow of gold from abroad or through the gold settlement fund merely goes into circulation as gold certificates, instead of being added to member bank reserves, such inflow would not directly affect the money market.[8]

The upper curve of Chart 43 shows the cumulative movement of gold into and out of the New York money market, corrected for gold circulation. Owing to lack of data for the movement of gold into and out of circulation in New York alone, data were taken for the country as a whole. The other curve shows the cumulative movement of Reserve bank credit into and out of the New York money market, corrected for that part of reserve bank credit which serves as money in the form of Federal Reserve notes instead of as credit base. Chart 44 gives the cumulative movement of the credit base in the New York money market, as adjusted for currency movements (a + b) on Chart 43; and is related on Chart 44 to member bank reserves of the Federal Reserve Bank of New York.

Defects in above method

As already noted, data are not available for correcting the net

[8] Consequently, before this portion of the credit base resulting from changes in gold stock can be combined with the Reserve credit portion of the credit base affecting the market, an adjustment must be made for currency movements. Similarly, the portion of Reserve credit "affecting the market" is that part *not* circulating in the form of Federal Reserve notes.

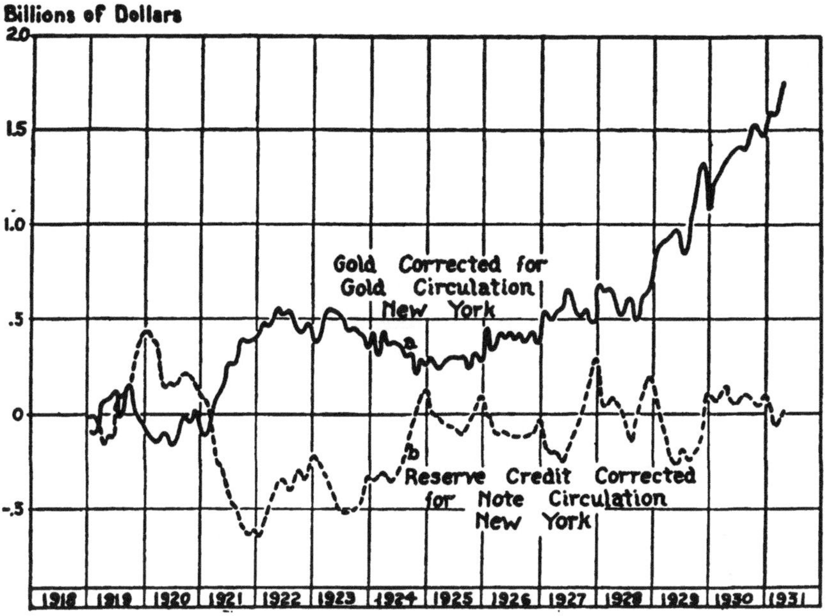

CHART 43. CUMULATED MOVEMENT OF RESERVE CREDIT AND GOLD TO AND FROM THE NEW YORK MONEY MARKET, CORRECTED FOR CURRENCY FLUCTUATIONS.

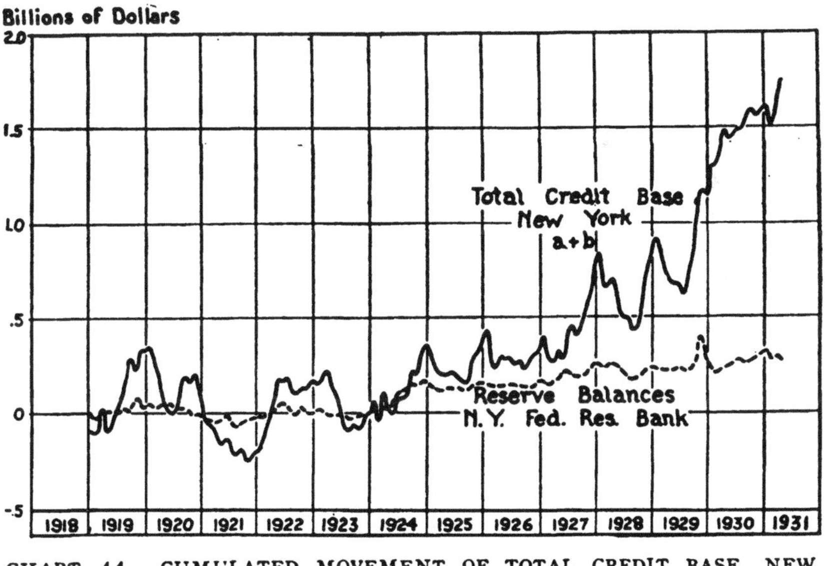

CHART 44. CUMULATED MOVEMENT OF TOTAL CREDIT BASE, NEW YORK, COMPARED WITH MEMBER BANK RESERVES.

THE CREDIT BASE CURVE ON THIS CHART IS THE ALGEBRAIC SUM OF CURVES "A" AND "B" ON CHART 43.

gold movement into and out of the New York money market by that part taken up by the circulation of gold and gold certificates of the New York district alone. For this reason the gold movement was corrected by taking the gold and gold certificate circulation for the country as a whole. In addition to this major defect, there are certain minor defects, in so far as the purpose here served is concerned. For example, the gold settlement fund data, as published and used, include the effects of inter-Federal Reserve bank rediscounting and participation by interior Federal Reserve banks in open-market purchases. These are also included in the series representing net movement of Reserve bank credit into and out of the New York money market. As a result, when the two are combined, as they are in Chart 44 in the line representing total credit base, duplication is involved. These defects probably account in part for the divergences between the total credit base and member bank reserve balances.

Alternative method of measuring New York money market gold movement

Because of the defects described above, it is necessary to attempt another method of measuring that part of the gold movement in the New York money market which affects the credit base. This method is based on the hypothesis that net movements of gold affecting the money market would be reflected in the cash reserves of the Federal Reserve Bank of New York. An inflow of primary reserve funds into the New York money market would either (1) increase the total cash reserves of the Federal Reserve Bank of New York; (2) increase the amount of money in circulation; (3) increase the cash reserves of nonmember banks; or (4) increase the volume of till money of member banks. Disregarding (3) and (4) as relatively unimportant, any net inflow of primary reserves affecting the money market and any outflow affecting the money market will be reflected in the cash reserves of the Federal Reserve Bank of New York. That part of the inflow or outflow reflected in increases or decreases in the amount of money in circulation would not affect the credit market.

Chart 45 is presented to show the relationship between the two methods of calculating the net gold movement affecting the New York money market. The curve labeled "corrected" shows the cumulated gold movement to and from the New York District, taking net imports or exports of the customs districts of

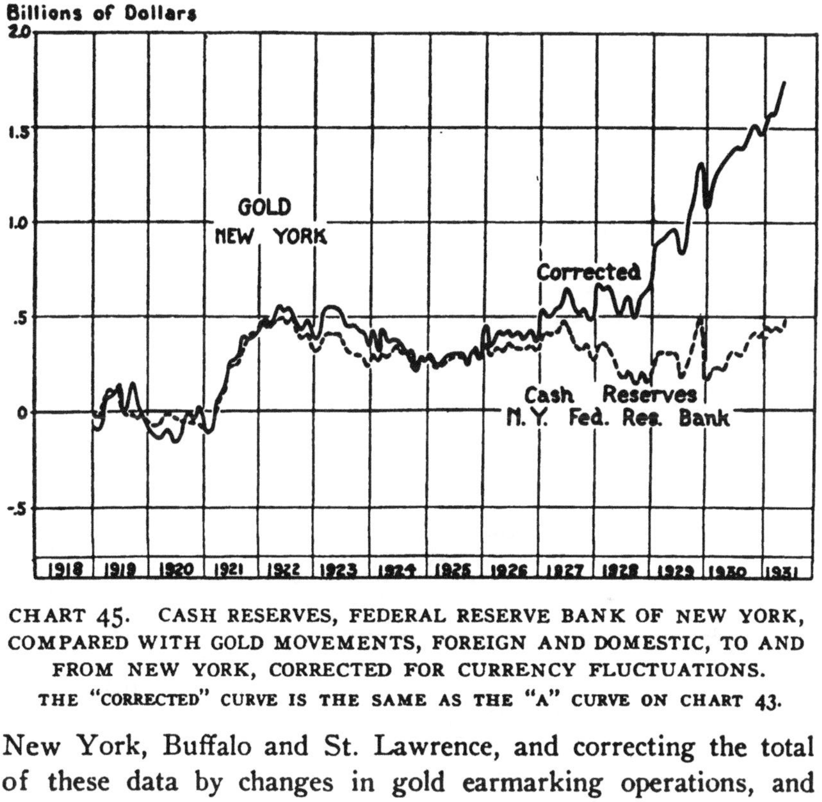

CHART 45. CASH RESERVES, FEDERAL RESERVE BANK OF NEW YORK, COMPARED WITH GOLD MOVEMENTS, FOREIGN AND DOMESTIC, TO AND FROM NEW YORK, CORRECTED FOR CURRENCY FLUCTUATIONS. THE "CORRECTED" CURVE IS THE SAME AS THE "A" CURVE ON CHART 43.

New York, Buffalo and St. Lawrence, and correcting the total of these data by changes in gold earmarking operations, and combining this movement with the domestic movement through the gold settlement fund. The other curve represents monthly cumulated increases or decreases, since the beginning of 1919, in the cash reserves of the Federal Reserve Bank of New York. It is to be noted that the two curves are in close agreement until the end of 1926; but since that time the "corrected" method reflects a far greater movement of gold to the New York money market than is reflected in the cash reserves of the Federal Reserve Bank of New York.

Combining the figures for the ebb and flow of Federal Reserve credit corrected for Federal Reserve note circulation, as calculated above,[9] with net changes in the cash reserves of the Federal Reserve Bank of New York, will presumably give the total net ebb and flow in the credit base affecting the money market. This

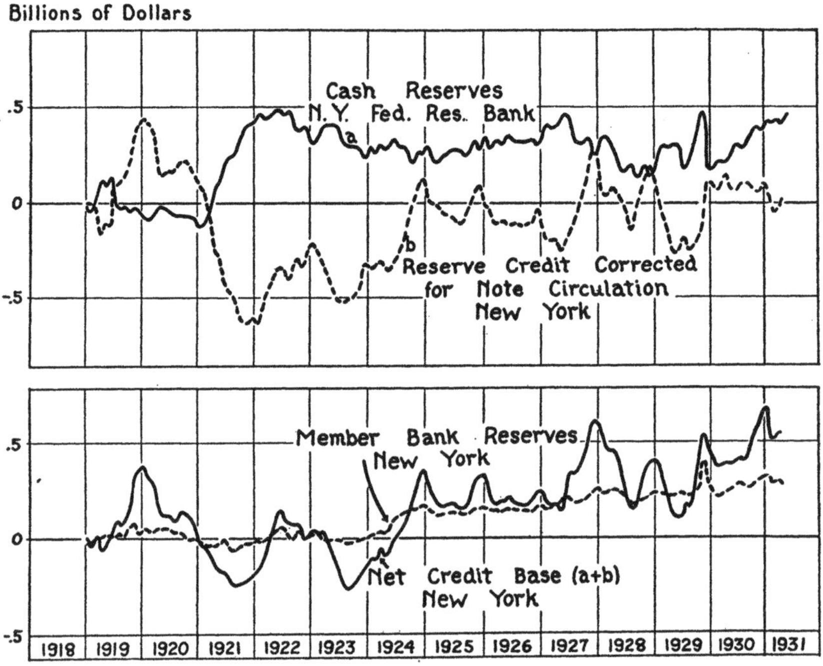

CHART 46. GOLD MOVEMENTS AS MEASURED BY CASH RESERVES OF THE FEDERAL RESERVE BANK OF NEW YORK, COMPARED WITH MOVEMENT OF FEDERAL RESERVE CREDIT.

THE "B" CURVE IS THE SAME AS THE "B" CURVE ON CHART 43.

makes use of the alternative method of measuring gold movements affecting the New York money market, which assumes that such gold movements would be reflected in the cash reserves of the Federal Reserve Bank of New York. This is shown in Chart 46. The lower portion relates the cumulative movement of the credit base (a + b) of the New York money market with member bank reserves.

[9] *Supra*, p. 342.

Comparison of two methods of measuring net credit base—New York money market

Chart 47 shows the results of an attempt to measure the movement of funds affecting the New York money market, in-

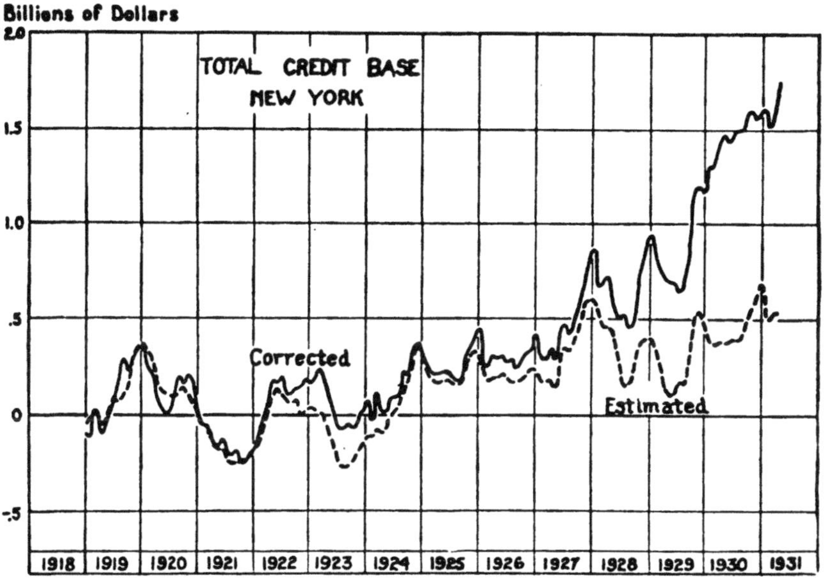

CHART 47. COMPARISON OF THE TWO METHODS OF MEASURING THE MOVEMENT OF CREDIT BASE TO AND FROM THE NEW YORK MONEY MARKET.

THE "CORRECTED" CURVE IS THE SAME AS THE "A + B" CURVE ON CHART 44.

cluding gold and Federal Reserve credit corrected for currency movements, by the two methods which have been outlined above. The curve labeled "corrected" represents the cumulated movement of funds affecting the New York money market since 1919, calculated by taking the sum of (1) and (2) as follows:

(1) *Gold movements* through the New York, Buffalo and St. Lawrence Customs Districts, corrected for changes in earmarked gold, added algebraically to gold movements to and from the Federal Reserve Bank of New York through the gold settlement fund (settlements, *i. e.*, transit clearings, government transfers and Federal Reserve note clearings). These results were then cor-

rected for gold and gold certificates in circulation in the United States. The final result constituted, presumably, the New York gold movement affecting the money market.

(2) *Federal Reserve credit* outstanding in the New York Federal Reserve district calculated as described above and then corrected for Federal Reserve notes in circulation in the New York district.

The curve labeled "estimated," on the other hand, is the cumulated movement of funds affecting the New York money market since 1919, calculated by substituting for (1) above the cumulated changes in the cash reserves of the Federal Reserve Bank of New York.

Shorter method of estimating volume of Federal Reserve credit in the New York money market

It is believed that it is possible to estimate fluctuations in the amount of Federal Reserve credit in the New York money market by a shorter method. The hypothesis is: total Federal Reserve credit in the New York money market = member bank reserves of the New York district + (Federal Reserve notes in circulation in the district — cash reserves of the Federal Reserve Bank of New York.) [10] Therefore that part of total Federal Reserve credit which affects the money market should equal member bank reserves minus the cash reserves of the Federal Reserve Bank of New York,[11] because Federal Reserve notes in circulation represent Federal Reserve credit which does not enter into the money market credit base. The cumulated movement in Federal Reserve credit was estimated in this way, and the result appears in Chart 48, together with a curve representing Federal Reserve credit movement in the New York money market calculated by the long method used above. The curve labeled "estimated" represents the movement of Federal Reserve credit in the New York money market cumulated from the beginning of 1919, calculated by taking the difference between member bank reserves in the New York Fed-

[10] Federal Reserve Bank of New York cash reserves is subtracted on the assumption that they represent the gold portion of member bank reserves.

[11] Cf. Burgess, W. R., *The Reserve Banks and the Money Market*, p. 313.

eral Reserve district and the cash reserves of the Federal Reserve Bank of New York; while the curve labeled "corrected" represents the movement of Federal Reserve credit in the New York money market cumulated from the beginning of 1919, calculated by the long method and corrected for changes in circulation of Federal Reserve notes in the New York district.

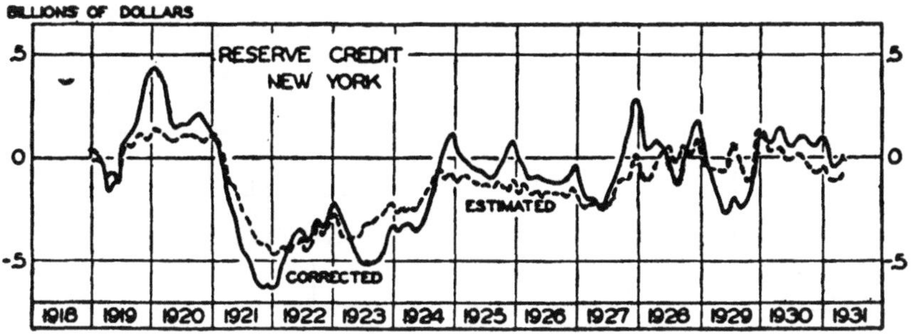

CHART 48. RESULTS OBTAINED FROM TWO METHODS OF MEASURING CHANGES IN THE AMOUNT OF FEDERAL RESERVE CREDIT IN THE NEW YORK MONEY MARKET.

THE "CORRECTED" CURVE IS THE SAME AS THE "B" CURVE ON CHART 43.

Federal Reserve Bank of New York data on movement of credit base

In recent years calculations have been made at the Federal Reserve Bank of New York of changes in the net credit base affecting the money market. Some of the data are published in *The Monthly Review of Credit and Business Conditions,* and in articles on the money market by Dr. W. Randolph Burgess in *The Harvard Review of Economic Statistics.*[12] These data are shown in Chart 49, with the monthly changes in credit base cumulated since October, 1925. Curve "B" represents the cumulated movement in Reserve credit affecting the money market while curve "A" consists of gold settlement fund transactions and other gold movements. It is not possible to check the results

[12] The data are not available in a continuous published series, but the authorities of the Federal Reserve Bank of New York very kindly furnished the authors with the series for the period 1926–1930. Cf. Federal Reserve Bank of New York, *Monthly Review of Credit and Business Conditions,* April 1, 1926, p. 3; July, 1926, p. 3. "An analysis of changes in the New York money market," *Harvard Review of Economic Statistics,* Jan., 1926, pp. 15–22.

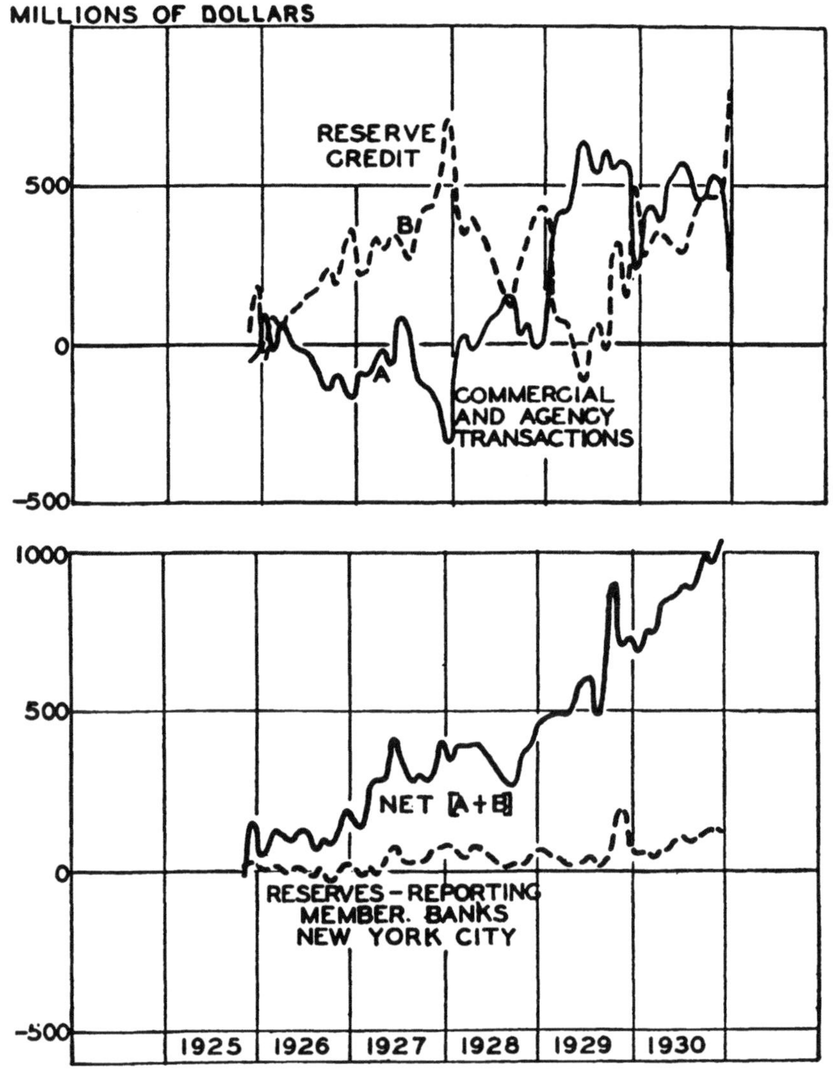

CHART 49. MOVEMENT OF RESERVE FUNDS TO AND FROM THE NEW YORK MONEY MARKET—FEDERAL RESERVE BANK OF NEW YORK DATA.

presented here with those obtained above, but it is to be noted that the Federal Reserve Bank of New York data show clearly the same inverse relationship in movement between Federal Reserve bank credit and gold. The combination of the two, which presumably gives the movement in the net credit base of the New York money market, is shown in the lower portion of the graph (A + B) and compared there with cumulated changes in the reserve balances of the reporting member banks of New York City.

According to the data plotted in the Charts 44 and 49, a large inflow of the credit base into the New York money market appears to have taken place since 1925. Apparently this inflow was not reflected in member bank reserves. Concerning this upward bias appearing in the data furnished by the Federal Reserve Bank of New York, the explanation is offered that these are based largely on transactions in New York City, rather than on complete transactions for the district as a whole.[13]

Revised statistics of changes in the net credit base have recently been prepared by the statisticians of the Federal Reserve Bank of New York. Data have been prepared for the entire of the New York district, as was attempted by the authors in the earlier pages of this chapter, rather than for New York City separately. The revised data, calculated in this manner and shown on the chart on page 352, correspond very closely with fluctuations in member bank reserves. The commercial and agency transactions include foreign gold movements, treasury transactions, the movement of funds through the gold settlement fund, currency withdrawals and deposits, changes in the balances of foreign central banks with the Federal Reserve Bank of New York, and changes in nonmember bank clearing accounts. The Reserve bank transactions include discounts for member banks in the New York district, acceptance and government security transactions in New York for all Federal Reserve banks, and the earnings and expenditures of the Federal Reserve Bank of New York. If the data appearing in these two curves were added algebraically, the result would be a curve exactly superimposed over the curve showing changes in member bank reserves.

[13] The upward bias in the data appearing in Charts 44 and 49 is in contrast to the downward bias which appeared in the cumulation of movement in the net credit base for the country as a whole (Chart 39), where there appears to be a more rapid rise in member bank reserve deposits than the growth in the credit base would indicate as possible.

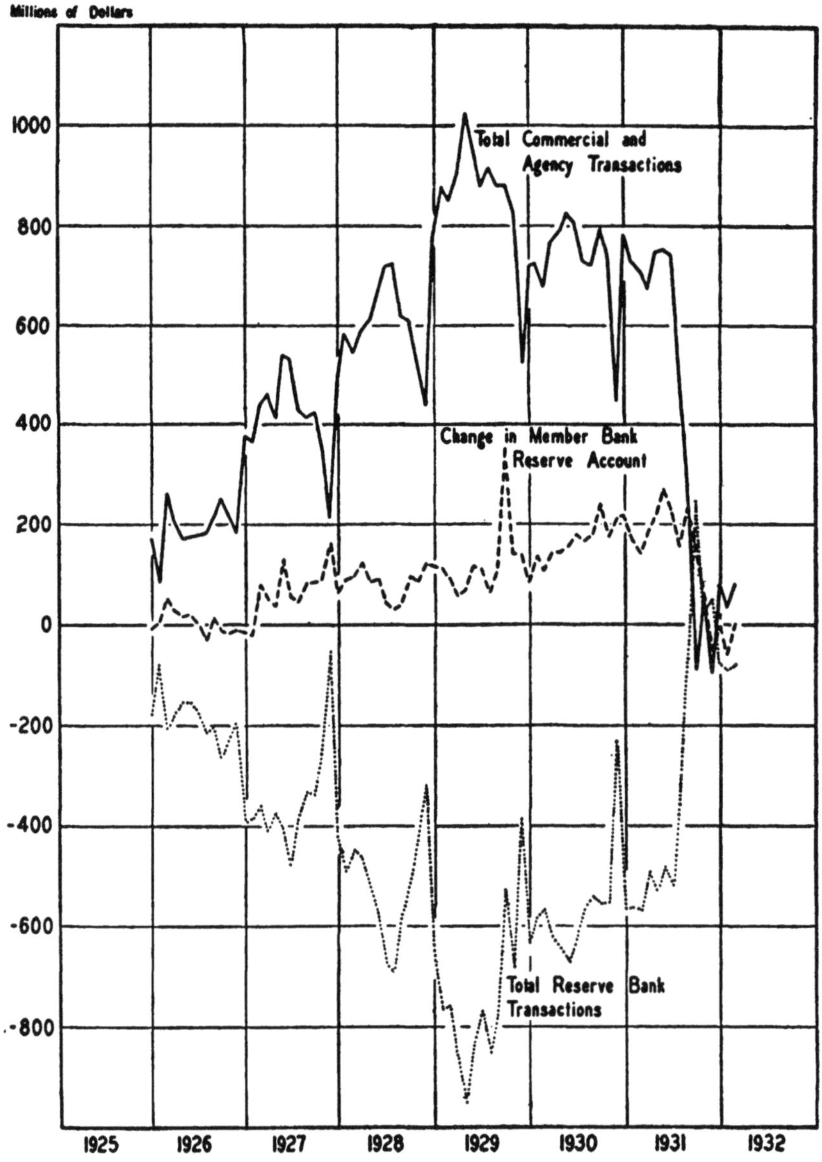

CHART 50. MOVEMENT OF RESERVE FUNDS TO AND FROM THE NEW YORK MONEY MARKET.

REVISED DATA, FEDERAL RESERVE BANK OF NEW YORK.

The importance of arriving at a method of analysis which will accurately picture the situation is obvious, since it relates to the whole question of Federal Reserve policy. If the Federal Reserve authorities are to act intelligently, and with sufficient timeliness, an exact method should be devised of measuring the movement of funds into and out of the money market, and it should be known what part of that movement is in the form of gold or its equivalent and what part is in the form of Reserve credit. Changes of an involuntary nature in other factors may be counteracting or aggravating a particular voluntary action on the part of the Federal Reserve banks, in either case throwing askew the calculations of the expected effect of the voluntary activities in the money market.

Summary

It has been the object of this chapter to present a statistical measurement of the net ebb and flow of the reserve funds of the money market, *i. e.*, the funds affecting the credit base. This was done by presenting the movement of funds to and from the United States through the visible and "invisible" ebb and flow of gold and the ebb and flow of Reserve bank credit. The ebb and flow of gold was corrected for currency movements and the total movement of Reserve bank credit was likewise treated. Thus was obtained a picture of the net movement of funds affecting the credit structure of the United States. This analysis was then followed by a similar study of the ebb and flow of the reserve funds of the New York money market. Data covering the movement of funds to and from the New York money market included: (1) exports and imports of gold of the Federal Reserve district of New York, and (2) movement of funds to and from New York through the gold settlement fund. This net gold movement was corrected for gold circulation and then combined with an estimate of the movement of Reserve bank credit to and from the New York money market, which was corrected for Federal Reserve notes in circulation. Two different methods of estimating the movement of the credit base were presented. All data were computed on a monthly basis and, in order to picture the trend and cycle in these movements, the data were cumulated from the beginning of 1919. It was found that the same characteristics are present in the data published by the Federal Reserve Bank of New York as regards increments and decrements to money market funds, so far as the inverseness of relationship between movements in Federal Reserve credit and gold movements is concerned. The combination of the two series into data purporting to represent the net changes in the credit base shows a residual trend or growth during the period studied, as well as various cyclical movements. In a later chapter these fluctuations will be related to money rates.

Chapter XVII

DOMESTIC MOVEMENT FURTHER ANALYZED

In preceding chapters the aggregate net movement of funds in and out of the New York money market was measured statistically in so far as possible. It was there indicated that the movement of Federal Reserve credit into and out of the money market serves to counteract or supplement, as the case may be, the movement of gold into and out of the money market.

In analyzing the domestic movement of funds, it is possible to regard each Federal Reserve district as a separate country, and apply by analogy the theory of foreign trade settlements to interdistrict movements of funds. Underlying explanatory data, in the form of commodity movements, financial transactions, the exchange of services and securities between the various districts, are not available; so that any explanation of the domestic movement of funds can be attempted only in very general terms. Little more may be done than to present data on the interdistrict movement of funds, to indicate the trends in such movements, and to hazard explanations of the behaviour of the curves.[1]

Statistical measurement of domestic movement of funds through the gold settlement fund—New York and the rest of the country

The movement of funds in domestic exchanges into and out of the New York money market may be studied, in accordance with available data, as follows: (1) the movement of funds through the gold settlement fund due to "government transfers"; (2) the movement of funds through the gold settlement fund due to currency movements, or "Federal Reserve note clearings"; and (3) the movement of funds through the gold settlement fund due to "transit clearings," which are the resultant of all other

[1] On economic characteristics of districts giving rise to the ebb and flow of funds. See Chap. XIV, *supra*, pp. 287–95.

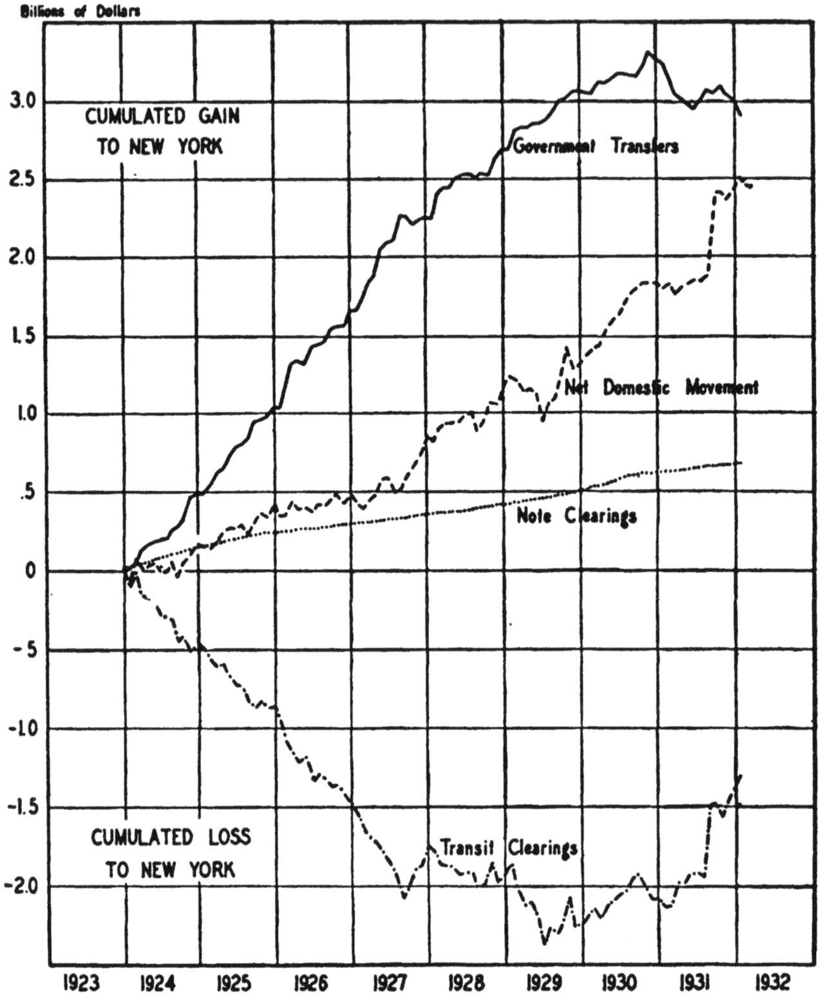

CHART 51. CUMULATED MOVEMENT OF FUNDS BETWEEN NEW YORK AND THE REST OF THE UNITED STATES, 1924–1931, DUE TO GOVERNMENT TRANSFERS. NOTE CLEARINGS AND TRANSIT CLEARINGS.

factors; namely, trade, services, investment, financial, speculative operations, etc.

Chart 51 is presented to show the cumulated movement in the ebb and flow of funds between New York and the rest of the country. The data are plotted from the beginning of 1924,

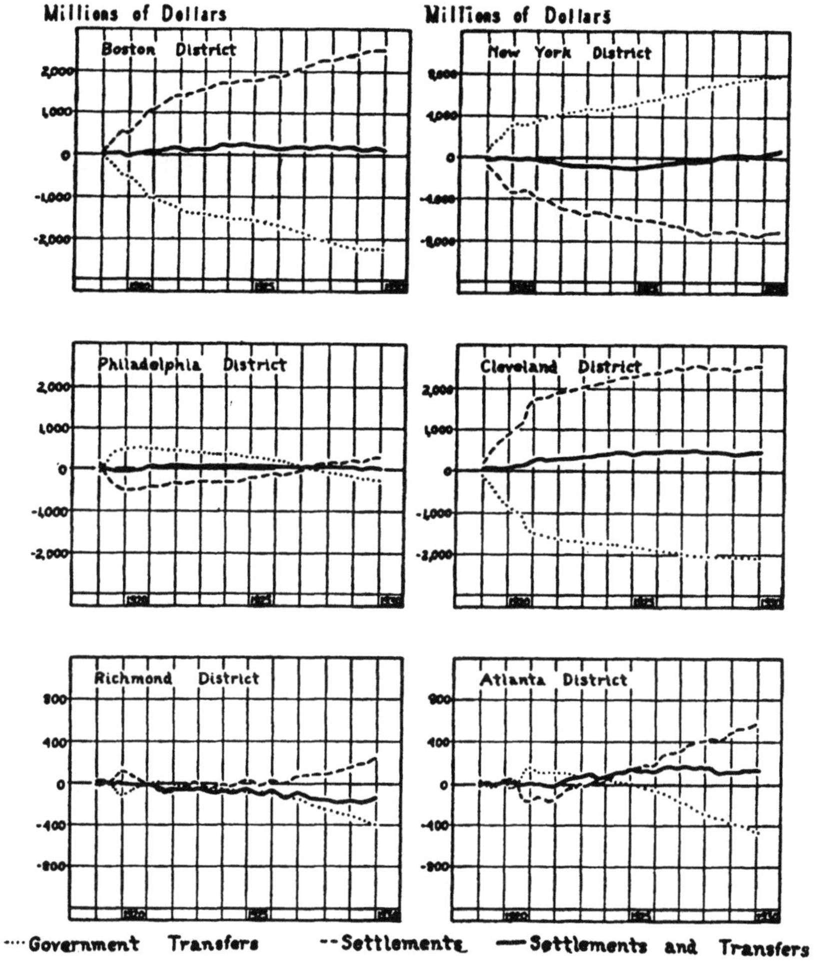

CHART 52. GOLD SETTLEMENT FUND TRANSACTIONS BY DISTRICTS—CUMULATED MOVEMENT OF FUNDS INTO AND OUT OF EACH DISTRICT IN RELATION TO THE REST OF THE COUNTRY, DUE TO GOVERNMENT TRANSFERS AND SETTLEMENTS.

inasmuch as data on Federal Reserve note clearings are not available on a monthly basis prior to that time.[2] As indicated in the chart, the New York money market tends to gain through government transfers and Federal Reserve note clearings, while it

[2] Cf. *Annual Report of the Federal Reserve Board*, 1922, pp. 110–11.

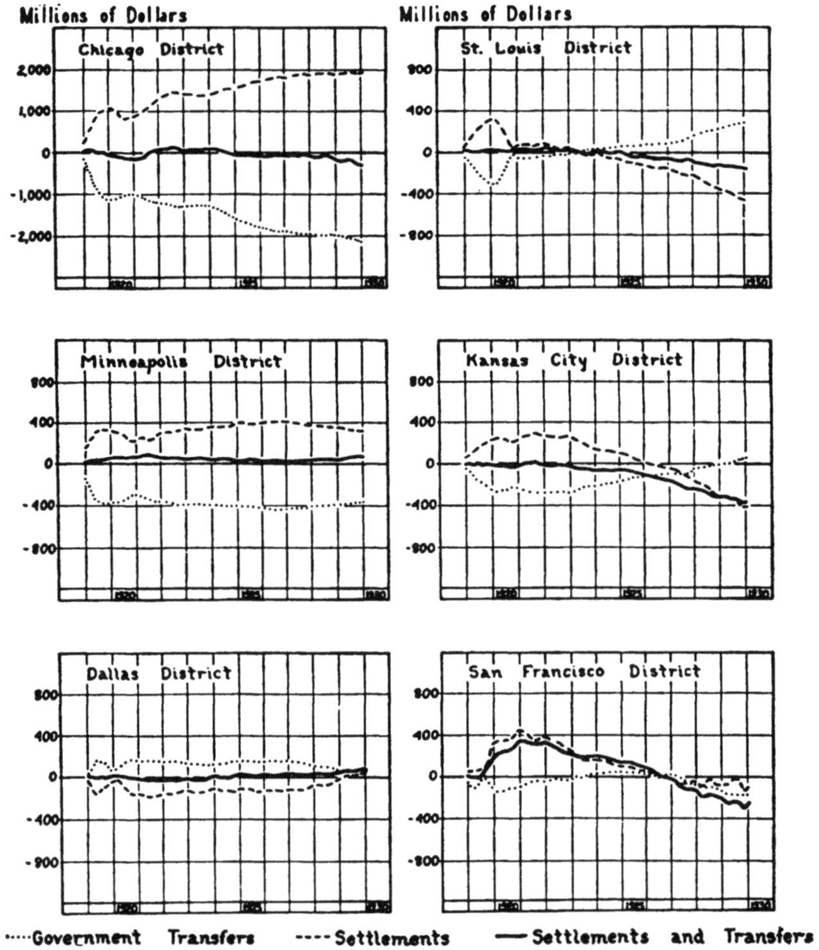

CHART 53. GOLD SETTLEMENT FUND TRANSACTIONS BY DISTRICTS—CUMULATED MOVEMENT OF FUNDS INTO AND OUT OF EACH DISTRICT IN RELATION TO THE REST OF THE COUNTRY, DUE TO GOVERNMENT TRANSFERS AND SETTLEMENTS (CONTINUED).

loses cumulatively through transit clearings.[3] The general discussion of the reasons for the cumulative gain from government transfers in the New York money market is contained elsewhere. As previously stated, the cumulative gain to New York from note

[3] Cf. Burgess, W. R., *The Federal Reserve Banks and the Money Market*, p. 162. *Supra*, pp. 302–3 and 316–20; *Annual Report of the Federal Reserve Board*, 1926, p. 250.

clearings is due to the fact that a larger amount of the note issues of other Reserve banks is spent by visitors in New York than notes of the New York Federal Reserve Bank are spent in other parts of the country. In a later part of this chapter, transit clearings between New York and each of the other Reserve districts will be considered separately.

Movement of funds between each Federal Reserve district and the rest of the country

Charts 52 and 53 show the cumulated movement of funds into and out of each of the twelve Federal Reserve districts, giving the cumulative movements due to government transfers (dotted line), due to settlements, including Federal Reserve note and transit clearings (dash line), and of the final net movement (solid line).

It will be noted that some of the districts lose cumulatively through government transfers, while others gain:

Districts which lose by government transfers	*Districts which gain by government transfers*
Boston	New York
Cleveland	St. Louis (since 1921)
Chicago	Kansas City (since 1921)
Richmond (since 1921)	
Atlanta (since 1921)	
Philadelphia (since 1920)	

The Philadelphia district gained through government transfers during 1919, though since that time the trend has been away from that district. The cumulative movement of government transfers seems clearly to be away from the Richmond and Atlanta districts, although the movement was confused in the years 1919–1921. The St. Louis district lost through government transfers during 1919, but since that time has gained. In the cases of the Minneapolis, Dallas and San Francisco districts, the trend in movement of government funds is not clear, although since 1926 Minneapolis has gained and the Dallas and San Francisco districts have lost. Attention should be called to the fact that the scales on these various graphs are different, so that the relative importance of the movement into and from New York is far greater than the relative sizes of the charts.

It is striking that the districts which lose cumulatively by government transfers tend to gain by settlements and vice versa. The Boston, Philadelphia, Cleveland, Richmond, Atlanta, Chicago and Dallas districts show a tendency to gain by settlements, although Philadelphia, Atlanta and Dallas lost from the first of 1919 to the middle of 1921. The New York, St. Louis, Kansas City and San Francisco districts show a tendency to lose steadily by settlements, although St. Louis gained largely in 1919; Kansas City gained from 1919 to the middle of 1921; and San Francisco gained during 1919 and 1920.

In most of the districts the final net movement of funds into and out of the district, in its economic relations with the rest of the country, shows little trend one way or the other. New York, however, has gained cumulatively since the beginning of 1924; Richmond has lost funds from the beginning of 1919; Chicago has lost funds since the beginning of 1924; Kansas City since the middle of 1921, and San Francisco since the beginning of 1921. Cleveland, Atlanta, and Minneapolis show cumulative gains.

In the case of the New York district the final net domestic movement must be considered in connection with foreign gold exports and imports in any interpretation of the effect upon the New York money market. This would apply also to the San Francisco district, inasmuch as large quantities of gold come into the San Francisco customs district as well as into San Diego. To some extent this qualification would apply to the Richmond district; to Dallas for gold coming from Mexico; and to the Minneapolis district for gold entering through the Montana and Idaho customs district. The New York and San Francisco districts are the principal ones which would be affected by gold imports and exports.

Monthly movement of funds between New York and the interior in 1928 and 1929 due to transit clearings

Charts 54 and 55 depict the movement of funds due to transit clearings by months during 1928 and 1929 between New York and each of the other eleven districts—the movement to New York is represented by a solid line; and the movement from New York, by a dotted line. It will be noticed how nearly equal in amount in most instances are the gains and losses. Transit clearings through the gold settlement fund include the entire movement of funds between the New York money market and the rest of the country, with the exception of (1) the movement of funds due to government fiscal operations, and (2) the movement of funds due to note clearings. Thus transit clearings represent funds coming into the New York money market to pay for imports; to pay for commodities bought by persons throughout the country from persons or firms in the New York district; to pay for securities purchased in the listed or unlisted markets; to pay for new issues floated by investment bankers in New York City; to pay for services rendered by persons or firms in New York to those outside the New York money market; to pay for foreign exchange purchased in New York; to increase call loans, bankers' balances, etc. They include also participation in open-market purchases by other Federal Reserve banks through the Federal Reserve Bank of New York.[4] Transit clearings represent the movement of funds out of the New York money market, on the other hand, to pay for goods and services and securities sold to New York (or through New York to other parts of the country or abroad); that resulting from withdrawal in open-market participation by the other Federal Reserve banks; and in general resulting from the reverse of all the above transactions mentioned. In brief, transit clearings in the aggregate constitute a measure of the total trade in goods, services and securities, in addition to financial transactions which take place between New York and the rest of the country. There is represented too that

[4] But in earlier years the inter-Reserve bank movement due to rediscounting was included in statistics on government transfers. See *Annual Report of the Federal Reserve Board, 1922*, p. 28.

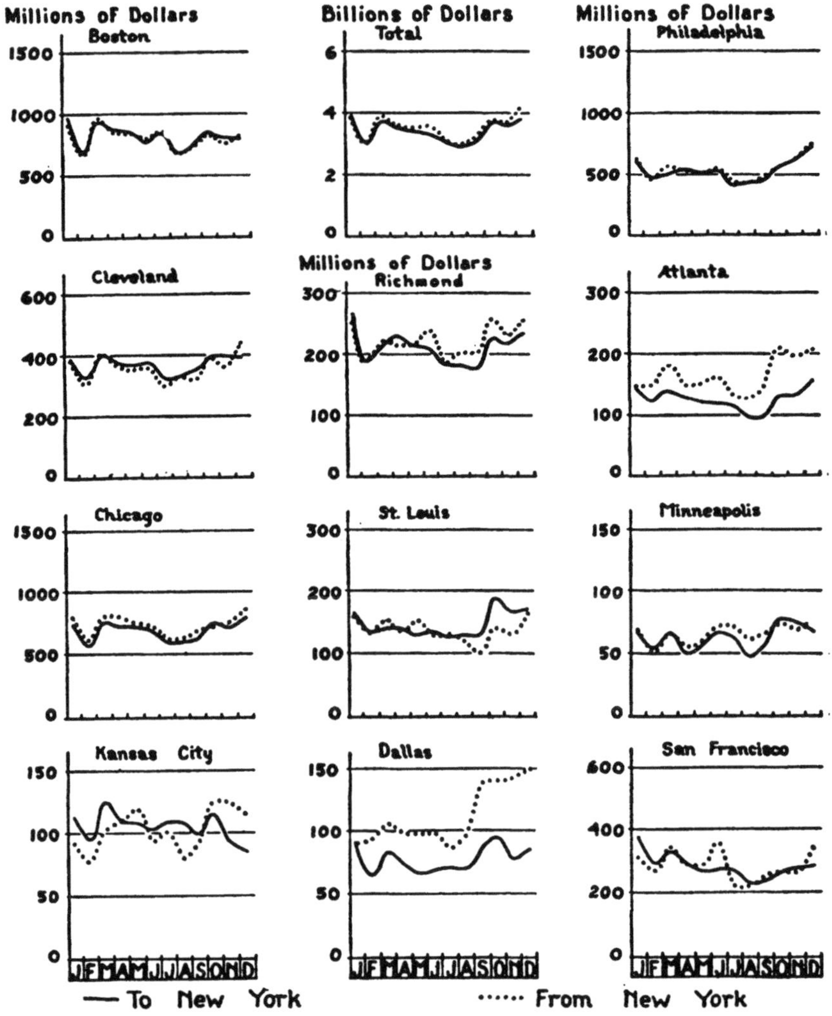

CHART 54. INTERIOR MOVEMENT OF FUNDS IN 1928 BETWEEN THE NEW YORK FEDERAL RESERVE DISTRICT AND THE OTHER FEDERAL RESERVE DISTRICTS, DUE TO TRANSIT CLEARINGS THROUGH THE GOLD SETTLEMENT FUND.

part of the import and export trade of the United States which is financed through the New York foreign exchange market.

From the point of view of industry and commerce and the business life of the nation, transit clearings are the most impor-

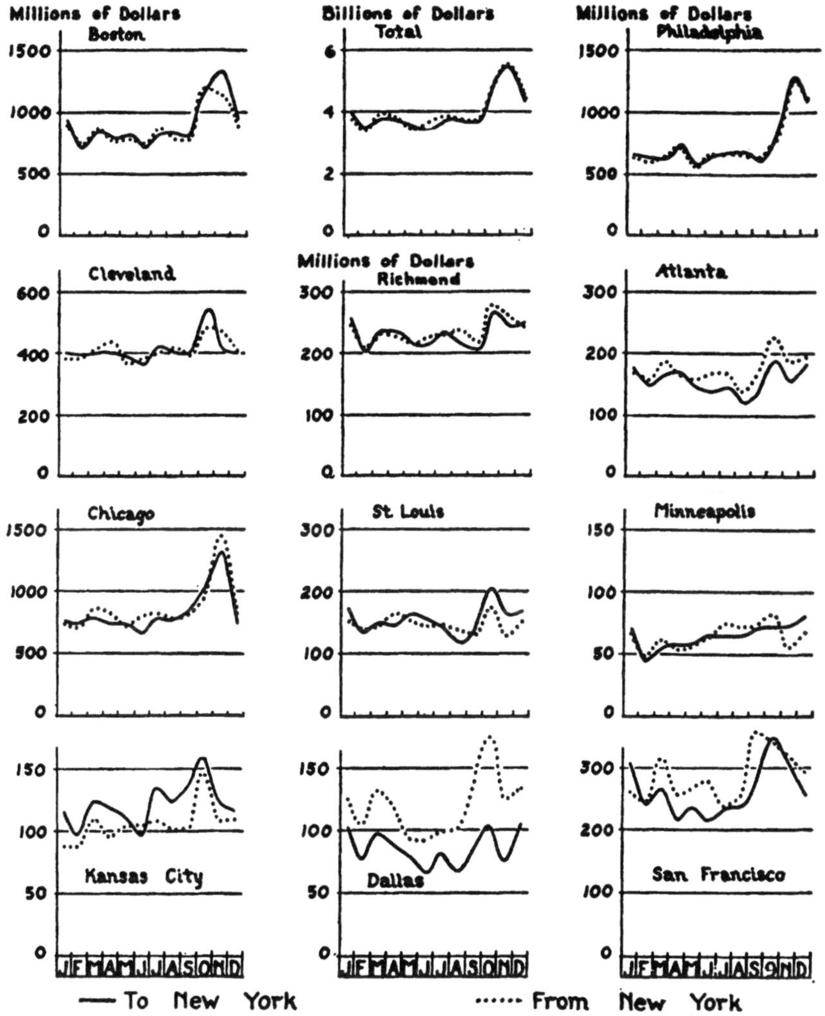

CHART 55. INTERIOR MOVEMENT OF FUNDS IN 1929 BETWEEN THE NEW YORK FEDERAL RESERVE DISTRICT AND THE OTHER FEDERAL RESERVE DISTRICTS, DUE TO TRANSIT CLEARINGS THROUGH THE GOLD SETTLEMENT FUND.

tant of the three types of gold settlement fund data analyzed. For this reason these data have been broken down, in order to show transit clearings between the New York Federal Reserve district and each of the other eleven Federal Reserve districts.[5]

[5] These data, 1919–1929, were supplied by the courtesy of the Federal Reserve

Annual data of net transit clearings between New York and each Reserve district

It has been seen that New York tends to gain funds from the entire country through the gold settlement fund by Federal Reserve note clearings and government transfers, while it suffers a heavy loss by transit clearings. To present a more complete analysis of the position of New York with reference to transit clearings, the data were broken down by Federal Reserve districts. It will be noted from Chart 56 that New York loses consistently to the Atlanta, Chicago, and Dallas districts, and since 1920 to the Minneapolis district. Gains are recorded through most of the period from the Philadelphia, Cleveland, St. Louis and San Francisco districts and in recent years from the Boston and Kansas City districts. In the following pages the movement with respect to each district will be studied separately and in so far as possible explanations of trend will be offered.

Boston district.—The explanation hazarded for the loss of funds by New York to Boston during 1919 and 1920 is that it was caused by the period of marked mill prosperity and represented a flow of money in return for sales of cotton and woolen goods. While in the following years, 1920–1925, the textile industries of New England were depressed, New England on the balance of funds movement was, nevertheless, able to maintain her own. The reason is that New England is a reservoir of capital and the steady flow of income on investments was sufficient to keep the gold settlement fund balance from turning against her.[6] In 1926 and again in 1929 occurred a rapid movement of funds to the New York money market.

Philadelphia.—The tendency has been for New York to gain from Philadelphia throughout the period with the exception of 1927 and 1928. The cumulative gain may be explained by: (1) the fact that the Philadelphia district is a large consumer of mis-

---

Bank of New York, and were compiled from the books of the Federal Reserve bank.

[6] Correspondence with Mr. F. H. Curtiss, Chairman, Federal Reserve Bank of Boston, Aug. 17, 1927; explanation given by Mr. Bowser, statistician of the Federal Reserve Bank of Boston.

cellaneous imported products for which remittance is made through the New York money market; (2) by capital investments through the New York money market; and (3) by the

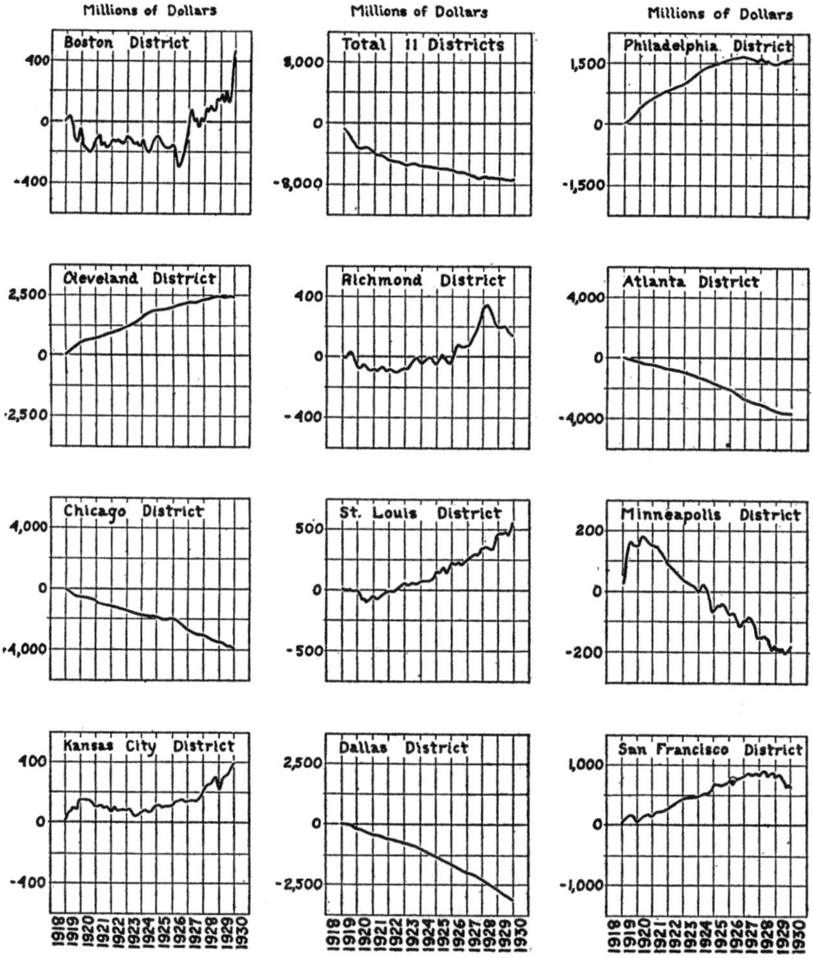

CHART 56. CUMULATED MOVEMENT OF FUNDS TO (+) AND FROM (—) THE NEW YORK FEDERAL RESERVE DISTRICT THROUGH THE GOLD SETTLEMENT FUND DUE TO TRANSIT CLEARINGS.

fact that the products of this district are not exported from the United States to an amount in value equal to imports. In addition, there is the fact that the Philadelphia district (which does not include Pittsburgh) does not sell an amount to the New York district equal to its purchases. The diversified products of Pennsylvania (that part lying in the Philadelphia district), with the exception of coal, are produced also in the New York district.[7]

Cleveland.—As the chart shows, New York gains funds steadily from Cleveland, the total cumulative gain since the beginning of 1919 amounting to almost $2,500,000,000. The Cleveland district is essentially manufacturing in character, producing a large part of its own raw materials, but with a market that is nationwide in extent. In addition there is the further consideration that the ownership of enterprise there, also, is virtually nationwide in extent. Profits are transferred to New York to build up corporation balances for distribution over the entire country in the form of interest and dividends. Large amounts of the funds accumulated by the industries and residents of this district are transferred to the New York money market for investment, on short-term and long-term account.[8] The Cleveland district is a large consumer of imported products and relatively speaking a small producer of products for export from the United States, and for this reason, in addition to the others mentioned, payments to New York would tend to be greater than receipts from New York. While Federal Reserve note clearings are not included in these figures, it is of interest to note that Cleveland also loses to New York in note clearings.[9]

Richmond.—From the middle of 1919 to the middle of 1922, New York lost cumulatively to Richmond. From the middle of 1922 until early in 1928, the flow was the other way, *i. e.,* from Richmond to New York; while since that time New York has lost to Richmond. The magnitude of total movement between New York and Richmond is small compared to that of the other districts, and the reasons for the fluctuations depicted obscure.

Atlanta.—The trend in the flow of funds is steadily from New York to the Atlanta district. Since the beginning of 1919 New

[7] Peterson, N. E., *American Industries by Geographical Sections.*

[8] Correspondence with George D. Camp, Chairman of the Board, Federal Reserve Bank of Cleveland, Aug. 16, 1927.

[9] *The Commercial and Financial Chronicle,* March 30, 1929, pp. 2010–11.

York has lost nearly $4,000,000,000 to Atlanta through transit clearings in the gold settlement fund. The reason for the loss apparently is that the bulk of the agricultural products of this district, cotton, for example, are exported, for which the producers are paid by remittance through New York. Thus Europe pays New York and New York remits to Atlanta. The bulk of the purchases of the district are from within the United States, for which payments would be made direct to the Federal Reserve district involved, so that the gain from New York is doubtless offset, in part, by losses to other districts. For example, purchases of automobiles manufactured in Detroit would be cleared between the Federal Reserve Bank of Atlanta and the Federal Reserve Bank of Chicago. In addition to the remittance of funds from New York due to the relatively heavy export trade of the district, there is the fact that investments of funds accompanying the rapid economic development of the district have been remitted through the New York money market.

Chicago.—The cumulative movement of funds due to transit clearings is from New York to Chicago. From the beginning of 1919 to the end of 1929, New York lost cumulatively to Chicago close to $4,000,000,000. This might be accounted for by the large exports of motor vehicles, grain and grain-mill products, and meat products from the Chicago district, as well as by New York purchases of these products for its own use.

St. Louis.—During 1919 and the first half of 1920, the trend in movement of funds was from New York to St. Louis, while since that time the trend has been the reverse. From the beginning of 1919 to the end of 1929, New York experienced a net gain of $500,000,000 from St. Louis.

Minneapolis.—In the case of Minneapolis, the trend in the movement of funds was towards New York throughout 1919 and through the first half of 1920. Thereafter, until the end of 1929, the trend was from New York to Minneapolis. New York lost cumulatively, from early in 1920 until the end of 1929, about $400,000,000. Considering the normal trading relations between the New York and Minneapolis districts, it is reasonable to assume that the trend of movement of funds should be consistently from New York because: (1) the New York district purchases huge quantities of grain, butter, cheese and other dairy products from the Minneapolis district; and (2) exports of wheat from the Minneapolis district would be paid for through the New York money market. On the other hand, purchases of the Minneapolis district would be spread over the entire country. It imports no important raw materials from the New York district or abroad which would cause a movement of funds from Minneapolis to New York. In addition to the flow of funds from New York to Minneapolis arising from trade relationships, there is the further fact that during the early years of the agricultural depression, banks in the district drew in funds from New York to liquidate the indebtedness to the Federal Reserve bank and to others. This explanation was contained in a letter received from Mr. Curtis L. Mosher, Assistant Federal Reserve agent of the Federal Reserve bank of Minneapolis:

> Undoubtedly the downward trend of the curve after the middle of 1920 reflects what we know to be true; namely, that the Northwest liquidated a very heavy debt to this bank, the War Finance Corporation, to its city bank correspondents in Minneapolis and St. Paul, Chicago, and New York, and liquidated in addition an undetermined but very large amount of private debts. Doubtless the downward trend of the curve reflects as well gradual liquidation under pressure of previous investments and war loan securities, which, considering the character and population of the district, were extremely heavy.

There remains, therefore, to be explained the rapid flow of funds from Minneapolis to New York during 1919 and the first part of 1920. This probably was evidence of the agricultural prosperity of those years, with Minneapolis banks and residents placing an increasing volume of funds in money market use in New York.

Kansas City.—The movement of funds through transit clearings between New York and Kansas City may be divided into three periods: (1) New York gained from Kansas City from the beginning of 1919 until early in 1920; (2) from March, 1920, until July, 1923, the trend in the movement of funds was reversed —New York lost to Kansas City, but still remained a net gainer from the beginning of 1919; and (3) from July, 1923, to the end of 1929, New York gained, the net gain to New York amounting to about $400,000,000 from the beginning of 1919. The explanation of the sharp movement of funds to New York during 1919 and 1920 is probably the same as that given in the case of the Minneapolis district.

Dallas.—The trend in the movement of funds between New York and Dallas has reflected a steady outflow of nearly as great a magnitude as the net outflow from New York to Atlanta. The outflow from New York to Dallas has arisen from payments for cotton and petroleum exports, but principally the former, and from the rapid industrial development and building program carried on in the Dallas district during the years 1919–1927, which was financed largely through New York.[10]

San Francisco.—Until the middle of 1928, New York gained from San Francisco, but since that time has lost. The cumulated gain of New York probably represents the flow of funds available for investment in the New York money market from the industrial and agricultural profits of the San Francisco district, from the savings of retired capitalists, and from the motion picture industry. Apparently more of these investable funds are utilized in the development of enterprise in other parts of the United States than are returned for investment in the San Francisco district.

Security and Investment Loan Fluctuations and Changes of Ownership in the Gold Settlement Fund

Since 1919, as shown in Chart 56, New York has lost funds consistently to some districts, consistently gained from a few, while in the case of other districts there has been no definite trend. When comparison is made between these cumulative movements and between increases or decreases in the security loans and investments of the reporting member banks, no striking positive correlation emerges. The reason is that investments and security loans, particularly loans extended to New York City brokers by interior banks, represent only two items

[10] Letter from Mr. W. J. Evans, Assistant Federal Reserve Agent, Federal Reserve Bank of Dallas, Aug. 18, 1927.

in the balance of payments between New York and each of the eleven Reserve districts. Changes of ownership in the gold settlement fund, on the other hand, represent the resultant of all forces in the interdistrict balance of payments, some of which are important enough in amount to offset increases or decerases in the volume of security loans and investments placed by interior banks in the New York money market.

The cumulative flow of funds between New York and Boston, it will be recalled, reflected divergent tendencies. Any attempt to trace a cause and effect relationship between the fluctuations in the volume of funds placed on call in New York by banks in the Boston Reserve district, and in changes of ownership in the gold settlement fund, could at best be only conjectural. The net loss of funds on the part of Boston to New York in the second half of 1924 might have been the result of the rapid increase that took place in security loans. On the other hand, even though the security loans of the reporting member banks in the Boston district continued to increase through 1925, New York lost to Boston through the first eight months in ownership in the gold settlement fund. The cessation of the loss, and the slight gain thereafter, might have been related to the continued increase in security loans. In 1926, when there was little appreciable change in security loans, the net gain in funds by New York from Boston, beginning in May, was amazingly large. Turning to an examination of the data for investments, there is as little correlation between these and the net movement of funds as there is in the case of security loans. The largest increase in investment holdings of reporting member banks in the Boston Federal Reserve district took place in 1922, when little net change occurred in ownership in the gold settlement fund as between the two districts. The gain of funds by New York in the second half of 1924 might have been reflective of the increase taking place in investment holdings, as it might have reflected the security loan rise. In 1925 the rapid increase in investment holdings towards the end of the year, together with the security loan increase, might have been the factor that checked the loss of funds by New York to Boston and that brought about a slight gain. The heavy loss of funds to May, 1926, and the subsequent gain to New York can not be related to changes in investment holdings any more than to changes in security loans.

In the case of the Philadelphia, Cleveland and San Francisco districts, it might be supposed that there would be greater relationship between gains to New York in the gold settlement fund and fluctuations in the investment holdings and the security loans of the reporting member banks. Upon comparing the year-to-year gain in funds with the changes taking place from the first to the last reporting date of each year in security loans and investments, little relationship emerges excepting in the case of San Francisco. In certain instances, as in 1923, when gains from Philadelphia and Cleveland were particularly heavy, security loan and investment increases were relatively small. When security loans and investments actually declined, as in 1921, New York's gain was very large and exceeded the gain in 1922, when the increase in security loans and investments was pronounced. In the case of these districts, as with Boston, no very definite relationship can be established. Even in the case of the San Francisco district, the relationship is not a particularly close one, though there is a tendency for New York's gain to increase with increases in the security loans and investments of the San Francisco reporting member banks. Evidently in the case of this district security loans and investments play a more important rôle in the balance of payments with the New York district, than is true for the other districts in their relationships with New York.

With a few interruptions in trend, the New York Federal Reserve district lost funds consistently to the Atlanta, Chicago, Minneapolis and Dallas districts. These are the districts in which relatively large increases in security loans have taken place. The fact that this has been the case gives added emphasis to the minor rôle that security loans play in the balance of payments between districts. It is true that the slowing down in the loss of funds to the Chicago district in 1924 and 1925 might be related to the very large increase in security loans and investments taking place through that period. Likewise the temporary gains by New York from Minneapolis in 1925 and 1927 might be related to the increasing volume of security loans and investments. However, during part of 1924, when New York was gaining from Minneapolis, the investments and security loans of the reporting member banks there were actually declining.

Those districts in which there has been no consistent trend in the net movement of funds include in addition to Boston, the Richmond and Kansas City districts. In the Richmond district, the increase in security loans were less than that in the case of any of the other districts. Even in the case of such increases as did take place, there is no manifest relationship between these and the gain of funds on the part of New York. For example, the gain from the Richmond district was particularly large in 1923, when the security loans and the investments of the reporting member banks of the Richmond district actually declined. Agricultural and commercial factors in the balance of payments evidently dominated.

Since the middle of 1920, with the exception of 1923 and 1926, New York has gained funds from the St. Louis district, where security loans increased relatively less than in most districts. Possibly the large gain in funds by New York in 1922 and 1924 might be related to the security loan and investment increases taking place in those years. In 1923 and 1926, when security loans plus investments showed a decline, New York's gain was less. Apparently in the case of this district some relationship does exist between the flow of funds to New York by reason of investments and security loans and the gain of ownership by New York in the gold settlement fund.

From 1920 to the middle of 1923 New York was losing to Kansas City, a period when both investments and security loans showed substantial gains. In 1924, when security loans and investments were increasing, New York gained; but in 1925 New York gained but little, though loans and investments continued to increase. In 1926 a substantial gain took place accompanying a smaller increase in these earning assets.

Over the period under review, there seems little definite relationship, in the case of most districts, between increases and decreases in the security loans and investments of the reporting member banks in each district and the gains and losses experienced by New York in the gold settlement fund. These financial items in the balance of payments apparently are submerged by other more important fluctuations.

To arrive at a final and complete explanation of the interdistrict flow of funds, further information is required as to the flow of funds between each district and the eleven others (similar to the study presented here for New York), and as to payments for goods and services between various parts of the country. If complete information on movements of funds were available, much could be concluded with reference to the movement of goods and services between various parts of the country. The data offered in this study illustrate strikingly the principle of triangular trade, with New York losing to some districts while gaining from others.

Summary

The object of this chapter was to present a more detailed study of the domestic movement of funds. A statistical analysis was first given of the three principal factors in the movement of funds between New York and the interior: (1) movement due to transit clearings; (2) movement due to Federal Reserve note clearings; and (3) movement due to government transfers. It was found that New York gains by government transfers and Federal Reserve note clearings, but loses by transit clearings.

The aggregate movement of funds to and from each Federal Reserve district, cumulated since the beginning of 1919, was then pictured, and it was found that in general there is an inverse correlation between movement of funds by government transfers and movement of funds due to settlements. Settlements include transit clearings and Federal Reserve note clearings.

The chapter then proceeded to a more detailed analysis of the movement of funds between New York and the interior by a study of the transit clearings between New York and each of the other eleven districts. In general it was found: (1) that New York loses funds cumulatively to predominantly exporting districts, such as Atlanta, Dallas, Chicago and Minneapolis; and (2) that New York gains funds from highly industrialized districts such as Cleveland, Philadelphia and Boston. New York loses to exporting districts the funds to pay for exports, New York then being reimbursed from abroad. Predominantly the sales of such districts are to or through the New York money market, while their purchases are scattered among all the districts. The gains of these districts from New York are presumably offset by losses to other districts.

In the case of the highly industrialized districts, funds move to New York in the form of cumulated earnings of enterprise for the payment of interest and dividends. These cumulated funds then are distributed to all parts of the country and abroad. The losses of such districts to New York presumably are made up by offsetting gains from other districts purchasing their manufactured products. Finally, in the case of districts developing rapidly industrially, there tends to be a movement of funds from New York, as capital from all parts of the country, realized by the proceeds of stock and bond issues floated by New York institutions, flows through the money market [11] to these developing parts of the country. These three factors are present in the relationship between New York and all other Federal Reserve districts to some extent, but in some cases one or the other of the factors is predominant and the flow of funds between New York and the respective districts is the result of some combination of the three major forces.

[11] Geographical distribution of the investments of life insurance companies is shown in an article entitled "Financing Economic Progress," by Thomas I. Parkinson, in the *Proceedings of the Twenty-second Annual Convention of Life Insurance Presidents,* New York, Dec. 13–14, 1928, pp. 28–50.

BIBLIOGRAPHY

BIBLIOGRAPHY

Anderson, B. M. "Some Major Forces in the International Money Market." *The Chase Economic Bulletin,* Vol. VII, No. 4, October 29, 1927.

——— "An Analysis of the Money Market." *The Chase Economic Bulletin,* Vol. VIII, No. 1, June 4, 1928.

——— "Bank Expansion versus Savings." *The Chase Economic Bulletin,* Vol. VIII, No. 2, June 25, 1928.

——— "Brokers' Loans and Bank Credit." *The Chase Economic Bulletin,* Vol. VIII, No. 4, October 31, 1928.

——— "The 'Free Gold' of the Federal Reserve System and the Cheap Money Policy." *The Chase Economic Bulletin,* Vol. X, No. 3, September 29, 1930.

Andrew, A. Piatt. *Financial Diagrams.* Publications of the National Monetary Commission. Washington, Government Printing Office, 1910.

——— *Some Facts and Figures Relating to the Money Trust Inquiry. Letters to the New York Evening Post.* Senate Document No. 1003, 62d Congress, 3d Session, Vol. 24. Washington, Government Printing Office, 1912.

Artman, C. E. "New England Manufactures in the Nation's Commerce." Bureau of Foreign and Domestic Commerce. United States Department of Commerce. Commerce Reprints. *Trade Information Bulletin No. 582,* October, 1928.

Bagehot, Walter. *Lombard Street.* 14th edition, with an introduction by Hartley Withers. London, John Murray, 1927.

Beard, Charles A. *The American Leviathan.* New York, The Macmillan Company, 1930.

Beckhart, B. H. "The 'Free Gold' of the Reserve Banks and its Relation to Credit Policy." *The Annalist,* Vol. 37, No. 939, January 16, 1931.

Burgess, W. R. *The Reserve Banks and the Money Market.* New York, Harper and Brothers, 1927.

——— "The Money Market in 1929." *The Review of Economic Statistics,* Vol. XII, No. 1, February, 1930.

Chicago as a Money Market. Published by the University of Illinois, Urbana, 1928.

Conway, Thomas, Jr., and Ernest M. Patterson. *The Operation of the New Bank Act.* Philadelphia, J. B. Lippincott, 1914.

Davenport, Donald H., Lawrence M. Orton, and Ralph W. Roby. *The Retail Shopping and Financial Districts in New York and Its Environs.* New York, Regional Plan of New York and its Environs, 1927.

Dulles, Eleanor. *The French Franc.* New York, The Macmillan Company, 1929.

Feis, Herbert. "Our Foreign Investment Position: An Analysis of Recent Capital Movements." *The Annalist,* Vol. 31, No. 788, February 24, 1928.

——— *Europe: The World's Banker 1870–1914.* New Haven, Yale University Press, 1930.

Gibbons, J. S. *Banks of New York and the Clearing House.* 10th ed. New York, Bankers Magazine, 1873.

Harlow, A. F. *Old Towpaths.* New York, D. Appleton and Company, 1926.

Jay, Pierre. "Federal Reserve Operations and the New York Money Market." *Trust Companies Magazine,* Vol. 42, No. 3, March, 1926.

Jenks, Jeremiah W. "An Analysis of the Question of the Retirement of the National Bank Notes." *Bulletin of the Stable Money Association,* Vol. II, No. 1, January–February, 1929.

Kemmerer, E. W. *Seasonal Variations in the Relative Demand for Money and Capital in the United States.* Washington, Government Printing Office, 1910.

——— "American Banks in Times of Crisis Under the National Banking System." *Proceedings of the Academy of Political Science in the City of New York,* Vol. 1, No. 2, January, 1911.

Keynes, John Maynard. *A Treatise on Money.* New York, Harcourt, Brace and Company, 1930.

Matthews, Ada M., and A. Ross Eckler. "Regional Business Conditions: A Study of Bank Debits." *The Review of Economic Statistics,* Vol. X, No. 3, August, 1928.

Parkinson, Thomas L. "Financing Economic Progress." *Proceedings of the Twenty-Second Annual Convention of Life Insurance Presidents,* 1928.

Peterson, N. E. *American Industries by Geographical Sections.* First National Bank of Boston, 1928.

Riefler, Winfield W. *Money Rates and Money Markets in the United States.* New York, Harper and Brothers, 1930.

Schacht, Hjalmar. "The Money Markets Before and After the War." *Harvard Business Review,* Vol. 8, No. 2, January, 1931.

Smith, James G. *The Development of Trust Companies in the United States.* New York, Henry Holt and Company, 1928.

——— "The Measurement of Time Valuation." *American Economic Review,* Vol. XVIII, No. 2, June, 1928.

Tippetts, Charles S. *State Banks and the Federal Reserve System.* New York, D. Van Nostrand Company, 1929.

Turner, Bernice C. *The Federal Fund Market.* New York, Prentice-Hall Inc., 1931.

Warburg, Paul M. *The Discount System in Europe.* National Monetary Commission. Washington, Government Printing Office, 1910.

——— *The Federal Reserve System. Its Origin and Growth.* New York, The Macmillan Company, 1930.

Watkins, L. L. *Bankers' Balances.* Chicago, A. W. Shaw Company, 1929.

Willis, H. Parker. *The Federal Reserve System.* New York, The Ronald Press Company, 1923.

——— and B. H. Beckhart. *Foreign Banking Systems.* New York, Henry Holt and Company, 1929.

——— and William Howard Steiner. *Federal Reserve Banking Practice.* New York; D. Appleton and Company, 1926.

Young, Allyn A. *An Analysis of Bank Statistics for the United States.* Cambridge; Harvard University Press. 1928.

Bank Publications

Federal Reserve Bank of Boston, *Monthly Review.*

Federal Reserve Bank of Boston, *Proceedings of the Annual Meetings of Stockholders.*

Federal Reserve Bank of Minneapolis, *Monthly Review of Agricultural and Business Conditions in the Ninth Federal Reserve District.*

Federal Reserve Bank of New York, *Annual Reports.*

Federal Reserve Bank of New York, *Monthly Review of Business and Credit Conditions.*

Federal Reserve Bank of Philadelphia, *Annual Reports.*

Federal Reserve Bank of Richmond, *Letters to College Classes in Economics and Banking Discussing the Practical Operations of the Federal Reserve System.*

Federal Reserve Bank of San Francisco, *Annual Reports.*

The Guaranty Trust Company (New York), *The Guaranty Survey.*

National Bank of Commerce (New York), *Commerce Monthly.*

National City Bank (New York), *Monthly Bulletin.*

Official Publications

Comptroller of the Currency, *Annual Reports.*

Federal Reserve Board, *Annual Reports.*

Member Bank Reserves. *Report of the Committee on Bank Reserves of the Federal Reserve System.* Washington, Government Printing Office, 1931.

Department of Commerce (United States). *Balance of International Payments of the United States.*

Hearings before a Subcommittee of the Committee on Banking and Currency. Investigations of Financial and Monetary Conditions in the United States, H. R. 429 and 504. Sixty-second Congress, Third Session, Washington, Government Printing Office, 1912.

Subcommittee on Banking and Currency. Sixty-second Congress, Third Session, House Report No. 1593. *Money Trust Investigation* (Pujo Report). Washington, Government Printing Office, 1913.

Hearings before the Committee on Banking and Currency. Sixty-third Congress, First Session, on H. R. 783 (S. 2639).

Hearings before the Committee on Banking and Currency. House of Representatives, Sixty-ninth Congress, First Session, on H. R. 7895.

Hearings before the Committee on Banking and Currency. House of Representatives, Seventieth Congress, First Session, on H. R. 11, 806.

Hearings before a Subcommittee of the Committee on Banking and Currency. United States Senate, Seventy-first Congress, Third Session, Pursuant to S. Res. 71.

Secretary of the Treasury. *Annual Reports on the State of the Finances.*

Miscellaneous Publications

Acceptance Bulletin, published by the American Acceptance Council, New York.

The Commercial and Financial Chronicle. A weekly newspaper. Wm. B. Dana Company, New York.

INDEX

INDEX

COLUMBIA UNIVERSITY PRESS
COLUMBIA UNIVERSITY
NEW YORK

FOREIGN AGENT
OXFORD UNIVERSITY PRESS
HUMPHREY MILFORD
AMEN HOUSE, LONDON, E. C.

Bei Fragen zur Produktsicherheit wenden Sie sich bitte an:
If you have any questions regarding product safety,
please contact:

Walter de Gruyter GmbH
Genthiner Straße 13
10785 Berlin
productsafety@degruyterbrill.com